The Philosophy of the Coen Brothers

THE PHILOSOPHY OF POPULAR CULTURE

The books published in the Philosophy of Popular Culture series will illuminate and explore philosophical themes and ideas that occur in popular culture. The goal of this series is to demonstrate how philosophical inquiry has been reinvigorated by increased scholarly interest in the intersection of popular culture and philosophy, as well as to explore through philosophical analysis beloved modes of entertainment, such as movies, TV shows, and music. Philosophical concepts will be made accessible to the general reader through examples in popular culture. This series seeks to publish both established and emerging scholars who will engage a major area of popular culture for philosophical interpretation and examine the philosophical underpinnings of its themes. Eschewing ephemeral trends of philosophical and cultural theory, authors will establish and elaborate on connections between traditional philosophical ideas from important thinkers and the ever-expanding world of popular culture.

Series Editor
Mark T. Conard, Marymount Manhattan College, NY

Books in the Series
The Philosophy of Stanley Kubrick, edited by Jerold J. Abrams
Football and Philosophy, edited by Michael W. Austin
Tennis and Philosophy, edited by David Baggett
The Philosophy of Film Noir, edited by Mark T. Conard
The Philosophy of Martin Scorsese, edited by Mark T. Conard
The Philosophy of Neo-Noir, edited by Mark T. Conard
The Philosophy of Spike Lee, edited by Mark T. Conard
The Philosophy of David Lynch, edited by William J. Devlin and Shai Biderman
The Philosophy of the Beats, edited by Sharin N. Elkholy
The Philosophy of Horror, edited by Thomas Fahy
The Philosophy of The X-Files, edited by Dean A. Kowalski
Steven Spielberg and Philosophy, edited by Dean A. Kowalski
The Philosophy of Charlie Kaufman, edited by David LaRocca
The Philosophy of the Western, edited by Jennifer L. McMahon and B. Steve Csaki
The Philosophy of Science Fiction Film, edited by Steven M. Sanders
The Philosophy of TV Noir, edited by Steven M. Sanders and Aeon J. Skoble
Basketball and Philosophy, edited by Jerry L. Walls and Gregory Bassham
Golf and Philosophy, edited by Andy Wible

THE PHILOSOPHY OF
THE COEN
BROTHERS

UPDATED EDITION

Edited by
Mark T. Conard

UNIVERSITY PRESS OF KENTUCKY

Copyright © 2012 by The University Press of Kentucky

Scholarly publisher for the Commonwealth,
serving Bellarmine University, Berea College, Centre College of Kentucky,
Eastern Kentucky University, The Filson Historical Society, Georgetown College,
Kentucky Historical Society, Kentucky State University, Morehead State
University, Murray State University, Northern Kentucky University, Transylvania
University, University of Kentucky, University of Louisville, and Western
Kentucky University.

Editorial and Sales Offices: The University Press of Kentucky
663 South Limestone Street, Lexington, Kentucky 40508-4008
www.kentuckypress.com

16 15 14 13 12   5 4 3 2 1

Cataloging-in-Publication data is available from the Library of Congress.

ISBN 978-0-8131-3445-1 (pbk. : alk. paper)
ISBN 978-0-8131-7323-8 (ebook)

This book is printed on acid-free paper meeting
the requirements of the American National Standard
for Permanence in Paper for Printed Library Materials.

Manufactured in the United States of America.

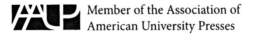

Member of the Association of
American University Presses

CONTENTS

Acknowledgments

First, I'd like to thank the contributors to this volume for all their hard work and patience, which are clearly evident in these terrific essays. Many thanks are also due to all the good people at the University Press of Kentucky, with whom it continues to be a real pleasure to work. Last, for all their love and support I want to thank my family and friends, especially Nayia Frangouli, Chris Landis, John and Linda Pappas, and Aeon Skoble.

INTRODUCTION

Mark T. Conard

Since arriving on the cinematic scene in 1984 with *Blood Simple,* Joel and Ethan Coen have amassed an impressive body of work that has garnered them critical acclaim and a devoted following. Their highly original works include both comedies and dramas and cover various genres (neo-noir, the romantic comedy, the western, the gangster film). However, most, if not all, of the Coens' films defy exact categorization, and they always bear the brothers' unmistakable stamp. From the Irish gangster morality play *Miller's Crossing* (1990) to the film blanc *Fargo* (1996), from the neo-noir comedy *The Big Lebowski* (1998) to the Odyssean *O Brother, Where Art Thou?* (2000), the Coens never fail to have something interesting to say and always say it in a unique and entertaining fashion.

As I've already hinted, much of the Coens' work can be characterized as neo-noir, whatever other styles or genres the brothers are working in. For those unfamiliar with the term, "film noir" refers to a body of Hollywood films from the 1940s and 1950s that share certain visual features, such as stark contrasts between light and shadow and oblique camera angles meant to disorient the viewer, as well as particular themes, such as alienation, pessimism, and moral ambiguity. Classic noirs include *The Maltese Falcon* (John Huston, 1941), *Double Indemnity* (Billy Wilder, 1944), and *Out of the Past* (Jacques Tourneur, 1947). Any film coming after the classic period that displays these themes and has a similar feeling to it we refer to as "neo-noir." Later films, such as *Chinatown* (Roman Polanski, 1974), *Body Heat* (Lawrence Kasdan, 1981), and *L.A. Confidential* (Curtis Hanson, 1997), fall into this category, as do many of the Coens' films. *Blood Simple* is a quite self-conscious neo-noir, for example, and *The Man Who Wasn't There* (2001) is clearly an homage to classic noir. As we'll see later, many or most of the brothers' other movies can likewise be identified as noirs.

This work investigates the philosophical themes and underpinnings of the films of these master filmmakers and uses the movies as a vehicle for exploring and explicating traditional philosophical ideas. It comprises eighteen essays from scholars in both philosophy and film and media studies. The essays are written in nontechnical language and require no knowledge of philosophy or media theory to appreciate or understand.

Part 1 of the volume, "The Coen Brand of Comedy and Tragedy," begins with Richard Gilmore's "*Raising Arizona* as an American Comedy," in which he argues that the aspirations for improvement of the outlaw protagonist of the film, Hi McDunnough, are quintessentially American in nature. Next, in "The Human Comedy Perpetuates Itself: Nihilism and Comedy in Coen Neo-Noir," Thomas S. Hibbs claims that the threat of nihilism, often prominent in classic noir, becomes a working assumption in much of neo-noir, revealing the various quests of the noir protagonist to be pointless, absurd, and thus comic and that the most representative examples of this turn to the comedic in noir are the films of the Coen brothers. In "Philosophies of Comedy in *O Brother, Where Art Thou?*" Douglas McFarland claims that the film's comic underpinnings can best be understood through concepts of the mechanical, the contradictory, and the absurd articulated in Henri Bergson's *Laughter* and Søren Kierkegaard's *Concluding Unscientific Postscript*. Richard Gilmore discusses the hubris and fatal flaws of Llewelyn Moss as he confronts his fate in the form of the killer Anton Chigurh in "*No Country for Old Men*: The Coens' Tragic Western." Last, in "Deceit, Desire, and Dark Comedy: Postmodern Dead Ends in *Blood Simple*," Alan Woolfolk argues that the Coens' first film has many of the classic noir conventions and themes but is at the same time thoroughly postmodern insofar as it frustrates the characters' attempts to make sense out of their lives and to communicate with one another.

Part 2, "Ethics: Shame, Justice, and Virtue," opens with "'And It's Such a Beautiful Day!' Shame and *Fargo*," by Rebecca Hanrahan and David Stearns, in which they claim that the film can be read as a meditation on shame, insofar as the primary characters are repeatedly presented with the chance to look at themselves through the eyes of others. Shai Biderman and William J. Devlin, in "Justice, Power, and Love: The Political Philosophy of *Intolerable Cruelty*," argue that the Coens' tale of love, marriage, betrayal, and divorce can explain much about competing theories of justice within political philosophy. "Ethics, Heart, and Violence in *Miller's Crossing*," by Bradley L. Herling, avers that the brothers' period noir is set in a gangster world run by an ethics of power that is enforced by violence but in which the primary characters at times display "heart," or attachment to one another based on positive emotions and sympathy. Matthew K. Douglass and Jerry L. Walls, in "'Takin' 'er Easy for All Us Sinners': Laziness as a Virtue in *The Big Lebowski*," examine the life philosophy of über-slacker Jeffrey Lebowski, a.k.a. "the Dude," and find that, especially in contrast to the hedonism, nihilism, and rugged individualism manifested in the other characters, the Dude's laziness is indeed a virtue. Last, Douglas McFarland, in "*No Country for Old Men* as Moral Philosophy," discusses the ethical landscape of the Coens' adaptation of the Cormac McCarthy novel set in a bleak and violent region of west Texas.

Part 3, "Postmodernity, Interpretation, and the Construction of History," begins with my chapter "Heidegger and the Problem of Interpretation in *Barton Fink*." In it I claim that the things and events in the life of the screen-writing protagonist lose their sense and meaning because he lives the "life of the mind" as an isolated Cartesian subject cut off from practical engagement with the world. Next, in "The Past Is Now: History and *The Hudsucker Proxy*," Paul Coughlin discusses how the Coens in their meditations on the past don't simply allude to or re-create history; rather, they cinematically investigate how history as a narrative is constructed and question the ideologies underpinning that narrative. Last, Jerold J. Abrams, in "'A Homespun Murder Story': Film Noir and the Problem of Modernity in *Fargo*," argues that the Coen noir *Fargo* reveals the isolation and alienation of humanity within modernity and its social fragmentation and radical individuation.

Part 4, "Existentialism, Alienation, and Despair," kicks off with "'What Kind of Man Are You?': The Coen Brothers and Existentialist Role Playing," in which Richard Gaughran discusses the dilemma of existential self-creation—the problem of the need to create identities for ourselves coupled with the lack of any hope of success, given the lack of a human nature and values to guide us in that self-creation—which is at the heart of so much of the Coens' work. Karen D. Hoffman, in "Being the Barber: Kierkegaardian Despair in *The Man Who Wasn't There*," uses Kierkegaard's account of various types of despair to examine the life of Ed Crane, the barber protagonist of the brothers' noir homage. Finally, in "Thinking beyond the Failed Community: *Blood Simple* and *The Man Who Wasn't There*," R. Barton Palmer discusses the alienation of the antiheroes of these two Coen films, which is a result of the failure of community that engenders in those protagonists a deep desire for connection to others. Palmer notes the influence of the great hard-boiled author James M. Cain and existentialists Sartre and Camus on these two fine Coen noirs.

I'm very pleased in this second, revised edition to include a fifth section, "God, Man, and Nature," comprising two brand-new essays on recent Coen films. This section reflects the Coens' increasing interest in religion and religious texts. In the first essay, "How Job Begat Larry: The Present Situation in *A Serious Man*," K. L. Evans discusses the Coens' updating and retelling of the Job story and argues that the conclusion the Coens wish to draw—that the world is chaotic and thus there is no truth—doesn't follow from the inscrutability of God's ways in the way they think it does. David LaRocca, in "'A Lead Ball of Justice': The Logic of Retribution and the Ethics of Instruction in *True Grit*," argues that the small but significant changes the Coens make to Charles Portis's story reverse and undermine the biblically inspired ethical lesson of the source text.

Whether you're a longtime fan of the Coen brothers or have seen relatively few of their movies, we hope and trust that you'll find this volume engaging and insightful and that it will deepen and enrich your understanding and appreciation of the work of these master auteurs.

Part 1

THE COEN BRAND
OF COMEDY AND TRAGEDY

RAISING ARIZONA AS AN AMERICAN COMEDY

Richard Gilmore

> We grew up in America, and we tell American stories in American settings within American frames of reference.
>
> —Ethan Coen

> Our American literature and spiritual history are . . . in the optative mood.
>
> —Ralph Waldo Emerson, "The Transcendentalist"

Raising Arizona (1987) begins with what sounds like the slamming of some prison doors. It is, to be sure, an ominous sound, and proleptic in at least two ways. First, it anticipates the sound that our protagonist is about to hear within minutes of our first meeting him, and second, it anticipates one of the major themes of the movie, which is, in the words of Ethan Coen, "family life versus being an outlaw." That is, presumably, to the outlaw, family life can seem like some prison doors swung shut. Immediately following the sound of the slamming prison doors there is banjo music and an image of what we learn is a police height measure for photographing suspected criminals. A young man (Nicolas Cage) is thrown into the point of view of the camera so that we can take his measure against the height chart. In a voice-over we hear, "My name is H. I. McDunnough. Call me Hi." I understand Hi's name (constructed from his first two initials) to suggest a spatial metaphor, a description of his ambitions, which are, I want to say, very American ambitions. The banjo music in the background is Pete Seeger's "Goofing Off Suite," which, like America itself, is a fascinating medley of American folk music, motifs from high European classical music (Bach and Beethoven), Russian folk music, and even yodeling.[1]

Hi is the central protagonist of the film and provides the voice-over narrative that accompanies the regular narrative of the film. Although Hi is the main protagonist, it is Ed (Holly Hunter), short for Edwina, who engages the action of the plot of the movie with her strong sense of what she wants and what constitutes natural justice, as did Antigone (except in this case the natural justice takes the form of stealing a live baby from a family that, it could be argued, has too many, rather than burying one's dead brother against the laws of the state).

Goofing off pretty much describes the sense one gets of what the Coens are doing in the opening sequence of the movie. There is one disjunctive discontinuity after another, each one constituting a kind of slapstick joke, and yet each one reverberates with a deeper truth. There is the overall structural discontinuity between Hi's voice-over narrative and what we see him doing. Hi sounds, in the voice-over, like he speaks from a place of detached, even philosophical, wisdom, but what we actually see him doing shows him to be a not very bright repeat offender, a petty criminal with an enthusiasm for robbing convenience stores. That disjunction is funny. His enthusiasm for robbing convenience stores is funny in itself, as is his evident incompetence at it, which is why he goes to jail so often. He seems to accept jail time as just part of life, and it is a significant part of his life. That he uses his time between crimes, that is, his time being booked for the crimes he has committed, to woo Ed, who is a police officer and the photographer for his mug shots, is funny and ridiculous. Their marriage, "starter home," "salad days," infertility, despair, and kidnapping scheme are all a little ridiculous, and yet, even though they are presented as basically funny, there is a sort of underlying truth to all of it. America does have a fascination or love affair with the image of the outlaw, so choosing to be an outlaw is not really that crazy. And it is hard starting a family in this modern world, even if, or especially if, you are an outlaw by trade. And starter homes sometimes are little mobile homes in the desert. And sometimes, in spite of your best efforts, nature does not cooperate; infertility is a fact of life.

When Hi says, for example, "I tried to stand up and fly straight, but it wasn't easy with that sumbitch Reagan in the White House. . . . I dunno, they say he is a decent man, so . . . maybe his advisers are confused," it is such a mishmash of deep political wisdom, weird, folksy compassion, and just raw, self-serving excuse that it is hard to find one's way with it. It is funny and true and crazy all at the same time. It also has a vaguely socialist ring to it, and of course Pete Seeger, the creator of the "Goofing Off Suite" we are hearing in the background, was a famous socialist and defender of the people, which further suggests some deeper political message behind the craziness. This, one might say, quoting the American poet Robert Frost, is "play for mortal stakes."[2]

The Optative Mood and America

We, in America, are weaned on the milk of aspiration. This is what I understand Emerson to mean when he describes our spiritual history as being in the "optative mood." "Optative," from the Latin *optio,* meaning "free choice," is Emerson's slightly archaic word for the American sense of being free to determine one's own life, to be whomever one wants to be. The great advantage of this spiritual history is the energy and the inventiveness it calls forth in American people. The downside of this ethos is how demanding and difficult it is on a person. There is very high expectation that everyone will be an "individual" and that a person will have high aspirations, but not much direction is given to us about what aspirations to have or how to achieve them, except that one should aspire to work hard. So much is expected of us to be something original and so little is given to us about how to do that that the problem of who we are to be can drive us a little crazy. We do not inherit an identity so much as find ourselves tasked with (to use a Coen expression from *Fargo* [1996]) creating an identity. That is an easier task for some than for others, and certainly there are some deep deceptions in the American mythos of self-creation, deceptions about the irrelevance of the conditions of one's birth, the role of social class, or money, or race. So, on the one hand, we have more freedom than most in history to make of ourselves what we will. On the other hand, that puts a considerable burden on each of us as individuals to come up with a unique self to be.

Part of the American mythos, part of the sense of what is especially unique about America, is captured in the idea of "American exceptionalism." This idea is usually traced back to Tocqueville's *Democracy in America* (originally published in two volumes in French in 1835 and 1840), but it can be found even earlier in a famous sermon given by John Winthrop in 1630, in which he describes a future for America in which "wee will be seen as a citty upon a hill."[3] This expression of American exceptionalism, of a future America as "a city upon a hill," is aspirational in at least two ways.

It is aspirational in the sense that it is describing not only a hoped-for state of the country that can be achieved if we are true to certain principles but also what we should aspire to for our future country; it expresses a dream of what America could be. It is also aspirational in the sense that this hoped-for state, once achieved, will itself represent an aspirational goal to the rest of the world.

The idea that there is something special about America, something not just unique but also superior, the idea of America as an idea of some kind of better possibility, seems to pervade our thinking about ourselves, as well as the thinking of others about us, and it is, as most things are, both a blessing and a curse. The blessing is the way the idea of America's exceptionalism empowers us to pursue our own dreams of what we want to be. It is part of the American ideal that we are not necessarily limited by birth or class or race. On the other hand, the expectations of individual achievement are very high, and often we fail to measure up. It is not an incidental detail, I think, that the first image we see of Hi is of him thrown against a height measure, which, under the circumstances, indicates a certain failure to measure up to the high expectations of society.

Comedy

Raising Arizona is a comedy.[4] I take it to be a comedy in at least two senses. First, it is a comedy because it is very funny. The second way that I see *Raising Arizona* as a comedy is in the classic sense of a comedy (which derives from Aristotle's definition of a comedy) as a narrative that begins in a bad place but, in its narrative unfolding, ends in a good place.[5] This is why Dante's narrative of a descent into hell and subsequent journey through purgatory and paradise is called *The Divine Comedy*.[6] It is not so much that it is a humorous work, although there are some very funny passages in it, but that it follows the classic trajectory of a comedy as described by Aristotle.

This claim, that *Raising Arizona* is a comedy in this classic sense, depends on an interpretation of the ending of the movie as being an affirmation of a better future for Hi and Ed. The ending of the movie seems to be ambiguous. Hi is having another one of his dreams (although all of his previous dreams in the movie have turned out to be connected with reality), and he is dreaming of a better and more fruitful future, but their actual situation seems to be worse: they are babyless, and Ed has pronounced, in her definitive way, their (Hi and Ed's) complete unsuitableness to each other and her determination to leave him. Whether they stay together or not remains undetermined by the narrative of the movie. To affirm the movie as having the form of a classic comedy means finding in this very ambiguity some kind of affirmation that transcends the early hopefulness and excitement of their original courtship and marriage.

I interpret the title of the movie, *Raising Arizona,* to indicate the most fundamental theme of the movie, namely, the aspirational theme of self-improvement that is so central to the American identity. The basic trope is the idea of height, so I take Hi's name to be a kind of spatial metaphor of his aspirations. What constitutes growth, what constitutes the necessary change in condition, from a worse to a better condition (so that the movie can fulfill the form of a comedy), will be a change in one's aspirations. At the beginning of the movie, I take Hi's aspirations to be relatively uncomplicated. What he wanted to be was also what he was, an outlaw. The outlaw is a kind of American aspiration, an American ideal. The outlaw is just an extreme form of the American ideal of the frontiersman, the adventurer, the one who braves the wilderness and does so because of the excess of wildness still in him or her. The classic American movie genre of the western is filled with figures that straddle the line between law and lawlessness, so that the good westerner is just barely across the line on the side of the law and the only one wild enough to go after the bad westerner, the one who has slipped to the far side of the law and into a lawless wildness. The connection with the American movie genre of the western is made explicit with some allusions to westerns in *Raising Arizona,* as, for example, the location of the film in the Southwest, the long-coat dusters worn by Gale (John Goodman) and Evelle (William Forsythe) when they rob the bank, and the showdown between Hi and Leonard Smalls (Randall "Tex" Cobb).

The problem of creating an identity for oneself can be framed in terms of the relationship between universals (or generals) and particulars. That is, to be something is to participate in some form of a universal: one is a lawyer or a teacher or a fifth grader or an American. But to participate too much in a universal, to identify oneself too deeply with a general idea, is to lack any particular identity at all.[7] On the other hand, to be too idio-syncratically particular is, in a way, also to lack an identity; it is to have no continuous identity at all. We construct our identities, therefore, out of a combination of some kind of general or universal idea inflected by our own particular characteristics. In part, our particularity is constituted by just the particular array of general ideas that we participate in, so one way to develop one's identity is in choosing which combination of general ideas in which to participate. So, one is a midwesterner or a teacher, someone who drives a Ford or likes baseball, and so on—our identity being, more or less, just the complete list of these general descriptions. A way to improve one's identity is to improve somehow on the complex array of universals that we participate in, making them all more harmonious or more beautiful or maybe just more complex.

Of course, many of the universals in which we participate we do not have a choice about, or not much of a choice. We do not choose (for the most part) our gender, whether we will be born rich or poor, in the Northeast or the Southwest. It seems clear that we make *some* choices, and it will be in those choices that such identity as we can make we do make.

Hi, at the beginning of *Raising Arizona,* has what seems to be a fairly simple identity structure. He seems to identify himself as an outlaw. He blames President Reagan (or his advisers) for his outlaw ways, but that really seems to be more a function of his outlaw ways than a real explanation of them. (When he really wants a job he seems to have no trouble getting one. When he wants a newspaper, he prefers to steal it than to pay the thirty-five cents, and that seems to be a matter of preference and principle rather than need.) The life of an outlaw is a kind of "primitive," pre-Christian, precapitalist kind of existence. It is lived in the present moment much more than toward any particular future. It is cyclical, like the seasons. There is the excitement of doing the crime, and then the over-structured time of being in jail, then back to the crime and back to jail. As Hi says, "Now I don't know how you come down on the incarceration question, whether it's for rehabilitation or revenge. But I was beginning to think that revenge is the only argument that makes any sense." We hear this voice-over as we watch Hi commit another crime after just seeing him being let out of jail. Furthermore, we see that he has pretty much botched this crime by accidentally locking himself out of his car, and the signs (we hear a police siren in the distance) indicate that he will soon be back in the slammer, and so his perspective pretty much mirrors his reality vis à vis the incarceration question.

In a sense, however, these simple primitive cycles and his relatively simple identity structure are already, for Hi, on their way to being things of the past, and they become that in, as it were, the blink of an eye. Heidegger speaks of how the possibility of a new encounter, a new way of encountering the world, will occur to us in the blink of an eye (an *Augenblick* in Heidegger's German).[8] The French philosopher Alain Badiou talks about a similar phenomenon as an "event."[9] An "event" is something that happens that does not quite fit into our established system of knowledge, and so it will appear to us as something unaccountable, something that we cannot quite get our minds around even as we recognize the great importance of the encounter. Badiou identifies four realms, four general categories, of events: politics, science, art, and love.[10] If we consider the final category, then, an event in love will be an encounter with another person that, as it were, opens up possibilities to us that we had never understood were possibilities; it creates a disturbance for us that we do not quite know how to quell. We will always be tempted, in the presence of an event, to turn away from the event, to pretend it did not happen, because the event is always experienced as being beyond us, beyond what we have the capabilities for. Ethics, for Badiou, is about having the courage to be true to, to be faithful to, the event.

The Event

I consider the flash of light when Ed first takes Hi's mug shot at the beginning of the movie to signal, as well, the occurrence of an event. What is the event? If Hi's identity is constituted according to the general idea of the outlaw, Ed's identity seems to be constituted primarily in terms of the law. Her cold-sounding, apparently indifferent, and oft repeated "Turn to the right!" is a kind of pure expression of the law. In that flash of a light, however, a mutual recognition seems to occur. Hi and Ed see in each other the possibility of another narrative, another way of being that would supplement and reconstitute their present ways, and in ways that neither quite understands, but for which both feel an attraction and a need.

Indeed, their marriage generates such a powerful sense of love for both of them, during what Hi refers to as "the salad days" of their marriage, that they felt, in Hi's words expressing Ed's feelings, "that there was too much love and beauty for just the two of us and every day we kept a child out of the world was a day he might later regret having missed." They feel, I want to say, the great potential of their marriage but do not yet understand how to unleash the power of this potential. The antilaw, joy-in-the-moment life of the outlaw has no future, and the pure form of the law is itself barren. The rocky road that Hi and Ed have to follow, then, is the road from the unworkable antinomy of trying to combine in their pure forms lawlessness and lawfulness, to a way of finding, for each, the virtue of the other that will unleash the potential powers of both. That is, Hi has to learn the value of law, and Ed, the value of ad hoc life in the moment in a way that makes possible a shared future to which they can both aspire.

The plot of the movie is all about the beginning of this journey. The beginning of this journey turns out to be quite funny. Perhaps it should not be, involving as it does a recidivist criminal offender, the kidnapping of an infant, a brutal "warthog from hell" biker who kills small animals with an indiscriminate zeal, and two escaped criminals, among other miscreants and malfeasance. Yet, as bad as a description of the characters and acts involved sounds, what we feel for these characters doing these things is, as Georg Seesslen says, "tenderness."[11]

This leads me to Plato's not exactly explicit theory of humor. In Book VII of *The Republic,* in the section known as the allegory of the cave, Plato describes two different kinds of laughter.[12] The first kind of laughter he describes is the laughter of the people who are trapped inside the cave, the people who take mere shadows for reality. They laugh at the people who return to the cave from outside because when those people return, from out of the bright light of reality back into the darkness of the cave, they stumble around, blinded by the darkness of the cave. To those inside the cave, those whose eyes are used to the darkness, this stumbling around looks like incompetence, and the people inside the cave think it is hysterically funny to see such bumbling. The second kind of laughter, however, is quite different. The second form of laughter is the laughter of the people outside the cave as they watch each new person who escapes from the cave and tries to walk in the bright light of day (reality) before his or her eyes have gotten used to all of the light. They stumble too, and this makes the people whose eyes are now used to the light laugh. On the surface these two forms of laughter seem quite similar, but, in reality, they are completely different. What is the difference? The difference is that the first kind of laughter is a laughter of ridicule, of supposed superiority at the expense of a supposed inferior. It is a laughter that separates and makes other. The second kind of laughter is like the laughter of parents seeing their child take her or his first wobbly step. It is a laughter of joy and love and inclusion. It is a laughter that welcomes and bonds.

Jokes

Raising Arizona is full of jokes. Some of the jokes are explicit. Although Hi woos Ed with a joke about a tipped cement mixer and some escaped hardened criminals (a joke Ed had heard before), most of the explicit jokes are of the "bad laughter" variety, and they are told by Glen (Sam McMurray). The rest of the jokes in the movie are implicit. They are not presented explicitly as jokes, but if you see them, if you get them, they are quite funny and also, generally, more or less tender, that is, including you and affirming our shared humanity rather than excluding or reinforcing a sense of otherness. Ted Cohen, in his book *Jokes: Philosophical Thoughts on Joking Matters*, describes the purpose of jokes in terms of "relief from certain oppressions, and the attainment of a very special kind of intimacy."[13] With jokes, one has to do some work, do some thinking. Frequently jokes work by ellipsis—something is left out that has to be supplied by the hearer. So, at first, the missing element occurs as just a sort of puzzling non sequitur, then you get it and see how the missing piece solves the puzzle. The result is an intimacy based on a shared understanding, based on "the sense held mutually by teller and hearer that they are joined in feeling."[14] So the philosophical importance of jokes has to do with the way they free us from things that oppress us, by giving us a certain distance, a certain detached perspective on those things, and by the way they foster intimacy and community between the teller and the hearer of the joke.

In a movie like *Raising Arizona*, the implicit jokes are frequently signaled only by an oddness, and one may laugh at them without being fully aware of what is funny, as though we got the joke subconsciously, if not quite fully consciously. Hi's enthusiastic and energetic seduction of Ed from the position of the one who is being booked and sent to jail is funny because it is a very odd situation in which to begin a seduction, since the very fact that one is a convicted criminal would seem to disqualify one as an appropriate partner, especially for a police officer. The tenderness, the good laughter of these sequences, resides in the way that it is in the nature of wooing to be, to feel, more or less unworthy, and yet we do it anyway. There is always something suspicious about wooing, a question of reliability and of motives that shades every wooer with a taint of criminality. The wooer understands this, as does the wooed, and yet we woo and are wooed. From inside the process, all of this causes anxiety, and from outside, it looks kind of funny. It is funny that Hi tells Ed that her ex-fiancé knows where to find him, "in the Munroe County Maximum Security Correctional Facility for Men, State Farm Road Number Thirty-One; Tempe, Arizona," since it is at once gallant and ridiculous. It is funny the way words work as things outside of us, with a kind of logic of their own that can be confounding, the way "Well, okay then" can be both the words that set Hi free by the head of the parole board and the identical words used to make him married. It is funny when someone says, "You're not just tellin' us what we wanna hear?" and you say, "No sir, no way," and then they say "'Cause we just wanna hear the truth," and you think, well, I am telling the truth, and so you say, "Well then I guess I am tellin' you what you wanna hear," and then they say, "Boy, didn't we just tell you not to do that?" Okay then. I hate it when that happens.

All of these jokes seem to be doing just what Ted Cohen says about jokes. In our laughter at these scenes from the movie we feel ourselves getting some distance from, and some perspective on, the kinds of things that cause us anxiety and oppress us. In our laughter, we feel a certain tenderness for Hi and Ed, and maybe even for Dot (Frances McDormand) and Glen, as well as for ourselves, and this feeling of tenderness is a feeling of an intimacy with these characters. If we are in a movie theater and our laughter is shared by others in the audience, this feeling of intimacy and shared feeling, shared community, is created in the actual movie theater itself.

There is at least one Freudian joke in the movie: the way the gynecologist (Ralph Norton) is using his cigar—what Freud would call a phallic symbol—as a pointer to the diagram of a woman's reproductive system. In the way he manipulates the cigar against the diagram he seems to be simultaneously explaining the problem of Ed's infertility and simulating sex. This is a doctor joke, a Freudian joke, and a joke on Freud (who famously said "Sometimes a cigar is just a cigar" and died, tragically, of oral cancer, suggesting that the great psychologist was not entirely in control of his own psyche).

Polysemousness

A narrative that has multiple levels of meaning can be called polysemous. Polysemousness not only characterizes the scene with the gynecologist but also is characteristic of *Raising Arizona* as a whole. Dante, in his famous letter to Can Grande, describes how his *Commedia* is polysemous. Dante says that each scene in the *Commedia* has four levels of meaning: first, the literal narrative, then the allegorical meaning, then the moral meaning, and finally the anagogical meaning (by which he means its spiritual significance). For example, the *Commedia* begins

> Midway in our life's journey, I went astray
> from the straight road and woke to find myself
> alone in a dark wood. . . . [15]

The four levels of interpretation for this opening scene would be, first, that the narrator, Dante, was literally sleepwalking and woke up after having veered off the road he had meant to be on, finding himself lost in a dark wood. The allegorical meaning is that this is a thing that has happened to virtually everyone and that many of us are, too, lost in a dark wood (of sin and error). The moral significance has to do with the recognition of this fact of our lostness and the need to recover our moral bearings and that the subsequent story may help us with this. The anagogical meaning is that this is not just a practical moral problem but also a spiritual problem and that our lostness is not just a reflection of our being out of sync with our own moral convictions but that we are also out of sync with the universe as whole, or with God, and that radical steps must be taken to remedy this dire condition.

Although the Coen brothers do not claim this kind of polysemous content for *Raising Arizona* as explicitly as Dante does for his *Commedia,* there are too many signs of it in the film to be ignored. I am not sure that *Raising Arizona* has the *same* interpretive levels as Dante's *Divine Comedy,* but certainly, I would say, there is more going on than just a literal story. There are too many odd parallels and peculiar events within the movie that seem to require some kind of interpretation, that seem to indicate other levels of meaning. Some quick examples are the tattoo (of Mr. Horsepower, but it also looks a lot like Woody the Woodpecker) shared by Hi and the Lone Biker of the Apocalypse, Leonard Smalls. There is the similar gesture of dragging someone out from under something by the foot, committed first by Hi, with one of the Arizona infants from under the crib, and the same gesture performed by the lone biker on Hi (dragging him out from under a car). There are weirdly unbelievable sequences like the whole Pampers-stealing, gun-blasting, dog-chasing sequence or just the strangely quiescent and unharmable baby who falls, twice (!), from the top of a moving car, yet survives untouched and unperturbed.

Take, for example, the polysemous character of the visit by Glen and Dot. The experience of their wayward undisciplined kids is a repetition of Hi's first experience with the unruly Arizona quintuplets when he is trying to kidnap one of them. It is a subjectivized representation of Hi's worst fear of what having a family will be like. It does not take a particular side on the nature versus nurture question, but it does definitely uphold the proverb about apples not falling far from the tree. Each of Glen's children seems to be an active embodiment of Glen's concept of a joke, a thing said or done at someone else's expense that can be laughed at. Not only does one of the children squirt Hi in the crotch with his squirt gun because he thinks it is funny but they also all laugh at their father's broken nose because they think it is funny. Empathy is not part of the family ethos. All of this is surely also a comment on American child-rearing practices, since, I would guess, most of us have encountered such a family in the United States, but I have never seen such a one, nor would I expect to, in Europe. And we laugh at this joke, and this is a good laughter. It is a laughter that, as Cohen suggests, frees us from certain oppressions, the oppressions of families, our own and other people's, the oppression of our guilt about feeling the oppressions of families, the oppression of anxiety about entertaining, which rarely turns out quite as badly as this experiment in entertaining turns out.

So there are many things going on simultaneously in this sequence, and all of them tie into different narrative levels that the movie sustains throughout. All of these narrative levels, however, address this question: how does one achieve happiness, how does one create a happy home, in this complex, wonderful, terrifying, maddening America? What is the answer to this question suggested by *Raising Arizona*?

The answer that this movie suggests seems to have something to do with the nature of comedy, something to do with the way seeing the comic can lead to a life lived as a comedy, that is, as ending better than it begins. This, it has to be acknowledged, would have to be the metanarrative lesson of the movie since no one in the movie itself seems to really pick up on the comic dimension of life.

Dreams and Freedom

An important and recurring theme in *Raising Arizona* is Hi's dreams. Dreams, if Freud is right, are inherently polysemous. They have, at the very least, two levels of meaning, what Freud called the manifest and the latent levels of meaning. The manifest meaning is what we literally dream, while the latent meaning is what the dream means, what an interpretation of the dream will tell us about ourselves. At least one commentator on the movie has raised the possibility that some, or all, of the movie may be a dream, which would make Hi's explicit dreams, dreams within a dream.[16] Nietzsche claims that metaphysics begins with the fact of dreams.[17] That is, with dreams we have a direct experience of a counternarrative, an alternative reality, to that of our everyday experience. This creates a need to determine which is the true narrative or the true reality, and that question calls forth metaphysics. If Nietzsche is right, this suggests a deep connection between dreams and philosophy. The idea of a counternarrative is what sets us free from the constraints of whatever narrative we happen to find ourselves in. This is the way in which philosophy can set us free, by empowering us to imagine other ways of being. Movies, in general, are very dreamlike—oneiric is the word for that—and, like dreams, seem to call for some interpretation and, also like dreams, can be a road to a new kind of freedom from what oppresses us.

"In dreams begin responsibilities," wrote Delmore Schwartz.[18] That is, in dreams we confront the pieces that are missing from the narrative that we are working with in our everyday lives. Hi's dreams are important to the movie because the movie itself is a kind of working through the issues that are raised in his dreams. The two escaped convicts, Evelle and Gale, are like emissaries from Hi's unconscious, come to remind him of his "true" nature. They emerge just as Hi is beginning to settle down into family life, and they can be seen as the part of his identity that he is not quite sure that he wants to give up yet. They are childlike, sloppy, and lawless, and they live only for the moment. They are literal and figurative remnants of Hi's earlier life, when all he lived for was to be an outlaw and when time moved in cycles so that he always knew where he was in time just by knowing where he was in a particular cycle.

At the beginning of the first section of Dante's *Commedia,* the "Inferno," after Dante awakes in the dark wood, he sees a distant peak with the bright light of the sun, representing goodness, shining atop it. He turns to make his way toward it, but his way is blocked by three beasts: a leopard, a lion, and a she-wolf. These beasts are, allegorically, his own sins that he is not yet quite ready to give up, things that he cannot quite convince himself are really evil. Similarly, Hi has to confront his own outlaw ways, which have been at the core of his identity. In some sense, he knows that he has to give up those ways, but in another sense, he does not know that at all and really wants to hold on to those parts of himself. That is part of the conflict within himself that Hi has to work through during the course of the movie. When Hi does manage to work through some of his issues, these two emissaries from his unconscious go back down into the dark hole from which they escaped. We are never completely free of those desires we once nurtured but now suppress, but we can keep them in a prison so that they never see the light of day.

The prison escape is also a kind of a joke. Their emergence from a viscous hole in the ground looks a lot like birth. As Gale explains in Hi and

Ed's living room, "We don't always smell like this, Miz McDunnough. I was just explainin' to yer better half here that when we were tunnelin' out we hit the main sewer," which is a lot like what William Butler Yeats has Crazy Jane say to the Bishop in the poem "Crazy Jane and the Bishop": "Love has pitched his mansion in / The place of excrement."[19] Life is a weird, messy business, and there is just no getting around that fact. Wisdom has to do with coming to grips with the messiness of it, the way it does not always go the way we would want it to go.

For Hi, *something* begins in that flash of light in which he first sees Ed, but that something takes an additional turn when Hi begins to process the remark by the prison counselor (Peter Benedek) about most people having a family at their age, that sets Hi to musing, then dreaming, then acting on an idea based on that remark. The hardest part of acting freely, if this is what freedom is, is staying true to one's original choice, remaining faithful, as Badiou says, to the event. The over-determining forces that would direct us along more predictable routes, including our own habits, do not suddenly vanish. On the contrary, they kick in with more force than ever. That is what Dante is talking about when he describes the three beasts that suddenly appear just as he tries to set off on a new direction in his life. The beasts overwhelm his resolve, and it is only with the intercessionary help of Virgil that he can go on. Hi will find himself driving past convenience stores on the way home from work, and, like Dante, he will find it too difficult to resist this particular beast in his own soul.

Andrew Pulver, writing for the *Guardian* about an encounter with Joel and Ethan Coen, identifies a passage from Ethan's book of stories, *Gates of Eden,* that Pulver suggests may have some biographical relevance but, in any event, does seem to tie in to a recurring theme in the Coen brothers' movies. In the story "I Killed Phil Shapiro" there is a summer camp director, Rabbi Sam, who says, as words of welcome to the new camp recruits, "If You Will It, It Is No Dream."[20] As Pulver mentions, this phrase occurs in *The Big Lebowski* (1998) when Walter (John Goodman) says to the Dude (Jeff Bridges), attributing it to Theodor Herzl, "If you will it, Dude, it is no dream."[21] This phrase captures the central metaphysical and narrative tension of *Raising Arizona,* which has to do with what is a dream and what is reality: are the two separable, or are they, somehow, intimately related?

To paraphrase Delmore Schwartz, reality begins in dreams. That is, insofar as our reality is to be really ours, is to be a reality of our own choosing rather than what simply happens to us, then it will begin for us as an event to which we will remain faithful. The act will have consequences, and those consequences will entail responsibilities. Our freedom, somewhat ironically, will depend on our being true to, upholding, our responsibilities. This strict notion of being responsible, however, is ameliorated by the fact that these responsibilities are *our* responsibilities, that is, our own chosen responsibilities, rather than inauthentic responsibilities that are imposed upon us by others or by the system at large.

The Uses and Abuses of America

Raising Arizona does present a fairly piquant critique of America. The Pampers-stealing, gun-blasting, dog-chasing sequence is, for me, one of the funniest pieces in the whole movie. It is so funny to me, in part, because it captures something of the wild craziness of life in America, the way that the simplest acts, like getting something from the store, can become a kind of race for one's life. It is also so funny to me because of the way it picks up on a particular fear that I have about my fellow Americans and their (our) love of guns and violence and their (our) desire to shoot and destroy things. The store clerk, his mouth full of braces, has a mad gleam in his eye at the opportunity to pull out the shotgun and start blasting away. The cops behave in the same way. Even the neighborhood dogs seem to pick up the scent of bloodlust and get into the chase.

All of this, also, reflects something deep in the nature of capitalism, which is at the very core of our democracy. Capitalism does foster a kind of Hobbesian war of all against all. On the surface all of us are (mostly) very polite and cooperative, but there is a kind of cutthroat competitiveness that lurks just below the surface and is deeply imbued in the spirit of capitalism itself. The Arizona family reflects many of the features of capitalism. Nathan Arizona's (Trey Wilson) relentless commitment to selling himself and his furniture is a paradigm of what it takes to be successful in a capitalistic system. The irony of his oft-repeated claim, "And if you can find lower prices anywhere my name ain't Nathan Arizona!" is, of course, that his name ain't Nathan Arizona, or it wasn't before he changed it, so I guess it is Nathan Arizona but, as it were, barely, which does put kind of a spin on his famous claim for his prices.

Nathan Arizona is an example of someone who has literally created his own identity out of his own dreams of what he wanted to be. I would say that what he wants to be seems a little shallow, and this is part of the movie's critique of America and American life, but he has been remarkably successful at achieving it. Clearly, to achieve his dream he has had to adopt a basically antagonistic stance with respect to virtually everyone around him. As he says, "My motto is do it my way or watch your butt!" It is an excellent, even a necessary, motto for being a successful capitalist, although it's less good for making friends. Nathan's relationship with his wife seems to lack all intimacy, but we learn that there is a *little* more to Nathan Arizona than just pure capitalist.

There is a kind of fairness to capitalism and a kind of unfairness. There is a sense in which those who are willing to devote themselves to accumulation deserve what they manage to accumulate. There is also a sense that in capitalism, some have much more than they need or deserve. The balance between these two notions associated with capitalism, of its fairness and its unfairness, is difficult to parse. Certainly, Hi and Ed feel the unjust side of it and decide to act to right it. Their act is a kind of underground socialism, a redistribution of the wealth from those with a surfeit to those with a dearth. Political scientists often remark that America has never had a really viable socialist movement, not, at least, in the ways Europe has. There are various speculations about why that is so. I see *Raising Arizona* as, as it were, raising the question of socialism and then turning in an ambiguous answer. The movie makes the idea of kidnapping another couple's child seem almost reasonable, almost a fair redistribution of wealth, and yet it really does not work out for anyone.

The Double Plotline or: The Good of the Bad

Dante's *Commedia,* much like Augustine's *Confessions,* can be described as having a double plotline. That is, one could diagram the narrative of these works in either of two ways. The first way would be in the shape of a check mark, that is, the first part of the narrative seems to be a descent, but then, at the crucial turning point, there is a turn for the better and that would be shown as an ascending line. That is the structure of a comedy in the classic sense. The other way of diagramming such a narrative, however, would be as simply an ascending line because the subsequent ascent is completely dependent upon the prior descent. This is what Augustine means when he refers to *"felix culpa"* (happy or fortunate sin). That is, in the case of Augustine, for example, he would not have reached his spiritual enlightenment if he had not fully experienced the degradation of his sin, so his sin was a great gift, a great boon to him. Dante has to descend through hell, the Inferno, because it is only by seeing it that he will be able to understand Heaven. So it is not just that the good comes after the bad but that the good is completely dependent on the experience of the bad.

Hi and Ed unquestionably experience a narrative descent. Their hopes for having a family are dashed. They have lost their jobs. Even their marriage seems to be in danger. And yet, they have become real people, something that neither really was at the beginning of the film. At the end of the movie they are complex enough to see how complex the pursuit of happiness is, they are complex enough to understand other people's pain and loss—even if those people do have a lot of babies already. To get to the way of thinking and feeling that leads Ed and Hi to return Nathan Jr. is an achievement, one that could not have been attained without all of the difficulties of their descent. Nathan Arizona, the unregenerate huckster and über-capitalist, reveals a surprising tenderness toward his returned son, toward Ed and Hi, and, most surprising of all somehow, toward his wife, Florence (Lynne Dumin Kitei). It is in this tenderness that I see the authentic aspiration of America, and maybe that is not just an American thing.

The real goal is not about money or fertility so much as about achieving this tenderness toward others. It may be that such tenderness can be achieved only through suffering and loss. Nathan Arizona expresses his feelings of tenderness for his wife in terms of his fear of losing her and suggests that Hi and Ed may yet discover such tenderness for each other and that they "should sleep on it" before they do anything rash like breaking up their marriage. I take it that they do sleep on it and that Hi's final dream is a dream of the tenderness made manifest in the world, specifically in Utah, the state above Arizona.

The Uberty of Liberty

There is some question about whether America really is exceptional and about the value of thinking about ourselves as exceptional. If there is something exceptional about us, it seems to me that it would have to do with the way we think of ourselves as being free, as having a right to our own opinions, as being both free to develop ourselves into the selves we want to be and responsible for what we become. It is quite true that, as a cynic might insist, many in America do not really have much freedom to develop themselves into anything other than what they were born to, that the idea that we are "free" in America, that this is a "free country," is a myth and a harmful one at that. Without denying that, I still want to say that there is a freedom that is not just granted, but in some sense honored, in America, and that is the freedom to dream.

"Uberty" is a somewhat archaic word for fruitfulness, for something that generates growth and abundance. The freedom merely to dream is, in one sense, no real freedom at all, but in another sense, in this philosophical sense in which any authentic choice must begin in something like a dream, then the freedom to dream is the only kind of real liberty that there is. Ultimate happiness may depend less on how much money we accumulate and more on having a sense that our life is our own life, that we have lived a life in which we have made some choices and lived according to the consequences of those choices. To accept responsibility for the consequences of our choices and actions is what makes us fully human, and it is what makes us tender. If there is any truth in that, then the stuff of comedy, the material to make the ends of our lives better than the beginnings, may be as accessible as our dreams. The most important thing, then, is to keep dreaming, and that is precisely what Hi is doing at the end of *Raising Arizona,* making it, in my estimation, a comedy not only because it is funny but also because it holds out the possibility, in the classic sense, that we can make our end better than our beginning. We can laugh in welcoming, like Plato's philosophers, the new recruits to the realm of tenderness for each other. As Walter says in *The Big Lebowski,* "If you will it, Dude, it is no dream."

Notes

Epigraphs: Peter Körte and Georg Seesslen, eds., *Joel & Ethan Coen* (New York: Proscenium Publishers, 2001), 172; Ralph Waldo Emerson, "The Transcendentalist," in *The Portable Emerson,* ed. Carl Bode with Malcolm Cowley (New York: Penguin Books, 1981), 99.

1. See the Smithsonian Folkways Recordings song list for the album *Darling Corey and Goofing Off Suite* by Pete Seeger (1993), catalogue #40018 at www. folkways .si.edu.

2. See the poem "Two Tramps in Mud Time, or, A Full-Time Interest," in Robert Frost, *Collected Poems, Prose & Plays* (New York: Library of America, 1995), 251.

3. John Winthrop, "A Model of Christian Charity" (1630), available as part of the Hanover Historical Texts Project, which is part of the Collections of the Massachusetts Historical Society. Available at http://history.hanover.edu/texts/winthmod .html, 47.

4. In the original VHS format the title had a colon followed by the phrase "An Unbelievable Comedy."

5. Aristotle, *Poetics I*, trans. Richard Janko (Indianapolis: Hackett, 1987).

6. Dante's own title was (in translation): "Begins the Comedy of Dante Alighieri, Florentine in Birth, Not in Custom." "The Divine" was added later. A translation of Dante's letter to Can Grande can be found at http://ccat.sas.upenn.edu/jod.cangrande .english.html.

7. This is what Jean Paul Sartre calls "*mauvais foi*" (bad faith).

8. Martin Heidegger, *Being and Time*, trans. John Macquarrie and Edward Robinson (New York: Harper & Row, 1962), 328.

9. Alain Badiou, *Ethics: An Essay on the Understanding of Evil*, trans. Peter Hallward (New York: Verso, 2002), 67–69.

10. Alain Badiou, *Infinite Thought: Truth and the Return to Philosophy*, trans. Oliver Feltham and Justin Clemens (New York: Continuum, 2004), 52.

11. Georg Seesslen, "Looking for a Trail in Coen County," in *Joel & Ethan Coen*, ed. Körte and Seesslen, 230, 277.

12. Plato, *The Republic*, trans. G. M. A. Grube, revised by C. D. C. Reeve (Indianapolis: Hackett, 1992), bk. VII, 516e–518c.

13. Ted Cohen, *Jokes: Philosophical Thoughts on Joking Matters* (Chicago: Univ. of Chicago Press, 1999), 10.

14. Ibid., 25.

15. Dante Alighieri, *The Inferno*, trans. John Ciardi (New York: Mentor Books, 1964), 28.

16. R. Barton Palmer, *Joel and Ethan Coen* (Urbana: Univ. of Illinois Press, 2004), 129.

17. Friedrich Nietzsche, *Human, All Too Human: A Book for Free Spirits*, trans. Marion Faber (Lincoln: Univ. of Nebraska Press, 1986), sec. 5. That section begins, "In ages of crude, primordial cultures, man thought he could come to know a *second real world* in dreams: this is the origin of all metaphysics."

18. Delmore Schwartz, *In Dreams Begin Responsibilities, and Other Stories* (New York: New Directions, 1978). Schwartz borrowed and adapted the line from an epigraph to W. B. Yeats's volume of poems, *Responsibilities* (1914). I am indebted to the anonymous reviewer of this manuscript for this citation.

19. William Butler Yeats, *The Collected Poems of W. B. Yeats* (New York: Macmillan, 1956), 251.

20. Andrew Pulver's original essay from the *Guardian*, entitled "Pictures That Do the Talking," is from 2001 and is reprinted in *The Coen Brothers: Interviews*, ed. William Rodney Allen (Jackson: Univ. Press of Mississippi, 2006), 158.

21. Pulver, quoted in Allen, *Coen Brothers*, 157

The Human Comedy Perpetuates Itself

Nihilism and Comedy in Coen Neo-Noir

Thomas S. Hibbs

> Bunny Lebowski: Ulli doesn't care about anything. He's a nihilist.
> The Dude: Ah. Must be exhausting.
>
> —*The Big Lebowski* (1998)

From their inaugural film, *Blood Simple* (1984), through the film blanc *Fargo* (1996), to *The Man Who Wasn't There* (2001), the Coen brothers have exhibited a preoccupation with the themes, characters, and stylistic techniques of film noir. By the time they made *Blood Simple* in 1984, neo-noir was already established as a recognized category of film.[1] Prior to Quentin Tarantino's darkly comedic unraveling of noir motifs in *Reservoir Dogs* (1992) and *Pulp Fiction* (1994), the Coens were already making consciously comic use of noir plots and stylistic techniques. Lacking Tarantino's penchant for hyperactive and culturally claustrophobic allusions to pop culture, the Coens focus, instead, on traditional noir character types and intricate plots whose complexity is bizarre.

Because it is so often characterized by self-conscious deployment of the techniques of classic noir, neo-noir evinces a strong inclination toward pastiche and the satiric. This makes comic themes more at home in the world of neo-noir than they were in the founding era of noir. Classic noir avoids overt moral lessons and leaves little room for well-adjusted, happy, virtuous types of Americans. The world of classic noir proffers a "disturbing vision . . . that qualifies all hope and suggests a potentially fatal vulnerability" against which no one is adequately protected.[2] Classic noir has deeply democratic instincts: no one wins because the unforgiving laws of the human condition apply universally to every individual. The grim pessimism of classic noir is hardly congenial to the sorts of comic films that flourished in America during the same time period.

This does not mean, however, that comedy is utterly alien to classic noir. The depiction of characters as trapped in a labyrinth at the mercy of a hostile fate can transform the tone of the action from the gravely tragic to the absurdly comic. What initially seems serious and ominous can, over time, come to seem humorous. Angst and fear can be sustained for only so long; endless and pointless terror becomes predictable and laughable. But the shift to a comic perspective involves more than the mere passage of time; comedy is more than tragedy plus time. What matters is the passage of time without any prospect of hope or intelligibility. Life in an absurd universe is rife with comic possibilities. Struggle and striving begin to appear superfluous and foolish. A classic noir film such as *Detour* (Edgar G. Ulmer, 1945) toys with its main character to such an extent that his continued gravity can come to seem a self-inflicted farce. Similarly, the degradation of affection—the perverse erotic attractions in which noir often wallows—lends itself to wry, detached irony, the dominant tone in *Sunset Boulevard* (Billy Wilder, 1950).

The baroque sensibility of noir has always contained the seeds of stylistic excess, even of the celebration of style for its own sake. In neo-noir, the accentuation of hopelessness and the overtly self-conscious deployment of artistic technique make the turn to dark comedy nearly inevitable. By contrast with classic noir films, whose style is reserved and less self-conscious, neo-noirs almost inevitably draw attention to their style, going so far in some cases as to make style itself the subject of the film. In the very act of recognizing the artifice, we are in on the joke, on the sleight of hand performed by the filmmaker. The result is amusement, even laughter.

As Foster Hirsch points out, one of the distinguishing features of neo-noir is a "cavalier amorality" that can steep viewers in a "depraved point of view."[3] Jean-Pierre Chartier's early and negative reaction to noir seems to apply more aptly to certain neo-noir films. Chartier lamented noir's "pessimism and disgust toward humanity." Devoid of even the most "fleeting image of love" or of characters who might "rouse our pity or sympathy," noir, he felt, presents "monsters, criminals whose evils nothing can excuse, whose actions imply that the only source for the fatality of evil is in themselves."[4]

Nietzsche and Nihilism

There are, then, important links between neo-noir and nihilism. According to its most trenchant analysts, nihilism involves the dissolution of standards of judgment; for the nihilist, there is no longer any basis for distinguishing truth from falsity, good from evil, noble from base action, or higher from lower ways of life. Nietzsche thought that nihilism would be the defining characteristic of the twentieth century, an epoch in which "the highest values" would "devalue themselves" and the "question 'why?'" would find "no answer."[5] Nietzsche is most famous for proclaiming the death of God. He certainly does not mean that a previously existing supreme being has suddenly expired; instead, he holds that the notion of God, created by humans to serve a variety of needs, is becoming increasingly less credible. But Nietzsche does not limit the effects of nihilism to religion; nihilism undermines all transcendent claims and standards, including those underlying modern science and democratic politics. The great questions and animating visions—those regarding truth, justice, love, and beauty—that previously gave shape and purpose to human life no longer resonate in the human soul. All moral codes are seen to be merely conventional and, hence, optional.

For most human beings, decline, diminution, and despair accompany nihilism. The bulk of humanity falls into the category of the *last man:* "Alas, the time of the most despicable man is coming, he that is no longer able to despise himself. Behold, I show you the last man. What is love? What is a star? Thus asks the last man and blinks. The earth has become small and on it hops the last man who makes everything small." The contented, petty last men create a society that is ruthlessly homogeneous ("everybody wants the same, everybody is the same") and addicted to physical comfort ("one has one's little pleasure for the day and one's little pleasure for the night; one has a regard for health").[6] These are the passive nihilists, the pessimists, the representatives of "the decline and recession of the power of the spirit."[7]

But nihilism is "ambiguous." If, in one sense, nihilism is the "unwelcome guest," it is also an opportunity, clearing a path for "increased power of the spirit."[8] Active nihilists see the decline of traditional moral and religious systems as an occasion for the thoroughgoing destruction of desiccated ways of life and the creation of a new order of values. Active nihilists, the philosopher-artists of the future, will engage in the "transvaluation of values." They stand beyond good and evil and engage in aesthetic self-creation, a project that is an affront to society's religious and democratic conventions, rooted, as they are, in moral absolutes or democratic consensus.

At times, Nietzsche's remedy for the nihilistic epoch, his path beyond nihilism, promotes a particularly virulent form of aristocracy. As he puts it frankly in the chapter "What Is Noble?" in *Beyond Good and Evil,*

> Every enhancement of the type "man" has so far been the work of an aristocratic society—and so it will be again and again—a society that believes in the long ladder of an order of rank and differences in value between man and man, and that needs slavery in some sense or another. With that pathos of distance that grows out of the ingrained difference between strata . . . keeping down and keeping at a distance, that other, more mysterious pathos could not have grown up either—the craving for an ever new widening of distances within the soul itself, the development of ever higher, rare, more remote, further-stretching, more comprehensive states . . . the continual "self-overcoming of man."[9]

What Nietzsche calls the *pathos of distance* is at work in a variety of neo-noir dramas, from *Body Heat* (Lawrence Kasdan, 1981) and *Cape Fear* (Martin Scorsese, 1991) and *Basic Instinct* (Paul Verhoeven, 1992) to *The Usual Suspects* (Bryan Singer, 1995).[10] In these neo-noir films, certain characters rise above the noir labyrinth, not by passing through it or learning to navigate its shifting waters but by acts of diabolical will. Impervious to the laws of the human condition, these characters get away with lives of criminality. This shift constitutes a movement in the direction of nihilism and a recoiling from the fundamentally democratic world of classic noir. The human condition is no longer universal; the noir trap is no longer seen as an indelible feature. Instead, it constrains only those who lack the willpower, or will to power, necessary to rise above, and control, conventions. Neo-noir's greatest departure from classic noir consists in a turn to aristocratic nihilism. The most resourceful of these characters are in control of the noir plot, using their cunning and artistry to ensnare others. Were it not so cumbersome, we might call this the *nihilistic myth of the American super-antihero.*

Nihilistic comedy has no limits on the targets of its humor; it turns the most atrocious of human acts—rape and beating in *Cape Fear,* cannibalism in *The Silence of the Lambs* (Jonathan Demme, 1991), and maiming in *Reservoir Dogs*—into quasi-comic expressions of exuberant amoral energy.

It mocks our longing for justice, for the protection of the innocent and the punishment of the heinous criminal, and for truth and understanding. The comic unraveling of the horror genre from within begins with the celebration of the evil antihero as beyond good and evil, as more interesting, attractive, and complex than the purportedly good characters in a story. Once this nihilistic move has been made, it is quite natural to repudiate and mock properly human longing for justice, truth, and love. Nihilism, as Nietzsche saw, entails the diminution of human aspiration to the vanishing point; it involves the death of man.

These are the consequences of the nihilistic turn in neo-noir, which repudiates justice, love, and truth in favor of aesthetic self-creation. Criticisms of conventional conceptions of justice, truth, and other ideals are not necessarily nihilistic. Indeed, the very notion of a critique presupposes that one has, implicitly at least, an awareness that things are not as they should be, that it would be better for things to be otherwise. As Shakespeare writes in *King Lear,* "This is not the worst, so long as we can say 'this is the worst'" (4.1). But thoroughgoing nihilism eviscerates any such standards or, what is more to the point, even the intelligibility of the quest for such standards. Gravity cannot be sustained. Audiences are entertained by the demonic superheroes who put on a good show and are much more clever and wittier than other, conventional characters. A character such as Hannibal Lecter (Anthony Hopkins) in *The Silence of the Lambs* is at first terrifying, then entertaining, and finally humorous as, in the film's final frames, he responds to a question as to his plans by saying, wryly, that he'll be having an old friend for dinner.

Noir, Nihilism, and Comedy in *The Big Lebowski*

The comic denouement of *The Silence of the Lambs* signals the unraveling of the hero genre from within, a point driven home with great gusto in such spoofs of the genre as *Scream* (Wes Craven, 1996) and *Scary Movie* (Keenan Ivory Wayans, 2000) and their sequels. If the gravity of the quest to understand and fend off evil produces no great insight about good or evil, just the surface aesthetics of the evildoer, then the audience, having become jaded, anticipates the aesthetics of evil and sees the whole drama as a farce. There is, thus, an opening for a democratic rejoinder to the sort of angst-ridden nihilism that celebrates the tragic heroism of the loner who faces the meaninglessness of life with gravity. The democratic and comic response is: Why bother? What's all the fuss about? If there is no meaning, then why get worked up about anything? And what, in a pointless universe, could possibly provide a basis for distinguishing, as Nietzsche wants to, between noble and base ways of facing the abyss? This sort of comedy mocks radicals of all sorts, whether they be nihilists or zealous reformers. Such is the inspiration for the Coen brothers' comic leveling of nihilism in *The Big Lebowski* (1998).

The Big Lebowski begins and ends with the noir commonplace: voice-over narration. As a tumbleweed blows down the streets of Los Angeles and over a beach, the narrator introduces "the Dude," a name no one else would "self-apply." "Our story," he relates, is set in the early 1990s, at the time of our national "conflict with Saddam and the Iraqis." Sometimes, the narrator continues, "a man is, I won't say a hero, but sometimes a man is just right for his time and place." That man is the Dude, the "laziest man in LA County," an achievement that puts him high in the "running for laziest worldwide." The camera turns to the Dude, wearing shorts and a bathrobe and shopping for groceries. A television in the store plays President George H. W. Bush's speech about the Iraqi threat: "This aggression will not stand."

Later that day, the Dude is attacked at home by intruders who call him Lebowski, stuff his head in the toilet, and demand that he repay the money his wife owes Jackie Treehorn. A perplexed Dude objects that no one calls him Lebowski and that he's not married—gesturing to the raised toilet seat as confirming evidence. The intruders suddenly come to their senses and one of them asks, "Isn't this guy supposed to be a millionaire?" In a parting gesture, they urinate on the rug—an act of defilement that the Dude regrets because "that rug really tied the room together."

These opening scenes introduce readily identifiable neo-noir themes. There is the theme of the loner, certainly not the hero of the old westerns, but rather the uprooted drifter, symbolized in the tumbleweed blown by chance forces beyond its control or comprehension. Then there is the motif of a shallow and artificially constructed political culture, suggested in the television coverage of the Gulf War. As we shall see, the film replays 1960s themes of the establishment versus the antiestablishment, especially in the contrast between the two Lebowskis. Finally, there is the noir staple of the "wrong man," the chance misidentification of an ordinary man as a culprit or criminal of some sort, a misidentification that sparks a series of trials on the part of the wrongly accused. Comic incongruity arises from the theme of the wrong man and from the repeated presence of the Dude in settings where he clearly does not belong, what the Coens call the *anachronism of incompatibility*.

The Dude's social life revolves around bowling with his friends Walter (John Goodman), a Vietnam vet and recent convert to Judaism, and Donny (Steve Buscemi), a pleasant, shy follower. Learning about the intruders, Walter insists that the issue is not the rug but the other Jeff Lebowski, whom the men were after. The Dude decides to visit the Big Lebowski (David Huddleston), a man confined to a wheelchair as a result of injuries suffered in the Korean War. When the Dude asks for remuneration for his destroyed rug and proclaims, "This aggression will not stand," Lebowski taunts him, saying that, when he lost his legs in Korea, he did not ask for a handout. He "went out and achieved": "Your revolution is over. The bums lost." Soon after this encounter, a humbled and weepy Lebowski invites the Dude back to the house and shows him a ransom note, indicating that his wife, Bunny, has been kidnapped. The Dude takes a drag off his joint and says, "Bummer, man." Lebowski offers the Dude twenty thousand dollars and his own beeper to act as a courier. An incredulous Dude asks Lebowski's assistant, "He thinks the carpet pissers did this?"

Throughout much of the film, someone in a blue car follows the Dude. Late in the film, he runs up to the car and yanks out the driver, who explains that he is a "private dick," working on the same case as the one the Dude's working on. He then admits fawningly, "I admire your work. The way you play one side against the other." Here, the Dude once again plays the wrong man role; this time he is misidentified as a professional, a private detective with the knowledge and cleverness to manipulate human character types for his own ends.

This is, of course, a complete illusion; to underscore the Dude's impotence, the Coens immediately shift to a scene in which a group of Germans break into his apartment and find him in his bathtub. As he complains that this is a "private residence," they drop a marmot into the tub just between his legs and announce, "We want the money. We believe in nothing. If we don't get the money, we will come back tomorrow and cut off your johnson." Walter shares the Dude's dislocation, but he, unlike the Dude, is troubled by his rootlessness. The Dude is often irked at Walter's strange Jewish devotion. When the Dude accuses him of living in the past, Walter responds, "Three thousand years of beautiful tradition from Moses to Sandy Koufax, you're goddamn right I'm living in the fucking past!" Walter wants to have an identity, to define himself in relation to a way of life, a tradition larger than himself. How badly he wants this is clear from his willingness to rate National Socialism above nihilism on the "ethos" scale. Yet his own embrace of Judaism, a result of his marriage to a Jewish woman from whom he is now divorced, serves to underscore the absurdity of attempting to introduce an ethos into a fragmented contemporary culture. His Judaism is an incoherent mixture of various elements, dislocated from contexts in which they originally may have made a kind of sense. Walter ranks bowling on about the same level as his religious devotion. Concerned about the Dude's preoccupation with the case of the missing wife, Walter exclaims, "We can't drag this negative energy into the tournament."

Without any direct contribution from the Dude, the case wraps up nicely. It turns out that Bunny was just on an unannounced vacation. Outside the bowling alley, the Germans, who think that Bunny is still missing, torch the Dude's car and demand money, claiming that, if they are not paid, they will kill Bunny. A timid Donny asks: "Are these the Nazis?" Walter replies, "No, these men are nihilists. There's nothing to be afraid of. . . . These men are cowards." When the Dude tells them that Bunny is alive and there will be no financial transaction, one of the Germans complains, "It's not fair." Walter taunts them: "Fair? Who's the fucking nihilist here? What are you, a bunch of fucking crybabies?" In the ensuing conflict, Donny has a heart attack and dies.

Walter here puts his finger on the problem of self-described nihilists and of the incompatibility between nihilism and human life, no matter how debased. Nihilism cannot, strictly speaking, be lived. An utterly amorphous and completely pointless life would deprive an individual not just of any inspiring sense of purpose but even of the basis for deliberating and pursuing anything whatsoever. Moreover, everyone complains about something, and this is rooted in some sense, however misguided and self-interested, of injustice or wrongs suffered. Full-blown nihilism cannot be lived; it can only be approached asymptotically.

Although the Dude is not foolish enough to proclaim himself a nihilist, his life borders on nihilism. He is skeptical of large-scale beliefs such as those to which Walter assents. He does not need an ethos, except insofar as that is mere style, which is about what the Jewish religion is for Walter. But the Dude has beliefs. He believes, for example, in private property, at least for himself. He thinks of himself as a respectable citizen; he is a low-class, minimally ambitious version of what the social critic David Brooks has called a *Bobo*, a bourgeois bohemian, someone who combines elements of

1960s counterculture with degrees of bourgeois conformity and standards of success.[11] Brooks's new social standard–bearers are much more bourgeois than bohemian; inversely, the Dude is more bohemian than bourgeois. He is little concerned with societal standards of success and insouciantly repudiates the work ethic. But, like Walter, he is also passionate about bowling and is deeply concerned with how his team will perform in the upcoming competition.

The Dude accepts the basic absurdity of the cosmos, of life in the most advanced civilization ever to grace the face of the earth. His way of life affirms the equal significance or insignificance of all human endeavors, but none of this stops him from judging certain things to be unseemly. The Dude has not so much an ethos as a style, a way of taking it easy, living lightly. Despite his lack of conscious planning and his absence of ambition, he manages to contribute to ongoing natural processes. At one point, he has sex with Maude, the Big Lebowski's libidinous and artistically rebellious daughter. Afterward, she asks a number of questions about his life and his habits of recreation. The zenith of his life was organizing campus protests in the 1960s; his recreation consists in car cruising and the occasional acid flashback. He gets out of bed and notices that Maude remains on her back cradling her legs, a strategy designed to increase the chances of conception. "What did you think this was all about?" she asks. When he expresses worries about the responsibilities of fatherhood, she explains that a deadbeat dad is exactly what she wants.

The Dude is a kind of comic hero, at least for our narrator (Sam Elliott), who shows up onscreen in the final scene at the bowling alley, where he and the Dude exchange pleasantries. The cowboy matter-of-factly reiterates the Dude's own self-referential proclamation, "The Dude abides," and offers some reflective, concluding observations:

> The Dude abides. I don't know about you, but I take comfort in that. It's good knowin' he's out there, the Dude, takin' her easy for all us sinners. Shoosh. I sure hope he makes the finals. Welp, that about does her, wraps her all up. Things seem to've worked out pretty good for the Dude 'n' Walter, and it was a purt good story, dontcha think? Made me laugh to beat the band. Parts, anyway. Course—I didn't like seein' Donny go. But then, happen to know that there's a little Lebowski on the way. I guess that's the way the whole durned human comedy keeps perpetuatin' itself, down through the generations,

westward the wagons, across the sands a time until—aw, look at me,
I'm ramblin' again. Wal, uh hope you folks enjoyed yourselves.

The Dude's abiding signals an escape, or at least a reprieve, from the world
of noir; in spite of the threats to his life, the Dude emerges from the noir
plot, from its labyrinth, unscathed. The tone of the ending, the suggestion that the human comedy perpetuates itself through the ongoing birth
of new humans, strikes a comic note different from that of mere satire or
denunciatory cynicism. Here, the impulses and resources of nature toward
reproduction and survival are seen as more powerful than the destructive
forces of noir. As Pascal puts it (a sentiment later stolen by Hume), "Nature
backs up helpless reason and stops it going so wildly astray."[12]

Basic Familial Instincts in Coen Comedy

As one critic has noted, *The Big Lebowski* is about "friendship and surrogate
families."[13] This strikes a note of comic affirmation absent in even the most
complex noir films, wherein the family is nearly always a source of the noir
trap, and marriages and the begetting of children provide no way out. If
surrogate families are at the heart of *The Big Lebowski*, real families figure
prominently in other Coen films, especially in the brothers' most critically
acclaimed neo-noir, *Fargo*. With a plot akin to that of *A Simple Plan* (Sam
Raimi, 1998), *Fargo* features criminals undone by their own futile, criminal
plans. The characters are *blood simple*, a phrase that the Coens borrowed
from Dashiell Hammett, who borrowed it from police talk to describe the
way criminals lose control of full rationality at the moment of committing
the crime and, thus, inevitably leave incriminating clues behind. Apparently
cold and calculating, they nonetheless act without adequate foresight; the
consequences of their acts quickly swirl out of control. Called a *film blanc*
because of the near-whiteout conditions that prevail in the film's setting in
the plains of North Dakota, *Fargo* features criminals who suffer "snow blind-
ness," the self-deceiving illusion of infallibility.[14] As in *Blood Simple*, here
too criminals are subject to a comedy of errors. Yet *Fargo* is a very different
film from *Blood Simple*; it inscribes the comedy of criminal error within
a more traditional structure of the detective who affirms the goodness of
conventional mores, a married and pregnant female detective named Marge
Gunderson (Frances McDormand in an Oscar-winning performance).

In the final scenes of *Fargo*, Marge's role as commentator eclipses in significance her role as investigator. Indeed, the criminals seem destined to destroy themselves. Marge's comments about her expected baby affirm a certain way of life as making sense, as bearing fruit, and as something worth preserving and handing on to the next generation. Her domestic life is void of the sort of calculating, radically individualist spirit that infects the families of the criminals in the film and the typical families that inhabit other noir films.

Despite its gruesome violence and somber tone, *Fargo*'s conclusion calls to mind certain features of classical comedy, which often ends with a wedding, an affirmation of order, especially of the marital bond as the cornerstone of hope in society. Affirming the reasonableness of conventions, classical comedy mocks radicals—be they criminals or well-intentioned reformers. Marge does not seek deeper meaning beneath the surface; committed to a conventional understanding of justice, she is not on a great quest to discern the nature and causes of evil. The causes, if there are any discernible (greed for a "little bit of money"), are readily available on the surface of criminal action; yet, given the risks, the cost, and the affront to natural goodness ("It's a beautiful day"), evil remains inexplicable: "I just don't understand it." Marge witnesses at close range the noir trap of criminality, but it does not destroy her—or even tempt her.

In a review of *Fargo* entitled "The Banality of Virtue," Laura Miller observes the "dullness of the Midwestern characters" and the essential emptiness of their values. She wonders, "In the universe of Fargo, where virtue is a kind of ignorance and wickedness a nullity, where do real people fit in?"[15] Indeed, the Coens' alternatives to nihilists, the characters who avoid entrapment by the noir vices of lust and greed, seem not so much virtuous as incapable of the complexities of vice. They seem to suffer from a sort of Forrest Gump syndrome, a sort of banality of goodness, a strange and comic counterpoint to Hannah Arendt's famous thesis concerning the banality of evil.[16] If this line of interpretation were correct, then we might see the substance, or lack thereof, in the Coens' films as a "knowing, highly allusive" form of filmmaking that is no more than "pastiche."[17]

Yet the gentle levity with which the Coens treat these characters and the way the characters embody natural tendencies, which they cannot themselves articulate, suggest the presence of something more than mere banality. Foster Hirsch, for example, describes McDormand's character as "a cockeyed optimist, wide-eyed but hardly stupid."[18] Indeed, the interweaving of comedy and fertility harks back to pagan and Shakespearean comedy, with the celebration of rites of fertility and marriage, of an order of nature that overcomes human vice and frailty and reconciles opposing forces and conflicting wills. No such complete reconciliation is possible in neo-noir, not even in the Coens' comic neo-noir. Yet the Coens' penchant for presenting fertility and, in some films, familial fidelity as ways of avoiding entanglement in the noir traps of lust and greed points in the direction of such comic reconciliation.

The themes of family and procreation are the preeminent issues in the Coens' early pure comedy, *Raising Arizona* (1987), the story of a recidivist petty thief, Hi (Nicolas Cage), and a female prison guard, Ed (Holly Hunter). Over a number of years and many return trips to prison, Hi falls in love with Ed, and she accepts his proposal of marriage. The film includes a number of noir themes—crime, repetition, entrapment, and the spoiling of the future by deeds committed in the past. Yet here those noir themes are, ultimately, inscribed within an overarching comic structure that contains both the theme of fertility and that of hopeful reconciliation. Throughout much of the film, Hi appears incapable of learning or altering his behavior. He admits in a voice-over that he is not sure where folks stand on the incarceration issue, whether it is about rehabilitation or just revenge. As we watch him being arrested yet again, he comments that he has begun to believe that revenge is the only possibility that makes any sense.

His marriage to Ed seems to have a salutary effect, at least until Ed is diagnosed as barren. Hi comments that her "insides were a rocky place where my seed could find no purchase." Seeing the announcement of the birth of the Arizona quints, born to the wealthy Nathan Arizona and his wife, Ed suggests that they kidnap one of the boys since the Arizona family has more than it can handle. Hi scales a ladder, enters the boys' bedroom, and takes Nathan Jr. In a surprise twist, Hi is the one who cannot live with the thought of their deed. His conscience exacts revenge in a dream where he is pursued by the "lone biker of the apocalypse," a vengeful giant of a man sporting a tattoo: "Mama Didn't Love Me." The tattoo is a whimsical statement of the core theme of the film, that familial love is the essence of human life. The crimes that Hi and Ed commit are but a perverse pursuit of properly human goods, one in which there is a twisted acknowledgment of the primacy of familial bonds.

The few noir elements in the film are subordinate to a larger narrative, a story of fidelity and the hope for fertility. Hi and Ed eventually come to their senses and return the baby. Relieved of their burden of conscience,

Hi has another dream, which may, he concedes, have been just wishful thinking, a dream of the future in which Nathan Jr. is happy and successful and Hi and Ed gather around a dinner table with their numerous offspring. What the Coen brothers hint at in a number of their noir films they explicitly embrace in *Raising Arizona:* the resilience of human nature's basic instincts, not the instincts for lust and domination of others, but those for love, affection, and procreation, instincts that steer human beings toward a happy ending, in spite of the damage done and the detours caused by their calculative misjudgments.

Notes

1. For a nice discussion of neo-noir and a division of it into modernist and post-modernist stages, see Andrew Spicer, *Film Noir* (Harlow, U.K.: Longman, 2002), 130–74. Also indispensable is Foster Hirsch, *Detours and Lost Highways: A Map of Neo-Noir* (New York: Limelight, 1999).

2. J. P. Telotte, *Voices in the Dark: The Narrative Patterns of Film Noir* (Urbana: Univ. of Illinois Press, 1989), 218.

3. Hirsch, *Detours and Lost Highways,* 10.

4. Jean-Pierre Chartier, "Les Américains aussi font des films 'noirs,'" *Revue du cinéma* 2 (1946): 67.

5. Friedrich Nietzsche, *The Will to Power,* trans. Walter Kaufmann (New York: Vintage, 1968), bk. 1, "European Nihilism," no. 2, 9.

6. Friedrich Nietzsche, *Thus Spoke Zarathustra,* in *The Portable Nietzsche,* trans. Walter Kaufmann (Harmondsworth, U.K.: Penguin, 1968), 129.

7. Nietzsche, *Will to Power,* no. 22, 17.

8. Ibid.

9. Friedrich Nietzsche, *Beyond Good and Evil,* trans. Walter Kaufmann (New York: Vintage, 1966), no. 257, 201.

10. For further discussion of the relation between Nietzsche, nihilism, and noir, see Mark T. Conard, "Nietzsche and the Meaning and Definition of Noir," in *The Philosophy of Film Noir,* ed. Mark T. Conard (Lexington: Univ. Press of Kentucky, 2006), 7–22.

11. See David Brooks, *Bobos in Paradise: The Upper Class and How They Got There* (New York: Simon & Schuster, 2000).

12. Blaise Pascal, *Pensées,* trans. A. J. Krailsheimer (London: Penguin, 1966), no. 131, 64.

13. James Mottram, *The Coen Brothers: The Life of the Mind* (Dulles, Va.: Brassey's, 2000).

14. Ibid., 124.

15. Laura Miller, "The Banality of Virtue," *Salon.com*, http://archive.salon.com/09/reviews/farg01.html.

16. I have discussed *Forrest Gump* (Robert Zemeckis, 1994), nihilism, and comedy in great detail in *Shows about Nothing: Nihilism in Popular Culture from "The Exorcist" to "Seinfeld"* (Dallas: Spence, 1999). On the banality of evil, see Hannah Arendt, *Eichmann in Jerusalem: A Report on the Banality of Evil* (1963; rev. and enlarged ed., 1965; reprint, Harmondsworth, U.K.: Penguin Classics, 1994).

17. Spicer, *Film Noir*, 149; James Naremore, *More Than Night: Film Noir in Its Contexts* (Berkeley and Los Angeles: Univ. of California Press, 1998), 214–15.

18. Hirsch, *Detours and Lost Highways*, 245.

PHILOSOPHIES OF COMEDY IN
O BROTHER, WHERE ART THOU?

Douglas McFarland

It is said that upon a visit to Berlin in the immediate aftermath of World War II, Groucho Marx was taken to the mound of rubble that had been the site of Hitler's bunker. Groucho stepped out of his jeep and climbed to the top of what constituted Hitler's gravesite, where he unexpectedly proceeded to dance the Charleston. On one level, the gesture is meant to defy evil, to assert the celebration of dance over the horrors of Hitler's madness, to demonstrate the irrepressible energy of the human spirit. Groucho, in short, thumbs his nose at the Führer. But his act of irreverence is also the staging of a radical and scandalous incongruity. Comedy is, as Kierkegaard asserted, "wherever there is contradiction."[1] In this case, the contradiction between a 1920s dance step and the perpetrator of the profound atrocity of twentieth-century Europe expresses the absurdity of the human condition. Groucho's gesture is ultimately as unsettling as it is liberating.

Within the overarching narrative framework of *O Brother, Where Art Thou?* (2000) the Coen brothers have generated their own complex set of comic absurdities. Although it has been called the "least serious" of the Coen brothers' oeuvre, the film is, in fact, one of their most thoughtful. With its fast-paced picaresque style and collection of zany characters, the film has undoubtedly delighted a wide audience, but its serious themes and at times disturbing contradictions also challenge that delight. The film has been fruitfully explicated in terms of pastiche, dissonance, and "engaged reinvention," but the film's serious comic underpinnings can best be understood through the overlapping concepts of the mechanical, the contradictory, and the absurd articulated by Henri Bergson and Kierkegaard. According to Bergson, we laugh when we see a human as a "set-up mechanism . . . a jointed puppet."[2] For Kierkegaard, the comic represents the unmediated contradictions of the human condition, incongruities that defy resolution but generate laughter. It is a blend of these perspectives that we experience in *O Brother*, as zany cartoon figures dance like mechanical marionettes across a landscape of existential incongruities, at times oblivious to their ontological status and at others struggling to resist the rigidity of law and the inflexibility of social roles and personal obsessions.

The philosophical explication of comedy runs its own comic risks. From Aristophanes to Rabelais and Swift, the scholar has been the natural butt and easy target of comedy. The philosopher's rigid obsession with his or her system of thought, a "hobby horse," as Sterne would put it, is potentially as laughable as Ulysses Everett McGill's (George Clooney) obsession with a particular brand of hair pomade. And no doubt, the Coen brothers would be amused by my own exegetical method. But my intention is not to impose an artificial intellectual category on what is visceral and alive but to provide a means to engage the social, ethical, and existential complexities of laughter in *O Brother, Where Art Thou?*

Generic Incongruities

The title of the Coen brothers' romp through Depression-era America comes from Preston Sturges's film *Sullivan's Travels* (1941). *O Brother, Where Art Thou?* is the title of the socially conscious film that Sullivan, after directing a series of successful musical comedies, now intends to make. He decides to move away from making films similar to Busby Berkeley's *Gold Diggers of 1935*, a celebration of sex, money, and dance, to ones similar to William Wellman's *Wild Boys of the Road* (1933), an indictment of social inequality, economic depravation, and railroad bulls. But after experiencing a transforming epiphany, Sullivan proclaims upon his return to Hollywood that there is as much, if not more, value in comedy as there is in working-class manifestos. On this "cock-eyed caravan" that we call life, laughter is a necessary tonic for its many trials and tribulations.

The Coen brothers' film, therefore, immediately confronts its knowledgeable audience with a generic incongruity. Although the film bears the title of the gritty film Sullivan originally intended to make, and indeed it does chronicle the travails of those facing economic hardship, social injustice, and political corruption, it is also a madcap comedy, perhaps the very comedy Sullivan decided to make after returning to Hollywood. We are left with an indecorous hybrid: *I Am a Fugitive from a Chain Gang* (Mervyn LeRoy, 1932) filmed as screwball comedy. Rather than therapeutic, the Coens would seem to have made a film that elicits a potentially jarring incongruity. This unresolved contradiction in generic perspective provides the ongoing comic dynamic of the film. What results is not a traditionally mixed generic form such as tragicomedy or pastoral epic but a self-consciously contradictory artifact.

The incongruity between comic high jinks and social commentary is addressed in an early self-referential scene. Three escapees from a chain gang, encumbered by the manacles that fasten them together, are struggling to climb aboard a boxcar of a moving train. Ulysses McGill, the apparent leader of the group, is first to pull himself up. But at the very moment of his triumph, as he pauses to ask if anyone of those already riding the train might be a smithy, the chain that binds him to his fellow fugitives tightens, and he is suddenly and unceremoniously yanked off the train. Satisfied that he is free and mobile, he forgets that he remains chained to his two companions and as a result takes a comic pratfall. To put it differently, he remembers that he needs a blacksmith's file to be unshackled, but he concurrently fails to remember that he is shackled.

The wide-eyed, exaggerated, and even goofy look on McGill's face, as well as the automated movement of his body as it is jerked down and pulled across the floor of the boxcar suggests Bergson's notion that we laugh when we see "something mechanical encrusted on the living."[3] The comic buffoon is one who has become a "lifeless automaton." Bergson's phenomenological understanding of comedy is an outgrowth of the contrast he makes between habit and recollection in *Matter and Memory*. He describes rote learning as a habitual type of memory: "Like every habitual bodily exercise, it is stored up in a mechanism which is set in motion as a whole by an initial impulse, in a closed system of automatic movements."[4] The comic figure is one given over to the "easy automatism of acquired habits."[5] This renders him a "jointed puppet . . . a set up mechanism," and the "more exactly these two images, that of a person and that of a machine, fit into one another, the more striking is the comic effect."[6]

In this context, it is important to note the twofold subtext that informs Bergson's explication of laughter. Written at the turn of the twentieth century, his treatment reflects his perception of a dehumanized culture, one in which the individual is increasingly enveloped in modern mechanization. This phenomenon was addressed as early as Marx's *Economic and Philosophic*

Manuscripts of 1844 and as late as Charlie Chaplin's film *Modern Times* (1936). The regulation of labor, aptly depicted by Harold Lloyd in *Safety Last* (Fred Newmeyer, Sam Taylor, 1923), and the bureaucratic configuration of mass society, addressed in King Vidor's *The Crowd* (1928), render man an automaton, not simply oppressed by a machine but transformed into one. Bergson's comic figure, manipulated from the outside as if it were a toy puppet and viewed as a depersonalized caricature, mirrors modern man caught up in social conformity, repetitive labor, and psychological habit.

This troubling side of Bergson's vision is accompanied by the prefigurement of an empowering one. Although Bergson wrote *Laughter* prior to the technological innovations of live-action animation, his understanding of the mechanized puppet looks forward to the cartoon figure. But the inherent sense of victimization in Bergson's characterization of the comic is replaced in animation by a sense of omnipotence. The flexibility and plasticity, termed "plamaticness" by Sergei Eisenstein, of this animated figure suggests an almost redemptive quality.[7] Its rubbery nature gives it the power to come back to life. As Steven Dillon puts it, "Cartoonism gives the impression of infinite repeatability. Cartoons tend to be serial, not singular. The cartoon world is cornucopian, overflowing, not empty."[8] This explains why an audience is not threatened by cartoon violence. Toons bounce back, immune from the physical violence perpetrated against them.

Both victimization and empowerment inform the opening scene on the train in *O Brother*. As I point out above, the freedom and autonomy that McGill believes he has attained once having pulled himself up onto the moving train is quickly proven to be not simply ephemeral but self-deceiving. McGill is a mere toy, not necessarily in the hands of modernity, but of the Mississippi state penal system. The chains, which bind the three prisoners together, are controlled by an external force, a puppet master who in this scene doesn't simply limit their movement but controls it as well. Although the sense of unease, of the innate cruelty of a certain form of comedy, at this particular moment remains enveloped in a comic pratfall, it nevertheless runs throughout the film with varying degrees of emphasis.

What I have referred to as cartoon empowerment enters the scene in a much more subtle manner and through a self-reflexive device. Once McGill has climbed on board and pulls himself up, he peers into the recess of the car and perceives a group of men huddled together. It is from this group that he seeks a smithy. The scene sets up certain expectations in the audience. It is of a type that moviegoers would have seen before in films ranging from the aforementioned *Wild Boys of the Road* to Hal Ashby's *Bound for Glory* (1976) and Clint Eastwood's *The Gauntlet* (1977), as well as countless other "road" pictures. The audience anticipates that McGill will discover a marginalized group of men and women, perhaps even sentimentalized as in a Frank Capra film, who will welcome McGill with the camaraderie of the road, or a group who will throw him off the train, hardened by their failures and unwilling to share with others what they have acquired for themselves.

McGill, however, faces neither friend nor foe. A collection of forgotten men with hollow looks simply stare back at him. Their faces express little more than indifference toward the new passenger. It is a disturbing commentary on the effects of the Great Depression. More importantly, the scene is constructed within a theatrical framework. McGill stands up on the floor of the car as if he were on a fully lit stage, while those already occupying the car sit back in the darkness as if they were themselves an audience for McGill's antics. The scene calls to mind the moment in *Sullivan's Travels* when the prisoners are marched into a church to enjoy a cartoon. Although this set piece from Sturges's film is used later in *O Brother* in an overt manner, it is here on the train that it raises serious issues concerning the comic nature of the scene. The prisoners in *Sullivan's Travels* watch a Walt Disney cartoon in which Pluto is shown at his most elastic. In one sequence he becomes attached to flypaper and chases his own body around in a frustrated circle before flopping on the ground. In another he is wrapped up in a window shade and then spat back out. The prisoners laugh uproariously at Pluto's mishaps, but Sturges does not seem interested in exploring why they laugh. One senses, however, that the laughter is therapeutic not because they are able to divert their victimization onto another entity but because violence itself has been relegated into the plastic world of animation, a medium in which elasticity and repeatability diffuse its threat to their bodies. Pluto is always restored to his original configuration.

The therapeutic empowerment of animation is conspicuous in its absence in the scene in the Coen brothers' film. Unease is generated not simply through the evocation of Bergson's automaton but in the inability of these men to respond to the animated caricature before them. It suggests that their apparent indifference to McGill's pratfall is symptomatic of their despair. The film viewer recognizes the elasticity of McGill and the lack of a real threat to his body when he falls off the train. The audience within the film, however, seems deadened to the possibility of laughter and hardened to the salutatory effect of cartoons.

One more aspect of the scene needs to be addressed. In his explanation of what constitutes the comic in *Concluding Unscientific Postscript to "Philosophical Fragments,"* Kierkegaard asserts, "If the reason for people's hustle-bustle is a possibility of avoiding danger, the busyness is not comic; but if, for example, it is on a ship that is sinking, there is something comic in all this running around, because the contradiction is that despite all this movement they are not moving away from the site of their downfall."[9] Men scurrying about hopelessly trying to save themselves would not on the surface seem funny, other than in a sadistic way. But for Kierkegaard it represents the contradiction that is intrinsic to comedy and to life. This is expressed in Kierkegaard's joke as the contradiction between freedom and necessity, between our infinite aspirations and the finite realities that confront those aspirations.[10] The crew on the ship, striving to keep itself afloat and yet helpless in its attempt, illustrates the contradiction between our need to take action and the ultimate meaninglessness of that action. It is the existential conundrum of the human condition.

The three convicts attempting to climb aboard the moving train fall neatly into Kierkegaard's comic scenario. They struggle for release and freedom but are bound to one another and in a sense bound to the earth. They reflect our innate belief in the need for action and the ultimate meaninglessness of action. Such a scene generates despair if one focuses on the frustration, but a comic understanding focuses on the absurdity of the moment. The utopian fantasy sung over the opening credits, "The Big Rock Candy Mountain," expresses the human need to imagine the possibility of redemption, and its lyrics hover over the attempted escape. The incongruity between the fanciful dream of a place where "bulldogs all have rubber teeth" and the frustrated cartoon characters of the film is precisely what Kierkegaard understood as comic. Perhaps Wylie Sypher best describes the dynamic at work in the scene: "Essentially our enjoyment of physical mishap or deformity springs from our surprise and delight that man's actions are often absurd, his energies often misdirected."[11] In *O Brother, Where Art Thou?* a host of characters are seeking freedom. That their attempts are more often than not cast as "absurd" and "misdirected" does not diminish their sincerity and expressiveness.

The opening set piece of *O Brother* depicting McGill and his cohorts failing in their attempt to board the train that would take them to freedom is a multifaceted comic staging and previews the complex and overlapping subtleties of the comic gestures that inform the film.

Challenging Postmodern Aesthetics

Although the climax of *O Brother* occurs with the Tennessee Valley Authority flooding the McGill ancestral "homeland," the picaresque set of adventures turns toward its conclusion at the Klan rally that McGill and his fellow escapees have infiltrated in order to rescue Tommy (Chris Thomas King), the African American blues musician they had met and befriended earlier in the film. But more importantly, through its rich collection of allusions to other texts, the scene provides its audience with the most striking and most unsettling set of comic incongruities in the film. These incongruities not only satirize the hooded Klansmen but also challenge the audience to move beyond the aesthetic pleasure of the film's postmodern wit. What has been called the "engaged reinvention" of popular mythologies that the Coen brothers demonstrate in *The Hudsucker Proxy* (1994) here takes on the form of a set of radical and disturbing contradictions.[12]

Allusions to *The Odyssey,* Busby Berkeley, Leni Riefenstahl, the Three Stooges, Robert Johnson, and *The Wizard of Oz* (Victor Fleming, 1939) all appear in the episode. Although these references play off one another in both obvious and subtle ways, the scene is grounded in a particular moment in American history: the activities of the Ku Klux Klan in the South in the 1930s. This is, of course, a particularly dark episode in the history of the republic and one that taken in isolation would generate some combination of outrage and guilt in the typically liberal audiences that the films of the Coen brothers might attract. The rich array of allusions, in short, cannot be separated from a historical context that elicits moral condemnation.

It is this historical grounding that undermines a postmodern reading of the episode. The assemblage of popular mythologies, pop culture references, and classical allusions does not, in this case, constitute what Fredric Jameson and others term "pastiche." Unlike parody and satire, pastiche, according to Jameson, is "the cannibalization of all styles of the past, the play of random stylistic allusion[,]" and thus constitutes a "neutral practice," an artistic and cultural form that has been emptied of any ethical perspective and "amputated of satiric impulse."[13] The postmodern pleasure of pastiche is the pleasure of recognizing references, so that engaging a text becomes a game of identification. Moreover, through this consumption of cultural signs, there emerges in the audience a sense of belonging to an "exclusive community," one detached from both traditional socioeconomic classifications and conventional ethical codes.[14] Membership in this sophisticated coterie group, which many in the audience of a Coen brothers film might expect, is sabotaged, I think intentionally, by the context of a Klan lynching of an African American. There is quite simply no possibility of avoiding the historical setting of the episode and the ethical response that that setting demands. Although the scene in question does expose the audience to a heterogeneous grouping of aesthetic styles and allusions, these do not occupy a neutral space devoid of normative values and of what Jameson refers to in this context as "real history."[15]

The most obvious consequence of this grounding is that the engaged and directed point of view of satire replaces the neutrality of postmodern wit. The scene opens with McGill and his two fellow travelers looking down from under cover at a Klan ceremony, which they soon learn is a lynching. The members of the Klan are marching in synchronized patterns that immediately call to mind a Busby Berkeley set piece. The Klansmen are, therefore, being mocked as silly men, in silly outfits, and in silly dance formations. Like Satan's band of devils in *Paradise Lost* who are compared to a swarm of insects, the self-importance of the Klansmen is deflated through a visual simile. The satire is reinforced through a Homeric parallel. The charlatan Bible salesman (John Goodman) who has robbed and beaten McGill and Delmar (Tim Blake Nelson) now shows up at the rally. His role as the uncultured and violent Cyclops of *The Odyssey* mocks the office of Grand Cyclops of the Klan.

The set of allusions taken together suggests, however, something more sophisticated than satire, something that relies on irreconcilable comic incongruities within that set of allusions. Perhaps the most outrageous and resonant reference in the set piece is to *The Wizard of Oz*. The rescue of Tommy from the hands of the Klan visually evokes the rescue of Dorothy from the Wicked Witch of the West. The three escapees take the parts of the Scarecrow, the Tin Man, and the Cowardly Lion. The Klan becomes the army of the Wicked Witch. This creates a jarring incongruity, one that is intensified by the contextualization of the allusion outside its original historical setting. Although *The Wizard of Oz* was made in the final years of the Depression and is in some sense a typical thirties "road" picture, its presence in the film will resonate with most of the audience in the context of the fifties, sixties, and seventies. For many years before the advent of home video technology, the film was annually shown on television and became an anticipated event, an almost ritualized staging in the living rooms of

American families. An allusion to the film generates not simply a memory but nostalgia for "a privileged lost object of desire."[16] In an impish and insidious manner, the Coens have uprooted this warm memory and relocated it to a 1930s Klan rally and execution.

The effect of the allusion on the audience is threefold. First, there is the pleasure in simply identifying the allusion, the sense of belonging to the sophisticated coterie group I mention above. Secondly, there is the pleasure in witnessing a childhood fantasy defeat evil. It is the Scarecrow, the Tin Man, and the Cowardly Lion who rescue Tommy from the clutches of the Klan and flatten its Cyclops. The innocence of a childhood fantasy proves stronger than racism. But thirdly, the allusion creates a disturbing and ironic incongruity: that between the dark recess of Mississippi in the 1930s and the living rooms of postwar baby boomers and their children.

Kierkegaard is instructive in understanding the effect if not the purpose of this irony. He asserts in the *Concluding Unscientific Postscript* that "irony is the *confinium* [boundary] between the aesthetic and the ethical."[17] The relationship between these two stages and the role that irony plays in the advancement from the former to the latter is treated extensively by Kierkegaard in *Either/Or*. In part I, a young man argues for the aesthetic point of view in a series of heterogeneous papers on topics as diverse as music, drama, crop rotation, and eroticism. In discussing these subjects, he asserts that one must distance oneself from commitment to any one particular form of artistic expression or to one exclusive human relationship. The aesthete is dimly aware of the existential contradictions of life, but he would avoid them by continually seeking out new experiences, preoccupying himself with the surfaces of life, and generally playing "shuttlecock with all existence."[18] "Everything in life," says the aesthete, "is regarded as a wager. The more consistently a person knows how to sustain his arbitrariness, the more amusing the combinations become."[19] The aesthete must constantly be changing his orientation to the world.

Part II of *Either/Or* consists of two letters written to the young man by a judge who represents the so-called ethical point of view. He challenges the self-styled aesthete not necessarily to adopt a specific ethical perspective but to act in the world, to overcome his indifference. "It is not," he explains, "a matter of choosing between willing good or willing evil as of choosing to will."[20] The aesthete should, in short, cease to be the "plaything for the play of his arbitrariness."[21] The task of the ethicist is to make the young man confront the comic contradictions of the human condition, the ironic incongruities between the body and the soul, the finite and the infinite, the necessary and the free, which inform the human condition.

Jameson's understanding of the postmodern world and the individual enmeshed within its plethora of signs is uncanny in its similarity to Kierkegaard's understanding of the young aesthete and his need for new and changing experiences. Jameson asserts, "What has happened is that aesthetic production today has become integrated into commodity production generally: the frantic urgency of producing fresh waves of ever more novel-seeming goods . . . at ever greater rates of turnover."[22] It is precisely this consumer of aesthetic commodities whom the Coen brothers confront in their staging of the Klan rally. They do it by fashioning a disturbing comic contradiction that defies the consumptive pleasures of their audience. The filmmakers' role is that of the judge in *Either/Or* who demands that the young, sophisticated aesthete confront the ironies of the human condition. Unlike *The Hudsucker Proxy,* whose comic perspective interrogates socioeconomic conditions of a specific era, the ironic incongruities of *O Brother* act against its own audience. The Coens are mischievous boys; in this instance, their mischief challenges the complacencies of the postmodernist aesthetic.

Comic Endings

The audience is informed of parallels between *O Brother* and *The Odyssey* in the opening credits, when the invocation from Homer's poem appears on the screen: "O Muse, sing in me and through me . . . that man . . . a wanderer, harried for years on end."[23] This is an invitation for the audience to search out specific references to the poem as the film progresses. And indeed, we do recognize versions of the Cyclops, the Sirens, the suitors, and others in the film. But the most significant borrowing from *The Odyssey* is an overarching narrative framework. The structural pattern of Homer's poem is one of loss and recovery, of wandering and return. The narrative begins with Odysseus hidden away on Kalypso's island and is set in motion with his decision to return to Ithaca. The tale reaches its conclusion with the recognition of the hero and the reordering of home and kingdom. The episodes of the poem are contained within an overarching narrative design that seeks and achieves closure. To the extent that the narrative reaches its conclusion with the reunification of the family unit and the reaffirmation of marriage, we might also say that its pattern is comic.

The Coen brothers' version of *The Odyssey* shares this narrative pattern.

The film begins with the hero's escape not from an exotic island but from a chain gang. It goes on to chronicle the "adventures" of our Odysseus as he makes his way back to home and family. Although he has told his cohorts that treasure awaits them, his real goal is to prevent his wife from remarrying and to restore his position as the true paterfamilias. Within this narrative structure we encounter others who are also seeking redemptive resolutions. When he learns that the wife of Pete's (John Turturro) cousin has run off, McGill suggests that she might have been looking for answers. And when Delmar sees the mesmerizing procession of initiates moving ceremoniously to the baptismal waters, he impulsively hurls himself into the river, insisting that he too be redeemed. And in something of an inversion of Delmar's passionate gesture, Tommy seeks out the Devil to acquire another form of redemption: the gift of music.

Unlike *The Odyssey,* however, the conclusion of *O Brother* is subverted. In the final scene of the film, McGill presents his Penelope (Holly Hunter) with the ring that he believes will reunite him with his wife and finally bring him the "repose" he has been seeking. But Penny refuses to acknowledge the symbolic value of the object and tells him that this particular ring, because it is not the original ring, lacks the magical charm that will restore their marriage. The ring, like her husband, is not bona fide. The family marches off across the screen with Penny in the lead and the aspiring paterfamilias tagging along behind. The comic resolution that the audience awaits and expects is undermined by the ironic representation of an uxorious Odysseus and of a family whose reordering remains in suspense.

Once again, Kierkegaard's distinction between the aesthetic and ethical points of view is instructive in understanding this apparently unresolved comic conclusion. In *Either/Or,* the young aesthete rejects marriage and asserts that eroticism should not be expressed in the context of a commitment to "everlasting love." He sees marriage as something "everlasting," not in the sense that it is immortal but in that it entraps one in temporal longevity. In other words, the resolution of the tension between the desire to transcend time and the reality that one necessarily lives within time is attained in the immediacy of the moment. And so the aesthete argues that "poetic infinity . . . can well be limited to one hour as to a month."[24] It needs to be stressed that this represents something more than a desire for instant gratification. It is the attempt to resolve through the immediacy of an aesthetic experience the fundamental contradiction of life: we necessarily live within time but can concurrently imagine ourselves outside time.

The ethicist responds that marriage is a means to "bind" time in a way that acknowledges longevity and mutability. The aesthete's "poetic infinity" is a fool's paradise, a vain attempt to gain release from the finite and material. Promiscuity, which the aesthete practices, is merely a form of consumption, a strategy to avoid the disturbing incongruities of life. These incongruities, however, are acknowledged in marriage: "The married man solves the great riddle, to live in eternity and yet to hear the cabinet clock strike in such a way that its striking does not shorten but lengthens his eternity . . . a contradiction."[25] Marriage is comic, not because it brings closure but because it acknowledges contradiction. Marriage "binds" time but simultaneously acknowledges the vicissitudes of time.

At the conclusion to *O Brother,* McGill has not reached the state of "repose" that he had imagined would await him. As I pointed out earlier, in the final scene the family literally is in motion, passing across the screen in a direction unknown to the audience. McGill is still pleading with his wife to accept the ring, but we suspect that he will never be truly bona fide in her eyes. But although marriage has not restored the paradise McGill thought he had lost, it does provide a context for his journey, which he lacked on the road. The irony that confronts the audience at the end of *O Brother* is that the marriage, although in some sense restorative, is nevertheless mired in the commonplace quirks of human character. Perhaps the Coen brothers have not reached the heights of existential contradiction, but they have provided an ending to their narrative that acknowledges the incongruity between our very real aspirations and our equally real limitations. It is surely not coincidental that the reconstituted family walks past a billboard announcing the introduction of electrical power to the Tennessee Valley and offering the implicit promise of a technological utopia. Electrical power may very well provide air-conditioning, but it does not end racism, purge us of crooked pols, eliminate difficult marriages, or resolve contradictions. Upon his return to Ithaca, McGill discovers no "Big Rock Candy Mountain," where "the sun shines every day . . . and the barns are full of hay." He encounters instead the inescapable comic ironies of life.

Comic Absurdities

I began with Groucho. Let me conclude with Joel and Ethan. In an interview in 1996, the brothers explained their understanding of comedy: "But it seems to us that comedy is a part of life. Look at the recent example of the people who tried to blow up the World Trade Center. They rented a panel truck to use for the explosion and then, after committing the crime, went back to the rental agency to get back the money they left on deposit. The absurdity of this kind of behavior is terribly funny in itself."[26] The whims of personality, the odd relationship between mind and body, the ludicrous conjunction of the transcendent and the ordinary, the disturbing incongruities of evil and innocence, the comic ironies of good intentions and awkward missteps are some of the contradictions that inform the human condition and are aptly represented in *O Brother, Where Art Thou?* How fitting that the title of the film should be posed as a question and not an answer.

Notes

1. Søren Kierkegaard, *Concluding Unscientific Postscript to "Philosophical Fragments,"* ed. and trans. Howard V. Hong and Edna H. Hong (Princeton, N.J.: Princeton Univ. Press, 2000), 523.

2. Henri Bergson, "Laughter," in *Comedy,* ed. Wylie Sypher (1956; reprint, Baltimore: Johns Hopkins Univ. Press, 1980), 80.

3. Ibid., 84.

4. Henri Bergson, *Matter and Memory,* trans. N. M. Paul and W. S. Palmer (New York: Zone Books, 1991), 80.

5. Bergson, "Laughter," 72.

6. Ibid., 80.

7. Sergei Eisenstein, *Eisenstein on Disney,* trans. Alan Upchurch (London: Methuen, 1988), 23, quoted in Steven Dillon, *The Solaris Effect: Art and Artifice in Contemporary American Film* (Austin: Univ. of Texas Press, 2006), 123.

8. Dillon, *Solaris Effect,* 125.

9. Kierkegaard, *Concluding Unscientific Postscript,* 555.

10. Thomas C. Oden, introduction to *The Humor of Kierkegaard: An Anthology* (Princeton, N.J.: Princeton Univ. Press, 2004), 12–13.

11. Wylie Sypher, "The Meanings of Comedy," appendix to *Comedy,* ed. Sypher, 209.

12. For "engaged reinvention," see R. Barton Palmer, *Joel and Ethan Coen* (Urbana: Univ. of Illinois Press, 2004), 158.

13. Fredric Jameson, *Postmodernism, or, The Cultural Logic of Late Capitalism* (Durham, N.C.: Duke Univ. Press, 1992), 17–18.

14. For "exclusive community," see Jonathan Raban, *Soft City* (London: Collins Harvill, 1974), 129.

15. Jameson, *Postmodernism,* 20.

16. Ibid., 19.

17. Kierkegaard, *Concluding Unscientific Postscript*, 501–2.

18. Søren Kierkegaard, *Either/Or*, in *The Essential Kierkegaard*, ed. and trans. Howard V. Hong and Edna H. Hong (Princeton, N.J.: Princeton Univ. Press, 2000), 57.

19. Ibid., 61.

20. Ibid., 75.

21. Ibid., 81.

22. Jameson, *Postmodernism*, 4.

23. The quotation at the beginning of the film is from Homer, *The Odyssey*, trans. Robert Fitzgerald (New York: Doubleday, 1961), 1. The Coens introduce only one minor rewording, changing Fitzgerald's "Sing in me, Muse, and through me" to "O Muse, sing in me and through me."

24. Kierkegaard, *Either/Or*, 60.

25. Ibid., 70.

26. Joel Coen, interview by Michel Ciment and Hubert Niogret for *Positif: Revue périodique du cinéma (Paris)*, September 1991, translated in Palmer, *Joel and Ethan Coen*, 192.

No Country for Old Men

The Coens' Tragic Western

Richard Gilmore

> The point is there aint no point.
> —Cormac McCarthy, *No Country for Old Men*

Coen Irony

No Country for Old Men (2007) is, one might say, one more step in Joel and Ethan Coen's cinematic effort to say something about this country and about being a member, a citizen of this country, the United States of America. *No Country for Old Men* feels like a very different kind of movie from every other Coen brothers film. It is more serious, or it is serious in a different way from their other movies. It is not unusual for the Coens to take on dark themes in their movies, but previous to *No Country for Old Men* there was always a level of what I will call meta-irony. That is, there was a level of detachment, a sense that their movies were meant to be taken as just stories, that you should not take them too seriously. To be offended by *Fargo* (1996) because it seems to be making fun of midwesterners is to take it too seriously. Irony, however, is a tricky business. People are suspicious of the ironic because those who are ironic never quite mean what they say. The ironic, for their part, are more or less invulnerable to attack, since to take them seriously is to miss the point, and not to take them seriously precludes an attack. With *No Country for Old Men*, the Coens have given up their ironic detachment and made a much more straightforward movie. Certainly, there is irony within the movie, but the movie itself lacks the sheen of ironic detachment that is a part of a movie like *Fargo*.

One reason for this change may be the fact that this is the first movie that they have made based on a novel. It is not irrelevant to the tone of the movie that that novel was written by Cormac McCarthy. That the Coens chose this novel by this writer, however, also reflects an evolution in their cinematic and storytelling concerns. It is a sign of their willingness to give up some of their ironic detachment, to give up a posture of invulnerability, in order to say something more straightforward about their perceptions of how the world is. This, it seems to me, is a step into philosophy.

The previous Coen brothers movie that has the most in common with *No Country for Old Men* is, in fact, *Fargo*. In *Fargo* there is an older, wiser police chief, Marge Gunderson (Frances McDormand) and her less experienced or savvy deputy, Lou (Bruce Bohne), just as there is in *No Country for Old Men*. In both movies, a local police officer is confronted with some grisly murders committed by men who are not from his or her town. In both movies, greed lies behind the plots. Both movies feature as a central character a cold-blooded killer who does not seem quite human and whom the police officer seeks to apprehend. *No Country for Old Men*, therefore, is not completely new territory for the Coens, but no one in *Fargo* has much of a sense of irony, although the movie itself is ironic, whereas Sheriff Ed Tom Bell (Tommy Lee Jones), for example, certainly does have a sense of irony although the movie *No Country for Old Men* does not feel ironic at all.

A great moment of Bell-ian irony is when he is reading a story from the newspaper to his deputy, Wendell (Garret Dillahunt), about a couple in California who were taking in older people as tenants, then killing them for their Social Security checks and burying the bodies in the backyard. After Bell reads aloud from the paper, "Neighbors were alerted when a man ran from the premises wearing only a dog collar," Bell comments sardonically, "You can't make up such a thing as that. I dare you to even try." Bell continues, appreciating the full irony of the story, "But that's what it took, you'll notice. Get someone's attention. Diggin graves in the back yard didn't bring any." When Wendell fights back a smile, Bell says, "That's all right. I laugh myself sometimes." There is a bittersweetness in that confession that shows the deep humanity that may be part of the ironist's position. His comment, "I laugh myself sometimes," links, for me, this nonironic movie with all of the Coen brothers' ironic movies, movies in which horrors (a Ku Klux Klan rally, a hooded kidnapped woman trying to run blindly from her killer kidnappers, the chopping off of a woman's toe, for example) are treated as things to be laughed at. There is a sadness to their funniest movies, and humor in their grimmest.

To Kill a Bird

O Brother, Where Art Thou? (2000) is another Coen brothers movie that is referenced in *No Country for Old Men*. The reference is indirect, as it originates in McCarthy's novel, but it nevertheless works on another level within the Coens' oeuvre. There is a sequence in *No Country for Old Men* in which we see Anton Chigurh (Javier Bardem) driving at night. He comes to a bridge and there is a hawk, a bird of prey, perched on one of the railing posts of the bridge. Chigurh picks up a pistol from the car seat, slows down, then, as he drives by, takes a shot at the bird. What is this about? On one level, it may be a foreshadowing: Chigurh, bird of prey to birds of prey, will ultimately miss his target, Llewelyn Moss (Josh Brolin). However, on a deeper level, the scene connects with other Coen brothers films.

In the movie *Cool Hand Luke* (Stuart Rosenberg, 1967) the über-boss, Boss Godfrey (Morgan Woodward) (with an ominously theocratic name), who oversees the chain gang working the Florida state back roads, is a mirror sunglasses–wearing, all but silent figure of ominous justice. There is a scene in the film when Boss Godfrey, standing in the middle of the road, raises the cane he uses over his head. One of the chain gang workers, Rabbitt (Marc Cavell), immediately runs over to the truck, grabs a rifle off a rack in the back window, hurries back, and hands it to Boss Godfrey. At first you think, "That's a pretty risky move, entrusting his rifle to one of these hardened criminals," but then you see Boss Godfrey take the bolt for the gun from his vest pocket. He slides the bolt home, raises the gun, and shoots a hawk flying just overhead. The scene begins with shots establishing a relationship between the chain gang workers and Boss Godfrey. One of the workers, Tattoo (Warren Finnerty), says, "Don't he ever talk?" After Boss Godfrey shoots the bird, Luke (Paul Newman) replies, "I believe he just said something." I take this scene to indicate how brutally and arbitrarily violent this man can be and that what he is saying when he shoots the bird is that he is the bird of prey to birds of prey. Just establishing the pecking order, as it were, so the members of the chain gang can see.

This figure of the lawman who is really beyond the law, beyond, even, as Nietzsche says, good and evil altogether, is picked up by the Coen brothers in *O Brother, Where Art Thou?* in the character of Sheriff Cooley (Daniel von Bargen). Sheriff Cooley wears mirror sunglasses just like Boss Godfrey in *Cool Hand Luke*, with the similar cinematic effect of showing reflections of the world in the glasses but never showing Boss Godfrey's, or Sheriff Cooley's, eyes. Sheriff Cooley is as relentless in his pursuit of the escaped chain gang convict, Ulysses Everett McGill (George Clooney), as Boss Godfrey is of Cool Hand Luke. Sheriff Cooley seems to be a representative of the law, but when it comes right down to it, when the law pardons Ulysses and his friends, Sheriff Cooley remains implacable in his pursuit of his own conception of justice. When Sheriff Cooley is about to string up Ulysses and his friends, even though they had been pardoned by the governor, Ulysses pleads, "It ain't the law!" To which Sheriff Cooley replies, "The law. Well the law is a human institution."

In *O Brother, Where Art Thou?* Sheriff Cooley is a direct lifting from, or a direct reference to, *Cool Hand Luke*. I would not be surprised if Sheriff "Cooley" was not an intentional reference to the title of the earlier movie. Anton Chigurh's arbitrary and violent shooting of the hawk (the bird of prey to birds of prey) on the bridge connects him to Boss Godfrey directly and to Sheriff Cooley, indirectly. To psychologize for just a moment, it seems clear that *Cool Hand Luke* made a powerful impression on the Coen brothers when they first saw it. What seems to have especially impressed them is the figure of a putative lawman who is motivated by an apparent concept of justice that has nothing human in it. This figure is not always a lawman but has its counterpart in the Coen brothers' *Fargo, O Brother, Where Art Thou?* and *No Country for Old Men.* There is a thin thread of allusion that connects these four films that is quite obvious once you see it but is invisible before you see it. Once you see it, this scene becomes richly allusive and deepens in meaning. This is why one frequently has the sense after watching a Coen brothers movie that there was more going on than one quite got. One has that sense because there *is* more going on than anyone ever gets. The more I see in *No Country for Old Men,* the more I am convinced that there is much more that I am not seeing. This is a very important realization to have in order to begin to really get what is going on in a Coen brothers film. In this sense, their films are like the world: there is always more to understand; there is always more to get. The goal, then, is, in the words of Henry James, to "try to be one of the people on whom nothing is lost!"[1] That is, perhaps, an unachievable goal, in life or in art, but it is that to which we should aspire, and certainly, the Coen brothers' movies richly reward the attempt to find more in them.

Westerns and Greek Tragedies

The stories that the Coen brothers are interested in telling all seem to be very American stories. Their approach of choice is the genre of film. Their favorite film genre is very American, a genre the French call *film noir*, but *No Country for Old Men* is of another classic American genre, the western. Genre is an interesting way to try to say something about something because, as Jacques Derrida has made explicit, the "law of the law of genre" is that every new member of a genre set will deviate from and violate the apparent established principles of that genre. This is how Derrida describes the "law of the law of genre": "It is precisely a principle of contamination, a law of impurity, a parasitical economy. In the code of set theories, if I may use it at least figuratively, I would speak of a sort of participation without belonging—a taking part in without being part of, without having membership in a set."[2] This description of each new member of a genre set sounds to me a lot like what it means to be a (new) member of the set of Americans. Just as each new Coen film that has genre elements adds to and transforms the genre it participates in, so too, each new American adds to and transforms what it means to be an American.

No Country for Old Men, then, is and is not a classic western. It takes place in the West and its main protagonists are what you might call western - ers. On the other hand, the plot revolves around a drug deal that has gone bad; it involves four-wheel-drive vehicles, semiautomatic weapons, and executives in high-rise buildings, none of which would seem to belong in a western. There is a beautiful moment when Sheriff Ed Tom Bell and his sidekick, Deputy Wendell, are riding along, following a trail, and Deputy Wendell remarks on the tracks they are following in a way that recalls for me a moment in John Ford's great classic (and revisionist) western, *The Searchers* (1956), when Ethan Edwards (John Wayne) and Martin Pawley (Jeffrey Hunter) are following some tracks that will be similarly fateful for everyone involved. It is an interesting connection (I won't claim it is a reference) because in *The Searchers*, Ethan says, "We'll find 'em. Just as sure as the turnin' of the earth"—and they do. They find 'em, sure enough; but in an odd, somewhat inexplicable twist, there is no final confrontation between Ethan and Scar (Henry Brandon), the hated Comanche chief he has been seeking for seven years. Instead, it is Martin who kills Scar, and he appears to have done it while Scar was asleep in his tepee. Sheriff Bell is pretty dogged for a while, but he will give up the search altogether before he finds his adversary, Anton Chigurh.

Anton Chigurh might as well be Melville's Moby Dick for all of the human compassion, or even human motivation, that can be found in him. It makes as little sense to speak of him as evil as it does to say that raw nature, a blizzard or a flood, is evil. He has principles, the equivalent in a man to the laws of nature. Given his principles, he does not act irrationally or from passion; he is more of an inexorable force. He is not a rampaging killer on the loose; he has been summoned by a human will, a human desire, to achieve a desired end. He appears only because he was summoned. The recognizable and clear evil lies with the one (or those, since there may be others involved; the film is not explicit on this point) who summoned him. He was summoned because of greed, lust for power, an indifference to the suffering of others, and personal gratification. He who summoned him will learn, too late, that, like the sorcerer's apprentice, he has summoned a power that he cannot control, that it was pure hubris to think that he could control it.

That evil man is of little interest to either Cormac McCarthy, the author of the novel, *No Country for Old Men,* or to Joel and Ethan Coen, the makers of the movie.[3] What is of interest to McCarthy and the Coens is rather what happens when a good, but flawed, man encounters this force of nature in human guise. In this sense, *No Country for Old Men* recapitulates the patterns of ancient Greek tragedy. As in ancient Greek tragedy, a good but flawed man will become enmeshed in events that will prove to be his ruin. It will be what is good in him as much as what is flawed that will engage him in these events, and his ruin will be complete. Oedipus is a kind of paradigm of the way the ancient tragedies begin and end. It is because Oedipus is so smart, self-confident, competent, and passionate that he ascends to the throne of Thebes and rules as a good and noble king. It is also because Oedipus is so smart, self-confident, competent, and passionate that he is able to complete the mysterious task sent him by the Oracle of Delphi and to find the murderer of the previous king of Thebes, King Laius.

Unfortunately, as it will turn out, it is Oedipus himself who killed the previous king, as predicted by the same Oracle of Delphi long ago. He has also married his mother and fathered his children/siblings. As a consequence, Oedipus's wife/mother commits suicide, he blinds and exiles himself, his incest-produced children will fight and be responsible for each others' deaths. Llewelyn Moss is similarly smart, self-confident, competent, and passionate. His intelligence and competence lead him to the "last man standing" (as Moss puts it to the man he finds dying in a truck, saying, "there must've been one") and to the money. His compassion compels him to return to the site of the drug deal gone bad to bring water to the dying man who asked for it. It is not at all clear whether or not Chigurh or the Mexicans would have ever picked up the transponder signals if he had not gone back, but it is certainly clear that once they have found Moss and his truck at the scene, they will be on his trail wherever he goes. A fate similar to Oedipus's disastrous ruin awaits Llewelyn Moss: both he and his young wife will be brutally murdered; all that he has will be lost.

Power, Hubris, and the Fatal Flaw

Anton Chigurh is a monster, in the sense that Emerson uses the word in his essay "The American Scholar," that is, in association with "monitory" and "admonition," drawing on its Latin derivation meaning a warning or an omen.[4] The ancient Greek tragedies were meant to serve that same function, that is, warning about especially human temptations that would lead to disaster. Tragedy was considered a source of wisdom as well as of entertainment, and the primary wisdom that the ancient Greek tragedies taught was also written on the wall at the famous and perhaps most holy of Greek temples, the Oracle of Delphi: "Avoid hubris." Hubris is a difficult word to recover from the Greek, but it means something like arrogant ignorance, thinking that you are better or more powerful than you really are. The Greek gods hated hubris, and one of their primary occupations as gods was punishing humans for their hubris.

Hubris was such a problem for the Greeks not because they valued timidity or even humility but because they loved power, and they loved powerful, proud people. As Aristotle says in the *Nicomachean Ethics*, "The man is thought to be proud who thinks himself worthy of great things, being worthy of them." The Greek ideal was to manifest all of your true power, and to be very powerful, without overstepping your own limits, without presuming to have more power than you really have. This is a very difficult ideal to achieve because one does not know what one is capable of until one tries to do things beyond what one has done before. And yet, the Greeks (Aristotle, for one) assumed that one could know what one is capable of and thereby avoid the calamities of hubris. The above quotation from Aristotle concludes, "for he who does so beyond his deserts is a fool, but no virtuous man is foolish or silly."[5] This Greek ideal, this wisdom, is, too, exhorted upon the wall at Delphi: "Know thyself."

Llewelyn Moss is a man of considerable resources, but his powers have been lying more or less dormant. He has innate powers of intelligence and determination as well as some acquired abilities learned while serving in Vietnam. Virtually all of these powers are banked, the way one banks a fire, because there is no way to exercise them in his day-to-day life. He has a good job as a welder that does not require all of either his intelligence or determination. He has a lovely young wife and a comfortable trailer home but no obvious way of improving his situation beyond this level of comfort. In many ways he seems to be happy and successful, but it is a difficult thing to have powers that you have no opportunities to use. Doing pretty well in America has never been the happiest of options if there is some chance that you could be doing better. Of course, that possibility of doing better becomes real for Llewelyn when he comes upon the briefcase full of cash. He barely seems to hesitate before he decides to go for it.

A key element of Greek tragedy is the idea of the protagonist's hamartia, the fatal flaw. *Hamartia* is a term derived from archery and literally means "off the mark," signifying that one's aim has been slightly off. The protagonist of a classic Greek tragedy must be essentially a good person, a person whose intentions are good but who does not really or fully know himself or herself, and this lack of self-knowledge is mixed with a bit of hubris, which puts off one's aim. This is quite literally suggested of Llewelyn at the beginning of the movie when he is hunting for antelope and ends up shooting one in the hindquarters. In a sense, the entire movie is prefigured in this scene. It is a scene that shows Llewelyn to be highly competent, an expert at hunting: the way he uses his boot for a barrel rest, the way he adjusts the sight for the distance of the shot, his patience in taking the shot, his picking up his shell after he takes the shot are all signs of his expertise. All are signs of his knowledge, his ability, his power, but the scene also shows his ultimate hubris, literally and figuratively. Instead of killing the antelope, he only wounds it, the worst possible outcome for a responsible hunter. He is clearly frustrated and annoyed with himself, and he heads out after the wounded antelope to try to finish what he has started.

It is a long shot that he thinks he can make. It is not a shot that he will make, but he is just good enough to actually hit the antelope at the distance of almost a mile. All of the elements of the movie are here, Llewelyn's talents as well as his misjudgments, as well as certain implacable facts of nature; distance, heat, the movement of the antelope are the facts of nature that will undo his best intentions. His aim is good but not quite good enough, and the worst possible consequences eventuate because he was willing to try the difficult shot. His experience is a Greek tragedy in miniature.

Our Place in the Universe

There is a problem in philosophy that is related to a problem in art and to one in science as well. The problem is, in part, epistemological, that is, it is a problem of knowledge, and it is, in part, a problem of communication. It is the problem of discovering and communicating new knowledge about the world. Take, for example, the phenomenon of gravity. Gravity is invisible. Before Newton, no one had thought of the concept of gravity to explain things as different as a falling apple and the movement of the moon. Of course, the signs of gravity were everywhere, but people did not know how to see them as signs of gravity. Then, once you have the concept of gravity and you see that this explains the movement of the moon, the movement of the planets, and even the movement of the earth, how do you explain it to someone else so that they can understand this new and powerful concept? Well, the way Newton did it was to talk about falling apples.

A more explicitly philosophical example can be found in the writings of Heraclitus. Heraclitus of Ephesus (585–525 BCE) was one of the more famous of the pre-Socratic philosophers. He was known as "the Dark One" and "the Riddler" because what he had to say about human life and the way he said it were so pessimistic, puzzling, and elusive. He said, for example (and most famously), "One cannot step in the same river twice," which seems to be factually false and yet strangely, provocatively true.[6] The structure that Heraclitus developed for conveying his cryptic ideas is based on a model that Hermann Fränkel calls the "geometrical mean," which has the form $A/B = B/C$. Using an example from Heraclitus—"Man is stamped infantile by divinity, just as the child is by man"—Fränkel notes that this would have the form divinity/man = man/child.[7] This is a way of trying to convey some very abstract wisdom about our human position in the universe. What he is trying to convey is the very difficult, nonhuman knowledge that we may not be the ultimate things in the universe, that not everything in the universe is about or for us. This is hard knowledge for us to see because so much of our attention is devoted to getting what we think we want, to finding in the world the things that we need, that it becomes our primary frame of reference: the world as the source of what we need. The world, in short, appears to us to be about us. Heraclitus is trying to convey a wisdom, a knowledge, that re-contextualizes our place in the universe for us. He is trying to communicate this to us so that we might understand ourselves differently, and having this knowledge will help us to live better, more satisfyingly, in this world.

There is a similar structure in the movie, and, I think, a similar wisdom. That is, the scene shift from Anton Chigurh killing the nameless car driver with his cattle stun gun to Llewelyn Moss hunting antelope is bridged with a virtually identical piece of dialogue, first uttered by Anton to the driver of the car he has pulled over, then by Llewelyn to the antelope he has fixed his sight on: "Hold still."[8] They are the words of the hunter to his prey. The basic formula seems to be that Anton is to human beings (and to Llewelyn, in particular), as Llewelyn the hunter is to the antelope. Just as the antelope can have little or no understanding of the principles that govern and guide its hunter, Chigurh's human victims can understand about as much of what governs and guides him. It is very hard to understand people who act from motives that are very different from our own. The default position is to label such people evil or morally reprehensible, but that is more or less just a throwing up of one's hands. It is more or less a confession of being confounded. The first step toward wisdom is an acknowledgment that there may be more going on than that of which we are aware. This has always been the central goal of philosophy, to figure out what the more going on might be.

Rules and Vulnerability

Anton Chigurh is like a walking abattoir. People are just cattle to him, which makes his weapon of choice especially appropriate. He is like a modern version, one updated for a heavily meat-eating American public, of the traditional figure of Death with his scythe. One of the most profound moments in the movie, or the moment that raises some of the most profound philosophical and, especially, ethical questions, is the moment when Chigurh asks Carson Wells (Woody Harrelson), "If the rule you follow brought you to this, of what use was the rule?" This is the great human question, the great philosophical question. It is the question that is central to Aristotle's *Nicomachean Ethics,* where he frames it in terms of the problem of how to live a life without regret.[9] It is what lurks under Camus's claim that the only real philosophical question is the question of suicide.[10] That is, is there a rule that we can follow and, in following it, be brought to a place where we can affirm our whole life? Are some rules better than others, and if so, which rules, or, what ultimate rule, is the best? The desideratum is to find a rule that will free us from the fear of death, because, following it, we will feel that we lived our lives in a way that left out nothing important. Wells seems, at the penultimate moment before his death, to regret the rule that had brought him to that place. Llewelyn Moss, with increasing awareness of just where his rule has brought him, clearly has increasing anxiety about the rule he has been following. At the very end of her life, Carla Jean Moss (Kelly Macdonald) is forced to evaluate the rule she has followed that has brought her to be sitting in a bedroom across from Anton Chigurh. There is a moment when a shadow seems to pass over her face as she considers it. Even Sheriff Bell, who has some very specific ethical rules he follows, which have worked for him, seems to be undone by the end of the movie.[11] It is as though Anton Chigurh comes as a kind of avatar of death, a remnant of the ancient Greek gods, and his function is to undo or to make irrelevant everyone's rules.

What rule, then, does Chigurh follow? There are two scenes that mirror each other and reveal something important about the rule that Chigurh follows. The first scene is the very powerful and very creepy one in which Chigurh gets annoyed with a friendly question from the proprietor of the gas station (Gene Jones): "Y'all getting any rain up your way?" What follows is a tense exchange that subtly escalates into what is clearly a life or death situation for the proprietor. Chigurh demands that the owner call a coin toss. After some resistance he does call it: "Heads." Heads it is. Chigurh leaves the coin and walks out. The proprietor gets a reprieve. In a similar scene, with Carla Jean, although we do not see the toss, it is pretty clear that she loses the bet and is killed. (As he leaves her house, Chigurh checks his boot soles for blood, an obvious danger in his line of work.) What is interesting about these two scenes is that in them Chigurh *has* vaguely human desires. In the first of the scenes, he really wants to kill the gas station proprietor. In the second scene, one feels as though he would really prefer not to kill Carla Jean. In both instances, he subjugates his desires to the flip of a coin, to chance. That is his principle. It is the principle that keeps him from a certain kind of vulnerability. As he tells Carla Jean, in the novel, when she says to him that he does not have to kill her, "You're asking that I make myself vulnerable and that I can never do. I have only one way to live. It does not allow for special cases. A coin toss perhaps."[12] That is, he recognizes that it is precisely his feelings, his desires, that make him vulnerable. His rule—that chance must trump any desire that he might have—is in the service of maximum invulnerability. I read the sudden and violent crash that occurs right after Chigurh leaves the house where Carla Jean was staying as a sign that there are higher laws yet in the universe than Chigurh's principle. As Chigurh is to Carla Jean, so are the higher laws to Chigurh. What the nature of those higher laws is I am not sure, but Chigurh's principle is no defense against them. Since these laws are higher and counter to Chigurh's principles, there is some reason to hope that they are also more sympathetic to human wishes and desires than Chigurh is, but that is a small hope indeed.

Apollo and Dionysus: Reason and Passion

The late nineteenth- and early twentieth-century philosophical movement known as existentialism can be understood, in part, as a reaction against the Enlightenment period of the seventeenth and eighteenth centuries. The Enlightenment was a period of great confidence in the human ability to use reason to shed light on the ways of nature. It is not that people thought they had all the answers but that they were convinced that all the answers would be forthcoming if methodological reason was applied to any given situation. This confidence applied to social contexts as well as to contexts of nature. The framing of the U.S. Constitution was an Enlightenment-influenced project producing a great Enlightenment document. Science produced technology, and technology created new industries, new factories, and new social structures. These industries and factories and social structures often resulted in new forms of abject poverty, human degradation, and war. The philosophical response to these unforeseen, unintended, but very real consequences of the Enlightenment was to question the very basis of Enlightenment ideals. Philosophers began to consider whether there might not be some fundamentally irrational principle in the world that will always evade rational accounting. Perhaps it is the very reliance on reason, at the expense of emotion and community and art, that is the problem.

Nietzsche's first book, *The Birth of Tragedy* (1872), explicitly takes on the conflict between science and art, between reason and passion. Nietzsche saw these late eighteenth-century conflicts as a recapitulation of a similar conflict that occurred in Athens in the fifth century BCE. According to Nietzsche's narrative, the great Greek tragedians Aeschylus and Sophocles were philosophers with a wisdom to teach, and that wisdom had to do with the importance of balancing reason and passion into a perfectly proportioned whole. Reason without passion was empty and meaningless, while passion without reason was chaotic and dangerous. Nietzsche invoked two Greek gods to represent the two sides of the equation: Apollo (for reason) and Dionysus (for passion). The need to balance these two energies within us is what Nietzsche took to be the sublime wisdom conveyed in the tragedies of Aeschylus and Sophocles. Greek tragedy, however, became corrupted, according to Nietzsche, by a rather unexpected figure: Socrates. The Socratic demand, according to Nietzsche, was that everything we do be rational. When Socrates questioned people in the marketplace of Athens, his expectation was that the person he questioned should be able to give good reasons for all of his beliefs. If he could not, Socrates implied that he should not believe those things. This spirit of Socratism, as Nietzsche calls it, began to infect Greek tragedy, especially in the plays of Euripides, where the sublime elevations of feeling and passion—in the plays of Aeschylus and Sophocles—were reduced to much more ordinary, everyday sorts of scenarios that were well explained by the chorus and ended with the ratification of some rational moral principle.[13]

For Nietzsche, dry Apollonian reason lacked all power of creativity. The Enlightenment emphasis on reason led to a kind of social sickness, a desiccated preoccupation with order and reason that made human life more or less pointless. His physicianly prescription was for a recovery of some of those lost or suppressed Dionysian energies. The Dionysian is associated with wild nature, which can be as violent as it is reproductively fruitful.

Wildness is a central tenet of our American identity. The word "wilderness" is from the Anglo-Saxon *wildëor*, a wild animal or beast, so that "wilderness" means "where the wild things are."[14] Europe, on the other hand, is associated with civilization. As Roderick Frazier Nash explains in his book *Wilderness and the American Mind*, "The largest portion of the energy of civilization was directed at conquering wildness in nature and eliminating it in human nature."[15] That is to say, it is the progress of civilization that creates the idea of wilderness. Before there was an idea of civilization, there was no differentiation between civilization and wilderness. "Civilization severed the web of life as humans distanced themselves from the rest of nature. Behind fenced pastures, village walls, and, later, gated condominiums," Nash writes, "it was hard to imagine other living things as brothers or nature as sacred. The remaining hunters and gatherers become 'savages.'"[16] Europeans were tamed by the social hierarchies of tradition, class, and family. To them, wilderness was something ugly. Americans, by contrast, had a wildness associated with them that came by way of the untamed land.

The history of the concept of wilderness is one primarily of opposition. The wilderness was considered a place both physically and morally perilous. The opposite of "wilderness" is "paradise," which is Persian for "luxurious garden" (nature tamed). The Bible is full of references to the wilderness as an accursed place. Adam and Eve are expelled from the garden into a desolate wilderness. Jesus experiences his trials with Satan in the wilderness. This was the attitude of the American pioneers as well. As Nash says, "The pioneers' situation and attitude prompted them to use military metaphors to discuss the coming of civilization. Countless diaries, addresses, and memorials of the frontier period represented wilderness as an 'enemy' which had to be 'conquered,' 'subdued' and 'vanquished' by a 'pioneer army.'"[17] The commitment of the American pioneers was to convert wilderness into civilization, a paradise.

Where there are gains, there are also losses. This is part of the wisdom of Nietzsche, that the suppression of some part of our nature can have dire consequences for our natures as a whole. The central trope of American wildness is the wild West. Early on Thoreau recognized the dangers of suppressing our own wildness and of the loss of wilderness. In his essay "Walking," he writes, "The West of which I speak is but another name for the Wild; and what I have been preparing to say is, that in Wildness is the preservation of the world."[18] I understand him to mean that, while rational Apollonian order and control are fine as far as they go, growth, creativity, and real human (and nonhuman) thriving depend on wildness, on a principle of chaotic, raw energy. To lose our wilderness, to lose our wildness, is to lose the world and ourselves.

The Westerner, Blood, and Death

In the classic westerns, there tends to be a divide between easterners and westerners. Easterners tend to be more civilized, more religious, more concerned with moral rules, more talkative, and much less committed to outright action. The westerner, by contrast, tends to be closer to something wild than civilized; has, at best, a very rudimentary piety, or none at all; is concerned with a pretty straightforward conception of justice that is based on leaving him or her alone; and is suspicious of words and is committed to doing what needs to be done.[19] Llewelyn Moss is a typical westerner in all these ways. His primary problem with Carson Wells seems to be that Carson Wells talks too much.

Peter French, in his book *Cowboy Metaphysics: Ethics and Death in Westerns,* says, "All westerners have something inside them that has to do with death."[20] Jane Tompkins, for her book *West of Everything: The Inner Life of Westerns,* takes the title from a passage in Louis L'Amour's *Hondo:* "the stark features of Lieutenant Creyton C. Davis, darling of Richmond dance floors, hero of a Washington romance, dead now in the long grass on a lonely hill, west of everything."[21] Tompkins explains, "To go west, as far west as you can go, west of everything, is to die."[22] French refers to ours as a "death-denying" culture, while the westerner is "death-accepting."[23] Part of the power of *No Country for Old Men*, it seems to me, comes from the primal themes that it addresses head on. Llewelyn Moss is a man who is not afraid of, is not really even put off by, death. When he comes across the death scene in the desert, he does not shake or flee or weep; he is simply cautious. When he finds the last man standing (now sitting and no longer a man) and takes the money, he knows exactly what he is doing, what he is risking. Sheriff Bell, too, knows what he is doing, knows that to do his job he must accept the possibility of his own death. As he says, "I always knew you had to be willing to die to even do this job."

There is, in *No Country for Old Men*, plenty of death and blood. In our culture today, we are as squeamish about blood as we are in denial about death. A skinned knee on a school yard is an emergency calling for rubber gloves and immediate containment procedures. There are reasons for this, to be sure. The omnipresent threat of AIDS is clearly one. For all that, however, such radical reactions to the sight of blood betoken an alienation from our own bodies and a terror of our own fluids. There is a sort of beautiful intimacy we see in the ways Llewelyn Moss attends to his own battered and bleeding body. There is a heroism, a revelation of his ferocious will, in his determination to continue to do what he intended to do, in spite of his severe and bleeding wounds. In a culture where our identities are largely determined by our shopping habits, where primary concerns have to do with what car we should buy, what television or house we can afford, to watch these primal struggles of a person with his own bleeding body and the attention demanded to stay alive, with a killer like Anton Chigurh on his trail, promises a kind of immediate and pressing reality that is pretty elusive for most of us. We have lost something real in our loss of the experience of wildness. I am not exactly saying that I would prefer to have someone like Anton Chigurh on my trail or that we should be cavalier about blood spilled on school yards, but I am saying that something gets lost when we lose the risks that wildness presents to us.

Fate

A movie like *The Man Who Shot Liberty Valance* (John Ford, 1962) can be thought of as an elegy for the loss of a certain kind of wildness. Tom Doniphon (John Wayne) is all that a westerner can be, a man in his prime, big, strong, and capable, as capable of tenderness as of violence. He really has no problem with the outlaw Liberty Valance (Lee Marvin), at least not until the easterner Ransom Stoddard (Jimmy Stewart) shows up. Ransom (with the faint suggestion of something rancid, something that is a sign of the death of something) comes to the western town of Shinbone as a lawyer and a talker, decrying lawlessness, which, for the westerner, is basically the same thing as freedom. Tom recognizes a certain degree of truth in the things that Ransom is saying, but he also recognizes what Ransom's truths will cost that country and especially the men like him who inhabit it. We, the audience, recognize the same things. We cannot deny Ransom's claims for the need for law, for the need to put a stop to men like Liberty Valance, but we also feel the sadness of the loss of a man as spectacular as Tom Doniphon. To be left only with people like Ransom Stoddard is a loss indeed.

Ed Tom Bell, too, is a westerner. He is similarly clipped in his speech, preferring understatement when words are absolutely necessary. His voice-overs, however, provide a whole new range to our understanding of the westerner. He sounds downright poetic in his thoughtfulness. This is not exactly new. It has always been an implied feature of the westerner that he is as sensitive as anyone to beauty and morality; it is just that talking about such things could pretty well ruin them. It is not so much that Bell is revealed to be a sensitive and thoughtful man via his voice-overs; rather, it is interesting to see the particular form his thoughtfulness and sensitivity take. The word that comes to mind to characterize the thoughts revealed in his voice-overs is *philosophical:* full of wonder and the attempt to put things together in the largest possible way.

There really are no easterners in *No Country for Old Men.* They are all, basically, westerners: tough, stoical, doers instead of talkers. There is one overarching wisdom that seems to be shared by Llewelyn, the old man Ellis (Barry Corbin), Bell, and even Anton Chigurh. It has to do with a sort of fatalism, which is very characteristic, I might add, of Greek tragedy. This fatalism is not quite a mechanistic inevitability, but it is definitely based on the idea that you are what you do and that what you have done cannot be undone, what decisions you have made cannot be unmade, and, finally, that what you do, what you have decided, will have its natural consequences in the world, and there is no avoiding or evading those consequences. This idea is conveyed explicitly and repeatedly in the novel, although it seems to be equally present in the movie, if somewhat more implicitly.

In the novel, there is a sequence of scenes that does not occur in the movie. Llewelyn picks up a young female hitchhiker. Llewelyn actually does more talking here than he does in the rest of the story. The woman is very young and is headed, somewhat vaguely, for California. At one point she says, "I guess I ain't sure what the point is." To which Llewelyn replies, "The point is there aint no point." After another short exchange, Llewelyn elaborates on a point he wants to make. "It's not about knowin where you are. It's about thinking you got there without takin anything with you. Your notions about startin over. Or anybody's. You don't start over. That's what it's about. Ever step you take is forever. You can't make it go away. None of it."[24] Later, when Bell goes out to talk to his Uncle Ellis, Ellis expresses a somewhat similar opinion about things. In response to a question Ed Tom Bell asks Ellis about what he would have done if the convict who'd shot him had been released, he says, "I dont know. Nothin. There wouldn't be no point to it. There ain't no point to it. Not to any of it." Ed Tom responds, "I'm kindly surprised to hear you say that." Ellis explains, "You wear out, Ed Tom. All the time you spend tryin to get back what's been took from you there's more goin out the door. After awhile you just try and get a tourniquet on it." Later, Ed Tom, in one of his ruminations, says, "I believe that whatever you do in your life it will get back to you. If you live long enough it will."[25] Anton Chigurh, explaining to Carla Jean why he, in fact, does have to kill her, says, "Every moment in your life is a choice. All followed to this. The accounting is scrupulous. The shape is drawn. No line can be erased. . . . A person's path through the world seldom changes and even more seldom will it change abruptly. And the shape of your path was visible from the beginning."[26]

Each of these characters is expressing a twofold understanding about the world. On the one hand, there is an inevitability, a sense that the world goes on in its way and that it does not have much to do with our human desires and concerns. On the other hand there is a sense that we contribute to our own inevitable futures with every decision we make, with every act we commit, that what is perhaps hardest to live with is not the inevitability that is the result of the turning of the earth but the inevitability that is associated with a future we are looking at that is the result of what we have done in the past. In biblical language, we reap what we sow.

There is a difference in the attitudes of the various characters to this wisdom. Uncle Ellis seems to be past guilt or shame or worry about what this wisdom means to his life. Llewelyn, who is still a relatively young man, seems to be pre-guilt, shame, and worry with respect to it. Ed Tom appears both most hopeful, in spite of this wisdom, and most haunted by guilt and shame because of it.

No Country for Old Men

At one point, Ellis says to Ed Tom, "What you got ain't nothin new. This country is hard on people. Hard and crazy. Got the devil in it yet folks never seem to hold it to account." I take "this country," first, to be a reference to the particular country that they are in at the moment, west Texas; then, second, to be a more general reference to the wild West; third, a reference to the United States; and, finally, to this world or even this universe, as a whole. There are several ways in which "this country" is no country for old men, although old men do inhabit it. It is a hard country, dry, hard ground, little water, not much there to keep a body alive without a lot of work. It takes the strength and resilience of youth to get on in such a landscape. That type of landscape is not just west Texas but the wild West in general, with its wild men, men who do not observe the social niceties and who grasp at what they want without asking and push others out of their way. Drug dealing is simply a more modern version of the lawlessness that has always been associated with the West, especially in Hollywood movies. Lawlessness is one way of conceiving freedom, and it is a very American way. The valence of a certain kind of freedom is a certain kind of lawlessness. The more laws there are, the less freedom. Such a freedom, however, is hard on the physically less robust. The wild West is indeed no country for old men.

The United States is a wild country in a similar way, not in being lawless, but in the way its laws are designed to encourage competition. The competition fostered by the laws of the United States is mostly economic, but we love competition in almost any form. A Sunday afternoon professional football game is not for the faint of heart. As Oliver Stone makes clear in his film *Wall Street* (1987) with Gordon Gecko's (Michael Douglas) paean to greed (the "Greed is good!" speech), Wall Street is, itself, a kind of wild West and no country for old men.

Senescence, the process of growing old, is part of every living species and has its evolutionary logic. August Weismann said, "I look at death as an adaptive phenomenon because an infinite duration of the individual would represent a very inopportune luxury. . . . Worn out individuals are of no value for the species; they are even harmful since they take the place of those who are healthy."[27] François Jacob continues this line of thinking:

In every species, the most important individuals are those which can reach sexual maturity, because they are the ones with the greatest capacity for propagation. Natural selection will, therefore, adjust the optimal state of animals to the time of their sexual maturity. In humans, for instance, maximal strength and resistance to disease is reached between twenty and thirty years. . . . Natural selection would tend to accumulate . . . harmful effects in the postreproductive period of the animal's life, thus favoring deterioration of the body with age. In other words, vigor in youth should in a way be paid for by senescence.[28]

Evolutionarily speaking, this is no country for old men.

Llewelyn Moss visits, as it were, the country of old men in the course of the movie. When the movie begins he is strapping strong, grown into his man strength, confident and at ease in his body. As the movie progresses, he is repeatedly shot and wounded, each hit diminishing his strength and bodily self-reliance. His bodily strength gets whittled away like Mr. Merriweather's (Martin Balsam) in *Little Big Man* (Arthur Penn, 1970). By the end of the movie, much of his strength has returned, but he has had a good taste of what old age is like. And, in the end, his strength will still not be sufficient to save him.

The title of the novel, and of the movie, comes from William Butler Yeats's poem, "Sailing to Byzantium." The poem begins:

That is no country for old men. The young
In one another's arms, birds in the trees
—Those dying generations—at their song,
The Salmon-falls, the mackerel-crowded seas,
Fish, flesh, or fowl, commend all summer long
Whatever is begotten born, and dies.
Caught in that sensual music all neglect
Monuments of unageing intellect.

The theme here is certainly consistent with Jacob's evolutionary evaluation of senescence. That is, the lament that can be heard in these lines is for no longer belonging to the country of the young. It is also a lament for the way the young neglect the wisdom of the past and, presumably, of the old. The poem continues in the second stanza,

An aged man is but a paltry thing,
A tattered coat upon a stick, unless
Soul clap its hands and sing, and louder sing
For every tatter in its mortal dress.

The wisdom here seems to be that when one has outgrown the world of the young, the world aflow with sensual music, one must make one's own music, presumably, as art; for Yeats, as poetry. The poem ends with the poet imagining himself, after he has died, being made into a golden bird by some ancient artisan,

set upon a golden bough to sing
To lords and ladies of Byzantium
Of what is past, or passing, or to come.[29]

Yeats chooses Byzantium because it was a great early Christian city in which Plato's Academy, for a time, was still allowed to function. The historical period of Byzantium was a time of culmination that was also a time of transition. In his book of mystical writings, *A Vision,* Yeats says, "I think that in early Byzantium, maybe never before or since in recorded history, religious, aesthetic, and practical life were one, that architect and artificers . . . spoke to the multitude and the few alike."[30] This idea of a balance and a coherence in a society's religious, aesthetic, and practical life is Yeats's ideal, and it seems to be the very same ideal that Nietzsche extolled. It is an ideal rarely realized in this world and maybe not even in ancient Byzantium. Certainly within the context of the movie *No Country for Old Men,* one has the sense, especially from Bell as the chronicler of the times, that things are out of alignment, that balance and harmony are gone from the land and from the people. It is Yeats's vision, and certainly Nietzsche's as well, that it is the artist/philosopher who is most needed to help restore the balance. It may not, in the end, be the doer as much as the thinker who is needed to help us see where our losses are and where we might find the gains to make us whole.

A Dream of Fire

The movie ends with Bell telling his wife Loretta (Tess Harper) about two dreams that he had had the night before. Both dreams have his father in them. The first is about some money that Bell loses. The second has his father riding past him in the night, carrying fire in a horn. Bell ends his description of the dream by saying, "And in the dream I knew that he was goin on ahead and that he was fixin to make a fire somewhere out there in all that dark and all that cold, and I knew that whenever I got there he would be there. Out there up ahead."

Prometheus stole fire from the gods to give to human beings in order to save them from extinction. To make a fire is an art. It is by the arts that human beings thrive, and I take that original art of making fire to stand, metonymically, for all the arts. Fire beats back the darkness, the darkness of fear, of ignorance, of hubris, of greed. I read Bell's dream of his father to be a dream of carrying on the fire of memory, the fire of the stories that one has of what one has seen in this world. It is the fire of the wisdom that those stories can yield with the telling of them. This, too, is an important role to play, to be the bearer of this fire. It is less heroic in the eyes of the world than that of lawman or outlaw, but it is probably more important to human survival and thriving than either of those.

Bell is himself a storyteller. There is a wonderful, funny, slightly unnerving scene in which Bell is talking to Carla Jean. She has contacted him in order to tell him where Llewelyn is hiding. She has been influenced to do this by a story Bell told her earlier, a complicated story of a man Bell said he knew, one Charlie Walser, who worked at a slaughterhouse. One day, as the story went, Charlie was trying to slaughter a cow. First, he'd hit it with a mallet, in the standard way, but the cow didn't die and started thrashing around, so he pulls out his gun and tries to shoot it. "But what with all the swingin and twistin it's a glance-shot and ricochets around and comes back and hits Charlie in the shoulder." The point of the story is that no matter how competent a person is, and Carla Jean has complete confidence in Llewelyn's competence, things can happen, things can go wrong. Carla Jean understands the point of the story, and it persuades her to go back to Bell to tell him where Llewelyn is so that he might be able to help Llewelyn. But before she tells Bell where Llewelyn is, she says, "Sheriff, was that a true story about Charlie Walser?" To which Bell replies, in part, "It's certainly true that it was a story."[31]

To say that it is true that it was a story amounts to saying that the story is not true. But, of course, the story *is* true, as an allegory about an aspect of the way the world is, even if it is not literally true, even if there is no Charlie Walser, or if there was such a man, even if he never shot a cow and ended up with the bullet in his own shoulder. It is true that sometimes bad things

happen in this world to even the most competent of people. There's no telling where that ricocheting bullet might end up.

Philosophy is full of stories that may not be literally true but are meant
to be understood as pointing to deeper truths. Plato, especially, puts these
kinds of stories into the mouth of Socrates in dialogues like the *Gorgias,* or
the *Republic,* or the *Phaedo,* to name just a few. How true a story is allegorically may even be the measure of a philosophy or of a work of literature, in
general. This is very much, it seems to me, the measure of the value of the
movies of the Coen brothers. Nearly all of their movies tell stories that are
unbelievable at the literal level. It is certainly true that they are stories, but it
is also true that they are in their own ways true stories, stories that reveal true
things about the way the world is and about our ways of being in the world.
It is precisely in this way that their movies function like philosophy.

If their movies are philosophical, the philosophy is very much about
America. The ending of *No Country for Old Men* may seem unsatisfying to
some and puzzling to others. One way to view the ending of *No Country*
is as a mixing of the two great American movie genres, the western and
film noir. These two great American film genres reflect the two sides of
the American psyche. On the one hand, there is the western in which the
westerner is faced with overwhelming odds, but between his perseverance
and his skill, he overcomes the odds and triumphs. This allegorizes the
optimism of the American psyche. In film noir, on the other hand, the hero
is smart (more or less) and wily and there are many obstacles to overcome,
the odds are against him, and, in fact, he fails to overcome them. He is
overwhelmed by the juggernaut of other people's evil or by the way the
world just happens to go. This genre reflects the pessimism and fatalism of
the American psyche. With *No Country for Old Men,* the Coens combine
these two genres into one movie. It is a western with a tragic, existential,
film noir ending. The western speaks to our youth (and nostalgically to us
in our old age); film noir speaks to the sadder wisdom of age. *No Country
for Old Men* speaks of both.[32]

At the end of the movie, Bell seems to be experiencing both regret and
chagrin: chagrin at how the world is turning out, regret that he could not do
more to have stopped it turning out so. Ellis refers to that regret as "vanity,"
which it is, and, no doubt, Bell knows that too. In one sense, Bell has failed.
He failed to protect Llewelyn and Carla Jean. He failed to capture Anton
Chigurh. And he failed to persevere to the end. He just more or less gives
up and retires from being sheriff. In another sense, however, there is great

wisdom in this apparent failure. Bell knows that he is no match for Anton Chigurh. What he has done, however, is bear witness to certain events. He has seen some aspects of the world, ways in which the world unfurls, that not many have seen. It is because he was, as it were, on the front line of those events, close enough to be killed, certainly, that he can see what he has seen about the world. This, too, is an important role to play, to play for the sake of humanity, the one who bears witness, the one who can tell the tales of what has happened in the past, of what is passing, and of what is to come.

Notes

I would like to express my gratitude to Tony McRae for comments he made on an earlier version of this chapter. I would especially like to thank Mark Conard for suggestions he made regarding the chapter title and the subheadings. I also owe a debt to Sarah McKee, the proofreader, who spotted an omission in the "To Kill a Bird" section of this essay.

1. Henry James, *The Future of the Novel: The Art of Fiction* (New York: Vintage Books, 1956), 13.

2. Jacques Derrida, "The Law of Genre," *Glyph* 7 (1980): 206.

3. Cormac McCarthy, *No Country for Old Men* (New York: Vantage, 2005).

4. I have in mind the following sentences from "The American Scholar": "The state of society is one in which the members have suffered amputation from the trunk, and strut about so many walking monsters—a good finger, a neck, a stomach, an elbow, but never a man. . . . In this view of him, as Man Thinking, the theory of his office is contained. Him Nature solicits with all her placid, all her monitory pictures." Ralph Waldo Emerson, *Ralph Waldo Emerson: Essays & Lectures* (New York: Library of America, 1983), 54.

5. Aristotle, *Nicomachean Ethics*, trans. Martin Oswald (New York: Macmillan, 1962), 1123b.

6. Heraclitus, in *The Presocratics*, ed. Philip Wheelwright (New York: Macmillan, 1966), 71 (fragments 91–92).

7. Ibid., 78 (fragment 79); Hermann Fränkel, "A Thought Pattern in Heraclitus," in *The Pre-Socratics: A Collection of Essays*, ed. Alexander P. D. Mourelatos (Princeton, N.J.: Princeton Univ. Press, 1974), 214.

8. It is worth noting that this is pure Coen brothers. This parallel between Chigurh and Moss is not made explicit in the book in the same way. In the book, Chigurh says to the man, "Would you step away from the car please." McCarthy adds the detail, "He placed his hand on the man's head like a faith healer" just before Chigurh pops him in the forehead with the cattle stun gun.

9. Aristotle *Nicomachean Ethics* 9.1166a29.

10. "There is but one truly serious philosophical problem, and that is suicide. Judging whether life is or is not worth living amounts to answering the fundamental question of philosophy." Albert Camus, "An Absurd Reasoning," *The Myth of Sisyphus*, trans. Justin O'Brien (New York: Vintage, 1955), 3.

11. In the book there is a passage in which Bell reflects on something his father once said to him: "My daddy always told me to just do the best you knew how and to tell the truth. He said there was nothing to set a man's mind at ease like wakin up in the morning and not havin to decide who you were. And if you done something wrong just stand up and say you done it and say you're sorry and get on with it. Dont haul stuff around with you." McCarthy, *No Country*, 249. Those same ethical rules are implicit for Bell in the movie as well.

12. McCarthy, *No Country*, 259.

13. Friedrich Nietzsche, *The Birth of Tragedy*, trans. Walter Kaufman (New York: Vantage, 1967), esp. secs. 11–12.

14. Roderick Frazier Nash, *Wilderness and the American Mind* (New Haven, Conn.: Yale Univ. Press, 1982), 1–2.

15. Ibid., xii.

16. Ibid., xii–xiii.

17. Ibid., 27.

18. Henry David Thoreau, *Walking* (Whitefish, Mont.: Kessinger, 2004), pt. II, sec. 14.

19. Jane Tompkins, *West of Everything: The Inner Life of Westerns* (New York: Oxford Univ. Press, 1992), 23–67; Peter A. French, *Cowboy Metaphysics: Ethics and Death in Westerns* (New York: Rowman & Littlefield, 1997), 1–45.

20. French, *Cowboy Metaphysics*, 47.

21. Louis L' Amour, *Hondo* (New York: Bantam, 1953), 59, cited in Tompkins, *West of Everything*, 23.

22. Tompkins, *West of Everything*, 24.

23. French, *Cowboy Metaphysics*, 57.

24. McCarthy, *No Country*, 227.

25. Ibid., 267, 281.

26. Ibid., 259.

27. A. Weismann, "La Durée de la vie," in *Essais sur l'hérédité* (Paris: C. Reinwald, 1892), quoted in François Jacob, *The Possible and the Actual* (Seattle: Univ. of Washington Press, 1982), 50.

28. Jacob, *Possible and the Actual*, 51.

29. William Butler Yeats, "Sailing to Byzantium," in *The Collected Poems of W. B. Yeats* (New York: Macmillan, 1979), 191.

30. William Butler Yeats, *A Vision* (New York: Collier, 1965), 279.

31. I want to thank Robert Angotti for drawing my attention to this line in the movie.

32. I am indebted to Tony McRae for some of the ideas in this paragraph.

DECEIT, DESIRE, AND DARK COMEDY

Postmodern Dead Ends in *Blood Simple*

Alan Woolfolk

> *Blood Simple* proceeded in a more organized, more conscious fashion. We did not deal with the real Texas, but an artificial version of it, an assemblage of texts and mythologies. The subject is "murderous passion." There have been so many cases of this sort that have occurred in Texas that it has become a part of the public imagination. But what resulted from that was important to us because the film was imagined as a slice of life, a deliberate fiction that it was normal to set within an exotic locale.
>
> —Joel Coen, interviewed in *Positif*

> We have seen that there is a way in which postmodernism replicates or reproduces—reinforces—the logic of consumer capitalism; the more significant question is whether there is also a way in which it resists that logic.
>
> —Fredric Jameson, "Postmodernism and Consumer Society"

As the inaugural film of Joel and Ethan Coen, *Blood Simple* (1984) is a startling exercise in transgeneric filmmaking that is difficult to characterize accurately not only because it draws upon the genres of film noir, comedy, the detective film, and the thriller but also because it is almost too obviously and pejoratively postmodern in its self-reflexivity, the use of obvious symbolism, and what Fredric Jameson calls the "omnipresence of pastiche" to the exclusion of any genuine "historicity."[1] Indeed, there is a strong and compelling case to be made that *Blood Simple* is an innovative product of the culture industry's postmodern neo-noir films, perhaps best exemplified by Lawrence Kasdan's *Body Heat* (1981) with its nostalgic recycling of noir motifs, compelling manipulation of seductive images, and persistent attention to the mastery of technique over content. According to this view, the Coen brothers simply bring macabre and comedic twists to their recycling of noir motifs that are calculated to jar and disturb the viewer. *Blood Simple* is, after all, what R. Barton Palmer calls a "visceral" film that reshapes the standard noir themes of greed, lust, and corruption, the jaded private detective, and the femme fatale at least in part because it so effectively employs techniques from comedy and thriller films.[2] Much like comedy and thriller films, this film works because it speaks to the body and is felt in the gut.

Nonetheless, *Blood Simple* is also arguably more deeply and resolutely postmodern in that it not only frustrates the attempts of its primary characters to achieve a coherent personal narrative and interpersonal communication, let alone trust in a saving metanarrative (all of which were already present in classic noir), but also lacks any significant intimation of resistance, however futile and self-destructive, to the corruption and profane ordinariness of late modernity that was present in classic film noir at its best.[3] From this perspective, the film's visceral quality may be seen as supporting a postmodern vision that connects with the history of our recent past precisely because it deconstructs and discredits prominent narratives of late modernity and what might be called late modernism that were exemplified in classic noir films. To be more precise, as a postmodern neo-noir film *Blood Simple* is a camp, over-the-top "blood melodrama"—blood is everywhere in the film—that severs the earlier, tenuous link between high modernism and film noir.[4] There is no implicit critique of modernity, no vestige of aesthetic revolt against the bourgeoisie, not even an allusion to the emptiness and corruption of conventional society. Rather, there is only the mundane, albeit comedic, present. *Blood Simple* ruthlessly burlesques the bourgeois myth of the self-made man to no other avail than affirming the healthiness of the clueless spouse/heroine. Instead of a detective with a questionable code of honor or perhaps an identity in conflict, it presents us with a low and venal parody of the corrupt Texas police detective Hank Quinlan from *Touch of Evil* (Orson Welles, 1958). Rather than charting the precarious and frequently fatal spiritual descent of a noir protagonist, *Blood Simple* gives us a hapless Marlboro Man who cannot even negotiate the flatlands of Texas. One looks in vain for a counternarrative, some evidence of the old tension between modernity and modernism, some remnant of the opposition between bourgeois and bohemian, but there is none to be found.[5] *Blood Simple* offers none of the authenticity of classic film noir because there is no gesture of rejection toward the extant society.

Yet *Blood Simple* advances beyond the inauthenticity of Fredric Jameson's "blank parody."[6] For the Coen brothers this film is a beginning point in their move toward the historical engagement and "new sincerity" of such films as *The Hudsucker Proxy* (1994) and *The Man Who Wasn't There* (2001).[7] As a sort of point zero, *Blood Simple* subjects one of the most popular myths of late modernity that is embodied in film noir—the noir myth of a fateful dark past and/or dark impulses intruding upon the conscious self and conventional society—to a merciless parody in order to move beyond it. In *Blood Simple,* the dark past becomes a dark and comedic present that casts no shadows. There is no "return of the repressed," nor even a *serious* return of that which has been denied or consciously rejected (although the cuckolded husband does prove stubbornly and comically difficult to kill and returns in the nightmare of the spouse/heroine). The noir myth is necessary to the film but only so that it may be negated. Paradoxically, *Blood Simple* relies upon the myth of a dark past and dark impulses that aren't there in any substantial form.

Minimal Philosophy and the Failure of Imagination

Blood Simple opens with a kind of common man's disquisition on life by an as yet unnamed private detective (M. Emmet Walsh), who is named Visser in the film and Loren Visser in the original screenplay (as indicated by his lighter), in the form of a voice-over in a country accent set against a barren Texas landscape: "The world is full of complainers. But the fact is, nothing comes with a guarantee. I don't care if you're the Pope of Rome, President of the United States, or even Man of the Year—something can always go wrong. And go ahead, complain, tell your problems to your neighbor, ask for help—watch him fly. Now in Russia, they got it mapped out so that everyone pulls for everyone else—that's the theory, anyway. But what I know is Texas . . . and down here . . . you're on your own." Visser's disquisition is vaguely reminiscent of Eric Hoffer's *The True Believer* (1951), a book notable for its articulation of a superficial sidewalk philosophy that gets nearly everything wrong. While the primary point of Hoffer's book in the 1950s was to attack early Christianity as a social movement made up of the riff-raff of society, the aim of Visser's comments is to articulate a crude philosophy of individualism.

Both present utterly profane views of the self, society, and world. Both bask in their anti-intellectualism, especially insofar as it supports a dismissal of any higher social philosophy.

Visser's minimal, lower social philosophy is depicted in *Blood Simple* as a comedy of hapless selves driven by desires. Indeed, historian Jerrold Seigel argues that the modern intellectual history of selfhood revolves around three dimensions of selfhood: the material or bodily, the sociocultural, and the reflective.[8] Defined in these terms, *Blood Simple* is an aesthetic experiment in which the sociocultural and reflective dimensions of the self have been elided and the bodily self has apparently been reduced to the simplest of impulses. In the opening scenes, a taciturn bartender named Ray (John Getz) begins a casual affair with his boss's wife, Abby (Frances McDormand), while driving her to Houston to escape from her marriage to Julian Marty (Dan Hedaya), a financially successful bar owner. From the beginning, the relationship between Ray and Abby is an exercise in failed communication, a series of misunderstandings and incorrect readings of each other. Initially, Abby has failed to recognize that Ray "likes" her. After the affair begins, both imagine that the other is involved with someone else. When Ray finds Marty shot and apparently dead, he imagines that Abby has committed the crime when in fact Marty has been shot and left for dead by Visser, who has been hired by Marty to spy on Abby. Later, Abby imagines that Ray is responsible for the death of Marty, for which he does share responsibility, but not for the reasons that she imagines. In short, the relationship between Ray and Abby is characterized by multiple failures of social imagination and misunderstandings, the inability to discern what the other person is thinking and feeling. If, as the American sociologist Charles Horton Cooley once wrote, "the imaginations which people have of one another are the *solid facts* of society," then there are but few solid facts between Ray and Abby and many insubstantial and misleading fictions.[9]

It is not an exaggeration to say that nearly every major action in the film is determined by unchecked passions—not just unchecked erotic impulses but raw motives of fear, greed, revenge, and anger that cause individuals to go "simple." Failures of social imagination and lack of self-reflection seem to explain much of the haplessness of repeated impulsive actions. On the surface of the narrative, Ray is initially driven by sexual desire, Marty by revenge, Visser by greed, Abby by fear and desire, and yet this is not the entire story. Visser's venality is intertwined with voyeurism (he takes pictures of Ray and Abby engaging in sexual acts and then gives the unsolicited pictures to Marty), and Marty's anger and vengeful motives are clearly inseparable from what he *imagines* other men are doing with Abby (which is made quite clear when he sees Visser's photographs). In fact, Marty's decision to hire Visser to kill Ray and Abby is the consequence of obsessive brooding about Abby, which is triggered by his viewing of the photographs. But the implications of Visser's photographs are even more complicated. Marty suspects Visser's voyeurism and reveals his jealousy when he asks, "How long did you *watch her?*" (emphasis added). Visser, in turn, not only shamelessly acknowledges his voyeurism but clearly takes pleasure in taunting Marty when he responds, "Most of the night. . . . They'd just rest a few minutes and then get started again. Quite something." In short, the imaginations Marty and Visser have of each other are the solid facts of their sordid relationship. In this closed postmodern universe, there is no glimpse of a moral society, not even the possibility of a genuine social relationship. Hence, there is not the sense of loss, the regret, about what might have been that is present in classic noir and even early neo-noir (e.g., *Chinatown* [Roman Polanski, 1974]).

The Complexities of Going "Simple"

On the one hand, the Coen brothers present us with a truncated view of individuals (who lack adequate social development, cultural context, and self-reflectiveness) that turns the major characters of the film into impulsive marionettes in a minimalist theater of the absurd placed at the mercy of a postmodern fate. On the other hand, the Coens have created an unpretentious Texan working-class universe that lacks what René Girard calls an external mediating authority.[10] There are no impersonal or sufficiently removed spiritual models regulating desire and emotion. Rather, desires and emotions run rampant. Jealousy and envy are unchecked among rivals in close social proximity to one another, with each imitating the other. For instance, Ray sexually desires his boss's wife, Abby, who then in turn is desired by her husband, Marty, resulting in an attempted rape. But in the interval between Ray's initial one-night stand with Abby and the attempted rape, Ray's desire for Abby is fueled by his perusal of the old photographs of Marty and Abby together hanging in the den of their home (recall that Ray caresses Abby's leg in one of the pictures). Consequently, Ray and Marty are jealous rivals whose desires for Abby each feed off the other. Moreover, Marty and Meurice (Samm-Art Williams), the African American bartender, are also to a lesser degree sexual rivals. Marty initially believes that Abby is having an affair with a "colored" man (quite possibly Meurice) and later unsuccessfully attempts to pick up Meurice's newfound girlfriend, Debra (Deborah Neumann). Meurice, for his part, meets Debra while working at Marty's bar and persists in bringing girlfriends back to Marty's place to party after hours, a seemingly innocent action, but not without significance given Marty's tendencies toward sexual jealousy and envy.

Photography obviously feeds the dynamics of what Girard calls "triangular desire" in *Blood Simple* and facilitates individuals going "simple" minded over more than just sexual objects. Visser's later photograph of Abby and Ray is doctored to make it look as though they have been shot while asleep in bed, all for the purpose of convincing Marty that Visser really has killed the couple. As such, the photo becomes a means of deceiving Marty so that Visser may collect his ten thousand dollars from Marty before he attempts to kill him. (Visser does not trust Marty not to go "simple" on him and reveal the murders.) Visser covets Marty's money more than his wife, but he is nonetheless the victim of his unchecked desires. Despite the fact that Visser is worried about Marty going "simple" on him, Visser himself goes "simple" out of greed, just as Ray goes "simple" out of desire and eventually affection for Abby, and Marty goes "simple" out of jealousy and rage. There is no room for self-reflection or self-critique. The unchecked desires of all three men simply and rather obviously lead to a dead end. Indeed, in a bit of self-conscious symbolism, the Coen brothers even have Ray living on a "dead end" street, which provides the setup for two humorous scenes in which Marty and Meurice angrily drive away from Ray's going the wrong way, only to come to an abrupt halt and turn around.

The Uncertainties of Postmodern Fate

As a postmodern film, *Blood Simple* is a film of self-parody. Self-conscious symbolism abounds, drawing attention to the fact that the narrative is constructed and relies on the manipulation of symbols by the director/writers. Just prior to being shot and left for dead by Visser, for example, Marty returns from his fishing trip with a string of fish, which remain on his desk rotting even after Ray has removed his body, signaling that something is "fishy" or that something "stinks." After seeing Visser's pictures of Abby and Ray apparently dead, Marty immediately vomits because he has "no stomach" for murder. And Visser himself is repeatedly depicted as a low and disgusting man who in his tactless yellow leisure suit and shabby personal demeanor resembles the (Volkswagen) "bug" that he drives. (Indeed, Visser even acknowledges that he is a repulsive creature, telling Marty that he can "crawl around" without his head if Marty wants to "cut it off.") Such camp symbols both draw attention to themselves in their obviousness and directness and prompt the sophisticated postmodern viewer to recognize them as bits of self-conscious humor inserted into the film by the authors for the amusement of the audience.

Of greater significance is the Coen brothers' self-conscious treatment of uncertainty and the irony of intentions, both bad and good, gone awry. As Palmer has argued, "What is most certain is uncertainty itself, the fact that 'something can always go wrong,' as the narrator wryly observes."[11] In the case of Visser, his criminal plans go awry on several occasions, most notably when he fails to kill Marty and leaves the photograph of Ray and Abby behind and when he disastrously underestimates the resourcefulness of Abby in the closing scenes. Likewise, Ray's plan to dispose of Marty's body in a misguided effort to protect Abby turns into a gruesome charade in which the mortally wounded husband is buried alive. But what is most important is not simply the irony of unintended consequences that runs like a red thread throughout *Blood Simple* and of course harkens back to classic noir films. Rather, it is the postmodern context within which these ironic consequences are set: the events of *Blood Simple* unfold within a universe of uncertainty, not fate, with the narrative of the film drawing attention to the sheer contingency of human action and events.

Blood Simple may be fruitfully contrasted with such classic noir films as *Double Indemnity* (Billy Wilder, 1944) and *Detour* (Edgar G. Ulmer, 1945), to which it bears a superficial resemblance. On the surface, all three films appear to emphasize the theme of an inexorable fate that is inseparable from the character flaws of the major characters. But the two classic noir films construct a modern notion of fate that, however contrived it might be, is set within the cultural context of a modernist critique of twentieth-century capitalist civilization. In *Double Indemnity*, as James Naremore has argued, the insurance agent Walter Neff (Fred MacMurray) "is little more than a cog in a bureaucracy, and he cannot resist the blandishments of sex and money." The film is "pervaded with grimly deterministic metaphors of modern industry: the lovers promise to remain committed to one another 'straight down the line'; Walter devises a clockwork murder involving a train, and when he puts his plan in motion he remarks that 'the machinery had started to move and nothing could stop it'; later, looking back over his crime, he claims that fate had 'thrown the switch' and that the 'gears had meshed.'" Even the femme fatale, Phyllis (Barbara Stanwyck), is "visibly artificial . . . a soulless, modernized female" who is "affectless."[12] Similarly, Ulmer's *Detour* is clearly influenced by the Frankfurt school and may be read as a critique of the American wasteland in which the lives of the major characters are dominated by cultural and economic forces embodied in Hollywood. As Paul Cantor explains, "The characters in *Detour* seem incapable of generating authentic desires; they are always setting their goals on the basis of the models that American society offers them."[13] Consequently, as in the case of *Double Indemnity*, the theme of fate is specifically linked to a critique of late modern capitalist civilization. The grim fatalism of Walter Neff in *Double Indemnity* and Al Roberts (Tom Neal) in *Detour* is a manifestation of the sickness of American society.

Blood Simple presents no such modernist critique. While the three male characters of Visser, Marty, and Ray all go "simple," the contingency of human action and events is unrelated to the context of late modernity; rather, contingency is universal, a fundamental fact of human existence. The rampant desires of a society created in the image of Visser's minimal social philosophy presuppose an uncertain world in which anything can and does happen by chance. "Something can always go wrong" is a primordial principle that precedes the social and cultural context. This uncertainty becomes explicit with regard to events associated with Abby's pistol, which Visser steals with only three bullets remaining in the six chambers. One bullet is fired when Visser shoots Marty with the gun in what appears to be an attempt to incriminate Abby. A second bullet is discharged when Ray accidentally kicks the gun upon entering Marty's office to find his apparently dead body. And the third bullet is not fired until Abby shoots Visser (thinking that he is Marty) in self-defense. During the time between the firing of the second and third bullets, Marty attempts to discharge the gun three times when he shoots at Ray from the grave, but in a stroke of remarkably bad luck he hits an empty chamber each time. Abby, on the other hand, has the remarkably good luck to fire the single remaining bullet on the first try exactly when she must to save her life. In *Blood Simple*, the universe is ruled by chance, not fate. Life is a gamble. Individual purpose and social order are fictions that may dissolve at any moment in the face of uncertainty to reveal not the bleak determinism of late modernity but the dark humor of the postmodern absurdity of life.

Multiple Burlesques

The postmodern humor of *Blood Simple* cuts more deeply because comedic inversions run throughout the film that not only parody and subvert the noir myth but also assume some familiarity with it. As a private detective, for instance, Visser retains none of the heritage of the dandy's impeccable self-control and aesthetic sophistication that classic noir drew upon beginning with *The Maltese Falcon* (John Huston, 1941).[14] Instead, Visser is clearly a villain and an inverted image of the dandy, an antidandy, a theme to which the Coen brothers return in *The Big Lebowski* (1998). As a postmodern cross between Hank Quinlan in *Touch of Evil* manufacturing evidence and Jake Gittes in *Chinatown* telling bad jokes, Visser possesses no sign of either the former's genius for framing the guilty nor the latter's unsuccessful aspiration to coolness and self-possession. In fact, going "simple" implies a complete lack of coolness and self-possession.

In contrast, Ray initially seems to be cool and self-possessed, but once he is confronted with the brute reality of Marty's body and concludes that Abby is responsible for the murder, he panics. From this point on, the whole dark comedy of cleaning up the seemingly endless blood and disposing of the body that is not dead unfolds. Ray's presentation of himself as the taciturn, laid-back Marlboro Man, contemporized with unlit cigarette, is exposed as a sham as he discovers how difficult it is not only to get rid of a body (à la Hitchcock in *The Trouble with Harry* [1955]) but also, more importantly, to dispose of one that is not dead. The disturbing farce of Ray's dance-of-death struggle with the nearly dead Marty on the highway and the ordeal of burying him alive are a brilliant, literal representation of the macabre with comedic twists that completely unnerve him. After these ghastly experiences, Ray never recovers his former composure as he seems to move inevitably toward his eventual death at the hands of Visser.

If Visser is rather obviously depicted as a lowly bug and Ray is exposed as a Marlboro Man overcome with panic, then Marty is mercilessly burlesqued as a conventional self-made man who is a "hard ass" and "anal retentive." Aside from the fact that Dan Hedaya bears a definite resemblance to Richard Nixon (the quintessential self-made man of American politics), Marty is repeatedly depicted as an uptight businessman who is obsessed with protecting his money and possessions (including Abby) to the point that he is deranged and "sick." Not only does Visser's scatological joke about anality and love seem especially appropriate for Marty but Abby explains later in the film in an unintentionally mock-serious scene at Ray's bungalow that Marty has confessed to her that he is mentally "anal." Here, it seems not unreasonable to conclude that the Coen brothers are burlesquing the pop psychology of the classic noir era (e.g., *The Accused* [William Dieterle, 1949]), as well as throwing in a bit of pop Freudianism that is incongruous for the time period of the film, once again drawing attention to the postmodern pastiche of *Blood Simple* as they subject the myth of the self-made man to a carnivalesque deflation.

The Triumph of the "Funny" Girl

In contrast to the three leading males who meet with their respective dead ends, Abby is a model of health and normality, and not simply because she tells Ray that the psychiatrist to whom Marty has sent her has told her that she is the "healthiest" person he has ever met. Despite the fact that she is driven by fear, desire, and loneliness, Abby is the only major figure in the film who does not lose her cool and go "simple." Even so, aside from the fact that she does not go "simple," Abby is still haplessly impulsive and clueless as to what is going on around her to the point that her misunderstanding of Ray's intentions results in his killing by Visser when she turns on the light in her new apartment, making her an unintentional femme fatale. Nonetheless, Abby's cluelessness is the key to her survival in this sordid society. As an unintentional femme fatale, she seems immune to the guile that leads others to their dead ends. In fact, Abby's lack of guile becomes an asset in a society in which most individuals are too clever for their own good, in which there is no working definition of the good.

Although Abby fails to understand and communicate with Ray clearly, her claim that "I ain't done nothing funny" is ironic precisely because it should not be read negationally. One should not assume that she *has done* something funny that needs to be revealed by removing or rejecting her denial (i.e., her "ain't"), despite her betrayal and humiliation of Marty (e.g., her adultery with Ray, the kick in the groin to Marty), which are openly carried out and not denied in the course of the film. The line is funny precisely in its straightness, given the deceit and paranoia that surround her. Abby is above suspicion.

Yet one must ask what "healthiness" means within the closed postmodern universe of *Blood Simple*. Noir films such as *Double Indemnity* and *Detour* offer bleak portraits of a sick society in which health is by implication dependent upon the rejection of late modernity. Fate may rule, but there is the possibility of a way out. *Blood Simple,* as stated earlier, presents no such modernist critique. There is no way out; there are only those who somehow keep from going "simple" and are momentarily lucky. Abby is lucky. In a world of uncertainty, she gambles and wins and, thus, is temporarily empowered.

Notes

The first epigraph is from an interview with Joel and Ethan Coen in *Positif* (July–August 1987), translated in R. Barton Palmer, *Joel and Ethan Coen* (Urbana: Univ. of Illinois Press, 2004), 160. The second epigraph is from Fredric Jameson's "Postmodernism and Consumer Society," in *The Anti-Aesthetic: Essays on Postmodern Culture,* ed. and intro. Hal Foster (New York: New Press, 1998), 144.

1. Fredric Jameson, *Postmodernism, or, The Cultural Logic of Late Capitalism* (Durham, N.C.: Duke Univ. Press, 1991), 18.

2. R. Barton Palmer, *Joel and Ethan Coen* (Urbana: Univ. of Illinois Press, 2004), 16.

3. On metanarratives, see Jean-François Lyotard, *The Postmodern Condition: A Report on Knowledge,* trans. G. Bennington and B. Massumi, foreword by Fredric Jameson (Minneapolis: Univ. of Minneapolis Press), 1984.

4. The expression is originally from Graham Greene. See James Naremore, *More Than Night: Film Noir in Its Contexts* (Berkeley and Los Angeles: Univ. of California Press, 1998), 45. Naremore makes a convincing case for the link between high modernism and film noir.

5. "For modernity, it is possible, without stretching customary usage too far, to distinguish between 'modernity' and 'modernism.' This is useful in separating a largely political or ideological from a largely cultural or aesthetic concept of modernity. They overlap, of course. . . . But there is sufficient tension between them, amounting at times to outright divergence, to make it helpful to consider modernity in this dual aspect. The same does not apply to the idea of post-modernity." Krishan Kumar, *From Post-Industrial to Post-Modern Society* (Oxford: Blackwell, 1995), 101.

6. Jameson, *Postmodernism,* 17.

7. See R. Barton Palmer, "The New Sincerity of Neo-Noir: The Example of *The Man Who Wasn't There,*" in *The Philosophy of Neo-Noir,* ed. Mark T. Conard (Lexington: Univ. Press of Kentucky, 2007), 151–66. See also Jim Collins, "Genericity in the Nineties: Eclectic Irony and the New Sincerity," in *Film Theory Goes to the Movies,* ed. Jim Collins, Hilary Radner, and Ava P. Collins (New York: Routledge, 1993), 242–63.

8. Jerrold Seigel, "Problematizing the Self," in *Beyond the Cultural Turn,* ed. Victoria E. Bonnell and Lynn Hunt (Berkeley and Los Angeles: Univ. of California Press, 1999), 281–314, esp. 285–89; Seigel, *The Idea of the Self* (Cambridge: Cambridge Univ. Press, 2005), 3–44.

9. Charles Horton Cooley, *Human Nature and the Social Order* (New York: Schocken, 1964), 121.

10. See René Girard, *Deceit, Desire, and the Novel,* trans. Yvonne Freccero (Baltimore: Johns Hopkins Univ. Press, 1966), 1–52.

11. Palmer, *Joel and Ethan Coen,* 17.

12. Naremore, *More Than Night,* 87–89.

13. Paul Cantor, "Film Noir and the Frankfurt School: America as Wasteland in Edgar Ulmer's *Detour,*" in *The Philosophy of Noir,* ed. Mark T. Conard (Lexington: Univ. Press of Kentucky, 2006), 146.

14. See Alan Woolfolk, "The Horizon of Disenchantment: Film Noir, Camus, and the Vicissitudes of Descent," in *The Philosophy of Film Noir,* ed. Conard, 107–23.

Part 2

ETHICS: SHAME, JUSTICE, AND VIRTUE

"And It's Such a Beautiful Day!"

Shame and *Fargo*

Rebecca Hanrahan and David Stearns

The drama of *Fargo* (1996) begins with a conversation in a bar. There, Jerry Lundegaard (William H. Macy) negotiates the kidnapping of his wife with two unsavory characters, Carl Showalter (Steve Buscemi) and Gaear Grimsrud (Peter Stormare). Carl asks Jerry, incredulously, "You want to have your wife kidnapped?" Jerry confirms his desire with an un-hesitant, untroubled, and unashamed "Yah." Carl, though, is concerned. And though his concern is primarily directed at the financial wisdom of the venture, he isn't mollified when Jerry reassures his two associates that the plan is "real sound. It's all worked out." The ransom, Jerry explains, will be paid by his father-in-law, Wade Gustafson (Harve Presnell), and Jerry will provide the two with a car. This isn't enough for Carl. He wants to know why Jerry would need to resort to such a scheme. Jerry feebly explains that it is "personal."

At this point in the conversation, Carl goes up to the edge of his concerns but can't seem to find his words. He stammers, "Okay, Jerry. You're tasking us to perform this mission, but you, you won't, uh, you won't—aw, fuck it, let's take a look at that Ciera." What is Carl grasping at, why can't it be said, and how is it that the Ciera is such a distraction?

The key to answering these questions, we contend, lies in the relation-ship between shame and friendship as put forth by Aristotle. In this movie, those who lack an appropriate sense of shame don't have the capacity to form friendships. Thus, each of the co-conspirators, to differing degrees, tends to relate to others merely instrumentally. They think in terms of what advantage they can get from the people around them and not in terms of the merit of those people on their own terms. Consequently, they don't have the regard for others that is needed for them to feel shame and hence regulate their behavior accordingly. The only character in the film who is morally upright is the sheriff investigating the kidnapping, Marge Gunderson (Frances McDormand). Her behavior gives her no cause to feel shame, for she has the ability to assume the good of others as her own, as demonstrated by her deep friendship with her husband. Moreover, this ability gives her a moral orientation that enables her to locate times when others should be ashamed. And with this knowledge in hand, she tries gently to instruct others as to how they should behave and feel.

To begin, we will consider Aristotle's theory of shame and its relationship to moral character. Next, we will draw parallels between Aristotle's theory and the various characters in the movie. Finally, we will show how shame and friendship are related both in the film and in Aristotle's work. There, we will argue that those characters who have the proper regard for others have the capacity for both shame and friendship, and those who lack this regard lack these capacities.

Aristotle on Shame

Shame, for Aristotle, is a feeling that accompanies one's recognition of having done something that would result in disgrace or discredit: "Shame may be defined as pain or disturbance in regard to bad things, whether present, past, or future, which seem likely to involve us in discredit; and shamelessness as contempt or indifference in regard to these same bad things."[1] Because shame is associated with disgrace, it necessarily involves our recognition of others as morally significant. Thus, to properly feel shame, we must care about our standing in relation to those who matter, specifically, those "persons whom we admire, or who admire us, or by whom we wish to be admired, or from whom we desire some service that we shall not obtain if we forfeit their good opinion."[2] We do not want to do wrong in front of these people, for when we do, we will be disgraced. We will have lost our honor and good reputation. Such a loss is felt as a pain, and this sort of pain is shame. Of course, these feelings of shame do not arise only in those contexts in which our bad actions are actually witnessed by those whom we respect. It also occurs when we imagine how such people would respond to that which we have done or that which we are tempted to do. In addition, we need not have any particular person in mind when engaging in these imaginative exercises. Merely imagining what respectable people would think of our poor behavior is enough to induce shame. For these reasons, Aristotle at times describes shame as "the imagination of disgrace."[3]

Now, this sort of pain is not something found in the most excellent people, "since it is consequent on bad actions," which the excellent do not do, nor are they even tempted to do.[4] But even so, there is still a way in which shame plays a role in moral goodness. For though the feeling of shame is not in and of itself praiseworthy, since it indicates either that you have done wrong or are tempted to do wrong, having a *capacity* for shame is. "But shame may be said to be conditionally a good thing; *if* a good man did such actions, he would feel disgraced."[5] If someone does something bad, we expect him to be disgraced by it. Conversely, we judge someone's character negatively if we observe him doing awful things and not feeling the slightest bit ashamed by it.

But though a capacity for shame is praiseworthy, it is obviously not a sufficient condition of moral excellence. "If shamelessness—not to be ashamed of doing base actions—is something bad, that doesn't make it decent to do such things and be ashamed."[6] In addition to a sense of shame, the morally upright individual must possess the disposition to act in accordance with what shame has taught him. For this reason, Aristotle thinks that shame is fitting "only for youth. For we think young people should be prone to shame because they live by passion and therefore commit many errors, but are restrained by shame; and we praise the young people who are prone to this passion."[7] By a "passion" (*pathos*), Aristotle simply means an emotion or desire. Some passions are directed at satisfying one's bodily appetites, but others are not. Anger and, as we can see from the quote above, shame are passions as well. Importantly, these feelings need not be particularly strong; they can be weak and still be considered passions.

Now, men of moral excellence have their passions in line with their right reason.[8] But the young are morally inchoate. While they may know right from wrong, their passions are too strong and draw them away from right action. Hence, there is no way to keep the young from acting poorly on occasion. Shame then allows the young to recognize bad actions, both those they have engaged in and those they are intending to do. And this knowledge can, of course, aid them in properly altering their behavior in the future. Moreover, if they properly alter their behavior, that is, if they correct their behavior to accord with shame's lessons, the young will in time master their passions and eventually bring them in line with right reason, thereby developing the disposition for good. But if they don't correct their behavior, they will develop the habit of doing shameful things, and in the end they will lose the capacity for shame.

From this short discussion, we see the outlines of a moral hierarchy emerging in Aristotle's works. The ideal is the man of excellence, whose passions accord with right reason, who never feels shame, but would if he ever did something deserving of it. The next step down is to those whose passions are out of sync with right reason. Both the morally continent and the morally incontinent in some sense know what is right. They reason well and to the good. But both have passions that tempt them to do what they know they should not. "We praise the reason of the continent and of the incontinent, and the part of their soul that has reason, since it urges them aright and towards the best objects; but there is found in them also another natural element, which fights against and resists it."[9]

The morally continent person has the self-control to do what is right, and shame has a hand here. For, again, our feelings of shame can be activated, not just by our doing wrong but by our imagining ourselves doing wrong. And our imagined disgrace can impel us to do what right reason demands. The morally incontinent can't overcome his passions. He knows what is right but only in the sense that "a man asleep, mad, or drunk" has such knowledge.[10] His passions preclude him from fully realizing his knowledge and acting as he should. He instead acts poorly and feels regret as a consequence.

Finally, the least moral are the shameless: they do shameful actions as they please and yet do not recognize that their actions are shameful. This morally self-indulgent person is one who is "led on in accordance with his own choice, thinking that he ought always to pursue the present pleasure."[11] This person does not know what is right. Instead, he thinks that the right always accords with his own pleasures and hence he always chooses to act for his pleasure. Such a person, again, might have failed to heed the lessons of his youth, acted contrary to his feelings of shame, and hence lost his capacity for shame.

Interestingly enough, the principal characters of *Fargo* fall rather nicely into these categories. Gaear performs acts of utter brutality and cruelty without a hint of shame. Jerry lacks self-control. He exhibits moments of moral awareness, some sense of shame, but acts reprehensibly nonetheless. Finally, as we have explained, Marge is the paradigm of excellence. Her behavior is beyond reproach, and her sense of shame allows her to feel the shame that others cannot. Let us now look more closely at these characters to discover the source of their differences.

Gaear Grimsrud

Gaear kills five "poor souls" in the course of this movie, and he does so with complete affective neutrality. He manifests no signs of any sort of inner conflict with regard to his violent behavior. With a wave of his hand, he explains why he killed Jean Lundegaard (Kristin Rudrüd), his kidnap victim: "She started shrieking, you know." This untroubled approach to violence points to Gaear's moral self-indulgence. The self-indulgent man "craves for all pleasant things or those that are most pleasant, and is led by his appetite to choose these at the cost of everything else."[12] The pleasure of Jean's silence is, in Gaear's estimation, worth her life.

Gaear is, thus, motivated solely by the most basic of human appetites: money, sex, and pancakes.

> GAEAR: We stop at Pancakes House.
> CARL: What're you, nuts? We had pancakes for breakfast. I gotta go somewhere I can get a shot and a beer—and a steak maybe. Not more fuckin' pancakes. [. . .]
> GAEAR: [Stares at Carl]
> CARL: Okay, here's an idea. We'll stop outside of Brainerd. I know a place where we can get laid. Wuddya think?
> GAEAR: I'm fuckin' hungry now, you know.

The only enticement Carl can muster to shift Gaear's focus away from pancakes is sex. His body takes precedence, while the needs and interests of others hold no weight for him. Gaear ignores Carl's protests that cigarettes are noxious and injurious, and he smokes throughout the drama. The two crooks never form any kind of true friendship. In fact, the two never make any personal connection whatsoever. And not for lack of trying on Carl's part. Carl explicitly rebukes Grimsrud for being reluctant to say anything in the way of conversation, despite extremely long hours on the road together.

A striking example of Gaear's indifference is seen when Carl returns to the cabin after shooting and being shot by Wade Gustafson. Gaear doesn't differentiate between his blood-soaked associate and the fuzzy soap opera on TV. Carl's injury is completely unremarkable in Gaear's opinion: he doesn't even ask if Carl is all right. His only concern is discussing how to split the ransom money and the car. And when the two disagree, Gaear resolves their dispute with the swing of an axe and puts his former associate in the wood chipper.

Gaear's indifference to others and consequent apathy toward social norms is further illustrated in the interactions between Gaear and Marge. Marge is not just the sheriff in charge of investigating Gaear's crimes but also an expectant mother. Thus, she occupies two roles that lend themselves especially well to bringing shame to bear on moral transgressors. As Marge approaches Gaear feeding Carl into the wood chipper, she identifies herself several times as a police officer. Her voice, though, is drowned out by the noise of the machine. The law, society's norms for governing behavior, is not able to make itself known to Gaear. He is deaf to Marge's invocations.

When Gaear is riding in the back of Marge's prowler, we see a more direct depiction of the incommensurability of the two characters. Marge tallies up the people that Gaear has killed, then remarks sorrowfully that it was all "for what? For a little bit of money." She continues, "There's more to life than money, you know. Don't you know that?" Her second iteration of the question seems more a recognition that, indeed, he might not know that. Gaear displays no reaction to her entreaty. Instead, he exhibits the same stony unresponsiveness during Marge's honest and sensible admonishment as he has throughout. Thus, the two seem alien to each other; her simple pronouncements about the moral corruption of his materialism and violence fail to move him in any way. Hence, Gaear's complete shamelessness is manifest. We watch him as his reprehensible actions are recounted to him by the best of people, and he is not affected at all.

Jerry Lundegaard

In his professional life, Jerry is a less than reputable car salesman. He has the habit of cheating not just his customers but his company as well. One of his schemes, which the movie indicates he regularly pulls, involves "TruCoat Sealant." During the bargaining, Jerry concedes that the car in question doesn't need sealant. Then when he calls the customer to come in for delivery, he nevertheless includes—and of course charges them for—the TruCoat. This obviously leads to angry customers. In the hyper-polite milieu of Minnesota, one of these customers even calls Jerry a "fucking liar." Jerry does not disagree; he concedes that he settled on a price that did not include paying for the TruCoat. Nevertheless, he sits in front of them, "talking like [they] didn't go over this already," and charges them four hundred dollars for it anyway. In general, Jerry seems untroubled by what he is doing, even leaving his office once in order to trick his customers into thinking that he is trying to get them a better deal from his boss. Only when he is sworn at does Jerry's facial expression reveal his shame. When the man accuses him of being a liar, Jerry's head drops and his eyebrows rise in unspoken assent.

The fact that the customer can bring Jerry—reluctantly—to some sort of realization of his shameful behavior shows that Jerry in a way understands what is wrong, that he has the correct rule somewhere in mind. But he acts without regard to the moral reasoning he seems at least capable of. In this way, Jerry fits Aristotle's description of the incontinent. Aristotle thinks that the incontinent knows right from wrong, but his knowledge is not put into action. Aristotle likens the incontinent to "a city which passes all the right decrees and has good laws, but makes no use of them."[13] Jerry in some sense knows what he is doing is wrong. But in another sense, he doesn't. His knowledge is shallow and hence it cannot counteract his desire for money. In fact, the money is, for Jerry, an incentive to ignore his shame. It is an acceptable compensation for his discomfort. Thus, he cannot and maybe even doesn't want that shame to shape his behavior.

Consider Jerry's interaction with his son, Scotty (Tony Denman). Jerry doesn't think about how the kidnapping of his wife is affecting Scotty until Wade's accountant, Stan Grossman (Larry Brandendurg), asks after Scotty's well-being. Crestfallen, Jerry responds, "Yeah, jeez, Scotty, yeah, I'll talk to him." Walking into Scotty's room, Jerry has an unconcerned grin on his face; no hint of angst registers in his voice. We are very much confronted by the fact that Jerry has put aside any shame he briefly felt.

> JERRY: How ya doin' there, Scotty?
> SCOTTY: Dad, what're they doing? Wuddya think they're doin' with Mom?
> JERRY: It's okay, Scotty. They're not gonna want to hurt her any. These men, they just want money, see.
> SCOTTY: What if—what if sump'n' goes wrong?
> JERRY: No, no, nothin's goin' wrong here. Granddad and I, we're— we're makin' sure this gets handled right.
> [...]
> JERRY: We're gonna get Mom back for ya, but we gotta play ball. Ya know that's the deal. Now, if Loraine calls, or Sylvia, you just say

> that Mom is in Florida with Pearl and Marty. . . . That's the best
> we can do here.

Scotty is the first one in the movie who expresses genuine concern for Jean's well-being. Even Wade, Jean's father, worries more over the money he will lose in paying the ransom. He goes so far as to entertain the possibility of offering the kidnappers half of what they asked for. But Scotty values his mother absolutely, not as an exchangeable or quantifiable good. He values her as one should value a member of one's family, for herself. Jerry witnesses the care Scotty has for his mother, and when he leaves his son's room, his body language conveys that he just might feel a modicum of shame.

It is worth noting here that for Aristotle, it is via the mediation of others that shame is felt. This fact is illustrated in these scenes. Stan Grossman is one of the few people in the movie who is respected by others. Thus, he is morally positioned to make Jerry recognize what he has done. And Jerry is for a moment shamed. Via his son, whom he loves, Jerry sees not just how he has harmed him but also how he has failed to properly value and care for his wife.

It is also worth noting *what* Jerry comes to recognize in these moments of shame. Through both Stan and his son, he recognizes the particularities of his wrong. He is made to confront the pain of his *one and only* son, who loves *his mother*, for herself, intrinsically. These are the people he should value in their singularity but hasn't, and for a moment he seemingly recognizes this fact. This illustrates Aristotle's conception of how the morally incontinent person comes to do wrong. For Aristotle, the incontinent person fully grasps universal moral truths, such as the truth that kidnapping is wrong. And he even has some vague sense of how that universal principle is applicable to the situation in question. But he doesn't fully grasp its application. Passions keep him from understanding in the moment the specifics of his wrong. Thus, he does wrong. Jerry's shame reveals to him what he didn't understand: how specifically he was harming *his son, his wife*. But his need for money doesn't allow him to act on his shame, and so he continues on with his plan, working now to ensure that he gets the ransom money he needs.

Thus, Jerry is close to becoming immune to the lessons of his own shame. He still feels shame, and it still points him to what he isn't sufficiently attending to, namely, the needs, values, and interests of particular others. But it doesn't affect his behavior. It is in this way that Jerry's shame is inert. Nothing in Jerry is preventing him from doing wrong.[14]

Two objections might be offered against this reading of Jerry's character. First, some might balk at the notion that Jerry could be overcome by his passions, for he is such a dull and tepid character. But is he really all that tepid? Jerry goes to his father-in-law for a loan that he would apparently use to both set up a small business, a parking lot, and get himself out of the trouble he has gotten himself into. Though Wade acknowledges that the deal looks good, he denies Jerry the loan, offering him only a "finder's fee." Afterward, alone in the parking lot as he scrapes ice from his car, Jerry is overcome by his emotions, and he feebly but violently attacks his windshield. Jerry doesn't often express strong emotion, but there is evidence here that he feels such emotion.[15]

Moreover, keep in mind that passion for Aristotle refers to one's emotions or desires, and these emotions can be either strong or weak. Consider also that for Aristotle a person can even be overcome by what would otherwise be thought to be a weak emotion: "It is possible to be in such a state as to be defeated even by those of them which most people master, or to master even those by which most people are defeated."[16] Thus, even if Jerry is considered tepid, even his weak emotions can lead him toward doing what his shame has taught him is wrong.

The second objection concerns shame's role in motivating Jerry's behavior. We argue above that Jerry is morally incontinent. He knows what is wrong and feels shame for the wrongs he does and intends to do, but this shame doesn't move him to behave as right reason demands. Instead, he acts on his passions. But might Jerry instead be doing wrong to avoid shame? He has gotten himself into trouble, so he has hatched this kidnapping scheme to get the money he needs to avoid the shame that will follow if his wrongs are discovered.

In response to this objection, note that avoiding public disgrace isn't the same as avoiding shame. For shame arises even when others don't know of your wrongs. To review, shame can arise either when others learn of your wrongdoings or when you merely imagine what would be thought of your bad actions or intentions by those whom you respect. Thus, Jerry can't avoid shame by doing more wrong; he can only avoid shame by avoiding wrong.

That said, avoiding public disgrace might, of course, be one of Jerry's motivations. But there is evidence that indicates that it isn't his primary motivator. Consider the money. Jerry is asking for $1 million in ransom money, yet he needs only $320,000, plus the cost of the kidnapping, to cover up his wrongdoing. If public disgrace is what he is seeking to avoid, he need not have asked for so much. Clearly, Jerry's greed is driving him here. Consider as well the last scene in which Jerry appears. He has fled, but the police have found him in a motel. If Jerry's primary motivation were to avoid public disgrace, once found he would try to explain away his crimes or he would at least try to lessen his disgrace by carrying himself with dignity. He would quietly and willingly surrender himself and confess his crimes. But this is not how Jerry is taken. Instead, he is found in his underwear trying to scramble out of the bathroom window. He is forcibly thrown on the bed and handcuffed, all as he screams and cries pathetically. His fear is moving him here, not his sense of right or wrong nor how his behavior will be seen in the public eye. Jerry, as we have shown, feels shame, but as we see in this scene it is his other passions—fear, greed, and pride—that move him.

Marge Gunderson

The first shot of Marge in the movie is preceded by the camera slowly panning over her husband's painting supplies. Marge is thereby introduced to us through Norm's interests. A phone call then awakens Marge, informing her of a triple homicide that she has to investigate. It is before dawn, but Norm (John Carroll Lynch) insists on cooking her eggs. She, though, wants him to stay asleep. He wins this battle and cooks her eggs that she begins to eat but which he finishes. Later, Marge discusses the crime scene with her partner Lou (Bruce Bohne):

> MARGE: I guess the little guy sat in there waiting for his buddy to
>   come back.
> LOU: Yah, it would have been cold out here.
> MARGE: Heck, yah. Ya think, is Dave's open yet?
> LOU: Dave . . . You don't think he's mixed up in—
> MARGE: No, no, I just wanna get Norm some night crawlers.

In this moment, Marge transitions from her own ends to her husband's ends fluidly and seamlessly. Though she intently inspects the crime scene, her interests never stray too far from Norm's interests, which include fishing. His interests and well-being are of concern to her, as hers are to him.

In these brief scenes, we see that between Marge and Norm there exists what Aristotle would call a friendship of the good. Aristotle distinguishes three kinds of friendships; two of them—the friendships of utility and pleasure—are deficient, while one—the friendship of the good—is excellent. Friendships of utility and pleasure are relationships in which the parties involved seek for themselves some benefit from the other. Either the one can provide some useful service to the other or he is merely entertaining company. Of course, those who are in a friendship of the good will similarly benefit from this relationship. The two will enjoy each other's company and find the other's counsel helpful. But, importantly, these friends don't seek out these benefits from each other. Instead, each wants only what is in the best interest of his friend and thinks not of himself.

This excellent type of friendship consists of "those who wish well to their friends for their sake."[17] Now, to want what is best for another for his own sake, you have to understand who that person is and what he values. In addition, you also have to respect him and his values. For if you do not and yet you still want what is best for him, you would end up contradicting your own values.

Thus, to be in a friendship of the good is to have someone in your life who matters to you, not because of what he can do for you but because of who he is. You value and respect him and, for his sake and his sake alone, you want what is best for him. This is how Marge and Norm care for each other. Each wants the best for the other. The one needs food and the other needs sleep, and they both want for the other what the other needs. Each supports the other in their respective daily tasks. Norm provides Marge with sustenance while she fights crime, and Marge provides Norm with encouragement as he makes art.

So, valuing and respecting others is central to friendship. It is also central to shame. It is only with regard to people we respect that we feel shame when we do wrong. To review: I feel shame when I recognize that those whom I respect would judge my actions (or even my intended actions) in such a way that would lead to my disgrace. Thus, I need to value others in order to feel shame. And I need to value them not in terms of what they can do for me but in terms of who they are: their opinions, values, characters. It is with regard to these people we so value that we fear our disgrace. Thus, we can now see the link between friendship and shame. To have friends is to have others matter to you, and it is only when others matter to you that you can be disgraced. Of course, we are not saying here that only those with friends can feel shame.[18] Rather, our point is that regard for others as goods in themselves is necessary both for having friends and feeling shame.

How, though, does this relate to Marge? As we have said all along, she does no wrong, so she has no cause to feel shame. She, though, is the one who in large part mediates other people's shame. In both big and small ways, she tries to get others both to see where they have gone wrong and to have the appropriate response to what they have done. We have already seen her do this with Gaear. She lists his crimes, trying to elicit in him some remorse, but to no avail. In an earlier scene, when Lou incorrectly deduces that the kidnapper's vehicle has a license plate that begins with the letters DLR, Marge confesses that she is not sure that she "100 percent agrees" with his police work, figuring instead that the letters DLR indicate dealer plates. Even with respect to her husband, she performs this function. Norm enters his paintings in competitions in which the winner's painting will be reproduced on a postage stamp. One of his paintings does win such a competition but only for a three-cent stamp. His main rival wins the larger denomination. Norm feels some sense of failure over this. But Marge soothes Norm by explaining to him how the little stamps are important when the post office changes the price of mail.

Fargo is peppered with scenes in which Marge gently cajoles others. In this way Marge is the moral center of the movie. She knows right from wrong and acts accordingly. She has the capacity to feel shame. She knows how one should feel if one has done wrong. And she tries to get others to feel and do as they should. Consider how Marge goes about correcting others. In most cases, she works to save face for those she instructs. Lou is embarrassed (and maybe a wee bit confused) by his failure to have figured out what "DLR" stands for, and Marge, recognizing this, lightens the moment with a joke. When an old high school friend makes a pass at her by changing seats so that he can touch her, Marge figuratively and literally puts him back in his place. But she explains that she is doing so only so that she won't need to twist her neck in order to talk to him. Marge has just rejected this man, and such a rejection is, of course, humiliating. Marge, knowing this, works to ameliorate her friend's embarrassment.

Some will say that Marge's behavior here is merely a product of her being "Minnesota nice," but her care for others shouldn't be dismissed so easily. It involves her empathizing with these people and wanting what is best for them while not compromising herself. Consider again how she treats her husband's loss. She doesn't inflate his ego. She doesn't deride the competition. She instead gives Norm honest reasons for feeling good about winning the three-cent stamp. She again is ameliorating his disappointment, and maybe even his slightly bruised ego, but in a way that shows that she both supports and respects herself and her husband.

Thus, Marge has the capacity for shame. And this capacity is shown not just in her ability to locate when one should feel shame but in the way she gently instructs others in how they should feel and behave. This capacity reflects the respect she has for others, and this respect is also what enables her to have the best kind of friendship with others.

In contrast, the other characters in this movie have at best only friendships of utility with the people in their lives. The co-conspirators each want something (money, sex, food), and they see others primarily in terms of how they will serve that end. And when these characters try to acknowledge another possible dimension of a particular relationship, a dimension beyond the bounds of utility, the attempt always fails. Carl hires an escort to accompany him to hear José Feliciano. At the concert, he tries to engage her in a conversation about her work:

CARL: Find that work interesting, do you?
PROSTITUTE: What are you talking about?

Carl is trying to treat this prostitute as if he weren't paying her, as if she were instead his date. And her response to this inquiry reveals that the nature of their relationship—he and she are exchanging money for sex—can't be gotten beyond. Consider again the scene in which Jerry seeks to comfort his son. Jerry's ability to care for him as he should is crippled by his desire to get what he needs from his son. Thus, as much as he wants to assuage his son's fears, he also wants his son not to jeopardize his scheme. So he gets Scotty to agree to lie for him about his mother's whereabouts. Jerry here can't do what is in his son's best interest because he instead needs his son to serve his own interests.

When our primary relationships with others are friendships of utility, we lose the ability to see others as selves worthy of our respect. Instead, we view them solely as instruments. That is, if we habituate ourselves to seeing other people (our spouses, our children, our coworkers, etc.) as possible means to ends, our sense of our place among other human beings becomes our place among potentially usable things. Now, one does not fear disgrace in the eyes of things, even when those things are people. Thus, such friendships of utility undermine the proper functioning of shame. Again, shame cannot work independently of the thought that people, and their opinions and values, *actually matter to us.* Thus, if we base our relations with others around their potential usefulness, their regard becomes more and more irrelevant.

Conclusion

Thus, the essential difference between Marge, on the one hand, and Jerry, Gaear, and Carl on the other is that the co-conspirators' actions flow from their appetites while Marge's actions flow from the concern and respect she has for others. The wellspring of Marge's basic decency is the part of herself that knows how others should be valued and treated. She knows not to treat others as mere instruments but instead to treat them with respect. And when she and others don't get the respect they deserve, she expects those in the wrong to feel shame. And if they don't, as is the case with Gaear, she is mystified.[19] On the other hand, by acting from their appetites, the co-conspirators isolate themselves from their sense of shame. Either they lose their capacity for shame, as is seemingly the case with Gaear, or this capacity persists, as is the case with Jerry (and it seems Carl as well), but the feelings of shame produced are inert. They no longer impel these men to act better.

With all of this in mind, return to the opening scene in the movie. Carl wants to know why Jerry would want to kidnap his wife. What would lead a person to do such a thing? But he can't bring himself to ask this question. Why not? To ask such a question is to acknowledge that Jerry's wife and in fact Jerry himself are worthy of moral concern, concern that outweighs what he will get if he agrees to this plot. But he doesn't want to acknowledge this, nor does Jerry want him to acknowledge this. Each has needs that won't be fulfilled if they do. Jerry needs the ransom money, and Carl needs the tan Ciera. So they let this question go unasked. They don't let themselves fully consider what they are about to do, thereby avoiding the shame that might have prevented them from moving forward.

Notes

1. Aristotle, *Rhetoric,* in *The Complete Works of Aristotle,* ed. Jonathan Barnes (Princeton, N.J.: Princeton Univ. Press, 1984), 1383b15–17.

2. Ibid., 1384b30–32.

3. Ibid., 1384a24.

4. Aristotle, *Nicomachean Ethics*, in *The Complete Works of Aristotle*, ed. Barnes, 1128b22.

5. Ibid., 1128b29–31.

6. Ibid., 1128b31–33.

7. Ibid., 1128b17–20.

8. Aristotle thinks that men are the only ones capable of true moral excellence. This accounts for our above reference to men and our use of the third person pronoun "he" when discussing Aristotle's theories.

9. Aristotle *Nicomachean Ethics* 1102b14–17.

10. Ibid., 1147a13–14.

11. Ibid., 1146b22–24.

12. Ibid., 1119a1–3.

13. Ibid., 1152a20–21.

14. In defense of Jerry, consider that for shame to function properly there must be the possibility of altering one's behavior in such a way as to avoid further shame. In Jerry's case, this requirement is not always met. Wade emasculates Jerry at every opportunity he gets. When Jerry approaches his wealthy father-in-law for money to invest in a parking lot that "could work out real good for me, Jean, and Scotty," he is abruptly shot down. Wade snidely asserts, "Jean and Scotty never have to worry." With these words, Jerry is overtly and unmistakably relegated to irrelevance. Even when Wade and Stan realize that Jerry's proposal is "pretty sweet," Wade offers Jerry a mere finder's fee rather than control of the project.

It is clear that Jerry is a disgrace in Wade's eyes. No matter what Jerry does, he does wrong. Worse yet, Wade is the family patriarch, so his judgment holds special weight. All this makes shame's call to change ineffectual. When no matter what an agent does, he is shamed, that shame loses its relevance as a moral guide. That is, a person might want to avoid feeling that shame (as Jerry clearly does), but since there is seemingly no way to do that, what one does or doesn't do no longer matters. Moreover, once shame loses it relevance in one context, the door is open to it losing relevance in others.

15. It is worth noting that expressions of strong emotions are condemned within the confines of the community depicted here. The husband whom Jerry cheats with his TruCoat scheme and who calls Jerry a "fucking liar" is quietly and clearly chastised by his wife for his display of emotion. Emotions are high but not to be expressed.

16. Aristotle *Nicomachean Ethics* 1150a11–13.

17. Ibid., 1156b10.

18. Those who don't have a capacity for shame also lack a capacity for friendship, for the capacity for shame depends on our respecting others, and respecting others is a necessary component of being someone's friend. But for Aristotle the reverse of this equation does not hold. Those who have a capacity for shame don't necessarily have the capacity for friendship. Having friends involves more than merely respecting others; it also involves having affection for them. Thus, there could be a person who respects

others and hence can experience disgrace yet has no affection for humanity. Such a person can be shamed yet can't have friends.

19. All of this might help put into context a comment from Marge that might seem otherwise mystifying. Consider again Marge's final scene with Gaear. After she lists his crimes, she wonders why he would do such a thing for mere money. She is even more incredulous, for after all "it's such a beautiful day." As she says this, she looks out onto a snow-covered landscape and appreciates the beauty that maybe only she can see. Why does Marge make this comment? Should it just be taken as a meaningless platitude? We don't think so. Consider a line from Nabokov's *Lolita:* "The moral sense in mortals is the duty / We have to pay on mortal sense of beauty." Vladimir Nabokov, *The Annotated "Lolita"* (New York: Vintage, 1970), 31. To appreciate beauty, one must be able to value that beauty noninstrumentally. You have to consider it, not for what it can get or do for you, but for itself. But, of course, this ability to value noninstrumentally is the very ability that one must have in order to treat others with the respect they deserve. Thus, Marge's ability to appreciate the beauty of the day is a reflection of her ability to show others proper moral concern.

JUSTICE, POWER, AND LOVE

The Political Philosophy of *Intolerable Cruelty*

Shai Biderman and William J. Devlin

What Is Justice?

What do we mean when we say that "justice must be served"? What is the difference between a "just act" and an "unjust act"? What is it that makes our relationships—whether they concern a family member, a loved one, or even a stranger—just and fair? Is it the case that justice is merely rooted in power, control, and domination, so that those who have the power determine what justice means? Or is justice rooted not in dominance but in agreement, where, through a sense of love, care, and concern toward others, we seek a balance of shared interests between the parties of the just relationship?

In *Intolerable Cruelty* (2003), we find that the Coen brothers tackle the question of justice in relation to the drive for power and the power of love. Ultimately, the film suggests that the strongest account of justice is one in which there is a sense of equality that obtains between both parties, irrespective of power and contracts. Miles Massey (George Clooney) is a successful and arrogant Los Angeles divorce attorney who is most famous for creating an ironclad and impenetrable prenuptial agreement known as the "Massey pre-nup." After completing a long list of victories in the courtroom, Massey endeavors to achieve a challenging winner-take-all battle against Marylin Rexroth-Doyle-Massey (Catherine Zeta-Jones), a beautiful and ambitious femme fatale whose goal is to con a man out of his money so that she can have her own financial independence. Though Miles leads the charge for the annihilation and destruction of Marylin, he succumbs to the taboo in the world of divorce attorneys, as he falls in love with her. Marylin, in turn, seeks revenge and her independence, as she dupes Miles into believing she married the oil tycoon, Howard Doyle (Billy Bob Thornton), so that she can marry Miles, using his own Massey pre-nup as a ploy to get half of his estate. However, we find that the struggle for power and complete independence is outweighed by the power of love as Miles and Marylin remain together, with all contracts and fear of deceit apparently left behind.

Through the adventures of Miles and Marylin, we see several interpretations of the notion of justice. The first interpretation, what we call "justice as power," suggests that justice is merely the manifestation of the Machiavellian sentiment that "might makes right." A second interpretation, "justice as compromise," maintains that justice is grounded in negotiation and agreement. A third interpretation, "justice as fairness," holds that justice is a balanced social system, which promotes equality for all members. These three interpretations reflect distinct philosophical traditions that illustrate the notion of justice. As we trace Miles and Marylin's journey from the notion of justice as power to justice as fairness, we explore how *Intolerable Cruelty* addresses these interpretations.

Justice as Power

When Bonnie Donaly (Stacey Travis) is caught cheating on her husband, Donovan Donaly (Geoffrey Rush)—the Hollywood producer of the soap opera, *The Sands of Time*—she turns to the services of the famous (and infamous) divorce attorney, Miles Massey. Upon learning that Donovan caught Bonnie with Ollie Olerud (Jack Kyle), the pool salesman, Miles is willing to serve as her legal counselor in the divorce. He explains to her that the "truth is so self-evident" that he'll "be able to make it equally as transparent to any jury." But Miles hasn't decided upon which "transparent truth" to give to the jury. Is it the case that Donovan's alleged spousal abuse drove Bonnie to have an affair? Or is it that Donovan mistakenly believed Bonnie was having an affair while Bonnie rescued Donovan from killing Ollie? Maybe it's the case that it is actually Donovan and Ollie who are having the affair. Miles, the legal counselor who is prepared to make a case in court (a place where one typically locates the proper administration of justice), is less concerned with what really happened and more concerned with victory. He will choose the "truth" that is most likely to promise him victory and even goes so far as to guarantee Bonnie that her spoils of this war will include the rights to *The Sands of Time*.

While it may come as no surprise to see a lawyer in a film depicted as being heartless, ruthless, and indifferent toward the notion of justice implicit in the law, Miles seems to be doing something more here. Rather than simply ignoring the idea of justice in the law, Miles rejects it and replaces it with an alternative account. Miles endorses the theory that justice is equivalent to power. This theory of justice can be found in Plato's *Republic*, where Thrasymachus (ca. 459–400 BCE) defines justice as that which "is nothing other than the advantage of the stronger." That is, justice serves the interests of those who are in power and is dictated by the powerful to maintain control and dominance over others.[1]

But what do we mean by those who are "powerful"? The most natural sense of being in power is understood as those who are superior in physical strength. That is, one can control and dominate others through brute strength, a large army, or having stronger weapons. But in order to be powerful, one need not necessarily have superior physical strength. One can maintain power by outsmarting others so that they will succumb to one's superior intellect. Or, one can wield power through the use of rhetoric and the knowledge of how to manipulate others and convince them to accept the conclusions of specious reasoning. Furthermore, one can control and dominate others through political strength in the form of legislative power. As Thrasymachus maintains, the rulers of each type of government set up laws that are in their own interest. The tyrannical ruler sets up tyrannical laws for his self-interest, the democratic rulers set up democratic laws for their own interests, and so on. Meanwhile, the citizens who are ruled by the given government uphold such laws, thereby enabling the laws to benefit the rulers, who are able to maintain their power, control, and dominance over those who are ruled.[2]

The view that justice is power can thus be implemented in various ways. What underlies these ways is the idea that justice is self-interested; it is the outcome of the perspective of the person who has subjective interests and wields power to achieve those interests. As such, supporters of this notion of justice find that justice is best achieved through the use of persuasion, rather than through truth telling. We see this to be the case with the ancient Greek group known as sophists. A sophist was an educator who, for a large fee, provided students with instructions on how to manipulate others, win debates, and achieve political success. Thrasymachus himself was one of the more dominant sophists of his time. As a sophist, Thrasymachus was less interested in finding genuine knowledge or truths about the world and more interested in defeating and dominating his opponents and accumulating wealth in the process. The practice of sophistry embodies the notion of justice as power, as it takes advantage of rhetorical and intellectual strengths to promote the self-interested desire for control over others.

Destruction of One's Opponent

As Miles puts the view of justice as power into practice, he is not concerned with the truth but with victory. In his pursuit of justice, Miles's methods and legal tactics mimic those of a military campaign. He treats his office as a "war room" for planning victorious strategies and evaluating the "enemy" (other lawyers, unlucky plaintiffs, etc.). Accordingly, he sees the courtroom as the ultimate battleground, where the warriors (i.e., lawyers) will engage in battle in pursuit of victory. But, as Miles points out to his associate Wrigley (Paul Adelstein), he doesn't simply want a victory where both parties compromise and find an equilibrium point based on the skill of the individual lawyers. Such compromises are more indicative of death than life. No, for Miles, life (and so also justice) is understood as the "struggle and challenge and ultimate destruction of your opponent." Miles lives for the battle—he lives for the struggle and the challenge of utterly annihilating, controlling, and overpowering his opponent in the courtroom. Like the sophist, Miles holds that such victories are based on a successful manipulation of the truth rather than the truth itself. They are rhetorical triumphs that indicate the superior power of the one who argues them.

Furthermore, Miles's own endeavor to maintain justice as power is not through physical strength. Rather, Miles's strategy is to dominate and control others through his superior skills of rhetoric. Whether it's his slippery slope reasoning in trying to establish an affair between Donovan and Ollie, his misuse of the "Kirshner precedent" in negotiations, his "arty-farty" introduction to cross-examining Marylin Rexroth, or his defenses against Freddy Bender's (Richard Jenkins) objections (such as "what's good for the gander"), Miles manipulates language to set up his opponents for defeat. His strength is not found in an ability to put together logically coherent arguments or an ability to deduce a valid conclusion from solid premises. Instead, his strength lies in his ability to construct dazzling, but fallacious, lines of reasoning, which persuade the judge and jury that he is correct, so that he is able to attain his victory.[3]

Miles's firm endorsement of the account of justice as power is most notably symbolized through the ongoing appearance and mentioning of teeth throughout the film. Miles is constantly preoccupied with his teeth, from the first time we see him on screen (through the ultraviolet light at a dentist appointment), to the point where Marylin's poodle sinks his teeth into Miles's hand. Also, Marylin's rottweilers bare their fangs when ordered to keep Rex and Miles out of her house(s). So does Elisabeta, the spoiled pet dog of Heinz, the Baron Krauss von Espy (Jonathan Hadary), whose teeth become the main concern of the baron during his testimony. In short, we find that teeth serve as a metaphor for power in *Intolerable Cruelty*. But while the dogs' teeth suggest that their power is in their physical bite, Miles's teeth do not indicate brute strength. Rather, as Marylin's friend, Sarah Battista-O'Flannagan-Sorkin (Julia Duffy), warns her, Miles is "no schnauzer"—he is rather renowned for his impressive skill and record of victories in divorces. Ever focused on how his teeth look, Miles is able to use his bright and handsome smile as a way to enhance his own appearance and the appearance of his arguments on his road to victory. Thus, Miles does have a bite, but this bite is characterized by his calculated presentation and manipulation of arguments. He sinks his teeth into his opponent in order to "nail his ass" and gain total victory.

Nailing Someone's Ass

Miles isn't the only one who espouses the notion of justice as power. Marylin shares this definition of justice as well. Marylin is introduced to us as a calculating, deceptive, and powerful woman who sees marriage as a "passport to wealth, freedom, and independence." That is, she enters marriage and plays the role of supportive wife as a means to achieve control over her husband's net worth. She manipulates her husband, deceiving him into believing that he is safe with her when, in fact, all she intends to do is "nail his ass."

While Miles's strategy to obtain domination and control is implemented through his skills of rhetoric in the courtroom, Marylin's strategy toward achieving justice as power is implemented through her ability to manipulate the notion of love in marriage. Love, for Marylin, is not a feeling of equality and care toward another. Rather, it is a commodity or a tool that can be used to mislead others into believing that she shares their feelings of equality and care. This deception allows her the opportunity to betray her husband's emotions in such a way that she is able to walk away with his fortune.

We can see Marylin's implementation of power come into play in her marriage to Rex Rexroth, the real estate mogul. Prior to their introduction, we discover that Marylin schemes with Baron von Espy to find a very rich husband. As the baron explains to Miles, this husband must be "a silly man . . . a man, though clever at making money, would easily [be] duped and controlled." Furthermore, this man must be "a man with a wandering pee-pee . . . a philanderer whose affairs would be transparent to the world . . . a man whom [Marylin] could, herself, brazenly cuckold." Marylin thus targets a wealthy but naïve husband who enjoys extramarital affairs out in the open. Marylin, in turn, would play the serving and loving wife who, in reality, maintains control over her naïve husband as she bides her time waiting for the right moment to "make hammer on his fanny." Given these criteria, the baron introduces her to Rex. Marylin proceeds to play the role she designed for herself. She proclaims that she loved Rex since they first met, as she cleverly steals Miles's earlier quote from Shakespeare's *As You Like It*: "Whoever loved that loved not at first sight?"

By duping Rex into thinking that she has fallen in love with him, she is able to marry him without any prenuptial agreement. Shortly thereafter, Marylin hires a colorful and tactless private eye, Gus Petch (Cedric the Entertainer), to catch Rex in an extramarital affair with another woman. Although Rex was under the impression that his relationship with Marylin does not preclude occasional affairs, he has no corroborating evidence to support this understanding. Moreover, as already mentioned, he also has no prenuptial agreement. As a result, Rex is completely exposed, "a sitting duck," and Marylin has unlimited access to his wealth. With the overwhelming evidence (supplied by Gus Petch), Marylin believes her plan will come to fruition: "I've invested five good years in my marriage to Rex and I've nailed his ass fair and square. Now I'm going to have it stuffed, mounted, and have my lady friends come over and throw darts at it."

Justice as Compromise

While Rex's ass was not stuffed and mounted, his victory in court and utter annihilation of Marylin was not by his own doing. Rather, in the war between Rex and Marylin, it was Miles who led the charge to victory *in spite of* Rex's ignorance. Particularly, regardless of Rex's wandering ways in extramarital affairs, one could point out two potentially fatal errors that Rex made in his marriage to Marylin. First, as mentioned earlier, Rex and Marylin did not have a prenuptial agreement that would allow Rex to leave the marriage with the amount of wealth with which he entered it. Second, though he and Marylin had an arrangement or understanding that they each could see other people, this arrangement was only verbally acknowledged and not put into writing. Rex, who—it is generally agreed—is easily duped and controlled, may have naïvely believed that justice would be served in a fair and appropriate manner should there be a divorce. But Miles immediately recognizes that this is not the case, as signed contracts would have been the only way for Rex to guarantee the security of his own estate.

The emphasis on signed agreements for the sake of security introduces another theory of justice known as the social contract theory. The social contract theory generally maintains that a just relationship is one in which both parties' obligations are dependent upon a contract or agreement made between them prior to entering the relationship. Both parties must honor the specified obligation to ensure that justice remains intact. In short, justice, according to this account, is rooted in a compromise that is typically exemplified by a contract.

One well-known social contract theorist is the British philosopher Thomas Hobbes (1588–1679). Hobbes's presentation of the social contract theory of justice can be divided into two stages: the state of nature and the contract. The state of nature is the hypothetical scenario of the human condition prior to the formation of a governed society. For Hobbes, the state of nature is very unpleasant, insofar as it is a "war of all against all." For Hobbes, all human beings, by nature, are self-interested, and, since there is no government to enforce any rules or regulations in the state of nature, it is as if each individual has a right to possess all things. This right to all things invites war among all people. Such a war can be characterized in three different ways. First, individuals must compete against one another to attain and preserve the basic human needs for survival: they "use violence to make themselves masters of other persons' wives, children, and cattle." Second, on the opposing end, individuals who have secured such goods must defend them. Thus, for the safety of their goods, they must engage in wars against any who would steal them. Finally, individuals in the state of nature fight for glory as they take pleasure in exercising their power over others: they engage in battle "for trifles, as a word, a smile, a different opinion, and any other sign of undervalue, either direct in their persons or by reflection in their kindred, their friends, their nation, their profession, or their name." Because of the constant battles for possessions, security, and glory in power, Hobbes maintains that the state of nature is characterized as a state of "continual fear and danger of violent death." He concludes that such a life is not worthwhile; rather, human beings should avoid it since life in the state of nature is "nasty, brutish, and short."[4]

Given the danger and violence that permeates the state of nature, the inhabitants are in great fear. But though they are self-interested, Hobbes maintains, they are also rational. Through the use of self-interested reason, they find that this state is a no-win situation and that they must seek an alternative scenario in order to prevail. This alternative scenario is the creation of a civilized society, which is founded upon the construction of a social contract. Inhabitants of the state of nature become members of a civilized society by entering into an agreement with one another whereby members renounce their originally perceived right to all things in exchange for a contractually based right to some of the things. A legislative sovereignty (in the form of a government) is established as the authoritative body whose role is to supervise and enforce the social contract. Members of society thus agree to live under common laws that are enforced by a government. All members have self-interested reasons to uphold the contract insofar as obedience to the law will ensure their own safety from others and from punishment. For Hobbes, then, the notion of justice is rooted in a compromise for the sake of security. The social contract creates justice for the civilized society in the sense that each party gives something up: members honor the agreement with one another to give up their original right to all things in the state of nature for the sake of safety and the security to pursue their self-interests.[5]

The account of justice as compromise seems to play an ambiguous role in *Intolerable Cruelty*. On the one hand, it underlies most of the social encounters in the film and is supported by the mere existence of a stable legal system, to which Miles and his firm owe their wealth and success. On the other hand, we can see that the notion of compromise does not play out well in the various opportunities in which it is presented. All of the players involved seem to prefer total annihilation over compromise whenever given the chance. That is, in Hobbesian terms, they prefer the disastrous state of nature to the civic state. This approach can be found in the various litigations and contractual negotiations that take place in the film, most notably the negotiation period before the trial between Rex and Marylin and in the father of all contractual agreements—the Massey pre-nup.

On the surface, the pretrial negotiation between Rex, Marylin, and their lawyers has the misleading appearance of being a congenial and open-minded discussion between parties who are willing to make a compromise in terms of an official contract between Rex and Marylin. The interaction is lightly referred to as an "ice-breaker," where everyone is friends and pastries are served. But this lighthearted spirit is just a ploy, as we soon come to understand that there will be a serious battle in the courtroom. The negotiation becomes a series of quips and rejoinders between Miles (Rex's lawyer) and Freddy (Marylin's lawyer):

> MILES: . . . At this point my client is still prepared to consider reconciliation.
> FREDDY: My client's ruled that out.
> MILES: My client is prepared to entertain an amicable dissolution to the marriage without prejudice.
> FREDDY: That's a fart in a stiff wind.
> MILES: My client proposes a thirty-day cooling-off period.
> FREDDY: My client feels sufficiently dispassionate.
> MILES: My client asks that you not initiate proceedings pending his setting certain affairs in order.

For Miles, however, such negotiations are nothing but idle chatter. Upon hearing that Marylin is willing to settle for 50 percent of the marital assets, Miles balks with disbelief, closing the negation period by saying, "Why only 50, Freddy? Why not 100? While we're dreaming, why not 150 . . . ?" Here, we can see that Miles balks not only at Freddy's offer but also at the very idea that justice is meted out through compromise. As seen earlier in the film, Miles maintains that compromise is indicative of death, not life, and so he has no intention of serving justice through negotiations: for justice to be served for his client, Miles must carry out the annihilation of Marylin. Miles thus dismisses the conception of justice as compromise. He does not believe that justice is properly served through a social contract in which one compromises his or her rights for the sake of security and safety.

Furthermore, we find that, throughout the film, the role of contracts is really a means for domination and control over others, which therefore implies that the notion of justice as compromise doesn't work. That is, the film suggests that the theory of justice as compromise is not the correct account of justice since it is ultimately parasitic on the theory of justice as power. The dismissal of the notion of justice as compromise can be seen through the famous marital contract, the Massey pre-nup, which "provides that, in the event of dissolution of the marriage for any reason, both parties will leave it with what they brought in and earned during." It is an impenetrable, ironclad, and romance-less agreement that protects the wealthier party insofar as "no one can profit from the marriage." The strict defense of the wealthier and more powerful party stands in direct opposition to the "everybody wins" agenda of a contractual compromise.

Now, the Massey pre-nup is presented in the film in two different ways: the signing of the contract and the tearing up (or, at times, the eating) of the contract. Both ways support the idea that the theory of justice as compromise is just a mask for the theory of justice as power. First, the signing of the contract indicates that the wealthier party wants security for his or her net worth. As Miles explains, the Massey pre-nup ensures that there is "no wiggle room" for compromise—it keeps the wealthy party from becoming "a sitting duck," naked and exposed. It helps the wealthy party "cover his ass," as it were, and so prevents the other party from nailing his ass during the struggle for power. Thus, when Howard signs the pre-nup before his marriage to Marylin, and Marylin signs the pre-nup before her marriage to Miles, it suggests that each one wants to maintain his or her power and control. In this sense, then, the contract ceases to be an instrument of compromise and reveals its true nature as a mask for justice as power.

Likewise, the tearing up of the contract reveals that the theory of justice as power underlies the theory of justice as compromise. When the prenuptial contracts are being torn (or eaten), it is a sign that power once more has overcome compromise. When Howard eats the pre-nup at the wedding reception, we are led to believe that Marylin has conned him out of his money by pretending to love him. That is, it appears as though Marylin has successfully achieved her own justice as power. Meanwhile, when Marylin tears up her pre-nup with Miles, we discover that she manipulated him, too, and deceived him into giving up the security of his fortune. This suggests that Marylin has used the contract as a means to dominate and control Miles. In other words, the justice that will be served is justice as power.

Thus, though the theory of justice as compromise is presented in *Intolerable Cruelty,* it is ultimately regarded as a conventional way to prevent the theory of justice as power from arising. This prevention continually fails, as is exemplified by the use of the Massey pre-nup: whether it is the signing or tearing up of the contract, in most cases the prenuptial contract becomes just another tool for maintaining control and domination over the other party.

Justice as Fairness

During Howard and Marylin's wedding reception, Howard gives an early wedding present to his bride: he eats the Massey pre-nup. Howard explains that he wants to prove wrong the priest's claim that "in today's cynical world, it's so hard to take that great leap of faith aboard the ship of love and caring." He wishes to show the audience that he and Marylin are "taking that leap . . . that they do have faith . . . that they do love." Thus, in order to prove that there is real love and trust between them, he tears up the contract, literally eats the pre-nup, and metaphorically eats the words that exemplify the notion of justice as power.

Though Howard's act of eating the pre-nup is part of Marylin's overall scheme to deceive and control Miles, this act allows us to conceive of a relationship that is not characterized by the drive for power or by contractual agreements of compromise. Rather, relationships can be carried out through love and equality. Such relationships reveal a third conception of justice: justice as fairness. This theory of justice is famously endorsed by the contemporary philosopher John Rawls (1921–2002). Following Rawls's account, the theory of justice as fairness can be presented in two steps. The first step examines what Rawls labels the "original position," an imaginary situation in which people who are free, rational, and equal come together to create a society and decide upon a proper theory of justice. We are to imagine that people in this position are "mutually disinterested" (i.e., only self-interested), that they put forward conflicting claims over who gets what, and that they have only a moderate scarcity of goods at their disposal. Furthermore, according to Rawls, we are to imagine that members of this position are operating under what Rawls calls the "veil of ignorance" as they determine the proper theory of justice. Under the veil of ignorance, people in the original position do not know where they will fall in society. They do not know what occupation or career they will have. They have no knowledge of their talents or skills. They do not know where they will fall in the distribution of income (if they will be better or worse off than others). This veil guarantees equality through ignorance: all members of the original position are equally ignorant of their characteristics and abilities, and they are equally unable to predict how they will be able to achieve what they want.[6]

Now that the scope and limits of what the members of the original position can know are defined, Rawls moves to the second step: finding out what such people would choose as principles of justice. Rawls presents two principles of justice that would be agreed upon by members of the original position. One principle is that each person has an equal right to the most extensive liberty. That is, each person has the right to do what he or she wants up until it impedes another person's freedom to do the same. The second principle, which is the heart of the theory of justice as fairness, is called the "difference principle." Rawls explains the difference principle as holding that socioeconomic inequalities of goods (such as income, wealth, opportunities, etc.) are just if and only if they attach to positions open to all, and if and only if they benefit all. In other words, inequalities are just, so long as everyone has a fair opportunity to achieve the available social goods. Given the characteristics of the original position, it is only fair for people to compete for and obtain scarce goods through the use of their natural talents. Legal inequalities and birth status inequalities are unjust. Furthermore, inequalities of goods must "benefit all" in the sense that they benefit the least advantaged. One must survey the inequalities across the field, and if one finds that a certain inequality does not benefit those on the lower end, then that inequality is unjust.

The theory of justice as fairness is exemplified in *Intolerable Cruelty* centrally through the love between Miles and Marylin. Though Miles endorses the view of justice as power initially, we find that once he meets Marylin, his attitude begins to change. Under the notion of justice as power, he finds great success: he has all the money and material goods he could want or need, he has a brilliant track record of court victories, he has earned the respect of Herb Myerson (Tom Aldredge), the senior partner of his law firm, and he has successfully achieved his dream of a victory through utter annihilation. But despite all of this success, he finds that he is still unhappy, and the reason for this despondency is that he does not have Marylin. Miles has fallen in love with Marylin and so dreams of marrying her.

Once Miles's dream comes true as he marries Marylin in Las Vegas, we find that his conception of justice drastically changes. In his speech to the National Organization of Matrimonial Attorneys Nationwide (ironically abbreviated as NO MAN), entitled "Nailing Your Spouse's Assets," Miles tears up his planned speech (another symbolic gesture of tearing up a contractual understanding) and instead "talk[s] to [them] from the heart because today, for the first time in [his] life, [he] stands before [them] . . . naked . . . vulnerable . . . and in love." He explains to them that, though matrimonial lawyers avoid the word "love" because they are afraid of this emotion, he is here to tell them that "love is good." He continues to say that the cynicism employed as "a cloak that advertises their indifference" is a cloak that "destroys everyone and everything." Under the notion of justice as power, Miles explains, he sought to "extinguish the flame" of love that his clients had so that he could "sift through the smoldering wreckage for [his] paltry reward." But now, he wishes to "fan this precious flame, this most precious flame, back into loving, roaring life" and to counsel trust between the disagreeing parties so that they can build or rebuild the love they have between them.

Miles's speech to NO MAN shows his new endorsement of the theory of justice as fairness. Miles's love for Marylin becomes his veil of ignorance. Though he thinks he knows Marylin's net worth after her divorce from Howard, he does not care about it. The self-interested drive for power in terms of the distribution of goods is irrelevant to him. He has no interest in nailing Marylin's assets because his love for her has blinded him toward such things. He thus signs the Massey pre-nup, acknowledging that a divorce would lead to an unequal, but just, distribution of goods. Though Marylin would retain her net worth from Howard's estate, Miles accepts this unequal distribution since she earned it through her talents of manipulation and Miles would not be worse off, given his own net worth. Thus, through the power of love, Miles discards the notion of justice as power in favor of the notion of justice as fairness.

While Miles's initial leap of faith into love and trust of Marylin becomes part of a clever dupe by Marylin to nail Miles's assets, we come to find that Marylin alters her theory of justice as well. Under the notion of justice as power, she too seems to have it all: she has achieved revenge upon Miles who utterly annihilated her in the courtroom, she has secured half of Miles's net worth, and she now has her "passport to wealth, freedom, and independence." But like Miles, she finds herself longing for something else. Even after the back-and-forth hiring of the hit man, Wheezy Joe (Irwin Keyes), Marylin finds that the love she pretended to have for Miles was not simply a manipulative tool for power. On the contrary, the love she has for Miles is real.

Her feelings of love and trust toward Miles come to fruition during the negotiation period after the dissolution of their short marriage. With Marylin's net worth now larger due to her inheritance of Rex's estate, Miles once again professes his love to her by signing another Massey pre-nup (once again indicating his endorsement of justice as fairness). Marylin, in turn, takes the pre-nup and tears it up. This act of tearing up the contract is different from previous occurrences as it reveals Marylin's sudden turnaround as she metaphorically tears up the notion of justice as power and instead endorses the notion of justice as fairness. In Marylin's case, her love toward Miles is also her veil of ignorance. But here, Marylin's love shows that she doesn't care about her financial estate. In the original position, her love made her blind to her assets. Instead, her love for Miles drives her to wish for a fair and equal distribution of goods between them, regardless of what they entered with. Thus, through the power of love, Marylin also rejects the notion of justice as power in favor of the notion of justice as fairness.[7]

All's Fair in Love and War

In *Intolerable Cruelty,* the separate and joint journeys of Miles and Marylin provide us with an exploration of the various theories of justice. This exploration ultimately centers on the tension between the theory of justice as power and the theory of justice as fairness, as brought out in the relationship between Miles and Marylin. And while it appears that, through their love for each other, the theory of justice as fairness prevails, this victory is not guaranteed.[8]

First, Miles and Marylin are now partners in the new television series, *Funniest Divorce Videos,* hosted by Gus Petch, with the tagline of "We gonna nail your ass!" Such a show, exploiting infidelities and broken hearts, suggests that while Miles and Marylin may endorse justice as fairness toward each other, they still embody justice as power toward others. But even though they share a love for each other, it is not certain that they will live happily ever after under the notion of justice as fairness. Given that both have been driven by their yearning for power most of their lives, we are left wondering whether or not either one will revert to treating justice as power. Since there is no Massey pre-nup between them, how do we know that Miles won't seek a divorce that earns him half of the new net worth, enabling him to walk away a richer man than before? Or, perhaps Freddy was actually able to tape up the torn pre-nup, allowing Marylin the opportunity to divorce Miles and keep her assets, including *Funniest Divorce Videos,* for herself. Since no reassurance is given, the ending of *Intolerable Cruelty* thus ironically suggests that, though three interpretations of justice have been presented and explored, no single account of justice is completely endorsed as the kind of justice that will always prevail.

Notes

1. Plato, *The Republic of Plato,* trans. Allan Bloom (New York: Basic Books, 1968), 338c.

2. Ibid., 338d–339a.

3. Furthermore, Miles's ability to manipulate language en route to achieving power and domination is not limited to his opponents—it even extends to his clients. We find a humorous back-and-forth banter among Miles, Wrigley, and their client, Rex Rexroth (Edward Herrmann), as Rex questions whether or not Miles has sat before the presiding judge in their case. The following clever and witty discussion leaves Rex all the more confused, which helps to keep Rex in his place—under the control of Miles:

> REX: Have you sat before her before?
> MILES: No. No, the judge sits first. Then we sit.
> REX: Well, have you sat after her before?
> WRIGLEY: Sat after her before? You mean, have we argued before her before?
> MILES: The judge sits in judgment. The counsel argues before the judge.
> REX: So, have you argued before her before?
> WRIGLEY: Before her before, or before she sat before?
> REX: Before her before. I said, before her before.
> WRIGLEY: No, you said before she sat before.
> REX: I did at first, but . . .
> MILES: Look, don't argue.
> REX: I'm not. I'm . . .
> WRIGLEY: No, you don't argue. We argue.
> MILES: Counsel argues.
> WRIGLEY: You appear.
> MILES: The judge sits.
> WRIGLEY: Then you sit.
> MILES: Or you stand in contempt.
> WRIGLEY: And then we argue.
> MILES: The counsel argues.
> REX: Which you've done before.
> MILES: Which we've done before.
> REX: Ah.
> WRIGLEY: But not before her.

4. Thomas Hobbes, *Leviathan* (1651; Mineola, N.Y.: Dover, 2006), 68–72.

5. Ibid., 72–80.

6. John Rawls, *A Theory of Justice* (Cambridge, Mass.: Harvard University Press, 1971), 118–19, 127, 131.

7. It should be noted that the love between Miles and Marylin only partially represents Rawls's veil of ignorance. Miles and Marylin are well aware of each other's occupation, skills, and talents—in fact, it may be the case that that is part of the reason they have fallen in love. However, their love represents the veil of ignorance insofar as neither one is concerned about their financial wealth. Thus, because their love has led them to disregard the financial wealth of each other, this love helps to represent, in a limited scope, Rawls's veil of ignorance.

8. It is important to point out that while Rawls's conception of justice is a universal conception of justice that applies to all rational beings, justice as fairness in *Intolerable Cruelty* applies only between Miles and Marylin. That is, Miles and Marylin exhibit the conception of justice as fairness only toward each other and not necessarily toward others. Though the scope of justice here is narrower than Rawls's version, justice as fairness still adequately explains the new conception of justice that Miles and Marylin have when they are with each other.

Ethics, Heart, and Violence in *Miller's Crossing*

Bradley L. Herling

Writing *Miller's Crossing* (1990) was no easy task. According to their own reports, the Coen brothers started with a set of images: big hats, men in overcoats, and—the woods. These glimpses, along with their fascination with Dashiell Hammett, led the Coens to a hard-boiled scenario involving crime, corruption, and thuggery, with a hero who is caught in the middle. But progress on the screenplay was fitful, and at one point it halted altogether. The brothers decided to take a break to work on something else and clear their heads. The result of this hiatus was *Barton Fink* (1991). As Joel Coen later said, apparently without irony, "That sort of washed out our brain and we were able to go back and finish *Miller's Crossing*."[1] It turns out that John Goodman's character "Madman Mundt" ("I'll show you the life of the mind!") helped *three* authors get over their writer's block: Barton, Joel, and Ethan.

We have to wonder about what made composing *Miller's Crossing* so difficult, beyond its complicated plot. Part of the answer, we might suppose, lies in the careful attention that the Coens paid to their film's genre-based world. If this was to be their take on gangster films, with a heavy dose of noir sensibilities, then it had to be true to form.[2] But *Miller's Crossing* is more than an ironic, technically proficient homage. When the brothers opted to infuse their genre-based tale with substantive concerns about the nature of its protagonist, a hero who is largely borrowed from cinematic convention, things must have gotten all the more difficult.

In this essay, I consider three central themes in the film—ethics, heart, and violence—and argue that the Coens weave them together to achieve a significant effect: we as viewers are compelled to reflect on the ethical status of the noir-style protagonist. From the outset, "ethics" is an explicit concern in *Miller's Crossing*. In the opening scene, Johnny Caspar (Jon Polito), "a brute posing as a philosopher," articulates the harsh code of conduct that dominates in the film.[3] But the Coens also return again and again to "heart," which signifies the capacity for positive attachment based on sentiment (sympathy). Finally, *Miller's Crossing* would not be complete without surreal and magisterial eruptions of Coenesque violence. These moments epitomize the deployment of an "ethics" of power, with sympathy-crushing results.

These features come together to make a cinematic proposal about a form of agency that is easy to be drawn to, that of the noir-style hero. As we will see, in *Miller's Crossing*, Tom Reagan (Gabriel Byrne) is very much in this mold, and we might see the resolution of the film as a dramatic success; Tom is autonomous, composed, stoic, and (admittedly) riveting—ready, in a Hollywood sense, for his next adventure. But the Coen brothers are careful not to allow his success to become this kind of cinematic apotheosis: he has succeeded in extricating himself from a bad situation in a corrupt moral universe, but he is also more alone than he was at the beginning. His impressive mix of reason and sentiment, it turns out, has been matched blow for blow by the disruptive effects of betrayal and violence.

In pursuing this reading of Tom Reagan's outlook I am influenced by David Hume's moral psychology, which pits "passion" and "reason" against each other but in the end affirms the inescapability of sentiment in moral deliberation. "*Passion,*" Hume writes, "is a violent and sensible emotion of mind, when any good or evil is presented. . . . By *reason* we mean affections of the very same kind . . . but such as operate more calmly . . . Which tranquillity . . . causes us to regard them as conclusions only of our intellectual faculties."[4] Deborah Knight has followed Hume's lead in suggesting that emotion can be seen as a stable foundation for moral reasoning, even in noir films.[5] But the twin-headed problem for Tom, which leads inevitably to his solitude at the end of the film, is *both* the deceptive coldness of reason *and* its reducibility to the dangerous instability of sentiment. In the face of passion's violent surpluses, whatever "heart" he has left at the end is vestigial—and no longer serviceable as an instrument of positive human connection.

Ethics: "I Ain't Embarrassed to Use the Word"

In the opening scene of *Miller's Crossing*, Johnny Caspar, the volatile Italian crime boss, informs Leo O'Bannon (Albert Finney), an Irish politico who is currently "runnin' things," that something needs to be done about Bernie Bernbaum (John Turturro). Bernie has been selling Caspar out, taking his bets but also revealing to "out-of-town money" which fights are fixed. Bernie makes a tidy little profit from this inside information, while Caspar's take is diminished. The complication: Bernie pays Leo protection money, so Caspar has to notify Leo about his intention to take action. Tom Reagan, Leo's adviser, observes.

Caspar makes an interesting argument for his proposal. The reason that he fixes fights is that he likes "sure things." But as soon as money starts flowing in, the cat is out of the bag, and the odds go down. What is the world coming to? "Now if you can't trust a fix, what *can* you trust?" If everyone has to revert to betting on chance, Caspar argues, "then you're back in anarchy. On account of the breakdown of ethics. That's why ethics is important, what separates us from the animals. . . . Whereas Bernie Bernbaum is a horse of a different color, ethics-wise. As in, he ain't got any."

It is of course comical that Caspar, a crime boss, invokes "ethics" in this exchange, but this is a common move for the Coens: deeper reflection (or fancier elocution) often comes from an unexpected source in their films. In fact, this particular "brute posing as a philosopher" seems to start by taking a page from Thomas Hobbes. Hobbes posited a "state of nature" within which all human beings are created equal and free, yet these very qualities breed tension. Nature is in fact "a warre . . . of every man against every man," and life in it is "solitary, poore, nasty, brutish, and short."[6] To keep things from spiraling downward, we enter into a primordial agreement that regulates our behavior toward one another. This "social contract" is the implicit foundation of morality and law, so when individuals break this contract, they are subject to reprisal. Because he breaks trust with Caspar, Bernie Bernbaum is subject to such punishment. If everyone started violating social covenants and conventions (e.g., the tacit ones surrounding bookmaking), then, as Caspar suggests, we risk descending into anarchy.

The reason for Leo's resistance to this argument is clear: he *also* has a contract with Bernie, one that is even more explicit. Because of this commitment, Leo engages in skeptical questioning. How does Caspar know that Bernie is the one leaking the information? Don't others know about Caspar's bets? Couldn't someone else be the grifter? In response, Caspar reverts to his premise: "this question of character . . . that's how we know it's Bernie Bernbaum. The Shmatta Kid. Because ethically, he's kinda shaky."

Caspar is unconcerned with the particulars of the case. Instead, he is intent on who "has ethics" and who does not, and with a little help from

Plato's *Republic,* his statements continue to reveal the dominant ethos in the world of *Miller's Crossing.* On one level, Caspar bases his judgments on a concept articulated very early on in Plato's text: justice is "doing good to friends and harm to enemies."[7] Later in the film, in fact, this notion proves to be central to Caspar's worldview. "Everything above board, that's how I like it," he proclaims, "so everybody knows who's a friend and who's an enemy." But as Socrates points out (and as *Miller's Crossing* constantly demonstrates), this is an unreliable foundation. Don't we confuse friends and enemies? And what constitutes a "friend" and an "enemy" anyway? Is a friend a good person? If so, then how do we know what a good person is, if we haven't already determined what justice is? Caspar wants to harm Bernie because he is perceived as an enemy, and that characterization depends on a prior judgment about Bernie's character. But Caspar doesn't articulate any criteria for what makes a bad character as opposed to a good one besides upholding contracts, and that indictment would require a convincing argument for Bernie's guilt in this particular case, which he does not present.

Of course the overarching irony of Caspar's reflections is that he wants to *kill* Bernie because Bernie is cheating him, or, to be more precise, Caspar wants to kill Bernie because Bernie is preventing *Caspar* from cheating the way *Caspar* wants to. When Caspar talks about "ethics," then, he is talking about a code of conduct that serves those powerful enough to influence the outcome of fights—people like him. Once again recalling Book I of *The Republic,* Thrasymachus offers the groundwork for this ethical view: justice, he says, "is nothing other than the advantage of the stronger." In other words, whoever is in charge dictates what's wrong and what's right, so all ethical systems are relative to who is in power.[8] This relativistic principle, supplemented first by making and enforcing contracts and second by helping friends and harming enemies, dominates the ethical landscape in *Miller's Crossing.* Bosses like Caspar and Leo are above the law; in fact, they make the law as they see fit.

As Plato suggests, this overcoming of conventional morality is a factor that leads to the tyrant's downfall. Everything for him is permitted, in a sense, so the tyrant is prone to being consumed by the rawness of his lower nature. This is true of Leo and Caspar from the outset. On the one side, Leo admits to being a man who does what his heart tells him—even if it isn't smart. In fact, as we later find out, his resistance to Caspar's initial proposal comes from passion: he is in love with Verna (Marcia Gay Harden), Bernie's sister, which influences his judgment. Caspar, on the other side, explodes with anger when

Leo rejects his proposal. When Caspar receives the "high hat" from people, we see the driving force behind his actions, which is pure, unadulterated rage. Any high falutin' talk about "ethics" among characters like these, as Hume would remind us, is window dressing for their passions.

Tom, our hero, knows the score, though as the "thinker" in the film, he may put more stock in the distinctiveness of reason—at the beginning, at least. After Caspar storms out of the room, Tom says, "Bad play, Leo." In his role as the hard-boiled, stoic adviser, Tom senses that Leo is not acting rationally, that is, in a way that will preserve his power. Leo has in fact introduced "heart" into the system, which leads to his attachment to Verna and thus attachment to her brother. It also makes him ready for a fight, anywhere, anytime. These outcomes are not advantageous in a world where Bernie *has* violated a contract with Caspar, where the increasingly powerful rival will now become a clear enemy, where actions have not been thought through dispassionately. Tom foresees trouble ahead, and it comes—but not quite in the way that he expected.

"Ethics" with a Twist

It doesn't take long for the plot to thicken. Leo appears at Tom's door very late one night because Verna is missing, as is the man who was supposed to keep an eye on her. From his desperation it is clear that Leo is smitten, but Tom sees Verna's "angle": she has seduced him for the sole purpose of gaining protection for her brother. Leo absorbs Tom's chiding for being such a "sap" and then departs.

So where is Verna? As we quickly learn, she is in Tom's bed, in the next room. He has also given in to her charms, in spite of (or perhaps because of) the transparency of her motives. "Did you put in a good word for my brother?" she asks, after hearing that Leo came and went without incident. "No," Tom says; instead, "I told him you were a tramp and he should dump you."

At this point, Tom's foothold in the world of Caspar's gangster/noir "ethics" is intact. He has used Verna for his own pleasure, knowing that he could manipulate her attempt to exploit a new angle for protecting her brother, namely himself; he is in the stronger position, so what is right has been dictated by his own advantage. Both have *attempted* to utilize each other as a means to a self-interested end, thus violating a basic prohibition within Immanuel Kant's moral philosophy, but that is a different world.[9]

The key at this stage in *Miller's Crossing* is that Tom has been successful in his manipulation, which determines the value of his action, whereas Verna has not. It should not be forgotten that Tom has *also* violated the trust of his friend Leo, because he is even more relativistic than Johnny Caspar. Who is a friend and who is an enemy anyway? As Tom says in one of his more nihilistic moments, "Nobody knows anybody."

Moral flexibility and unfeeling cynicism are markers of Tom's noir heroism early in the film, but his outlook starts to shift after Rug Daniels (Salvatore H. Tornabene), the man trailing Verna for Leo, turns up dead in an alley—sans his hairpiece.[10] In a meeting at his club, Leo quickly decides that Caspar was responsible and orders a reprisal. Tom disagrees, this time angrily, and he urges that Leo give up Bernie to keep the peace. Once again, Leo's attachment to Verna leads him to reject this proposal, and Tom storms out. Soon after this exchange, Tom barges into the ladies' room in search of Verna. After some snappy verbal sparring, she comes clean to Tom: sure, she's cozying up to Leo to protect her brother, so what of it? Tom claims that he is simply looking out for Leo, who is getting "twisted" around by Verna. Tom grabs her. "You're a pathetic rumhead," she says. He responds, "And I love you, Angel," before giving her a rough kiss.

Verna answers by punching Tom in the mouth, but now it seems that "heart," the marker of positive emotional attachment, has broken through Tom's tough exterior. Soon after this episode, the two of them stop dancing around the issue. After getting beaten up by Caspar's henchmen, Tom forces his way into Verna's apartment and accuses *her* of killing Rug. Verna denies the charge and changes the subject: "That's not why you came. . . . Admit you don't like me seeing Leo because you're jealous. Admit that you've got a heart—even if it's small and feeble and you can't remember the last time you used it." Tom responds blithely, "If I'd known we were going to cast our feelings into words I'd have memorized the Song of Solomon."[11] Yet he once more gives in to her (after she flings his hat across the room), despite the fact that there is no "angle" to getting involved with Verna; there is only further vulnerability to *becoming* one.

"Jesus, Tom": Violent Interlude (1)

One of the most distinctive elements in the work of the Coen brothers is their staging of violence. Many of the most memorable scenes in their films depict violent struggles that oscillate between choreographed slapstick and grisly realism. Pacing is often slow and unnatural, and the gore is thick and gruesome, heightening the immediate, uncanny effect that violence has on us. At the same time, the sheer constructedness of these scenes makes us self-consciously aware that we are watching violence on film, that it is artifice meant to achieve some aesthetic purpose, even if that purpose is merely the impish delight of the directors themselves.

The violence in *Miller's Crossing* fits into this pattern with precision. In the first stylized staging of violence in the film, for example, Tom is subject to a beating by Caspar's henchmen. The doors of a warehouse close as Caspar departs, and Tom is left with an "ape" of a man, Frankie (Mike Starr), who is supposed to work him over. The Coens film Frankie from below in a long, wide shot that places him at the far end of the warehouse interior. Shot from below, the man should look huge and imposing, and in some sense he does, but he is also diminished by the empty space of the warehouse, and he comes off as comical and pathetic as he marches forward, toward Tom (and the viewer). As soon as he draws near, Tom asks him to wait as he takes off his coat, and he picks up a chair and breaks the thug's nose with it. Frankie looks like he is about to cry as he says, "Jesus, Tom."

Frankie turns around and marches away, giving Tom a quick, hurt glance before he heads out the door. Tom stands like a statue, still poised with the chair in its follow-through. After a couple of beats, the door opens again, and Frankie's much shorter partner, Tic-Tac (Al Mancini), strides right up to Tom, with the behemoth in tow. Tom again tries to use the chair, but Tic-Tac blocks the blow and subdues him. Now the two begin to beat Tom viciously—but they are stopped as one of the police raids instigated by Leo breaks down the warehouse doors, just in time.

Tom's exchange with Frankie is comical: the "ape" strides up to Tom like Citizen Kane but is hurt like a child when hit with the chair. When he mutters, "Jesus, Tom," he is saying, implicitly, "Aww, you didn't have to do that," suggesting that beatings like this are routine, businesslike, almost collegial in the film. In fact, Tom is never seriously hurt, though he is beaten down again and again. Yet this is a real, visceral pummeling that he absorbs and that we absorb with him. It is Tom taking punishment, in this case, because he adheres to Leo, to whatever moral force binds him to Leo's side. It may be arbitrary, but this loyalty has consequences. Heartfelt attachments always do.

The hurt that comes as a result of this positive attachment needs comfort and care, so Tom finds it and, in some sense, pays Leo back. He goes to Verna again, and they solidify their bond, as discussed above, with the Song of Solomon hanging in the air.

How to Philosophize with a Chisel: "Look in Your Heart"

The scene depicting Tom and Verna's second romantic encounter moves smoothly into one of the most memorable sequences in the film. Armed men sent by Caspar invade Leo's home, and he defends himself brilliantly with a tommy gun to the strains of "Danny Boy." Leo has escaped this time, but the attack reveals weakness. The power of the tyrant/boss is a matter of perception, as Tom affirms: "You don't hold elected office in this town. You run it because people think you run it. Once they stop thinking it, you stop running it."

So what should Leo do? Once again, Tom recommends giving Bernie up, kicking back, and waiting for Caspar "to show a weakness." Leo hesitates again—and then reveals his plan to marry Verna. His obligation to Bernie now has become all the more intense. Tom can't stand to see sentiment blind his boss any longer. He accuses Verna of killing Rug Daniels and then explains why: "Rug knew something she didn't like him knowing. . . . He knew where she was sleeping, and who with." "Maybes don't make it so," Leo says, but this is no "maybe." Tom confesses to Leo that Verna was at his place the night that Rug was killed, the night that Leo came by, looking for advice from his trusted adviser.

Tom's willingness to come clean manifests a dichotomy in the outlook of this character. On the one hand, Tom lays bare his violation of the trust between the two men, revealing that he is in fact a "son of a bitch," not only in his relationship with Verna but also in his friendship with Leo. Because he has broken this covenant, he is subject to a vigorous response. Leo gives Tom another beating and then banishes him. "It's the kiss-off," he proclaims. "If I never see him again it'll be soon enough." At the same time, Tom has made a persuasive point by sleeping with Verna; he has shown empirically that she is receptive to advances from men besides Leo. Perhaps she is not worth his trust and should be guarded against. In this sense, Tom's disclosure maintains a fundamental obligation to protect Leo, even against Verna, and even against himself. In response, Leo does take forthright action, suppressing his "big heart" in favor of realism: he also banishes Verna.

Tom and Verna are now out in the cold, and it appears that this "kiss-off" drives our hero into full-blown cynicism and amorality. After first tricking

Verna into telling him where Bernie is, Tom goes to *Caspar* to offer his services—and the first piece of information he serves up is Bernie's whereabouts. Tom thinks that this will be enough to get him in with Caspar, but a further test is demanded. Tom must kill Bernie himself, out in the woods, at a place called Miller's Crossing.

What ensues is one of the most striking scenes in the film and, indeed, within the entire Coen brothers corpus. Frankie and Tic-Tac drive Bernie and Tom out to a deserted spot in the woods; Tom receives a gun and is instructed to "put one in his brain." As the two of them wander deep into the trees, Bernie, played brilliantly by John Turturro, begs for his life:

> Tommy, you can't do this. You don't bump guys. You're not like those animals back there. It's not right, Tom. They can't make us do this. It's a wrong situation. They can't make us different people than we are. We're not muscle, Tom. I never killed anybody. I used a little information for a chisel, that's all. It's in my nature, Tom, I couldn't help it. Somebody hands me an angle, I play it. I don't deserve to die for that. Do you think I do? . . . [now weeping] I'm praying to you! I can't die! Out here in the woods! Like a dumb animal! I'm praying to you! Look in your heart!

Turturro improvises and repeats these last few lines to great effect, yet the cuts to Tom reveal a stoic demeanor, eyes barely visible beneath the brim of his hat, gun mechanically pointed at the pleading con man. In the end, however, the appeal works: Tom fires two shots—but not into Bernie. Tom instructs him to disappear, to leave town and never show his face again.

Why does Tom refrain from eliminating Bernie, something he has been advocating for the entire film? What makes Bernie's appeal so powerful? Perhaps because it includes some rationally persuasive arguments. Bernie first speaks to Tom's sense of character and identity. In undertaking this action, Bernie asks him to consider *who he is* and whether this self-concept is compatible with executing other human beings. If it is not, Bernie argues implicitly, Tom should not perform this act. If Tom subscribes to the character-based theory of ethics that grounds this argument, Bernie has a point; Tom is an adviser, not "muscle."[12] In fact, when it comes to his own dealings, Tom rarely harms anyone himself—but he is *subject* to beating after beating. In a world that trades on thuggery, Tom has always been a "thinker," so why would he start resorting to violence now?

Bernie also argues that his *own* character and actions should mitigate the response. On the one hand, "chiseling" is a fixed disposition in his character, to use Aristotelian language, because he simply can't help "playing an angle" if it is presented to him. To his mind, this makes him less culpable for his violations of others. While this is an unconvincing attempt to shirk responsibility, it does represent a substantive response to Caspar's vendetta against him.[13] If everyone knows that "ethically speaking, he's kind of shaky," and that he's a "horse of a different color, ethics-wise," as Caspar argues at the beginning of the film, then why did Caspar lay bets with Bernie in the first place? In light of Bernie's "nature," doesn't Caspar also implicate himself? Bernie makes an even stronger claim, now about his actions. Does grifting—skimming a little extra off the top—warrant a death sentence? Here, as a simple matter of retributive justice, the punishment does not seem to fit the crime.

Bernie quickly abandons these arguments because Tom remains unmoved, and the death march continues; it seems that reason will not win the day. The register of Bernie's voice changes once again, and he slumps to his knees. He identifies the incongruity of the scene: Tom is a man in a hat, suit, and overcoat, standing in the woods, and he is about to shoot Bernie "like an animal." The connection with Caspar's opening argument, which proposed that behavior like Bernie's could lead down a slippery slope to "the state of nature," is transparent. "Ethics," it was claimed, was what *separated* us from the animals, but at Miller's Crossing, Bernie presents a counterappeal. *Caspar's* ethical vision, the dominant system of ethics in this world, is actually the one that leads to barbarity and subhuman behavior. This emotional appeal is meant to repel Tom from the action he is about to undertake.

But Tom's capacity for deliberation still resists. In the realm of binding agreements and contracts, benefits to friends and harm to enemies, might makes right, and cool calculation, "whacking" Bernie makes sense, or, at worst, it is a matter of relative indifference. So what should Tom rely on to guide his actions, in lieu of these conventions? Bernie's proposal: "Look in your heart. I'm praying to you." This final, desperate call for mercy forces Tom to confront both the vulnerable humanity of the man before him and his own basic moral intuitions, which do not turn out to be rationally calculable, as Hume famously argued.[14] Even if Tom refrains from killing Bernie because in this moment he thinks of Verna, he still has recourse only to his "heart," not to any sensible, realistic, deliberate foundation for this (lack of) action.

Tom's decision is a "bad play." He knows that it will come back to bite him, and we can well imagine that he has surprised himself with this sudden rush of sympathy.[15] Bernie is also surprised—and a bit embarrassed—by his pathetic appeal, as he later admits. It represents, after all, the interruption of a very different kind of ethics from the one that constitutes the premise of the film (and so many others that it emulates), for it suggests that genuine sympathy is an option in the midst of gangsterism.

Out in the woods, this heartfelt moral orientation is in radical surplus, right up front, pressing the issue, almost uncomfortably so. It is, the Coen brothers seemingly admit, *too much,* for they quickly allow this aperture into the "heart" of the two characters to be closed as their film heads toward its conclusion.

"An Artist with the Thompson": Violent Interlude (2)

We should recall that the middle act of *Miller's Crossing,* leading up to the striking episode in the woods, is kicked off by a small masterpiece of cinematic mayhem: the attempted hit on Leo at his mansion.

The Coens open this scene with a gesture that presents violence as the explicit counterbalance to "heart." Tom and Verna start kissing and "doing plenty" for the second time, and Tom's hat enters the shot as it is tossed across the room and lands on a chair. Then the camera directs the viewer's gaze to the window, which is framed with two lace curtains. The opening strains of "Danny Boy" come up, and the shot fades into curtains surrounding one of the windows at Leo's mansion. His guard is killed off camera, and then the shot catches up to his body on the floor as blood pools around his head and his cigarette ignites the newspaper he was reading. In this series of shots, passion literally leads into violence.

Upstairs, Leo is in bed, listening to the plaintive Irish air on the Victrola as the hit men make their way up the stairs. Leo notices a wisp of smoke making its way through the floorboards, and he sits up, dons his velvet slippers, and grabs the pistol on his nightstand. Just then, the killers burst in, machine guns blazing. Leo rolls under the bed; he shoots one of the men in the ankle and then in the head when he hits the floor. Now the other one retreats, and Leo scoops up the dead man's tommy gun. He races out of the bedroom and across the hall, dodging bullets as he goes, and makes his way out a window.

Now on the front lawn, looking up, he trains the machine gun on the window, in which the thug soon appears. Leo unloads his weapon, and in the cuts to the man being hit above, we witness the "Thompson jitterbug," "a gruesome dance performed involuntarily by a hood who's being riddled with bullets while his dead fingers continue to squeeze the trigger of a Thompson submachine gun."[16] Now a car careens around the corner, and someone inside opens fire on Leo, who stands his ground, unfazed, in front of his burning mansion. Framed by the flames, he starts marching deliberately toward the car as it speeds away from him down the avenue, firing his machine gun the whole way. Eventually he hits the vehicle, and it slams into a tree, bursts into flames, and explodes. Leo stands in the street in his brilliant red robe and slippers, the weapon still smoking, and he reaches into his pocket and retrieves the cigar that he put there just before the attack began.

The brilliance of this episode stems largely from Leo's composure, conveyed so fantastically by Albert Finney. As one of his retainers says later, "The old man is still an artist with the Thompson." Leo is "an artist," an artist of power politics, as this sequence is meant to illustrate. As he unloads the bullets from the tommy gun, the Coens cut to him, sometimes from below, reinforcing his mastery and authority, and sometimes from above, zooming down on his position in front of the house, while also cutting to the victim inside. This zoom magnifies the center of force that is tearing the hit man to shreds—Leo.

But we must notice that the premise for all of Leo's brilliance and artistry is his being dislodged from a position of strength. First he is forced to roll out of the bed, then he must leave his own house (which burns), and he ends up in the street. While masterful in its orchestration, this eruption of violence signifies his dislocation and vulnerability. The presence of the classic Irish tune, which makes the sequence so effective, renders this explicit. The song, after all, is written from the perspective of the one who has been abandoned, who expects death before reunion with the prodigal beloved. Leo *has* in fact been abandoned by the police and mayor who are supposed to prop up his authority—and, more importantly, by Verna and Tom, as the previous scene has revealed.

The attempted hit on Leo, in the end, stages the next act in the film, leading up to Tom and Bernie's scene at Miller's Crossing. Like Tom after his beating at the hands of Caspar's men, Leo seeks comfort in the face of his suffering and weakness; his "heart" expands and he decides to ask Verna to marry him. But this turns out to be a surplus of sentiment, an overcompensation for the brush with death that Tom just cannot abide. Reading Leo's vulnerability from his own perspective, Tom confesses to his relationship with Verna. This act repels all three characters from each other, suppressing the "heart" in/of the middle of the film, until it makes it appearance again, out in the woods.

"Mr. Inside-Outsky": Tom's Play

Tom's decision to spare Bernie does in fact go sour. Bernie said himself, "It's in my nature, Tom. . . . Somebody hands me an angle, I play it." Now he has an angle, so instead of leaving town, as he agreed to do, he decides to stick around. If he leaves, he has nothing, but if he stays, he has Tom, whose survival now depends on Bernie being dead. So his first demand turns the tables: Tom is to kill Caspar, or else Bernie threatens to "start eating in restaurants." But he wants more than Tom's services. He wants Tom, who "put the finger" on him in the first place, to "squirm," to "sweat a little bit."

So why does Bernie turn on Tom so viciously? This is not just a simple business decision, Bernie acting on his "nature" to get rid of a threat (Caspar); it is also driven by malice. "I guess I made kind of a fool of myself out there," Bernie says, "bawling away like a twist. I guess I turned yellow. . . . It's a painful memory. And I can't help remembering that you put the finger on me." Now the energetic "vivacity" of Bernie's appeal (to use Hume's term) is channeled in a different direction. His vulnerability has degenerated into pain and embarrassment, which in turn leads him to play his angle with an edge of sadistic pleasure. In this sense, Bernie urges the film to return to its dominant ethical mode, the "ethics" articulated by Caspar in its opening scene. Because of the betrayal Bernie is perpetrating on him, Tom is only too happy to join in this effort, and the Coen brothers oblige the both of them.

In fact, even before Bernie reappears, our hero has been doing some maneuvering to undermine Caspar's right-hand man, "the Dane" (J. E. Freeman). The Dane is closely linked with Mink (Steve Buscemi), who makes only one brief appearance very early in the film. Mink is "the Dane's boy," but unbeknown to him, Mink has recently gotten mixed up with Bernie also.[17] This triangle turns out to be central to the action of the film. Mink, because he is vouched for by the Dane, has inside information about Caspar's fixed fights, and Bernie has apparently colluded with Mink (extorted him, more likely) to engage in the swindle that got everything started.

Tom has figured all of this out, and he places a call to Mink in which he lies and suggests that he has spilled the beans to Caspar and the Dane.

Tom urges Mink to disappear. Later, after Mink is nowhere to be found, Caspar reaches the conclusion that Tom wanted him to: Mink and Bernie were in on the swindle together. Now it's only a small leap to assuming that the Dane was *also* betraying Caspar, and Tom plants the seed of this idea, but Caspar is not yet sold. He wants to talk to Mink first, and he orders Tom to find him.

Before Tom can get much further, however, the Dane intervenes. Realizing that his colleagues never actually *saw* Bernie's execution, he picks Tom up and takes him for a "little ride"—out to Miller's Crossing. This was an eventuality that Tom had to foresee; he perhaps thought that the Dane could be taken care of before he became skeptical. But now Tom is in Bernie's former position as the Dane marches him out into the forest. There is no pleading this time. Tom for the most part maintains his cool exterior, but at a certain point he vomits, which is all the Dane needs to see. Just as he is about to execute Tom, one of the men calls out. They have found a fresh body, a body with the face shot off. This corpse, for the moment anyway, satisfies the Dane. "I said put one in his brain," says Tic-Tac, laughing, "not in his stinking face."

In his next meeting with Caspar, Tom uses this episode to press his case. The Dane's plan, according to Tom, was to *miss* the corpse, kill Tom for not doing the deed, and then blame another fix on Bernie. Caspar continues to hesitate, but the stress is getting to him: "Since last we jawed, my stomach's been seizing up on me. The Dane saying we should double-cross you; you double-cross once, where's it all end? An interesting ethical question." Caspar is uncomfortable knowing that his tyrant's power cannot help him clarify who is a friend and who is an enemy. In fact, his position makes things worse. "Runnin' things," he laments, "it ain't all gravy."

Meanwhile, Tom is also working on his Bernbaum problem. He manages to track Bernie down through a hulk of a man named Drop Johnson (Mario Todisco), a boxer who has placed a suspiciously large bet on another fighter, a terrible hack. Tom confirms that Drop placed this bet for Bernie.[18] Soon Bernie calls Tom, and the mystery of the miraculous corpse is solved: Bernie killed Mink and dumped him at Miller's Crossing to give Tom "some insurance"—and to keep his own "play" with Tom alive. But Tom has had enough. He tells Bernie that he's leaving town and demands payment to keep quiet until he's gone. Bernie must come to Tom's apartment at 4:00 A.M. to complete the transaction.

Tom inches ever closer to resolving his problems, and the next step is finishing off the Dane. In a remarkable scene (discussed further below), Tom enters the great room of his mansion, and the Dane is there, lying in wait. Tom is on the short end of a violent struggle until Caspar rises and beats the Dane mercilessly, for Tom has in fact convinced Caspar that the Dane was double-crossing him all along. Now Caspar wants a piece of Mink too, and Tom tells him that the Dane's supposed accomplice will be at his (Tom's) apartment at 4:00 A.M. Then Caspar finishes off his loyal henchman with a pistol shot to the head.

Tom has finished his setup. At four o'clock, Caspar goes to Tom's apartment, with Tom hanging back to avoid the fireworks. After Caspar enters the building (which is called the Barton Arms, by the way), shots ring out, and Tom slowly makes his way up the stairs. Caspar hasn't even made it into the apartment: he lies splayed out in the hallway, shot, his bloody bald head wedged into the banister. And of course Bernie is there, waiting in the doorway. Tom's plan has worked. Bernie arrived early, "looking for blood," and he shot Caspar, mistaking him for Tom. Now everything is smoothed over. The Dane, Tom proposes, can be blamed for everything, including Caspar's death, and it turns out that there's enough money in the boss's wallet to wipe out Tom's gambling debt.

There's only *one* problem, Tom suggests, once he has the money and all of the guns. "We can't hang this on the Dane," he says. "The Dane's already dead, halfway across town. . . . It's got to be you." For the second time, Tom turns a gun on Bernie, but this time there will be no reprieve. Bernie slumps down, pleading once again: "So what's in it for you? There's no angle! You can't just shoot me like that! Jesus Christ! It don't make sense! Tommy! Look in your heart!" Tom responds, "What heart?" and he shoots Bernie through the forehead ("one in the brain"), planting the gun that killed him on Caspar and the one that killed Caspar on Bernie.

"A Deep, Dark Place": Violent Interlude (3)

The climactic and most surreal staging of violence in the film is the scene in the great room of Caspar's mansion. This scene seals the fate of the Dane, but more importantly, in the hands of the Coen brothers, it is a vivid demonstration of the sympathy-crushing effect of passion gone wrong, which constitutes the true foundation of the "ethics" of power in *Miller's Crossing*.

When Tom enters the room, he walks with Caspar toward a chair by the fireplace, and a relatively tight shot follows them, so we as viewers have no sense of the space behind them. Tom's vision is narrow, too. Because he is fixated on making his case to Caspar, he fails to notice that the Dane is there. A shot now follows the Dane from right to left as he announces his presence and traverses the previously unnoticed space behind Tom. The Dane directs Tom's (and the viewer's) attention to the fact that Drop Johnson is also in the room, in the space he just vacated, on the right. A zoom now takes us straight up to Drop's bludgeoned, swollen face, and his eyes widen horribly as he gazes at Tom. Now the next shot zooms in on Tom in the same manner, mirroring the way we have just seen the "gorilla" sitting in the corner. These sudden directorial interventions are disorienting. For much of *Miller's Crossing,* the Coens have avoided the careening shots that their other films (like *Raising Arizona* [1987], for example, the film that preceded *Miller's Crossing*) lead us to expect, but now that we have arrived at the violent core of the film, the stable, stately subjectivity bestowed on the viewer for much of its duration is disrupted.

The Dane begins to assault Tom by choking him, and now the shot from below has its standard effect: the thug is diabolical and imposing as he announces, "I am going to send you to a deep, dark place. And I am going to have fun doing it." The Coens cut to a hideous close-up of Johnny Caspar's gigantic bald head; he sits by the fire, seething, the very manifestation of the rage behind the Dane's violence. But this rage, the viciousness of the tyrant behind the "ethics," is greater than the film, *qua* "nostalgic gangster/noir homage," can bear. Johnny suddenly smashes the Dane's face with the fireplace shovel. Like his friend, Mink, the Dane is now faceless as he covers his shattered visage, hat knocked off and blood streaming between his gloved fingers.

Meanwhile, Drop Johnson begins screaming, howling like a wounded animal. Caspar approaches him, ready to pummel him too, demanding that he shut up. The camera again zooms in on his horrible, howling face. Tom nods to him to make him shut up—and he does—and now the shot strangely, artificially zooms out on a silenced Drop, the reversal of the earlier shot. Tom convinces Caspar to come to his apartment at four, supposedly to take care of Mink, and meanwhile the Dane begins to stir. Drop begins to scream once again, and Caspar strides up to the Dane and shoots him in the head. The terrifying, final zoom brings us right up to Caspar's bloody mug as he says, "Always put one in the brain."

In *Miller's Crossing,* we have come to recognize this statement as the mantra of thoughtless, businesslike violence. It also manifests the gravely negative effect (thoughtlessness) of excessive passions gone wrong—the passions that form the true basis of Caspar's "ethics," which dominate the world of the film. But Caspar's rage (like Bernie's pleading at Miller's Crossing) is, in the end, *too much* for this genre-based tale to absorb, even though it is about crime and gangsters. Drop's terrible howl is at once both *so* Coen brothers and *so* out of place in the world they have created: it bears witness to the indecipherable force that drives Caspar's brutality and, when rationalized, that pulls itself together in codicils of gangster/noir "ethics"—which are, as Tom now fully understands, consumed in an instant by the horrifying passion that is their premise.

The overarching effect of this episode is to steel Tom forever against the dangers of the "heart," which completes his journey toward noir stoicism and autonomy. In Leo's love for Verna and his readiness to fight, in Tom's own desire for Verna and sympathy for Bernie, and in Caspar's demented rage, our hero has witnessed a downward spiral into confusion and cruelty that is conditioned on the instability of passion and sentiment. But cool Machiavellian calculation has hardly saved the day. The smooth surface of Caspar's "ethics"—indeed, Tom's job as a thoughtful adviser—was always premised on the raw deployment of mastery, punishment, and power, the force that manifests itself in a disorienting swirl of shots and surreal howling of a "gorilla" of a man.

But the real nightmare here is the implication of this protagonist in the traumatizing violence to which he is constantly subjected. Can Tom control this horrible, howling force, the origin of all power politics, in himself? The pairing of shots that ends in Tom silencing the beast suggests that he can. But does Tom in fact have this animal within him? The mirrored pairing of shots, with Drop on one end of a zoom and Tom on the end of the next, suggests that he does. These ambiguities resolve in Caspar's blood-streaked face, which is the emblem of the madness behind this corrupt world. Caspar too will soon be dead as a result of his own rage, which seems all too appropriate, but Tom kills Bernie himself, without mercy, not only because it makes sense: it also satisfies his own bloodlust. It is, we might assume, a "deep, dark place" that Tom *never* wants to visit again.

Conclusion: "Do You Always Know Why You Do Things?"

When questioned about the character he played in *Miller's Crossing*, actor Gabriel Byrne observed, "All through the picture, Tom is battling with the idea of love and idea of giving himself to another person. The turning point for Tom is at Miller's Crossing—Bernie gets through to his heart and he lets go. From then on, everything goes haywire, and he is determined never again to be ruled by his heart."[19] As this essay has suggested, Byrne was largely right: Bernie's betrayal of Tom's heartfelt sympathy sends him down a path that, in the end, leaves him steely and alone.

To gather the impact of the film's conclusion, however, we have to render Byrne's observation with further precision. Despite his last words to Bernie, the latter stages of the action are in fact *driven* by Tom's "heart" and, in particular, his abiding sense of loyal, sentimental attachment to Leo. Toward the end of the film, for example, Tom tells Verna that he had to give Bernie up to Caspar because it was the only way he could "straighten things out for Leo." Verna responds, "You said you didn't care about Leo." Tom's answer is telling: "I said we were through. It's not the same thing."

A job, a duty, an obligation determined at first on contractual grounds— or founded on random contiguity and mutual need—can move us toward heartfelt connection. That is surely the case with Tom and Leo, who share ethnicity, experience, and a longstanding relationship. "Care" for Leo in fact drives Tom's play all along, even his illicit affair with Verna. Following through on this impulse in the last half of the film, Tom repairs the original covenant by enacting Leo's interest; he aims to return Leo to the advantages of power; he upholds their friendship while destroying Leo's enemies; and he does most of this through careful, dispassionate calculation. Thus Tom proves to be quite adept at maneuvering within the confines of Caspar's "ethics" while maintaining some measure of his own character and identity. Like the tyrants themselves, however, Tom's "passion" (in Hume's sense) is the ultimate foundation of his decision making, as rational as it often is. In particular, his heartfelt, organic connection with Leo is the compelling interest.[20]

But Tom swears off this connection in the final sequence of the film. A significant factor in this decision, of course, is the revived betrothal of Leo and Verna. Even if he began the affair with Verna to make a point, Tom feels for Verna, and now it would be impossible for him to restore his friendship with the man who is married to her. In this sense, Tom has become the archetypal hero who has lost the girl, which evokes our pity and sympathy. At the same time, we as viewers secretly wish this misfortune upon him, so he can continue to be the cynical, wisecracking free agent that the conventions of his genre dictate. We would rather that characters like Tom *not* live happily ever after, so we can imagine them as they are, ready to get into and out of trouble again and again with dexterity, humor, and aplomb.

But in the hands of the Coen brothers, it is difficult to imagine Tom Reagan as reproducible and serialized—it is difficult to see his noir-style stoicism and freedom without thinking of the trauma that made it. Leo and Verna's mutual attachment cancels out Tom's feelings for both of them, surely, but the deeper, darker journey in the last half of the film is truly what places a seal—an unassailable closure—on Tom's heart (to make creative use of the phrase from the Song of Solomon). How can one make heartfelt connections when they are so brutally punishing? How can one adhere to a system of "ethics" when we know that its origin is always shifting passions, often horrifyingly negative ones? And what about action based on cool calculation of interest or even on higher dictates, arrived at through reason? These too mean nothing in a world where love, greed, fear, or rage—or "one in the brain"—can blow away the "tranquillity" of our "intellectual faculties" (to invoke Hume once again) in an instant.

Our celebration of this hero, which is conditioned by our expectations surrounding genres so precisely invoked by the Coens, swells in the last shot of the film. We see Tom leaning up against a tree in the woods where Bernie's funeral has taken place, and he gazes off into the distance, watching Leo walk away. Now he tilts his head down slightly, so his eyes are obscured by the brim of his hat, which he adjusts in a highly stylized gesture. This would be a great place for the film to end, with Tom's freedom and composure vividly symbolized by his hat being on just right. But the Coens take a brilliant next step, insisting that we look at this figure again. Slowly Tom removes his hands from the hat, he raises his head so his eyes become visible, and we zoom in on his face, which continues to gaze—sadly, we realize—into the distance.

We may treasure the first Tom Reagan who stares out at us at the end of the film and adjusts his hat, as well as all the heroes he so closely resembles—and the gangster/noir stoic in all of us. But in offering a second look, the Coen brothers remind us about the traumatic excesses that go into this kind of lonely autonomy. We should probably hesitate before it, even as we continue to engage the "struggle of passion and of reason" that is at the center of our moral life.[21]

Notes

1. Quoted in James Mottram, *The Coen Brothers: The Life of the Mind* (Dulles, Va.: Brassey's, 2000), 55.

2. The hard-boiled gangster noir precedents are transparent: Hammett's work inspired *Miller's Crossing* (particularly *The Red Harvest* and *The Glass Key;* for analysis of this link see Mottram, *Coen Brothers,* 64–65, and Steve Jenkins, "Miller's Crossing," in *Joel & Ethan Coen: Blood Siblings,* ed. Paul A. Woods [London: Plexus, 2000], 71–72), and the film also strikes all the right notes as an example of "stylized crime realism," to employ Jason Holt's definition of noir. See Holt, "A Darker Shade: Realism in Neo-Noir," in *The Philosophy of Film Noir,* ed. Mark T. Conard (Lexington: Univ. Press of Kentucky, 2006), 23–25. R. Barton Palmer has in fact argued that noir provides a conceptual and aesthetic space for the whole body of the Coens' work. See Palmer, *Joel and Ethan Coen* (Urbana and Chicago: Univ. of Illinois Press, 2004), 46–50.

3. Richard T. Jameson, "Chasing the Hat," in *Joel & Ethan Coen: Blood Siblings,* ed. Woods, 80.

4. David Hume, *A Treatise of Human Nature* (1739–1740; London: Oxford Univ. Press, 1965), 437.

5. Knight argues against "the view that hard-boiled detectives are dispassionate reasoners," suggesting instead that "there is something special about the hard-boiled detective . . . something that has to do with his personal and emotional investment in the events and people he is investigating." Deborah Knight, "On Reason and Passion in *The Maltese Falcon,*" in *Philosophy of Film Noir,* ed. Conard, 208.

6. Thomas Hobbes, *Leviathan* (1651; London: Penguin, 1985), 185, 186.

7. Plato, *The Republic,* trans. Allan Bloom, 2nd ed. (New York: Basic Books, 1968), 332d.

8. Ibid., 338c–339a.

9. "Act in such a way that you treat humanity, whether in your own person or in the person of another, always at the same time as an end and never simply as a means." Immanuel Kant, *Grounding for the Metaphysics of Morals,* trans. James W. Ellington (1785; Indianapolis: Hackett, 1981), 36.

10. Rug's toupee does fit into a relatively straightforward frame of symbolic reference in *Miller's Crossing.* The removal of head coverings is a sign of vulnerability and lack of control. Hats get removed or fall off when Tom is beaten, for example, and when he goes to bed with Verna. The reason for Tom and Verna's initial encounter, in fact, is that Tom is *looking* for his lost hat after a night of boozing with Verna and friends. So when Rug Daniel's hairpiece is removed from his corpse by a random kid, it is an emphatic sign that serious chaos is about to ensue as the result of something absurd: losing a hat is one thing ("foolish," Tom says), but a man without his hair is another! Rug's death does prove to be empty of meaning in and of itself; Bernie later reveals that his murder was "just a mix-up." Meanwhile, characters often speculate about Rug's missing hair, as if wondering about the strange directorial hand that put them in the situation they are in.

11. The text, which Tom has not "memorized" but here lets on that he knows, is of course a testament to the overriding power of passion and sentiment. Cf. Song of Solomon (8:6–7, NRSV):

Set me as a seal upon your heart,
as a seal upon your arm;
for love is strong as death,
passion fierce as the grave.
Its flashes are flashes of fire,
a raging flame.
Many waters cannot quench love,
neither can flood drown it.
If one offered for love
all the wealth of his house,
it would be utterly scorned.

12. Recall *The Republic* once again, in which Plato makes a classic argument for the importance of character in the formation of moral action. The just man "really sets his own house in good order and rules himself; he arranges himself, becomes his own friend. . . . Then, and only then, he acts, if he does act in some way." Plato *Republic* 443d–e.

13. Aristotle describes virtues and vices as fixed dispositions or "characteristics" (*hexis*) that are formed by repeated actions. See Aristotle, *Nicomachean Ethics,* trans. Martin Ostwald (Upper Saddle River, N.J.: Prentice Hall, 1999), 1103b. While these dispositions do become fixed (e.g., Bernie's "nature"), Aristotle insists that we are ultimately responsible for them, since we have a free choice about the direction of our character when they first get started. See ibid., 1114b–1115a.

14. "Morals excite passions, and produce or prevent actions. Reason of itself is utterly impotent in this particular. The rules of morality, therefore, are not conclusions of our reason." Hume, *Treatise of Human Nature,* 457.

15. Another reading might suggest that Tom is not *actually* moved by Bernie's appeal at all; instead, he calculates and determines that Bernie will be useful to him down the road—and this does in fact turn out to be the case. But other, intervening events suggest that Bernie's later role in Tom's "play" is improvised. The fact that Caspar's men take him out to Miller's Crossing to verify the kill, for example, is an eventuality that Tom must have thought possible as he let Bernie go, and yet he did it anyway, endangering himself in the process. It does seem that "sympathy," in Hume's classic sense of the term, has in fact been awakened in this scene.

In one place in *A Treatise of Human Nature,* for example, Hume discusses the "vivacity" with which another's "condition" is presented as central to eliciting sympathetic reaction, and this analysis applies quite precisely to the effectiveness of Bernie's appeal: "When the present misery of another has any strong influence upon me, the vivacity of the conception is not confin'd merely to its immediate object, but diffuses its influence over all the related ideas, and gives me a lively notion of all the circumstances of that person, whether past, present, or future. . . . By means of this lively notion I am interested in them; take part with them; and feel a sympathetic motion in my breast, conformable to whatever I imagine in his." Ibid., 386.

16. Steven Levy, "Shot by Shot," in *Joel & Ethan Coen: Blood Siblings*, ed. Woods, 74.

17. The homosexual overtones of the connection between Mink, Bernie, and the Dane are submerged in innuendo (anything explicit would disturb the surface of the film's genre-based setting too much), but it is clear that the Coen brothers aim to get this subtext across. In his early exchange with Tom, for example, Mink reveals that he has taken up with Bernie. "We're just friends," he says, "you know, amigos?" Tom responds, "You're a fickle boy, Mink. If the Dane found out you had another 'amigo' . . . I don't peg him for the understanding type." Later, in the scene in the ladies room, Verna hints at Bernie's leanings: "Yeah, sneer at him like everyone else. Just because he's different. People think he's a degenerate. People think he's scum. Well he's not." Then, when Bernie first appears in Tom's apartment he reveals—rather shockingly—that Verna has in fact attempted "to teach [him] a thing or two about bed artistry." "Some crackpot idea about saving me from my friends," he says. In other words, it appears that Verna has attempted—through incest—to dissuade Bernie from his sexual proclivities. Later, when Tom accuses the Dane of double-crossing Caspar with Mink, he suggests that "there's always that wild card when love is involved." And finally, in his last encounter with Tom, after having killed Caspar, Bernie admits to blackmailing Mink with the fact that the two of them "were jungled up together."

18. In a lovely cinematic footnote, when Tom enters Drop's apartment we catch sight of the poster advertising his next bout along with the fight he is betting on, which is much lower on the card. In the headliner Drop Johnson will apparently be fighting "Lars Thorvald." If the makers of the poster have made a small typographical error and "Thorvald" is actually supposed to be "Thorwald," Drop will in fact be fighting the villain from Hitchcock's *Rear Window* (1954), the murderer (played by Raymond Burr) who cuts up his wife!

19. Quoted in Mottram, *Coen Brothers*, 63.

20. Here the comparison with Sam Spade (Humphrey Bogart) in *The Maltese Falcon* (John Huston, 1941) becomes quite helpful, especially in light of Deborah Knight's analysis. We recall that Spade gives up Brigid (Mary Astor) at the end of the film not simply because his reason masters the temptation that she represents; instead, his emotional attachment to his old partner (whom she killed) will not let him stay with her. As Knight suggests, Spade acts on a "moral commitment . . . to his dead partner, despite the fact that he didn't like him and that Miles wasn't particularly smart." Knight, "On Reason and Passion in *The Maltese Falcon*," 218. Tom *also* acts a sentiment-based "moral commitment" to Leo, to which his rationality is subservient. Why else would Tom remain in the fray after Leo's "kiss-off"?

21. Hume, *Treatise of Human Nature*, 438.

"Takin' 'er Easy for All Us Sinners"

Laziness as a Virtue in *The Big Lebowski*

Matthew K. Douglass and Jerry L. Walls

"Drifting along with the tumbling tumbleweed"

The opening scenes of *The Big Lebowski* (1998) portray a lonely tumbleweed as it rolls aimlessly down the streets of Los Angeles. The tumbleweed, once verdant and firmly planted, has long since surrendered to the wind and now goes wherever it blows. Immediately thereafter we see an unabashed loafer, a man whom the narrator describes as "quite possibly the laziest [man] in Los Angeles County, which would place him high in the running for laziest worldwide." Like the tumbleweed, this man has long since taken the path of least resistance. He may have once been vigorous and idealistic, but blithe resignation has replaced all of that. Now this man is content to let life carry him along wherever it wills.

Although this man's real name is Jeffrey Lebowski, he insists that people call him "Dude." Apparently, laziness for the Dude (Jeff Bridges) is not a simple habit. It is a distinct, chosen ethos—"dude-ism," to give it a name. Naturally, the Dude never develops his philosophy, nor does he proselytize. That would take too much effort. Hence, if we are to understand the Dude's philosophy, we must speculate somewhat. Even so, the tumbleweed imagery provides a guiding metaphor, and the Dude's actions and conversations should allow us to infer the basic doctrines of dude-ism.

The tumbleweed metaphor and its link with the driving wind lead us to recognize the first tenet of dude-ism: *Reality is inherently chaotic and purposeless.* The wind has no will and thus no reason to push the tumbleweed around; it is simply the effect of trillions of tiny, chaotic molecular interactions. Yet these interactions, when added together, create a mighty force that the tumbleweed is powerless to resist. In the same way, life is blind and purposeless, the effect of billions of (mostly) mundane yet chaotic events. Yet, when added together, these events create a force that no individual can resist. Additionally, it is easy enough to describe *how* the Dude got to where he is today, just as it is easy to explain how the tumbleweed got to Los Angeles. However, just as it is absurd to wonder *why* the wind has brought the tumbleweed to its current location, it is absurd to wonder why the Dude is here or even why he exists at all.

The second tenet of dude-ism is: *One should expend effort only on simple, short-term goals.* This follows from the first tenet, for if life is irresistibly chaotic, one's effort might bring order to life, but only for a short time. Attempting anything too grand will ultimately end in frustration. In addition, there is no way to know if a seemingly mundane decision might have drastic effects. For example, the Dude's decision to get justice for his urine-soaked rug sets the rest of the film's plot in motion. Things continue to get worse and worse for the Dude, who eventually complains, "I could be sitting here with just pee stains on my rug." In the Dude's mind, all of this trouble stems from his audacious decision, which he made against his better judgment.

Along these lines, the "laws" of chance dictate that each person will have a mixture of good and bad experiences. As the Stranger (Sam Elliott) explains to the Dude, "Sometimes you eat the bear. And sometimes the bear, well, he eats you." The third doctrine of dude-ism follows from that fact: *Since one can do very little to affect this mixture of good and bad, one should accept life as it is and learn to be content.* Granted, a little effort is sufficient to solve some problems. Hunger, for example, can be eliminated simply by eating. Other problems are either unsolvable or they take more effort than is worthwhile. A successful dude-ist is one who can tell the difference between these two types of problems.

The fourth dude-istic dictum runs as follows: *The purpose of life is to be as happy as possible in any situation.* If life (like the wind) is blind, chaotic, and purposeless, then the purpose of life does not come from anything metaphysical or external to the individual. If life is to have purpose, therefore, each individual must decide what that purpose is. The other characters in *The Big Lebowski* find meaning in various things: sensual pleasures, money, and duty, to name a few. Yet the Dude reacts with detached amusement to each of them. These things are fine, he seems to say, but none of them is essential to make life worth living. Nevertheless, while it might be tempting to say that the Dude does not value anything, it is more accurate to say that he values *everything*, but no particular thing is supreme.

Dude-ism's practical implications can be summarized as "principled laziness" or in a pithy motto: "Why chase the wind when it will carry you to the same place?" As an ethos, dude-ism simply describes an easy way to be happy. Since it does not appeal to external, universal standards, it has very little to say about what is morally good or bad. Even so, dude-ism is a benign philosophy; kindness is much more pleasant and much less disturbing than rudeness or selfishness. When other people act like jerks, the Dude reacts the same way as if someone had spilled a drink: he is frustrated by the needless unpleasantness of the situation more than the "immorality" of someone's actions. Life would be so much easier, the Dude believes, if everyone would just relax.

In short, laziness is a virtue for the Dude—that is, laziness is a trait that ultimately leads to happiness and fulfillment—and it has been working for him until we first meet him in a supermarket. However, from the moment two thugs mistake him for another Jeffrey Lebowski (that is, "The Big Lebowski") and urinate on his rug, his principled laziness faces a series of trials. As the film unfolds, the Dude encounters several alternative worldviews and increasingly difficult situations, each testing his basic assumptions about life. Our goal, then, will be to evaluate dude-ism in light of these trials and to determine whether, according to *The Big Lebowski,* laziness can be truly virtuous.

"We believe in nothing, Lebowski. Nothing!"

The Dude's apathy toward pretty much everything places him in the same philosophical neighborhood as *The Big Lebowski*'s principal villains, the nihilists (played by Peter Stormare, Flea, and Torsten Voges). In general, nihilists agree on three points. First, there are no standards with which to distinguish right from wrong, good from bad, beautiful from ugly, and so on. Second, life has no intrinsic meaning, value, or purpose. Third, "truth" is ultimately incomprehensible, and thus our quest for ultimate knowledge is pointless. Most nihilists are atheists, but this is not necessary, so long as "God" remains a thoughtless, impersonal entity.

The nihilists' thick German accents suggest a kinship with Friedrich Nietzsche (1844–1900), whose reputation as a nihilist is due largely to this famous declaration: "God is dead; but given the way of men, there may still be caves for thousands of years in which his shadow will be shown.—And we—we still have to vanquish his shadow, too."[1] God's "death"—clearly a metaphorical pronouncement—refers to society's loss of faith in God. In other words, God was "alive" only while people believed in God, but now, as Nietzsche put it, "*We have killed him—you and I.*"[2]

As the first quote shows, Nietzsche's goal was not simply to announce God's demise; he wanted to eradicate all evidence that God ever existed. These traces, or "shadows," refer to the values that humanity inherited from its belief in God—free will, moral obligation, the value of life, and so on. If God does not exist, Nietzsche argued, humanity must accept that such cherished ideals are nothing but comforting illusions.[3]

With the abolition of humanity's past cherished values, it is easy to see why Nietzsche is often called a nihilist. Yet Nietzsche detested that title and, ironically, accused almost everyone else of nihilism. Granted, Nietzsche did not believe that life has intrinsic value; however, for Nietzsche this did not imply that life has no meaning whatsoever. Whereas true nihilism must reject all values, Nietzsche attempted to create values that correspond to a God-less reality.

In place of God's decrees, Nietzsche built his values system on what he considered the first principle of reality: the will to power. Simply put, the will to power refers to an eternal struggle that drives all things, even natural laws.[4] Because the will to power is a brute fact of nature, Nietzsche believed that anyone who rejected it was rejecting reality itself and was, therefore, a nihilist.[5]

It should be clear now that Nietzsche was not, in fact, a nihilist, even though sometimes he is regarded as such. Consequently, if *The Big Lebowski*'s "nihilists" are genuine nihilists, they are not philosophical heirs of Nietzsche. They claim to care about nothing and attempt to prove it by smashing things, torching cars, and cutting off toes. This sort of disdain for the physical world is in line with what Nietzsche considered nihilism, but it is antithetical to his own tastes. In addition, the self-proclaimed "nihilists" do not live according to the will to power. Instead of exerting power over those around them, these characters are little more than inept thugs who make impotent threats.

In *The Big Lebowski*'s final altercation, the nihilists confront Walter Sobchak (John Goodman), the Dude, and Donny (Steve Buscemi), demanding the money that they feel is due them. Walter, completely fed up and unafraid of these "nihilists," calls their bluff and refuses to give them anything. However, the nihilists, who had been counting on the money, strongly protest:

NIHILIST #1: His girlfriend gave up her toe!
NIHILIST #2: She thought we'd be getting million dollars!
NIHILIST #1: It's not fair!

In this moment, Walter identifies the nihilists' hypocrisy.

WALTER: Fair?!?! Who's the fucking nihilist around here, you bunch o' fucking crybabies!

As it turns out, these "nihilists," who value money and appeal to "fairness," are not true nihilists. However, we should not be too hard on them. While nihilism is possible in theory, it is not possible in practice. If life truly has no purpose or meaning, why keep living? It seems that, to avoid suicide, nihilists must willfully deceive themselves: they must live as if *something* makes life worth living, even while preaching that life is worthless.

The Dude, meanwhile, seems even more apathetic than the nihilists, and if one equates "nihilism" with "apathy," then the Dude is even more nihilistic than they are. Yet the Dude is less extreme in his views, so no self-delusion is necessary. Even if he does not find intrinsic value in life, he does not go so far as to reject all values. The Dude finds purpose in whatever life gives him, and the fact that there is no transcendent, metaphysical reason to live is irrelevant.

"Viva Las Vegas!"

Whether by personal choice, fortuitous heredity, or years of drug use, the Dude is able to enjoy the simple things in life: bowling, White Russians, smoking weed, a good, long bath, and a nice little rug that "really ties the room together." Such simple pleasures, however, are not enough to satisfy Bunny Lebowski (Tara Reid), the beautiful trophy wife whose disappearance drives the film's plot. Her only purpose in life is to experience as much pleasure as possible.

This philosophy, known as "hedonism," is generally attached to the Greek philosopher Epicurus (341–270 BCE). According to Epicurus, our sensations arise from perturbations of the "atoms" that compose our bodies, and it is only reasonable to make these atoms interact in a pleasurable way.[6] The highest form of pleasure, Epicurus taught, was intellectual, not sensual. Thus, Epicurus' sophisticated hedonism might suit Maude

Lebowski (Julianne Moore), the Big Lebowski's feminist daughter, but certainly not Bunny.

Instead, Bunny follows the original form of hedonism, founded by Aristippus of Cyrene (ca. 435–366 BCE).[7] Ancient historians describe Aristippus as a scandalous figure, supposedly the first of Socrates' disciples to charge for his teaching.[8] After garnering a measure of notoriety, Aristippus infiltrated the court of Dionysius of Syracuse where, like Bunny, he lived luxuriously at another's expense.[9]

Unlike Epicurus, Aristippus' hedonism celebrated sensual delights and denigrated intellectual pursuits. For him, anything that was not immediately practical was a waste of time. Aristippus argued that the *psyche,* which motivates the body, naturally strives for pleasure and avoids pain. Further, since the *psyche* naturally inclines itself toward the good, it follows that pleasure *is* the good. Actions are thus moral if they work to increase pleasure and bad if they either reduce pleasure or cause pain.[10]

The problems with this type of hedonism are easy to identify. First, it is very easy to indulge oneself in excess, causing desensitization or addiction. Bunny suffers from both effects. As Maude Lebowski points out to the Dude, "There are some people—it is called satyriasis in men, nymphomania in women—who engage in [sex] compulsively, and without joy. . . . These unfortunate souls cannot love in the true sense of the word. Our mutual acquaintance, Bunny, is one of these." As the law of diminishing returns states, any pleasurable experience, if repeated often and mechanically enough, will eventually lose its appeal, making ever-increasing forms of stimulation necessary.

Second, Bunny's hedonism is expensive, but one who slavishly seeks pleasure lacks the restraint and foresight necessary to make money. Bunny consistently finds herself in debt, and since she depends on the kindness of others, her lifestyle is sustainable only while she has something to offer in return. Once the effects of partying take their toll on Bunny's appearance, she will not be worth supporting, and she will be forced either to change her lifestyle or find another way to make money.

The Dude is a hedonist insofar as he strives for ephemeral pleasures; however, he successfully evades hedonism's pitfalls. Because he is too lazy to chase after pleasure, the Dude has learned to enjoy every moment as it happens to him. He has not developed an addiction, and his experiences are mild and varied enough to keep him from jadedness.[11] His simple tastes allow him to enjoy life even though he is unemployed and has almost no money. Finally, because the Dude finds pleasure in leisure, he is able to live a consistently slothful life, no matter how old and frail he becomes.

"I went out and achieved anyway."

Standing in stark contrast to the Dude, the nihilists, and Bunny is the Big Lebowski (David Huddleston), a crippled Korean War veteran whose sensibilities are steeped in capitalism and the American dream. His worldview has several euphemistic aliases—"rugged individualism," "egoism," or "social Darwinism," to name a few—though in his case, "pitiless, selfish bastardism" may be more accurate. Not surprisingly, very few philosophers have been audacious enough to espouse egoism, even the pitiless and selfish ones. One notable exception is Nietzsche, whose "master morality" was a classically informed defense of egoism and who claimed that it was the ethics of the noble class.[12] Drawing inspiration from classical Greek and Roman culture, Nietzsche stated that aristocrats respect only those qualities that they prize in themselves. Thus, pride, ambition, and power are "good" in the noble mind, while their opposites are dubbed "bad." Importantly, Nietzsche wanted to move beyond our common ideas of "good" and "evil." Consequently, the terms "good" and "bad" for Nietzsche and the noble class are *aesthetic* terms, not moral ones. In other words, "good" and "bad" in master morality mean "noble" and "vulgar," not "right" and "wrong."[13]

The Big Lebowski, with his exquisitely decorated mansion and wall of plaques, faithfully demonstrates master morality. Brandt (Philip Seymour Hoffman), Lebowski's personal assistant, reverently describes some of Lebowski's most notable awards to the Dude: a key to the city of Pasadena, the Los Angeles Chamber of Commerce Business Achiever Award, and a picture of Lebowski taken with Nancy Reagan, "when Mrs. Reagan was First Lady of the *nation* . . . not of California." The most prized picture shows the Little Lebowski Urban Achievers, "inner city children of promise" who receive college money from Mr. Lebowski.

Since pity is "vulgar" in master morality, Lebowski's charitable acts might seem odd. However, Nietzsche conceded that aristocrats will sometimes give to the poor but only from an excess of power, not from pity.[14] In other words, as Lebowski's wall of awards demonstrates, rich people give money precisely to show how rich they are. In place of compassion, Lebowski values self-sufficiency. As he explains to the Dude, "Every bum's lot in life is his own responsibility, regardless of who he chooses to blame."

Despite his noble talk, Lebowski's egoism fails in many ways. First, very few people are bold, talented, and ambitious enough to build their own wealth. The Big Lebowski, Maude reveals to the Dude, is not as self-made as he sounds. He is an incompetent businessman who inherited his wealth from his late wife and even steals money from the Little Lebowski Urban Achievers, ostensibly to pay Bunny's ransom, though in reality Lebowski keeps the money for himself and tries to pin the theft on the Dude. Although his wealth is unearned, Lebowski admires all the "noble" traits of master morality; however, because he is too impotent to gain his own power, he exhibits none of these traits in his own life.

Since master morality proceeds from the will to power, an egoist will always be in conflict with those around him, even when the other person is not looking for a fight. In their first encounter, all the Dude wants from Lebowski is compensation for his ruined rug. Lebowski, meanwhile, takes the Dude's request as an attack and erupts into a paint-peeling tirade. Realizing that a heated confrontation is not worth the effort, the Dude calmly puts on his sunglasses and walks out. Sensing victory, Lebowski hollers after the Dude, "Your revolution is over, Mr. Lebowski. Condolences! The bums lost! . . . The bums will always lose! Do you hear me, Lebowski? The bums will always lose!"

Because the Dude cares nothing about power, he is generally at peace with the world around him, and because he cares nothing about awards or legacy, he is content even when no one takes notice of him. In fact, he seems to prefer being left alone. Overall, therefore, the Dude's attitude makes him much happier than the Big Lebowski, and often he prevails, even without putting up a fight. For instance, despite Lebowski's declaration of victory, it is the Dude who prevails. Leaving Lebowski behind, the Dude informs Brandt, "The old man told me to take any rug in the house," and he even has a servant carry the rug out for him.

"Smokey, this is not 'Nam. This is bowling. There are rules."

Of all the major characters in *The Big Lebowski*, only Walter Sobchak follows a philosophy that is not fundamentally individualistic. Instead, Walter defines himself in relation to larger groups: he is at once Jewish, American, a veteran, and part of a bowling team, and he finds his purpose in following each group's rules. For Walter, it is the rules themselves that determine right and wrong, and nothing else.

The philosophical term for rules- or duty-based morality is *deontological ethics.* The epitome of deontology is Immanuel Kant (1724–1804), who said, "If any action is to be morally good, it is not enough that it should *conform* to the moral law—it must also be done *for the sake of the moral law.*"[15] Like most Enlightenment philosophers, Kant believed that objective reality exists beyond individual human experience and that the human mind could apprehend this reality through reason alone. For Kant, objective reality included a universal "moral law," which applied to all people in all situations. Since this law could be discerned through reason, Kant argued that every rational person has a duty (or, as Kant called it, a "categorical imperative") to obey this moral law *for its own sake,* regardless of that individual's personal interests.[16]

According to the categorical imperative, an action is morally good only if everyone else should act the same way.[17] Suppose, for example, that you are tempted to break an oath. According to Kant, you can break an oath only if you want every person to break his or her oath as well. Clearly, this would be absurd, for if everyone broke their oaths, there would be no point in making oaths in the first place. Thus, breaking oaths is immoral, and by implication, if we make an oath, we are obligated to keep that oath *no matter what.*

With the categorical imperative in mind, many of Walter's outbursts start to make sense. During the league bowling tournament, Smokey (Jimmie Dale Gilmore), a member of the opposing team, knocks eight pins down, but Walter insists that since Smokey crossed the line, no score should be entered. As the situation escalates, Walter produces a gun from his bowling bag and declares, "[If] you mark that frame an eight, you're entering a world of pain." The other characters are dismayed at his fanaticism, but according to the categorical imperative, Walter cannot tolerate Smokey's transgression: if everyone crossed the line, it would be pointless to have a line at all. Granted, the line's distance from the pins is arbitrary, but it must be placed *somewhere,* and it must be respected. Otherwise, a bowler could stand as close to the pins as he or she wants.

This example and others that could be cited notwithstanding, Walter's sense of duty differs markedly from the categorical imperative. Rather than universal maxims, Walter follows specific rules that are, in most cases, simply a matter of convention.[18] Apparently, what these rules are about is irrelevant for Walter; all that matters is that the rules are rules. This raises a serious question: if the rules are not universal truths, and if Walter did not help write the rules, why is he so devoted to them?

Some examination of another deontological ethicist's views might be helpful here. The British philosopher John Locke (1632–1704), in his *Second Treatise of Government*, stated that rules express a "social contract" among members of a group. These rules, he continued, are necessary to keep the group stable. His reasoning began with humanity's "state of nature," a state characterized by perfect liberty and equality. Importantly, however, while people in their natural state have liberty, they do not have license to do whatever they will. The state of nature is governed by natural law, which humans can discern through reason. Among other things, people in the natural state have a duty to preserve themselves and, since all people are equal, to preserve others as well, whenever possible. Lastly, in the state of nature, each person has the right to punish those who harm another's life or property, in order to bring the wrongdoer to repentance, deter others from acting wrongly, and to rectify the injustice that the victim has suffered.[19] However, it is often difficult for one person to execute punishment, especially if the perpetrator is stronger than the victim. Thus, while life in the state of nature is free, one's rights are best defended with help from a society.

In order to enter into a society, Locke continues, each person must give up his or her right to enforce the natural law. When conflicts arise, each person's judgment is inevitably clouded by personal interest, so an impartial third party must adjudicate between disputing parties, and everyone must agree that this decision is final. To be fair and consistent, the group must also agree upon standards (that is, "rules" and "laws"), and *everyone* must agree to follow them.

Walter defines himself according to the groups to which he belongs, so it is not surprising that he would fervently defend their rules. However, because Walter belongs to multiple groups, problems arise when Walter must choose between conflicting rules. For instance, when Walter points a gun at Smokey, he is defending the rules of the game, but he is breaking the rules of society.

The Dude's attitude toward Walter reveals another critique of rules-based ethics. Each time Walter feels that a rule has been broken, he quickly erupts into fits of righteous indignation, spewing torrents of obscenities and terrifying everyone around him. Meanwhile, the Dude futilely attempts to calm Walter down. According to the Dude, rules-based ethics overestimates the law's contribution to social order. Allowing a minor transgression here and there will not destroy society. In fact, since forgiveness often prevents conflict, it can actually promote unity. Nevertheless, Walter always responds the same way: "Am I wrong? Am I wrong?" Realizing that Walter has the rules on his side, the Dude can only reply, "You're not wrong, Walter. You're just an asshole."

"Takin' 'er easy for us sinners"

Throughout *The Big Lebowski,* the Dude encounters several alternative philosophies, but as we have seen, the Dude abides in his dude-ism. This does not imply, however, that dude-ism is vindicated. To determine whether laziness is a virtue, at least according to *The Big Lebowski,* we must consider whether the Dude's philosophy is compatible with *The Big Lebowski's* overall message. To this end, it may help to review the tenets of dude-ism and evaluate them according to *The Big Lebowski's* plot.

Reality is inherently chaotic and purposeless. Like the tumbleweed that seems out of place as it rolls down the streets of Los Angeles, the Dude consistently finds himself in awkward situations, and, like the tumbleweed, there does not appear to be any reason *why* he should be there, though it is easy to see *how* he got there. The Dude is, after all, the wrong man for just about any job, yet each character attempts to use him.[20] Unlike most movies, which are predictable because of a clear sense of purpose, *The Big Lebowski* can be confusing and unpredictable. The action does not seem to work toward a particular goal. Instead, the action grows ever more complicated, and the Dude's situation grows increasingly dire as the film progresses.

One should expend effort only on simple, short-term goals. This tenet follows from the assumption that if life is chaotic, then one's efforts will only temporarily succeed; eventually, chaos will frustrate any person's attempts to determine his or her fate. *The Big Lebowski* clearly affirms this belief. As the plot unfolds, each character attempts to take advantage of Bunny's supposed abduction and the million-dollar ransom. Yet, for all their struggling, perhaps *because* of their efforts, things deteriorate. Granted, peace is restored by the end of the film, but only because Bunny gets bored and decides to return home.

One should accept life the way it is and be content, and *the purpose of life is to be as happy as possible in every situation.* The Stranger's wisdom, as he expresses it to the Dude, confirms these final tenets: "Sometimes you eat the bear. And sometimes the bear, well, he eats you." When the Dude sees the narrator again in the final scene, it is clear that he has taken this wisdom to heart:

STRANGER: How's things been goin'?
DUDE: Well, you know, strikes and gutters, ups and downs.

At this point in the film, the principled laziness that sustained the Dude throughout his trying ordeal continues to make him happy. Insofar as a "virtue" is a trait of the soul that provides happiness, *The Big Lebowski* concludes that laziness is indeed a virtue, and thus a lazy person is, oddly enough, righteous. Conversely, as the rest of the scene attests, work can be a vice, and those of us who work too hard are "sinners."

DUDE: . . . Well, take care, man. Gotta get back.
STRANGER: Sure. Take it easy, Dude. I know that you will.
DUDE: Yeah, well, the Dude abides.
STRANGER: The Dude abides. I don't know about you, but I take
    comfort in that. It's good knowin' he's out there—the Dude, takin'
    'er easy for all us sinners.

Of course, laziness is not truly virtuous just because a comedic film says so. Indeed, *The Big Lebowski* is humorous precisely because it departs so dramatically from real life. We would be remiss, therefore, to endorse laziness without considering its real-world implications. Not surprisingly, philosophers condemn laziness almost unanimously.[21] Aristotle, for example, wrote that virtues are traits of the soul, cultivated by habits of the body. In other words, to become a "good" person, one must work for it, consistently acting in a way that leads to happiness and fulfillment. However, according to Aristotle's own definition, a virtue is something that brings about happiness, and thus the true test of one's virtue should be one's overall happiness.[22] If a slacker is truly happy to work part-time menial jobs and relax for the rest of the day, then, arguably, laziness could be virtuous for that person.[23]

Kant would argue that laziness cannot be virtuous, for if everyone were lazy, very little would ever get done and our economy, which depends on labor, would soon collapse. However, dude-ism is a personal ethos, not a worldwide movement. Since most people want more than just bare necessities and simple diversions, our society is safe from the ills of universal laziness. According to dude-ism, if hard work makes one happy, then work is a virtue for that person, just as laziness is a virtue for a dude.

Ironically, this individualism is dude-ism's greatest flaw. Because dude-ism has little to say about how other people should act, it provides no objective standard for right and wrong behavior. As we have seen, the Dude evaluates particular actions according to pleasantness. This standard is acceptable in most situations, but it fails when confronted by true evil. When Walter ruins the ransom transaction, the Dude is convinced that Bunny is in grave danger. Certainly, Bunny's murder would be much worse than "unpleasant." Yet without an objective standard (such as God's will, or Kant's categorical imperative), it is difficult to see how dude-ism can say that murder (or rape, or slavery, etc.) is genuinely wrong. Granted, this flaw stems from dude-ism's assumption that life is purposeless, not from laziness itself. Since murder requires either meticulous planning or intense passion—both of which dude-ism flatly rejects—whether to murder or not should never be a problem for a dude-ist. However, making a decision over whether to struggle to prevent someone's murder is a serious problem. In the end, the Dude chooses to do what he can to save Bunny, but his decision probably has more to do with assuaging his conscience (since guilt is terribly unpleasant) than doing the right thing.

If a dude-ist can avoid such sticky moral dilemmas, laziness can have an aura of virtue. Furthermore, if dude-ism is correct about the nature of life and reality (and this is a very important if), then it seems like a plausible middle ground between nihilism, which arguably leads to suicide, and hedonism, which ultimately leads to addiction and desensitization. Suppose, on the other hand, that there is something external to us that provides purpose and meaning to life. For example, one might argue that natural selection has instilled in us a simple command: be fruitful and multiply. By implication, the purpose of our lives is to create future generations and to be the best parents we can so that our children have the best chance at success. Natural selection could also explain how we have developed inclinations toward friendship, cooperation, and so on: people who are likeable "team players" are more likely to survive. A problem with this notion is that natural selection is a blind, though complicated process, much like the wind that blows the tumbleweed. Likewise, since natural selection has no intention, it does not "want" us to survive any more than the wind "wants" the tumbleweed to roll through Los Angeles. In short, like the wind, it can explain *how* we inherited feelings like parental love and cooperation, but it cannot explain *why* or *if* the human race is worth perpetuating.

A more traditional philosophical move is to appeal to God to give meaning and purpose to life. If God exists (this, too, is a very important *if*), then our purpose would follow from God's purpose in creating us. If, for example,

God simply wants to watch us, then our purpose is nothing more than to be entertainers. If God simply wants us to be happy, we could live much like the Dude and find as much happiness as possible in whatever comes our way. On the other hand, if God has some purpose for us—being stewards of the earth, loving partners with God and others, working to manifest God's will, and so on—then laziness is unacceptable.

"Well, that about does 'er."

While *The Big Lebowski* suggests that laziness can bring happiness, a closer look at "quite possibly the laziest [man] in Los Angeles County" leads us to the ultimate questions: Is life *actually* purposeless and meaningless? And if so, is it up to each of us to find our own purpose? According to *The Big Lebowski*, we must answer "yes." Unless we can identify some objective or transcendent source of purpose or meaning, we may be hard pressed to disagree.

Notes

1. Friedrich Nietzsche, *The Gay Science*, trans. Walter Kauffman (New York: Vintage, 1974), 167.

2. Ibid., 181–82.

3. Friedrich Nietzsche, *The Genealogy of Morals*, trans. Francis Golffing, in *The Birth of Tragedy; and, The Genealogy of Morals* (New York: Anchor, 1990), 228–29.

4. Ibid., 210.

5. An inveterate rhetorician, Nietzsche was quite fond of his charge that Christianity is a disguised form of nihilism. In light of the will to power, it is easy to see why. Consider, for example, Matthew 5:5 (RSV), "Blessed are the meek, for they shall inherit the earth," and 2 Corinthians 11:30 and 12:9 (RSV), "If I must boast, I will boast of the things that show my weakness . . . for [God's] power is made perfect in weakness."

6. The notion of atoms, far from being a new idea in physics, was actually suggested in the fifth century BCE by another Greek philosopher, Democritus, who also coined the term *atom*, which literally means "not cuttable."

7. Information here about Aristippus' life and teaching is from W. K. C. Guthrie, *A History of Greek Philosophy*, vol. 3, *The Fifth Century Enlightenment* (Cambridge: Cambridge Univ. Press, 1969), 490–98. See also D. A. G. Fuller, *History of Greek Philosophy: The Sophists, Socrates, Plato* (Westport, Conn.: Greenwood Press, 1931), 115–36.

8. Socrates (470–399 BCE) is widely known as the founder of western philosophy. Much of what we know of Socrates comes from Plato, who portrays him as a passionate seeker of truth. While he does not appear to have made money as a philosopher, he was

quite influential in Athenian society—so influential, in fact, that he was sentenced to death for corrupting the youth of Athens.

9. One anecdote about Aristippus and Dionysius is particularly enjoyable, and runs something like this:

ARISTIPPUS: Good Sir Dionysius, I would like to borrow some of your money.
DIONYSIUS: But, Aristippus, you have said that a wise man will never be in need.
ARISTIPPUS: Good Sir, first give me some money, then we will talk about that.
(Dionysius hands him some money.)
ARISTIPPUS: You see, Good Sir, I am not in need!

10. Hundreds of years later, Jeremy Bentham said that a choice was moral if it brought about the most pleasure (in both amount and degree). Another utilitarian, John Stuart Mill, modified Bentham's hedonistic calculus, stating instead that a choice was moral if it brought about the greatest amount of *good* for the greatest number of people. Jeremy Bentham, *Principles of Morals and Legislation* (1780; Buffalo, N.Y.: Prometheus, 1988), chap. IV; John Stuart Mill, *Utilitarianism, Liberty, and Representative Government* (New York: Dutton, 1950), chap. I.

11. Of course, the Dude might be addicted to his White Russians and the drugs, but the film does not suggest this. In any case, even if he is addicted to drugs, these drugs only add to his laid-back demeanor. According to the film, at least, the drugs do not dominate his life in the way that sex dominates Bunny's life.

12. As it turns out, there are several proponents of egoism in popular culture. The most popular egoist is Ayn Rand, whose novels have inspired Reagan-era "big-business" conservatives. In all likelihood, the Big Lebowski's ethos is patterned after Rand's philosophy; however, since Nietzsche anticipated many of her ideas, and because Nietzsche is more influential in the field of philosophy, we will focus on his moral theory.

13. Nietzsche, *Genealogy of Morals,* 159–61. For further discussion of Nietzsche's concepts of master morality and egoism, see Robert C. Solomon, *Living with Nietzsche: What the Great "Immoralist" Has to Teach Us* (New York: Oxford Univ. Press, 2003), 44–47, 171–74.

14. Friedrich Nietzsche, *Beyond Good and Evil: Prelude to a Philosophy of the Future,* trans. Marion Faber (Oxford: Oxford Univ. Press, 1998), 157.

15. Immanuel Kant, *Groundwork of the Metaphysic of Morals,* trans. H. J. Paton (1785; New York: Harper & Row, 1953), 57–58.

16. Ibid., 68.

17. Ibid., 104–6.

18. Recall, for example, Walter's preference for the term "Asian American" over "Chinaman" as well as his reference to the "rules" of ransom situations.

19. John Locke, *Second Treatise of Government* (Indianapolis: Hackett, 1980), chap. II.

20. Interestingly, only Maude uses the Dude successfully. She recognizes that he is only good for easy, short-term tasks. With this in mind, she seduces the Dude in order to get pregnant, reassuring him that she does not want him to take any responsibility for the child once it is born.

21. One notable exception is Bertrand Russell, who wrote an essay called "In Praise of Idleness." In this essay, Russell wrote, "I want to say, in all seriousness, that a great deal of harm is being done in the modern world by belief in the virtuousness of work, and that the road to happiness and prosperity lies in an organized diminution of work." Bertrand Russell, "In Praise of Idleness," in *In Praise of Idleness, and Other Essays* (London: G. Allen & Unwin, 1935). Quotation from online version, http://www.zpub.com/notes/idle .html. However, for a number of reasons, we will not discuss the essay here. The first reason, aptly enough, is laziness. Second, Russell also wrote a mammoth work called *Principia Mathematica,* in which he attempted to unite the fields of mathematics and formal logic. Anyone who would undertake such a task, is, almost by definition, not lazy. Therefore, Russell was a hypocrite, and, to be shamelessly fallacious, we should simply ignore him. Third, "In Praise of Idleness" was more an attention-grabbing title than a serious philosophical statement. Russell was not endorsing laziness as such; he was advocating socialism over capitalism, which, in his opinion, places too much value in hard work and turns the working class into slaves. Another proponent of laziness is Jean-Jacques Rousseau, who late in his life expressed that he found joy in solitary idleness, which left him free "to muse all day long without order or coherence and follow in everything only the caprice of the moment." Rousseau, *The Reveries of the Solitary Walker,* trans. Charles E. Butterworth (Indianapolis: Hackett, 1992), 251.

22. Aristotle, *Nicomachean Ethics,* in *The Ethics of Aristotle: The Nichomachean Ethics Translated,* trans. J. A. K. Thomson (Baltimore: Penguin, 1955), 66–67.

23. It is doubtful that Aristotle would recognize the slacker as *truly* happy given his view that we are not truly happy unless we properly fulfill our nature.

No Country for Old Men
as Moral Philosophy

Douglas McFarland

Amid the eruptions of violence and carnage in their adaptation of Cormac McCarthy's *No Country for Old Men* (2007), the Coen brothers address fundamental questions concerning the place of duty, responsibility, necessity, and luck in human affairs. These questions are addressed in a rich and what one might call philosophical manner through a fictional narrative charting the interactions among three principal characters and their involvement in a drug deal gone murderously wrong. The film maintains an austere tone without references to popular culture and the self-conscious reimaginings of traditional genres that one normally associates with a Coen brothers film. Perhaps its salient formal characteristic is the absence, with one telling exception, of a musical soundtrack, creating a mood conducive to thoughtful and unornamented speculation in what is otherwise a fierce and destructive landscape.

Sheriff Bell and the Moral Imperative

The film opens with the voice-over narration of Ed Tom Bell (Tommy Lee Jones), who in 1980 is the sheriff of a west Texas county. His voice will appear throughout the film in reflective conversations, providing a point of reference and raising questions to which the film repeatedly turns. The voice that initially speaks to the audience is a weary one, concurrently expressing nostalgia for what has passed and dread of what lurks on the horizon. When he was younger, Bell felt pride in being part of a family of lawmen. In those days a sheriff did not need to wear a gun and would know everyone's phone number by heart. But now that world and its communal standards have collapsed. Sheriff Bell has lost the means to "measure" crime. Violent acts are inexplicable, defying reason and moral categories of assessment. He quite simply does not "know what [crime] is anymore." While he is able to understand how things happen, and this aids him in catching criminals ("my arrest, my testimony"), he has no categories for understanding why things happen. He has always been ready to die in the line of duty, but he no longer understands the basis of duty, the source and meaning of obligation. Before the opening narration ends, Bell goes one step further to declare, "I don't want to know. A man would have to put his soul at hazard . . . he would have to say, okay, I'll be part of this world." For the remainder of the film, Bell will be preoccupied with the boundary he has set between himself and the world, oscillating between reluctance and duty.

In terms of moral philosophy, we might say that Bell has found himself in a post-Kantian predicament. For Kant, ethical conduct is not based on a transcendent set of rules—Platonic, Christian, or otherwise—but rather on reason, which he believes is the essence of human nature. Kant identifies in his system of morality universal a priori laws based on rationality that provide a basis for judging human actions. As Kant puts it in *Groundwork for the Metaphysics of Morals,* "The law is the objective principle valid for every rational being, and the principle in accordance with which he ought to act, i.e., an imperative."[1] The obligations that are derived from the categorical imperative require the suspension of self-interest in favor of rational moral law. Moreover, and perhaps most importantly for Bell's situation, Kant makes a fundamental distinction between reason that can explicate a causal chain of events to show how things happen and reason that can judge why actions are taken by individuals. At the crime scene, the sheriff is able to sort through the evidence and establish a narrative of what has transpired. His deputy Wendell (Garret Dillahunt), in fact, compliments him for his "linear" thinking. But Bell self-deprecatingly responds, "Old age flattens a man." Bell cannot draw upon a set of moral categories to understand the carnage he encounters. It is not simply that individuals have violated an ethos, acted immorally, and broken a rule but that there are no boundaries of demarcation. Bell cannot apply the clarity of linear reconstruction to the "why" of human affairs. The miasma of the crime scene, littered with decomposing bodies, is something that he cannot "measure."

As I point out above, Bell is continually confronting the boundary between action and inaction. Hovering throughout the film is the temptation for him to retire, to insulate his soul in a protected enclave of home, overseen by his wife, Loretta (Tess Harper), and her seemingly unambiguous set of moral imperatives. As Bell is preparing to go to the scene of the crime, Loretta tells him, "Don't get hurt . . . don't hurt no one." These commands are expressed as generalized rules, apparently applicable to any situation. She imposes a sense of duty and obligation to a shared code of conduct. Bell confirms their universality by responding that he "always" does obey them, but there is another implied obligation that is a personal one. Loretta essentially asks him to promise that he will take care of himself. And this can be turned into something conditional, not universal: if you care about me, you won't get hurt. She forces him to weigh his duty to his job as an enforcer of the law against his duty to her as a husband. And subtly woven into this moment is another conditional: if you stay with me, you will be safe. As if she had heard his words to the audience earlier in the film, she tells him that here at home his soul will not be at risk. As the film progresses, Bell will discover himself to be ensnared in increasingly intricate and overlapping obligations.

The first of these occurs when Bell decides to go to Odessa to meet with Llewelyn's (Josh Brolin) wife, Carla Jean (Kelly Macdonald). After it has become clear to Bell that Llewelyn is in possession of the drug money and that at least two groups are trying to find him, he arranges to meet Carla Jean in the hope that she will tell him her husband's whereabouts. As he is leaving his office, he tells the secretary that "I think I'm goin' to commence dedicatin' myself twice daily" to "truth and justice." But in his conversation with Carla Jean his dedication to universal imperatives becomes something else. In his attempt to persuade Carla Jean to reveal Llewelyn's location, he promises, "I can make him safe." These words are the most significant Bell will utter in the film. They propel him across a threshold and he becomes "part of this world." His promise to Carla Jean rests on his ability to bring about a particular end. As Kant puts it rather succinctly, duty rests "in the principle of the will without regard for the ends that can be brought about by such an action."[2] In *High Noon* (Fred Zinnemann, 1952), Will Kane (Gary Cooper) decides that staying in town and confronting the tide of lawless revenge that is about to arrive is the right thing to do. His duty does not depend on the success or failure of his attempt; it is enough that he chooses to stay. Bell, however, links duty to a specific outcome and by so doing brings into play another set of categories: responsibility, intention, trust, and shame. The issue becomes not whether he is willing to sacrifice himself in the line of duty, as it is for Will Kane, but whether he can fulfill a promise to bring about a particular outcome. In some real sense, it is at this moment that he puts "his soul at risk." Once he makes this promise, there is no turning back.

Eventually Carla Jean reveals to Bell that Llewelyn is in El Paso. By the time Bell arrives, however, Llewelyn has already been killed. He fails, therefore, to keep his promise to Carla Jean. He becomes accountable for an outcome for which he is not directly responsible. It was his intention to make Llewelyn safe, and he set out to fulfill that obligation without doubt or hesitancy, but intention is overshadowed by outcome. To put it another way, he has fallen short of what he hoped and intended to accomplish. For Bell, shame and guilt now rear their heads. The moral imperative for Kant stipulates that one be freely willing to choose duty. The outcome does not undermine, threaten, or qualify that choice. But because Bell has made his promise dependent on what he had hoped to accomplish, and because that hope has not been fulfilled, he fails in fulfilling his duty. He has stepped out of Kant's system of categorization and made himself vulnerable in a way that Will Kane, who simply chooses to follow his duty, does not. As a result, when Bell faces Carla Jean, he feels ashamed. It is written in his face. Shame is a quality that defies rational and quantitative measurement. Moreover, as Bernard Williams has argued, shame does not simply reflect how one is seen by others but also how one sees oneself.[3] Bell has fallen short of his own expectation of himself. Near the end of the film he laments that God has ignored him in his old age and then adds that he expects he would do the same. His self-deprecation is genuine. In his eyes, he has tainted himself with his own failure, and thus his promise, contingent on his ability to enact an outcome, has put his soul as risk.

After viewing Llewelyn's body, Bell makes a decision to return to the crime scene. His reasons are not explicitly stated. He may feel a sense of obligation to the dead; earlier he had admonished a truck driver for not properly tying down the corpses that had been removed from the site of the massacre. But I believe that there is also the desire to bring about a quantifiably just conclusion and to establish, in Kantian terms, a means to restore "an intrinsically just conception of responsibility."[4] He wants, in short, to make an arrest. He knows there is someone out there apart from the Mexican drug dealers and that someone may be returning to the motel in order to gather evidence. But human motives are invariably complex. He needs not only to "measure" the crime but also to assuage his shame, as if apprehending Chigurh (Javier Bardem) could mitigate his failure in making Llewelyn safe.

When he arrives at the entrance to the motel room where Llewelyn was killed, he sees that the lock has been blown out and understands that Chigurh may be in the room. Bell is now confronted with the choice of crossing a literal threshold. He does decide to enter the room but does so in an unexpected manner. Throughout the film, the danger of entering such rooms and the necessary precautions are repeatedly shown. But rather than kicking the door open, holding himself out of sight, and then entering cautiously with gun drawn, Bell opens the door and pauses on the threshold. The camera looks up at him from inside the room, and we see him perfectly framed and back lit, offering a ridiculously easy target. Is this a gesture of sacrificial atonement? Is he momentarily addled? Perhaps it is more plausible to think that for a brief moment he does not care whether he lives or dies. It is ultimately not the tide of inexplicable evil that frightens him. He is simply weary of living with himself. Bell stands on the threshold of the room caught in a moment of utter vulnerability.

In the final scene of the film, Bell recounts two dreams he has had during the previous night. In each dream he has been infantilized and made vulnerable. The first dream is only briefly described but suggests a sense of shame in the eyes of his father. The second is longer and given in more detail. In it his father passes on horseback carrying with him into the darkness fire in a horn. He is telling this to Loretta, but at some point it takes on the quality of a soliloquy. You can read in his eyes that he believes there will be no fire in the darkness, that his father will not be waiting. It is too easy to say that west Texas in 1980 is no place for an old man. Bell's recognition is deeper and more disturbing than that.

Llewelyn and Moral Authenticity

If Bell struggles to maintain a set of normative values, Llewelyn Moss is searching for authenticity in the context of betrayal and moral hypocrisy. But unlike other so-called existential heroes, who attempt to create meaning in a meaningless world, Llewelyn remains entangled in ethical categories and will ultimately be judged according to those categories. The distinction between Abraham and the tragic hero made by Kierkegaard in *Fear and Trembling* is helpful. Kierkegaard argues that in choosing to obey God's command to sacrifice Isaac, Abraham suspends the ethical obligation he has toward his son. Once he has decided, therefore, to carry out God's will, he has "transgressed the ethical altogether and [has] a higher telos outside of it."[5] Maintaining an ethical standard, in short, is the temptation. As an example of the tragic hero, Kierkegaard offers, among others, Brutus, who as consul of Rome must order the execution of his two sons for their part in a conspiracy against the state. When he does have them put to death, he carries out his duty to Rome but violates, not suspends, his duty to his sons. He is tragic because he remains entangled in two horribly conflicting obligations. For the tragic hero, Kierkegaard concludes, "there can be no question of a teleological suspension of the ethical." Similarly, Llewelyn is unable to avoid the entanglements of a situation that has a "dialectic in its relation to the idea of moral conduct."[6] In his need to authenticate himself by asserting his freedom and autonomy, he overlooks the demands of ethical obligation.

As the film progresses it becomes clear that the trauma and betrayal of Vietnam hover over Llewelyn. He is first encountered taking aim with a long-range rifle on a herd of antelope in the dry and open landscape of west Texas. The position of his body and the routine he goes through suggests, however, something other than recreational hunting. He lies on his stomach, apparently keeping himself hidden from the herd, and carefully judges distance and wind speed in preparation for taking a shot. He has the appearance of a sniper and the aura of a military veteran. And, indeed, later in the film we learn that he had served two tours of duty twelve years earlier in Vietnam. His commitment to a collective national ethos has proven in the aftermath of the war to have been wasted. His sense of futility is figuratively reflected in his failure to hit the antelope. As he walks across the landscape, apparently in the general direction of the scattered herd, he seems aimless and without bearing.

Llewelyn, however, soon crosses the path of a wounded dog and is confronted with a choice. He decides to follow the blood trail back to what will later be called the "goat fuck." In McCarthy's novel the scene of carnage that Llewelyn discovers is explicitly compared to Vietnam by Bell's deputy: "It must of sounded like Vietnam out here."[7] Llewelyn has stepped into what remains of a firefight, a miasma of blood. And before he knows any of the reasons for the massacre, before he knows anything of drugs and money, and before Chigurh comes onto the scene, Llewelyn becomes part of this world. One senses that what hunting antelope has not provided, this spectacle of violence does. This Hobbesian nightmare quickly provides Llewelyn with purpose. This will never be about the money per se but about who controls the money. It will become his chance to hit the mark.

The contest, however, almost immediately shifts to a moral one. Llewelyn discovers a lone survivor who pleads for water. Llewelyn has no response other than to disarm him and to ask in which direction the last man standing went. That the dying man asks for water *"por Dios"* is conspicuously underscored by a crucifix hanging on the dashboard, a deeply ironic reminder of another context for the spilling of blood. Although Llewelyn steps into a cradle of violence in a bleak and indifferent landscape, he must confront almost immediately an obligation to a transcendent set of moral values, based not on an Enlightenment faith in reason but on a faith in the redemptive power of Christ's sacrifice. His cool indifference to human suffering casts a shadow over his need to authenticate himself in what he perceives to be a valueless world. At this moment, he seems to be contributing to the shortcomings of that world.

The audience's perception of Llewelyn as the existential loner, an understanding perhaps conditioned by literature and film, is contradicted once he returns home with the guns and money he has taken. It is almost as if he had stepped into another fictional space, another genre. After hiding the case of money in the bedroom, Llewelyn sits on the couch with Carla Jean, and they begin to banter flirtatiously back and forth. They generate an atmosphere of ease and familiarity. Llewelyn's role as a marginalized figure is qualified by his duty and obligation to another part of his life. Against her will and without her knowledge, Carla Jean has been drawn into the killing field that he has discovered in the barren landscape of west Texas. Whether he immediately recognizes it or not, Llewelyn's apparent compartmentalization of his identity now begins to break down. He has defiled his home and put his family at risk.

The film's insistent exploration of moral imperatives is taken up again in the ensuing scene. The camera is looking down on Llewelyn as he suddenly starts up out of sleep. The film cuts to the kitchen, where he is filling a gallon container with water. Carla Jean enters and asks him what he is doing. He replies, "I'm fixin' to do somethin' dumber 'an hell, but I'm goin' anyways." It is clear that he means to return to the scene of the killings with water for the survivor. Two aspects of his decision are important. First, he does not base it on self-interest. And secondly, it is not conditional on the outcome. It is not a question of "If I do not go, the Mexican will die," but rather, "If I do not go, I will not be able to live with myself." Like Will Kane, he puts himself at risk because of his duty to a set of values.

Llewelyn's decision making in the context of ethical choices is not finished. As Kierkegaard might put it, he is unable to suspend the ethical in order to assert his own set of meanings in a context that seems absurd. Moreover, in the end he will be judged through the perspective of the ethical. The first of these choices is made during his telephone conversation with Chigurh in the hospital. Chigurh tells him that he will not harm Carla Jean if he brings him the money. The offer carries with it the implicit understanding that Llewelyn will be killed. There is nothing to be done about that, but Llewelyn does have the choice of saving his wife. If he doesn't comply, Chigurh promises that he will kill Carla Jean, regardless of recovering the money. It will, in fact, be his duty to do so. Llewelyn chooses to have his cake and eat it too. He will keep the money, but he will take steps to protect Carla Jean. His critical error is to link his need to authenticate himself with a particular moral obligation.

Llewelyn fails on both counts. He and Carla Jean will both die. Along with Bell, the film audience first sees the Mexicans frenetically fleeing the crime scene and then the body of Llewelyn sprawled on the threshold of a motel room. Here, the filmmakers have significantly departed from the novel by deleting a lengthy exchange between Llewelyn and a girl he has picked up hitchhiking. He recognizes her naïveté and her vulnerability and gives her money so she can make her way to California without hitchhiking. Although she offers herself to him several times, he is never tempted, maintaining an almost parental relationship to her. The most telling difference comes in the shoot-out in which Llewelyn and the girl are killed. In the novel, the reader is told that one of the Mexicans grabs the girl by the hair, points his gun at her head, and tells Llewelyn that he will kill her if he does not lay his weapon down. He does put down his gun, and immediately the Mexican shoots the girl and then turns and shoots Llewelyn. Surely he knows he cannot save the girl regardless of what he might do with his weapon. And surely he knows that he will die if he does put it down. His act becomes a gesture of impotent responsibility; it will have no effect in preventing the death of either himself or the girl. Although the drug dealer sets a conditional ("If you put down the gun, I will not kill the girl"), Llewelyn acts knowing there is really no conditional at all. He knows that no matter what he does, she will die. He does not sacrifice himself to save another life. He acts purely out of duty. A moral imperative orders him to do this. It is the defining moment in the novel for Llewelyn.

The filmmakers have chosen to alter this scene significantly in their adaptation. The sixteen-year-old hitchhiker becomes an older woman (Ana

Reeder) who is sunbathing and having a beer alongside the pool of a two-star motel. She is clearly experienced in picking up men. The scene is shot in harsh light, giving it a hard and glaring look. When she first begins to flirt with Llewelyn, he tells her that he is married and lifts up his hand to show her his wedding ring. She persists, telling him he can stay married and that beer only leads to more beer. Llewelyn looks up with a half smile on his face, and at that moment the camera pans up into the sky, and the light fades to a blur. The film immediately cuts to a point-of-view shot of Bell's arrival on the scene. Like the novel, the deaths of Llewelyn and the woman are reported to Bell. Unlike the book, however, the film shows nothing of Llewelyn's gesture, and the audience is left to surmise what transpired between the woman and Llewelyn in that missing interval. Although the location of the bodies suggests that nothing did follow the beers, there is the impression that at the very least Llewelyn has let down his guard. When one considers what is at stake—the life of Carla Jean—it is difficult not to recognize some degree of a moral failing. In an earlier scene in which Llewelyn calls Carla Jean to tell her to meet him in El Paso, as he is speaking to her, he turns his head to follow a woman almost as if he were involuntarily distracted. The filmmakers have deliberately chosen, at the very least, to suggest that Llewelyn has compromised himself, that his need for authenticity, his need not to back down, is entangled with his own shortcomings. Llewelyn exits the film as he entered. He takes aims and then misses his mark.[8]

The Philosopher Who Fell to Earth

In an interview published in the *New York Times* upon the release of *No Country for Old Men,* Joel Coen describes his conception of Chigurh: "He's like the man who fell to earth. . . . He's the thing that doesn't grow out of the landscape."[9] This rings true as far as it goes. Chigurh does seem to be some alien menace who operates outside categories of human understanding, certainly ethical categories. And although he bleeds and his bones can be broken, he exudes a certain physical invulnerability. He is almost robotic in his single-minded focus on completing his agenda. There is also something perversely alien in his choice of weaponry: a device for slaughtering cattle that resembles a portable oxygen tank. The characters within the film have a frustrating time pinning him down. At various times he is called a "psychopathic killer," a "homicidal lunatic," and a "ghost." It is said that he "lacks a sense of humor" and is a "man of principle." He eludes clinical and ethical categories of human understanding. But more importantly, in a series of dialogues with other characters, Chigurh raises fundamental philosophical questions concerning choice, necessity, chance, and justice in human affairs.

The proprietor of a gas station where Chigurh stops asks a simple, offhanded question concerning the weather in Dallas. He has noticed the license plate of Chigurh's car and is completely unaware that it has been stolen. It almost immediately becomes clear that Chigurh means to kill the proprietor over what he thinks is meddling. Their encounter offers a quick lesson in the violent contingencies of modern life. A chance remark can change one's life forever. After instilling terror in the heart of the proprietor, Chigurh shifts his focus. He flips a coin and asks his would-be victim to call it, clearly meaning that if the proprietor wins the coin toss, Chigurh will spare him. Chigurh has almost sadistically transferred responsibility from himself to chance. In an instant he has created a world with its own arbitrary and simple rules that exclude ethical categories. The proprietor pulls back in disbelief and refuses to make his life dependent on the flip of a coin. If he is to save his life, he must abandon the world he knows and enter a space that, if not absurd, is at least arbitrary. If he is to live at all, it will be at the behest of luck. Categories of justice and assumptions of responsibility cease to have meaning. But of course, he has no choice but to call the coin flip. It's his only chance. After the proprietor has won the toss, Chigurh mystifies the coin. He tells the proprietor that he must keep it separate from other coins and that he and the coin were destined to meet at this crossroads. The coin is, in short, his talisman. As Chigurh leaves, however, he pauses at the door, cocks his head back, and with a wry and mischievous curl to his lip, takes it all back. The coin could be special, but then again it may be just a coin. The gesture belies the notion that Chigurh has no sense of humor. In a masterful manner and in the space of a few minutes Chigurh has shattered complacency, dispatched categories of ethical and religious belief, and catapulted the proprietor into a realm of contingent circumstances, random eruptions of violence, the dehumanized face of chance, the grim necessity of luck, and the quirkiness and perversity of life. It is a sudden and succinct tutorial in that world which Bell fears will put his "soul at risk."

In Chigurh's encounter with Carson Wells (Woody Harrelson), different questions are raised. Wells understands that Chigurh now means to kill him, and he argues, "We don't have to do this." Wells means, of course, that Chigurh can have the money without killing him. But there is the more subtle point that Chigurh is under no mandate, that he is free to act in any way that he desires. Wells does not raise moral concerns by asserting that it would be unjust to kill him. Perhaps he recognizes that there would be some justice in it since Wells has himself been paid to hunt down Chigurh. Chigurh then suddenly asks a question that initially feels inappropriate. He says to Wells in an almost pensive manner, "What good is a rule, if it got you here?" The question explicitly addresses the value and purpose of codes of conduct and ties them directly to "good" outcomes. That "good" would seem to be based on self-interest. It is, of course, a direct refutation of Kant's understanding of the unconditional moral imperative. Although the question is addressed to Wells, it speaks also to Chigurh's decision to kill Wells. He implicitly dismisses ethical considerations in his decision. He also suggests a criterion based on simple assessment of what can be gained in choosing one way or another. By doing so, he creates a necessity based not on ethical obligations but on pragmatic ones. He will kill Carson Wells because it is necessary. It is in his self-interest to do so. His position is eerily similar to that of the Athenians when they ask the Melians to tell them why they should not be destroyed. When the Melians claim that the Athenians have unfairly required them to "speak of expediency apart from justice," the Athenians respond that justice is never an issue unless the two sides are equal in power.[10] It is the same cool and perverse rationality that informs Chigurh's relationship to Wells.

The final dialogue takes place between Chigurh and Carla Jean. She finds herself in the same bind as the gas station proprietor, having the chance to save her life by calling the flip of a coin. Before that offer is made, she tells Chigurh what Carson Wells had told him: "You don't have to do this." Chigurh perversely responds that he must fulfill a promise that he has made to Llewelyn: if Llewelyn did not give himself up, he would kill Carla Jean. He has hunted down Carla Jean to make good on his promise. Chigurh has perversely taken us back to Kant's ethical system. A promise must be kept, Kant argues in the *Groundwork*, for no other reason than that it is a promise. It is kept out of duty, and so it is Chigurh's duty to kill Carla Jean. He is obliged to her husband; it is necessary that he do this. Chigurh is being deeply ironic and in so doing problematizes human categories of morality based on a priori imperatives. He mischievously contradicts his earlier understanding of obligation based on self-interest and instead suggests that his obligation is to keep a promise no matter what the outcome. In this instance, Chigurh is less a man of principle, as Wells describes him to Llewelyn, than a man of irony. He seems to have dropped out of the sky, with the purpose not to espouse a philosophical position but to bedevil human attempts to construct their own philosophical models.

After this exchange, Chigurh does give her the chance to call the coin flip. Unlike the gas station proprietor, however, Carla Jean ultimately refuses to do so. Her decision is one of the most significant moments in the film. As he did earlier, Chigurh not only provides her with a chance to live but also relinquishes responsibility for his act. Carla Jean, however, recognizes what is at stake and refuses to participate in his game. She will not give her life over to chance and insists that the responsibility for her death lies with Chigurh, not the coin. She forces him to make the choice. In so doing she restores moral judgments to the situation. She will not, in short, speak of "expediency apart from justice." She defies the irrational flip of a coin and retains her integrity. She hurls Chigurh's ironic perversity back into his face: "I knew you was crazy." Although Carla Jean is neither an existential nor a tragic hero, she is, nevertheless, heroic in her unwillingness to abandon the human need to construe the world in moral terms.

Coda

Minutes after leaving Carla Jean's house, Chigurh has his own bad luck. A driver runs a red light and smashes into the side of Chigurh's car. Ironically, Chigurh has been following a basic rule of interaction: stop on the red, go on the green. Issues of responsibility, intention, accident, and chance converge at the intersection. Perhaps later Chigurh will ponder the implications of the collision, but for now he does what he needs to do in order to survive and go on to the next task. The accident suggests that justice may eventually assert itself into human affairs. During the time Chigurh has been tormenting Carla Jean, this accident was waiting to happen. One might wryly ask him, "What good is a rule, if it got you here?" But as I said, he does not contemplate the philosophical implications of the moment. He seems to be philosophical only when he interrogates others. It is ultimately left to human beings to struggle with the moral and ethical complexities of their condition. And it is that struggle the filmmakers have chosen to explore in *No Country for Old Men*.

Notes

1. Immanuel Kant, *Groundwork for the Metaphysics of Morals,* trans. Mary Jane Gregor (1785; Cambridge: Cambridge Univ. Press, 1996), 73.

2. Ibid., 4:400.

3. Bernard Williams, *Shame and Necessity* (Berkeley and Los Angeles: Univ. of California Press, 1993), 102.

4. Ibid., 95.

5. Søren Kierkegaard, *Fear and Trembling,* trans. Howard V. Hong and Edna H. Hong (Princeton, N.J.: Princeton Univ. Press, 1983), 59.

6. Ibid.

7. Cormac McCarthy, *No Country for Old Men* (New York: Vintage, 2005), 75.

8. The word that Aristotle uses in *The Poetics* to describe the flaw of the tragic hero is *hamartia,* which literally means "to miss the mark."

9. Quoted in Lynn Hirschberg, "Coen Brothers Country," *New York Times Magazine,* 11 November 2007.

10. Thucydides, *The Peloponnesian War,* trans. Steven Lattimore (Indianapolis: Hackett, 1998), 295.

Part 3

POSTMODERNITY, INTERPRETATION, AND THE CONSTRUCTION OF HISTORY

HEIDEGGER AND THE PROBLEM OF INTERPRETATION IN *BARTON FINK*

Mark T. Conard

> In interpreting, we do not, so to speak, throw a "signification" over some naked thing which is present-at-hand, we do not stick a value on it; but when something within-the-world is encountered as such, the thing in question already has an involvement which is disclosed in our understanding of the world, and this involvement is one which gets laid out by the interpretation.
>
> —Martin Heidegger, *Being and Time*

> Contrary to present tendencies to think of the reading of texts as the paradigm case of interpretation, Heidegger's paradigm cases are everyday activities like opening a door or hammering.
>
> —David Couzens Hoy, "Heidegger and the Hermeneutic Turn," in *The Cambridge Companion to Heidegger*

The Coen brothers' *Barton Fink* (1991) is the story of a New York playwright who desires to create a new, living theater about and for the common man and who sees it as his job "to make a difference." The year is 1941, and upon the success of his (presumably) first produced play, Fink (John Turturro) is lured into a Faustian bargain to go to Hollywood and write for the movies. Upon arriving in Los Angeles, however, and despite his newly formed friendship with his next-door neighbor and common man Charlie Meadows (John Goodman), and despite counsel from another writer, W. P. Mayhew (John Mahoney), whom Fink considers to be the "finest novelist" of their generation, Fink finds himself blocked up on the B wrestling picture he's supposed to be scripting.[1] The situation goes from bad to utterly bizarre as events unfold: Mayhew's secretary and lover, Audrey Taylor (Judy Davis), turns out to have authored the great writer's books; in attempting to be Fink's muse, Audrey seduces him and then ends up dead in his hotel room; Charlie helps Barton dispose of Audrey's corpse; supposed common man Charlie turns out to be a homicidal maniac who may have murdered Audrey; and Charlie entrusts Barton with a box that may very well contain Audrey's head. Despite, or more likely because of, these events, Fink overcomes his block and is able to write his wrestling picture, which ends up sounding an awful lot like his New York play. As Fink's descent into hell is complete, the hotel where he is staying bursts into flames, and Charlie shotguns to death the police detectives who are investigating Audrey's murder. Barton escapes the inferno as Charlie disappears back into his flaming room. In the closing scenes, Barton enters another sort of purgatory as the head of the movie studio refuses to release him from his contract and thus retains the rights to all of Barton's writing. Finally, Barton winds up on a sunny beach and becomes a part of the picture that throughout the movie has decorated the wall of his hotel room.

The movie is clearly about the nature of creativity and art, the deceiving nature of appearances, compromises in the creative process, and the problem of an artist who is cut off from reality while he is attempting to create. But there is much about the film that seems to resist interpretation.[2] What's the significance or meaning of the box that may contain Audrey's head? Or of the picture of the girl staring at the ocean that becomes real at the end of the movie? Or of the emphasis on shoes (feet, and other body parts) in the narrative? Or of the mosquitoes that seem to plague Barton? In this essay, I use the film as a springboard into a discussion of Heidegger's theory of interpretation. I then use that theory to shed some light on these puzzling elements of the movie.

A Day or a Lifetime

Certain elements and themes of the film are clear. As I note, the movie is about creativity and the relationship between art and life. Indeed, it is a jab at artists and intellectuals who remove themselves from real life. Barton is supposedly writing about the common man, but any time Charlie—a common man himself, at least as far as Barton knows—tries to tell him about the life of the working stiff, Barton refuses to listen. When Charlie attempts to relate to Barton some experience or other he's had, he begins with "I could tell you some stories," and Barton always cuts him off. Consequently, alienated from his supposed subject, Barton really only has one story to tell: the B wrestling picture he writes seems to be exactly the same narrative as his Broadway play. (We don't know the details of the story, but both the movie script and the play are set on the Lower East Side of Manhattan, both at least mention fishmongers, and both end with the line: "We'll be hearing from that kid, and I don't mean a postcard.")

Further, *Barton Fink* is clearly a Faustian tale. Barton makes his deal with the devil (he sells his soul in agreeing to go to Hollywood and write for the movies) and ultimately descends into hell. There are clues to this descent in the Hotel Earle, where Barton is residing. Recall, for example, that the motto of the hotel is "A day or a lifetime," a reference to eternity. When Barton first enters the hotel, he rings for the attendant, and the bell seems to chime on forever. Only when Chet (Steve Buscemi), the desk clerk, emerges out of the floor like some imp or demon from the underworld and lays a finger on the bell does it stop ringing. The hotel's elevator operator (the only other person we see inside the hotel) is named Pete (Harry Bugin), a probable reference to St. Peter, and Barton's room is on the sixth floor, perhaps a reference to the number of the beast. Of course the conflagration in the hotel at the end of the movie is confirmation that Barton has reached the fiery depths of the underworld.

To get a little more philosophical, the movie also seems to be a fuzzy sort of meditation on the relationship between mind and body. Note that there are several references to the mind and many references to the body. First, Barton says he lives the life of the mind, and at the end of the film, in the inferno, Charlie shouts, "I'll show you the life of the mind!" In addition, as an insurance salesman, Charlie says that he sells "peace of mind." It's also pretty clear that Barton's hotel room resembles the inside of a skull, with the two windows acting as eye sockets, and so it's likely that we're to think that we're inside Barton's head (or mind). There seems to be an ambiguity in this metaphor, however. Recall that Charlie's ear leaks pus, and this clearly echoes the wallpaper glue that melts in the heat in Barton's room. So, are we inside Barton's head or inside Charlie's head?[3] Or is Charlie a figment of Barton's imagination? These seem to be further issues that resist interpretation.

There are also, as I mentioned, lots of references to the body. These include references to feet and shoes. Shoes line the hallways of the hotel, waiting to be shined; the studio head, Lipnick (Michael Lerner), kisses

Barton's foot; and Barton realizes that he's been given Charlie's shoes when he tries them on and they're much too large for his feet (clearly meaning that Charlie's shoes are too big for Barton to fill). In addition, there are a number of references to the head. Charlie claims a few times that "things are all balled up at the head office." Remember that the serial killer decapitates the bodies and that we suspect it's Audrey's head in the box Charlie leaves with Barton. When Charlie mentions his ear infection, he says that "you can't trade your head in for a new one." Charlie misquotes a cliché when he says, "Where there's a head, there's hope," and Barton corrects him: "Where there's *life,* there's hope." The cops say that Madman Mundt (Charlie's real identity) is a little funny in the head. In other mentions of the body, at the beginning of the film, Barton claims that a writer's gut tells him what's good, and when Barton talks about the phoniness of the theater, Charlie says, "I can feel my butt getting sore already."

The Life of the Mind

At this point it would be helpful to discuss René Descartes and Cartesian dualism, the idea that the mind and the body are two different substances, since, as we'll see below, Descartes will make a nice foil for Heidegger.

With his famous "I think, therefore I am," Descartes revolutionizes philosophy insofar as he institutes what's known as the "subjective turn." This is not "subjective" in the negative sense that we use it, meaning just a matter of opinion (as opposed to being objective and valid). Rather, it refers to the subject of thought or perception (*I* who am thinking or perceiving, as opposed to the *object* being perceived). In other words, Descartes in a radical way brings the subject into the picture. Prior to Descartes it was possible to do metaphysics and talk about the world and the nature of reality without talking about the knower or the perceiver who's grasping the world. After Descartes and his revolution, that's no longer possible. Now we have to take the subject into account and discuss how it is that we know, perceive, and understand the world that we're talking about.

Descartes constructs his metaphysics as you would a mathematical system, by starting with one necessarily true axiom and then deducing everything else he knows from that one principle. But how do you find that one truth, the one axiom that's beyond all doubt? Descartes does it by postulating, for the sake of the argument, an "evil genius," a being who's all-knowing and all-powerful (like God) but who's malicious and whose sole intention is to deceive Descartes about everything. The genius can implant perceptions, thoughts, beliefs, emotions, and memories directly into his mind. Thus, Descartes's entire life, everything he thinks he knows about the world, could be a fiction.

Given the thesis of the evil genius, Descartes's skepticism is so radical that he claims he can even doubt the existence of his own body (as part of the physical world). But now we get to the ultimate skeptical question: is it possible that he, Descartes, too, doesn't exist? Could the evil genius make him believe he exists when he really doesn't? And the answer is no. Descartes can doubt his existence, but he must exist in order to do the doubting and thus, "I think, therefore I am." Doubting is an act of thinking, and for thinking to be going on, there must be a thinker. This is Descartes's one indubitable axiom (from which he intends to deduce everything else he knows about reality). Now, what he concludes from this is that, because he can doubt the existence of his body but not the existence of his mind, he is essentially his mind. I *am* a mind, says Descartes; I *have* a body.

From this Descartes further concludes that mind and matter (the body is material or physical) are radically different substances (types of stuff). The body is material and takes up space, for example; the mind is immaterial and doesn't take up space (thoughts and ideas have no physical or spatial dimensions). This is what's known as Cartesian dualism. Further, this substance dualism (the idea that the universe is made up of two radically different kinds of stuff) leads ultimately to what's called the mind/body problem, the question of how the mind and body interact, if they're of such radically different natures. If the mind is immaterial and has no physical dimension, then it has no physical location either: it can't *be* anywhere in the sense of being located in space. Consequently, it's difficult to see how the mind could interact with any part of the body, since it can't physically be there in the presence of that part. Descartes didn't have a satisfactory solution to this problem. Further, substance dualism also leads to the problem of other minds. That is, I have direct and immediate access to my own mind and my own thoughts, but I have no such access to yours. I directly perceive your physical body, but I can't think your thoughts. So how do I know that you even have a mind? How can I be certain that there are in fact other minds, that mine is not the only one in existence?

So Descartes's revolutionary beginning seems to turn us into atomistic, detached mental substances, unsure of whether we're all alone in the universe. Indeed, this seems to be the situation in which Barton finds himself. Living "the life of the mind," an artist and an intellectual cut off from reality, Barton lives inside his head, symbolized by his hotel room. His isolation is so complete, in fact, that there are no other guests at the hotel (besides Charlie, who, as I note, may just be a figment of Barton's imagination).[4] As we'll see below, this is quite important for my Heideggerian interpretation of the film.

The Dream and Its Interpretation

As I note above, what we're interested in here is an interpretation of the film or at least of those puzzling elements of the film that I mention. The branch of philosophy explicitly concerned with the theory of interpretation is known as hermeneutics, which originally referred specifically to the interpretation of scriptural texts but which is now used in philosophy to refer to the interpretation of any text whatever. Now, the fact that I'm talking about hermeneutics and interpretation may suggest that I've drifted far from *Barton Fink*; however, there's a suggestion in the film that this is not at all so. First, recall that Mayhew presents Barton with a signed copy of one of his novels, which is entitled *Nebuchadnezzar*. Subsequently, in his hotel room, Barton opens the Bible to a passage in the Book of Daniel, "Nebuchadnezzar's Dream." The passage reads:

> In the second year of Nebuchadnezzar's reign, Nebuchadnezzar dreamed such dreams that his spirit was troubled and his sleep left him. So the king commanded that the magicians, the enchanters, the sorcerers, and the Chaldeans be summoned to tell the king his dreams. When they came in and stood before the king, he said to them, "I have had such a dream that my spirit is troubled by the desire to understand it." The Chaldeans said to the king [in Aramaic], "O king, live forever! Tell your servants the dream, and we will reveal the interpretation." The king answered the Chaldeans, "This is a public decree: if you do not tell me both the dream and its interpretation, you shall be torn limb from limb, and your houses shall be laid in ruins. But if you do tell me the dream and its interpretation, you shall receive from me gifts and rewards and great honor. Therefore tell me the dream and its interpretation."[5]

The dream is told and interpreted correctly by Daniel and concerns the fate of the kingdom and several kingdoms that will follow it.

Barton subsequently turns to the first lines of Genesis, and (at least in his imagination) they have been transformed into the beginning of Barton's story: "Fade in on the Lower East Side," and so forth. This seems to be further evidence of what I note above: because Barton is cut off from real life, he has only one story to tell. An artist is supposed to draw inspiration from real experience, and because Barton is living in his head and is alienated from that real experience, he has no inspiration or motivation and thus can conceive of no other story (the biblical story turns into his story).

The fact that the Coens reference this passage in Daniel, with its focus on dreams and interpretation, could be a hint that much of the film is actually a dream of Barton's.[6] This is certainly an interpretive possibility and one way to read the film (I'd suggest, if one were to go in this direction, that everything after the first shot of California, the waves of the Pacific crashing against a rock, should be read as the dream). This would certainly solve all the questions and problems about the film, since in our dreams nothing has to make sense.[7] The head in the box, the photo that becomes reality, the hotel that spontaneously bursts into flames—all of this might just be the illogic of a dream world.[8] On the other hand, the fact that the Coens make reference to this biblical story could be a clue (likely with a definite wink) that they're aware of the difficulties of interpreting the movie. In any event, this scene in the film at least hints that we're not too far afield in discussing theories of interpretation.

The Metaphysics of Presence

Before discussing Heidegger's radical take on interpretation, it would be helpful to describe briefly what it is that he's arguing against, what he calls "the metaphysics of presence." Most of us tend (unreflectively) to believe that the beginning of philosophy and of science is when someone takes a look at the world, or things in the world, from an objective, theoretical viewpoint. That is, the philosopher or scientist becomes disengaged from practical concerns and from his or her own subjective interests and examines something objectively; only in doing so does he or she *really* understand that thing, and only then does he or she *get it right*.

This way of thinking goes back at least to Aristotle, who claims that the real is the actual. That is, if you want to know what's real, what reality is, the answer, according to Aristotle, is: what's real is what's actually existing *here* and *now*. In other words, traditional metaphysics takes the world to be an aggregate of objects that are *present,* both in the sense that they are really existing now in the temporal present and in the sense that they are spatially present here before us. Hence, the metaphysics of *presence.* History (and thus reality) is a series of "nows": the past is gone forever, and the future doesn't yet exist.

In addition to a physical object present in the here and now, there is, set over and against it, the subject who knows and perceives that object. As we see above, Descartes is an important proponent of the metaphysics of presence. He divides the universe into two substances: the material and the mental. We are isolated, individual mental substances separate from each other and from the physical objects that surround us. Again, this is the position in which Barton finds himself: living in his room at the Hotel Earle is symbolic of his retreat into his own mind and his alienation from others and indeed from reality itself.

Now, note importantly that if we conceive of the reality of things in this "objective" fashion, and we're committed to the scientist's picture of the world, then things are really just brute collections of atoms and molecules and thus they can have no meaning or sense in and of themselves. A hammer, a typewriter, a great work of literature—these are all simply clusters of atoms, which are themselves mostly empty space (so the physicist tells us). Thus the only meaning these things could possibly have is that which we, as mental subjects, foist upon them. In other words, in this view, meaning in the world is only a subjective, mental construct. The world in and of itself, and things within the world, are inherently without meaning and sense.

Heidegger completely rejects this traditional view of human subjects and their relationship to the world. He argues that the metaphysics of presence is derivative of a more fundamental way to understand human nature and the universe in which we find ourselves.

Dasein

Part of the difficulty Heidegger faces in laying out his understanding of human nature is that we've become so accustomed to thinking of ourselves, and talking about ourselves, in the traditional way that it's difficult to conceive of ourselves in any other fashion. Consequently, Heidegger believed he needed to coin new words and create new expressions in order to discuss his revolutionary way of thinking. To designate human beings, then, he uses the term *Dasein,* which is the ordinary German word for "being."

One of the fundamental characteristics of Dasein, according to Heidegger, is that it is constituted by potentiality. That is, as opposed to objects like tables and chairs that have fixed natures or essences, human beings do not have a determinate essence or nature.[9] We are our own possibilities. What's definitive of Barton is not that he is a writer, a friend, happy, or sad. No one is a writer or is joyful in the way that a table is a table (Barton could certainly take on another profession if he wished, and his moods change from moment to moment). What's definitive of him as a human being is rather that he *can* be these things and many more besides. Thus Heidegger completely rejects the idea that the real is the actual. At least for human beings, potentiality is more fundamental than actuality. We *are* what we *can be.*

What's more, Heidegger further rejects the metaphysics of presence by arguing that the other two temporal dimensions, past and future, far from being nonexistent (as the tradition would have it), are in fact constitutive of the being of Dasein. That is to say, in no way is it the case that everything that's present here and now, in this spot and in this moment, is definitive of who and what I am. My past is an essential part of me; it defines and limits me in certain important ways, and thus I am my past.[10] My decision to go to grad school and study philosophy, for example, and my decision to become a college professor provide the context in which my current decisions and actions make sense. I teach and write about Heidegger in a university setting in order to make a living, for example, rather than write movie scripts, wrestle big men in tights, or run a movie studio. Further, my future is also a part of me; it makes sense out of my present. I am always projected out into the future. I'm working toward finishing this essay, anticipating meeting a friend later for lunch, and thinking about what I have to do to prepare for the beginning of the fall semester, and so on. These projections give sense and meaning to the present and to my actions and decisions in the present (I have to read a few pages of Heidegger, go to the ATM to get cash, and revise my syllabi, for instance). Thus I am also my future.[11] "We shall point to temporality as the meaning of the Being of that entity which we call 'Dasein,'" says Heidegger.[12]

"A Tourist with a Typewriter"

In addition to the new conception of human beings outlined above, Heidegger also has a novel understanding of nonhuman things in the world, which he refers to as "equipment." As I said, he claims that this understanding is more primordial than the theoretical or "objective" view of those things. Rather than being at bottom clusters of atoms, things in the world *are* what they do, what they're used for. Heidegger's favorite example is the workshop and the tools within the workshop. The hammer that the carpenter uses just *is* its function of hammering. To be more explicit, in Heidegger's view, the workshop is a meaning-filled context, and the equipment's very existence is constituted by the role that it plays within that workshop in fulfilling some project or another: building a bookshelf, a table, or a chair, for example. When you look around the workshop at the equipment, you don't see pieces of wood and metal, much less collections of atoms and molecules. What you see are hammers, screwdrivers, and saws, which are *for* hammering nails, screwing in screws, and cutting wood, *in order to* build a bookshelf.[13] The tool or piece of equipment is its own meaning (what it is for) and nothing more, and again it takes this meaning from the context of the workshop. Thus meaning is not something subjective that we arbitrarily foist upon some brute, meaningless object. It is already a part of the world and a part of the equipment within the world.

Given the nature or essence of equipment, then, our most primordial "understanding" of things is when we use them in our normal, everyday activities. The carpenter understands the hammer best when he uses it fluidly to pound nails, without thinking about it. This mode of the hammer is what Heidegger calls "ready-to-hand."[14] A thing is ready-to-hand when we use it expertly to fulfill our projects: I use the pen to take notes on Heidegger to write this essay, I use the doorknob to enter the next room to retrieve a book that I need, and so forth. This is obviously a much different sense of "understanding" than we're used to. It's a noncognitive, or precognitive, sense of that term. We're not even explicitly aware of the tool when it's ready-to-hand. We're rather aware of the task we're trying to complete, and the equipment in a sense disappears (I'm not explicitly aware of the pen as I'm taking notes). However, again, Heidegger argues that this is a more primordial or fundamental understanding of the thing than the so-called scientific, theoretical, or objective view of it.

Now, says Heidegger, we become aware of the real existence and nature of equipment when things go wrong in a certain way. That is, for example, I'm in the midst of taking notes on Heidegger to write this essay and my pen runs out of ink. The work comes to a halt, and I suddenly become explicitly aware of the pen, and its role in my project and plans, for the first time. I perceive its character *as* equipment. In this mode, the tool is what Heidegger calls "unready-to-hand."

There's a nice example of this contrast between the ready-to-hand and the unready-to-hand in *Barton Fink*. Note that Barton and Ben Geisler's (Tony Shalhoub) secretary have different relationships to their respective typewriters. We see the secretary (Gayle Vance) expertly typing letters for her boss. She's not explicitly aware of the machine itself; she's focused on the task she's been given. For her, the machine is ready-to-hand. Barton, on the other hand, is blocked on his wrestling picture, and so we see him sitting passively and staring at the typewriter. In this case, there's nothing wrong with the machine itself—it hasn't run out of ribbon, nor has a key fallen off, for example. Rather, because the ideas aren't coming to Barton, the machine is taken out of play. He's explicitly aware of it now that he's not using it. He's aware of the role it should be playing in his creation of the script and thus in his writing career.

The last step, then, is the movement from the unready-to-hand to what Heidegger calls the "present-at-hand." This occurs when we take the "objective," theoretical view of a thing and, for example, weigh and measure it, forgetting for a moment its essence as equipment. Heidegger doesn't deny that the scientific or theoretical view of things as present-to-hand is useful for certain purposes. What he rejects is the idea that on this view we have a better understanding of the thing, that in scientifically observing it we're really getting at its true nature. Rather, as I note, he claims that this view is derivative upon our most primordial understanding of equipment as ready-to-hand. Further, Heidegger argues, you can clearly derive the present-at-hand from the ready-to-hand by ceasing to use things and taking a theoretical view of them. However, starting from the present-at-hand, things as viewed scientifically and "objectively," there's no way to account for how those things show up as truly meaningful in the world and in our lives.

Interpretation, Understanding, and *Barton Fink*

So far I've been discussing Heidegger's novel conception of understanding, which for him is our skillful comportment in the world, our ability to expertly use equipment like hammers, doorknobs, and typewriters to complete our everyday tasks and long-term projects. However, I haven't yet said anything about his notion of interpretation, which is the stated topic of this essay. Note that in our ordinary conception or use of these terms, there's a very close relationship between understanding and interpretation. One might even argue that every understanding *is* an interpretation and that every interpretation is at least based in some understanding (for me to understand a text means that I have to interpret it; for me to interpret it, I have to have some understanding of it).

In Heidegger's special use of these terms, there is likewise a very close relationship.[15] He says, "When something within-the-world is encountered as such, the thing in question already has an involvement which is disclosed in our understanding of the world, and this involvement is one which gets laid out by the interpretation."[16] A piece of equipment, the typewriter, for instance, already has its involvement, its role and meaning within the context of the secretary's office, and that involvement is revealed in our understanding of the world, in our skillful comportment in using the machine (when the secretary uses the typewriter to type letters for the boss, in conducting business, its use and meaning is revealed). Interpretation, then, lays out or makes explicit that involvement.[17]

Above I refer to the workshop as a "meaning-filled context," because in Heidegger's example it is the network or web of relations in which the equipment is constituted. Again, the hammer's meaning, and therefore its existence, is constituted by the role it plays in pounding nails *in order to* make a table or bookcase. This is what David Couzens Hoy is referring to when he says,

> "Meaning" for Heidegger thus involves the holistic way in which something can become intelligible as something in a web of relations. . . . Independent of the web of meanings, entities are not meaningful. . . . In other words, unless objects inhere in an interpretive context, they could not be understood. So they cannot be said to have meanings that are prior to and independent of their interpretive uses.
>
> The context of meaningfulness is thus what makes it possible to interpret something *as* something. For the most part this context is not explicit, but makes up the background of understanding.[18]

The "web of relations" or the "context of meaningfulness," in this case a workshop, is the "interpretive context" in which the hammer is meaningful and in which we're able to understand the hammer and to interpret it *as* a hammer. To put this another way, if there were no such thing as woodworking and carpentry, and thus no such thing as a workshop, there would be no network of relations or interpretive context in which the hammer would find its meaning (provided for the sake of the example that we ignore any other uses to which the hammer might be put). The hammer would then have no meaning or use, and so it would in that case be impossible for us to understand and interpret it. It would be like handing a cell phone to an ancient Roman gladiator. He obviously wouldn't know what it was or what to do with it.

Okay, so what does all this have to do with *Barton Fink?*

Here's my stab at a Heideggerian reading of the movie. Because Barton is a Cartesian-like subject, he lives "the life of the mind" and cuts himself off, not only from the common man, the supposed wellspring of his inspiration, but also more and more from life and reality itself. Consequently, he removes himself from any kind of practical engagement with the world and is thus cut off from those networks or contexts of meaning in which equipment is understood and interpreted. Consequently, the things around him lose their meaning and cease to make sense (like the cell phone would for the gladiator). In other words, the elements of the film (like the box or the picture) that resist interpretation aren't supposed to make sense. That's the whole point. Indeed, in interviews the Coens themselves reveal that not everything in the movie has a clear-cut meaning: "What isn't crystal clear isn't intended to become crystal clear, and it's fine to leave it at that," says Ethan Coen; Joel adds, "The question is: Where would it get you if something that's a little bit ambiguous in the movie is made clear? It doesn't get you anywhere."[19] I'm not suggesting, of course, that the brothers had anything like Heideggerian interpretation on their minds as they made the film. Rather, they acknowledge that not everything in the film is interpretable or makes sense, and I'm using Heidegger to suggest a way to understand why those things lack meaning or sense. Again, things in the world must have a network of relations, a context for practical engagement (like an office in which a typewriter is used, or a workshop in which a hammer is employed), in order for them to have sense and meaning. Because Barton lives more and more in his own head (symbolized by his hotel room), cut off from reality and practical engagement with the world, the things around him cease to have sense and meaning. They're not understandable or interpretable.

This may perhaps be frustrating, since most of us tend to like to understand and be able to interpret the meaning of everything in the stories we experience. However, as I said, my exposition above at least provides a reason why certain things in the film don't make sense. Further, though the film seems dreamlike and fantastical in certain ways, the fact that it contains elements that are ambiguous and lacking in sense and meaning makes it that much more like real life.

Notes

My thanks to J. J. Abrams for many very helpful comments on an earlier draft of this essay.

1. Critics note, and the Coens confirm, that the character of W. P. Mayhew is at least partly based on William Faulkner.

2. "If *Miller's Crossing* offered spectators difficulties of presentation (Who did what, and why?), *Barton Fink* presented them with difficulties of interpretation. Are Barton's horrific experiences in the film's gothic hotel real? If so, what is in the box given him by a serial killer?" R. Barton Palmer, *Joel and Ethan Coen* (Urbana: Univ. of Illinois Press, 2004), 10.

3. Recall also that Charlie hears things in the hotel (like the "love birds" in the room next to Barton) that would seem to be impossible for him to hear, suggesting that all of this is occurring in his head.

4. Note that supposed common man Charlie, who perhaps lives in Barton's head and turns out to be demonic, is rather like Barton's version of the evil genius (or evil demon, as he's sometimes called). It's via the evil genius that Descartes comes to grasp his own mind as a pure intellectual intuition. Similarly, it's Charlie who reveals Barton's alienation to him, the fact that he's trapped inside his own head: "I'll show you the life of the mind!" Charlie yells. My thanks to J. J. Abrams for pointing this out to me.

5. Daniel 2:1–6 (NRSV, Catholic edition).

6. It's interesting to note that in his Meditation I, prior to his introduction of the evil genius, Descartes discusses dreams and wonders whether our entire lives might be a dream. If that's at least logically possible, Descartes argues, then we can't trust any of our sense perceptions to be true or real. This skepticism isn't quite radical enough for Descartes's purposes, and so he goes on to introduce the evil genius.

7. I'll note as I'm writing this, and I'm not making this up or joking, that just last night I dreamed of a flying lobster. So, go figure.

8. In an interview, Joel Coen all but denies that they explicitly meant the sequence of events in California to be a dream, but he confirms that they wanted those events to be irrational and illogical. He says, "Some people have suggested the whole second part of the movie is only a nightmare. It certainly wasn't our intention to make it a literal bad dream, but it's true that we wanted an irrational logic. We wanted the climate of the movie to reflect the psychological state of its hero." Quoted in William Rodney Allen, ed., *The Coen Brothers: Interviews* (Jackson: Univ. Press of Mississippi, 2006), 49.

9. As we'll see later in this chapter, the essences of things are fixed relatively and are conventional. They depend upon Dasein and human agency. That is, a table is a table because people use it for that purpose, and for no other reason is it a table.

10. "In comporting ourselves toward an entity as bygone, we retain it in a certain way or we forget it. In retaining and forgetting, the Dasein is itself concomitantly retained. It concomitantly retains its own self in *what it already has been.* That which the Dasein has already been in each instance . . . belongs concomitantly to its future. This having-been-ness, understood primarily, precisely does *not* mean that the Dasein no longer in fact is; just the contrary, the Dasein *is* precisely in fact what it *was.* That which we are as having been has not gone by, passed away, in the sense in which we say that we could shuffle off our past like a garment. The Dasein can as little get rid of its [past as] bygoneness as escape its death. In every sense and in every case everything we have been is an essential determination of our existence." Martin Heidegger, *The Basic Problems of Phenomenology,* trans. Albert Hofstadter (Bloomington: Indiana Univ. Press, 1982), 265.

11. "The Dasein understands itself by way of its own most peculiar capacity to be, of which it is expectant. In thus comporting toward its own most peculiar capacity to be, *it is ahead of itself.* Expecting a possibility, I come from this possibility toward that which I myself am. The Dasein, expecting its ability to be, *comes toward itself.* In this coming-toward-itself, expectant of a possibility, the Dasein is *futural* in an original sense. This coming-toward-oneself from one's most peculiar possibility, a coming-toward which is implicit in the Dasein's existence and of which all expecting is a specific mode, is the *primary concept of the future.*" Ibid., 265.

12. Martin Heidegger, *Being and Time,* trans. John Macquarrie and Edward Robinson (New York: Harper & Row, 1962), 38.

13. "[Heidegger] thinks that we grasp entities as entities in their webs of relations with other entities, not as aggregates of perceptual qualities. Thus, we do not first see some colors or hear some noises and only secondarily infer that we are seeing or hearing a motorcycle. Instead, we first encounter a motorcycle, and only secondarily (if at all) do we abstract its properties (perhaps to hear its 'noise')." David Couzens Hoy, "Heidegger and the Hermeneutic Turn," in *The Cambridge Companion to Heidegger,* ed. Charles Guignon (Cambridge: Cambridge Univ. Press, 1993), 183.

14. To be more precise, this is a common English translation of Heidegger's original German.

15. "Heidegger [insists] that all forms of interpretation in real life and in the human sciences are grounded in understanding and are nothing but the explication of what has already been understood." Kurt Mueller-Vollmer, ed., introduction to *The Hermeneutics Reader* (New York: Continuum, 1988), 35.

16. Heidegger, *Being and Time,* 190–91.

17. "When I interpret something, I do not add on to an experience an external meaning or significance. I simply make clear what is already there. What is already

there in the world's objects is the manner and purpose for which I make use of them." Michael Gelvin, *A Commentary on Heidegger's "Being and Time"* (New York: Harper & Row, 1970), 94.

18. Hoy, "Heidegger and the Hermeneutic Turn," 183.

19. Quoted in Allen, *Coen Brothers,* 58. In regard to their including ambiguous and uninterpretable elements in the film, Joel Coen says, "We're definitely guilty of teasing." Ibid., 94.

THE PAST IS NOW

History and *The Hudsucker Proxy*

Paul Coughlin

> Well, the future . . . that's something that you can never tell about. But the
> past . . . that's another story.
>
> —Moses in *The Hudsucker Proxy*

When Moses (William Cobbs) utters this phrase in the opening sequence of
the Coen brothers' *The Hudsucker Proxy* (1994), his commentary is intended
to launch the film's "story": Norville Barnes's (Tim Robbins) rise and fall and
rise again as the corporate stooge cum genius of Hudsucker Industries. But
it also establishes a critical element that characterizes all representations of
the past: their fundamental textual character. History (the past) is a story.
The postmodern age has decreed that history is something of the present,
rather than the past: we access history through the texts that define it, the
texts that conduct it. Linda Hutcheon argues that "there is no directly and
naturally accessible past 'real' for us today, we can only know—and construct—the past through its traces, its representations."[1] Postmodernism
exposes the human complicity in the construction of history and, as such,
in the representation of "truth" and "fact." It is no longer acceptable to conceive of history as pursuing a single linear route, and the possibilities for
other expressions of the past are now wound up in issues of power, authority, and control. Those who control the means and ordering of expression
determine our history.

The Hudsucker Proxy is the Coen brothers' most farfetched film. Elements of fantasy and wonder abound, culminating with the literal stopping
of time at the story's conclusion. It is also a work that references other films
and filmic styles. *The Hudsucker Proxy* adopts the generic conventions of

screwball comedy while drawing directly on the works of Frank Capra. It is for reasons like these that the works of the Coen brothers are regularly criticized as being artificial, empty of meaning, of failing to engage with reality or history and thus ignoring moral and ethical concerns. Emanuel Levy condemns the Coens as "clever directors who know too much about movies and too little about real life."[2] *The Hudsucker Proxy's* mixture of artificiality and allusion suggests a disconnection with customary notions of history and reality. Yet it is precisely *The Hudsucker Proxy's* textual qualities—its intertextual cues, generic conventions, use of allusion, and self-reflexive narrational tools—that guarantee its engagement with history and "real life." Postmodernism contends that history is a text like any other and as such is open to interpretation. History is unstable, and postmodern representations and theory regard it as a cultural construct. History and fiction are discourses, serving to remind us that we name the past as historical facts by selection and positioning. And, even more basically, we know the past only through its representation, through its traces in the present.

The Politics of Postmodernism

Postmodern theory promotes the notion that the past (history) is in a state of constant flux. When quizzed about the postmodern aspects of his and his brother's work, Ethan Coen's declaration, "The honest answer is I'm not real clear on what postmodernism is," mirrors the confusion that confronts much of the critical theory that surrounds the term.[3] Coming to grips with the notoriously unstable definition of postmodernism is a challenging commission. For many, postmodernism is an extension and repudiation of the tenets of modernism, adopting the processes of modernism yet rejecting its wish for absolute truths. Others see postmodernism in art as characterized by a loss of meaning, the collapsing of typically binary oppositions, and a suspicion of absolute truths. Postmodern texts often operate by adopting the styles of past representations in order to investigate them, as exemplified in the rampant allusion and widespread referencing that adorns *The Hudsucker Proxy*.

Postmodernism is often criticized as being apolitical, promoting emptiness, a loss of meaning, and as such, a waning of history. Hutcheon, however, suggests that irony, historical reference, an interest in textual structures, and the collapsing of boundaries between art and reality are all typical of the processes by which postmodern representations can subvert prevailing views of the world and culture. Hutcheon argues against the contention that postmodernism is impotent and ahistorical when she declares "that postmodernist parody is a value-problematizing, denaturalizing form of acknowledging the history (and through irony, the politics) of representations."[4] Hutcheon believes that parody is precisely the tool that will unlock the frameworks of representation (the tools used to construct stories), and it does so by foregrounding and examining the structure and organization of texts. The Coens' application of a screwball comedy design that also draws heavily upon the work of Frank Capra in their construction of *The Hudsucker Proxy* demonstrates how self-reflexivity and irony can operate to investigate and even challenge accepted representations of the past and the ideologies upon which these representations are grounded. Postmodern parody imitates an existing work of art that is familiar to its readers and reconsiders it with an ironical, critical, or antagonistic purpose. Distinctive features of the work are retained but are often mimicked with an antithetical intention. Parody changes the texts it imitates, questioning and sometimes corroding the ideologies that they convey and challenging the authority of historical representation.

A film such as *The Hudsucker Proxy* foregrounds the nature of history as a plural creation. The Coen brothers mix fact and fiction, truth and fabrication, the real and the unreal. They construct texts that are at once completely in tune with history but entirely fictional. The technically precise and culturally astute recreation of America's Deep South in the 1930s framed by Homer's epic narrative *The Odyssey* in their film *O Brother, Where Art Thou?* (2000) is a model of postmodernism. The merging of authenticity with classic fiction highlights the link between the story structures of both fictional and historical representation. James Mottram suggests that when the Coen brothers adapt Homer they "are reminding us that fragments of literature—like the past itself—exist in our subconscious to be reinterpreted."[5] Yet to be aware of the structures of storytelling does not require an exchange of the real for the unreal; rather, it recognizes that the real is always constructed, its temporal plot always "told," our understanding of it a matter of tone and perspective. The manipulation of time is precisely what is achieved when Moses stops the clock's gears (and the narrative action) in *The Hudsucker Proxy,* an act that saves the life of Norville by halting his suicide fall mid-plunge. Moses not only disrupts the illusion of continuity but also breaks out of character to address the audience: "Strictly speaking, I'm never s'posed to do this." This action reinforces the artificiality of *The*

Hudsucker Proxy as well as demonstrates the way texts are controlled by a creator, their trajectory formed and altered at a whim.

Remembering the Past

If, as Hutcheon argues, postmodern texts are preoccupied with history, it is also true that they are obsessed with memories. Postmodern film exploits the vast resources of the spectator's remembrances, using memories and recollections of the past to construct meaning in the present. Memory and reality interconnect in the process of ordering experience. Giuliana Bruno claims that *Blade Runner* (Ridley Scott, 1982) constructs an environment in which the status of memory has changed from "Proustian madeleines" (those somewhat distant, involuntary, and sensory-induced recollections) to "photographs," arguing that the postmodern viewer, like the replicants in Scott's film, is "put in the position of reclaiming a history by means of its reproduction."[6] Yet Bruno's contention is not simply a symptom of the postmodern malaise: history has only ever been accessible in its reproduction, whether it is in the oral narratives of the ancient eras or the literary texts that followed. What has changed has been the dominant mechanism for reproducing the past. Changes in technology have altered the way we access the past, though such changes have not revised the nature of history. History is, and has always been, a story.

Since the 1960s Hollywood films have exhibited an increasing stylistic self-consciousness, referencing cinema history and quoting from other styles. Carolyn R. Russell declares that *The Hudsucker Proxy* "is the most insistent delegate in a progression of films which synthesize the aesthetic past. In virtually every frame of the film may be recognized what theorist Fredric Jameson has termed 'the imitation of dead styles, speech through all the masks and voices stored up in the imaginary museum of a new global culture.'"[7] By drawing on Jameson, Russell is arguing that *The Hudsucker Proxy* must fall into the category of the apolitical, for Jameson believes postmodern texts to be incapable of engaging with the "real" world and its concerns. But to recall past representations does not mean to do so without irony or critical commentary. And surely a film such as *The Hudsucker Proxy*—blatantly drawing from the "dead style" of screwball comedy and from the mythology of Frank Capra, which represents the "museum of a new global culture"—operates at a critical level with regard to these allusions.

The Hudsucker Proxy's parody of the screwball comedy and the works of Capra demonstrates a rather acute satire on the values associated with each of these representational forms. One of the reasons for the critical and commercial failure of *The Hudsucker Proxy* was that it parodied a genre that is committed to romantic ideals, upsetting and alienating the genre's supporters. The Coens are less interested in the emotional connotation of convention and more concerned with the *memory* of pleasure they expect to find in their audience's consciousness. But the Coens deny their audiences this enjoyment by taking their film in contrary and subversive directions. Joel and Ethan Coen use the genre in order to examine its processes, expose its traditional agendas, and highlight its inherent ideologies. The intention is not to ridicule the genre but to identify the manner by which the screwball comedy reflects ideology, history, and meaning. The Coens' modern screwball comedy works somewhat like the revisionist western, in which quotation, referencing, and allusion can be used to identify ideological and social change. The variations between the original and the reworking are indexes of changes in attitude toward certain cultural values. The Coens' satirical view, as represented in *The Hudsucker Proxy*, dismisses many of the assumptions made in past representations of the screwball genre and challenges the values that these assumptions support. Through the use of irony, parody, and subversion, the Coens expose these older representations to scrutiny and examine the ideologies upon which they were constructed.

The Hudsucker Proxy may at first seem to be a film that is overloaded with the components of other film styles, genres, and intertexts, but its allusions are not limited to cinema. The intertextual web is strung in such a way that connections are drawn from a series of diverse sources. Early in *The Hudsucker Proxy*, when Norville finally secures employment, he is stationed in the mailroom at Hudsucker Industries, situated in the bowels of the enormous company building. The mailroom is a darkly cavernous chamber that extends beyond the line of sight; its walls are lined with a labyrinthine arrangement of steel pipes representing the nerve center of a bureaucracy that winds its way to the executive offices. Norville's instructional introduction to the mailroom is a litany of double-talk and bureaucratic mumbo-jumbo. The scene is an allusion to *Brazil* (Terry Gilliam, 1985), a film in which a bureaucratic slip leads to a series of nightmarish misadventures. Director Gilliam constructs a universe that is so belabored with organization that it becomes distinctively chaotic, as symbolized by a visual design that is both futuristic and primitive. The relationship between *The Hudsucker Proxy* and *Brazil* can be extended further to include George Orwell's *Nineteen Eighty-Four*.

Orwell's novel itself deals with a dystopian view of a future society ruled by a totalitarian regime. The state's stubborn reliance on a deficient bureaucracy is a major theme that reappears as the central motif in Gilliam's film. As this winds back to *The Hudsucker Proxy* the connections established through the suggestive imagery provide an immediate referent, or cinematic shorthand. For Jim Collins this is evidence of the "ever-expanding number of texts and technologies" that is "both a reflection of and a significant contribution to the 'array'—the perpetual circulation and recirculation of signs that forms the fabric of postmodern cultural life."[8] Postmodern films are replete with cinematic allusions that identify the usable past as a means of establishing a relationship with history and its various representations.

The *Hudsucker Proxy* relies on intertextual cues for meaning to be made. But it is not merely a film made from the pieces of fictional texts and narratives from popular culture. This is illustrated when the Coens acknowledge "legitimate" history in their ironic summoning of the cultural memory of J. Edgar Hoover. When Chief (John Mahoney)—the editor of Amy's (Jennifer Jason Leigh) newspaper—barks the angle on a report about Hoover, he proposes the question, "When will he marry?" The contemporary image of Hoover details a moral crusader who concealed his own homosexuality and transvestitism in a climate when such a lifestyle was considered a moral deviation. The irony generated by the historical setting of the film and the viewer's contemporary knowledge creates a particular intertextual connection based upon a double meaning. This example also highlights the responsibility of the viewer/reader to complete the text, to exercise its ironic component. Intertextuality substitutes the disputed author/text dynamic (in which the author is considered to be the sole creator of a text's meaning) with one between reader and text, where meaning resides within the discourse of history itself. John Biguenet refers to a verbal exchange in *Les Enfants du paradis* (Marcel Carné, 1945), similar in context to the J. Edgar Hoover quip, that recalls Monsieur Ingres's aptitude for playing the violin—which was apparently dreadful (Biguenet suggests an analogy to Jack Benny and his fiddling). But Biguenet believes this reference is almost lost on modern audiences who know little of this cultural memory: "Unfortunately for Marcel Carné, he hitched his wagon to a dying horse. With each passing year, those lines of the film become ever more obscure."[9] And the same applies with the reference to Hoover in *The Hudsucker Proxy*. Its cultural currency will inevitably fade as the memory becomes more and more irrelevant to a contemporary audience. Notwithstanding, it remains a historical document, a remembrance that constructs a bridge to the past and sets up a reference that alternates two perspectives of history: one based in 1959 (the film's setting) and the other in 1994 (the year of the film's release). Meaning, and in this case its apparent irony, is consequently drawn from a history that competes with itself.

Intertextuality in the films of Joel and Ethan Coen places a significant emphasis on the viewer's ability to "complete" the text by drawing from an accumulation of remembered texts—"the array." The Coens' films privilege the cine-literate viewer because the majority of references are drawn from film history. *Barton Fink* (1991) depends to some extent on an audience that can recognize the characters' connections to moments and themes in *The Tenant* (Roman Polanski, 1976) and *The Shining* (Stanley Kubrick, 1980). *O Brother, Where Art Thou?* initially presupposes an understanding of Homer's *The Odyssey* but also draws on the films of Preston Sturges. And *The Hudsucker Proxy* relies squarely on a knowledge of the screwball comedy genre and the films of Frank Capra. However, to not recognize these sources does not mean that a viewer will find the Coens' films unfathomable. And to recognize only cursory details of the textual allusions may be exactly enough for one to engage critically with the material. A knowledge and understanding of Capra's films and his legacy is not limited to those viewers who have seen his work. Capra has a prominent cultural position, and it may be enough for a spectator to be familiar with television's *The Simpsons* (1989–) or a film like *Hero* (Stephen Frears, 1992) or even *Mr. Deeds* (Steven Brill, 2002) to know Capra and his mythology. The vast network of intertextuality is not just constructed upon a familiarity with particular key texts but rather with all texts that in one way or another refer to myriad other representations.

Every text depends on some prior knowledge of other representations. A genre is developed and canonized via the recognition of particular tropes and repeated conventions. *The Hudsucker Proxy* is the Coen brothers' most literal genre film in its recreation of the themes, conventions, and iconography of the screwball comedy. Thomas Schatz defines the screwball comedy as a genre that supports the status quo even when "it's espousing enlightened capitalism or enlightened marital-sexual relationships," and the genre is often distinguished by the romantic communion of a disparate pairing having overcome initial antagonism. Schatz also maintains that the morality of the characters is inspired by conventional ideals: "the hero's or heroine's traditional values and attitudes are attributed directly to a rural background and small-town sensibilities."[10] The application of this limited taxonomy to

The Hudsucker Proxy is fairly straightforward: Norville arrives from Muncie, Indiana (read small-town America, or "Chumpsville," according to Amy), and falls in love with Amy, who at the outset despises him as a corporate buffoon (read initial antagonism) but ultimately falls for his humble and modest value system based on humane ideals (read traditional values and attitudes). That *The Hudsucker Proxy* falls so neatly into the category of a genre film is significant to the Coen brothers' parodic agenda. Parody requires the anchoring of the narrative in an identifiable context to cue the spectator to a regulated conventional viewing pattern. Once established, the genre's assumptions are challenged using devices rich in irony and subversion, reestablishing textual structures (employing the genre's typical conventions and tropes) in a way that favors scrutiny rather than commemoration.

Identity, memory, and history are affected and informed by "the array"; our understanding of the world is dependent upon our recycling of remembrances and ideas through disparate media. Almost every episode of *The Simpsons* is made up of a series of allusions that seek to parody old television programs, previous films, past representational forms, and popular culture. For a viewer of *The Simpsons,* the infamous television debates between Richard Nixon and John F. Kennedy are remembered through their parody in an archived Duff beer commercial. In this commercial Nixon's legendary nontelegenic image is lampooned. But the sequence also carries a satirical edge as visual imagery is shown to supersede the mechanics of the democratic process. The Coen brothers tap into that same vein that recognizes that history is accessed through its images and its remembered texts. And these memories can provide a site for ironic reworkings that interrogate the past, its texts, and their ideologies.

Challenging the Past

Michel Foucault notes that "where there is power, there is a resistance, and yet, or rather consequently, this resistance is never in a position of exteriority in relation to power."[11] Foucault suggests that the tools used to maintain power are often the same tools used to challenge it. This notion identifies the reason why parody is often considered a conservative transgression: it works within the parameters of the targeted texts and styles in order to criticize and satirize them. Unlike the more artistically bold avant-garde, parody uses conventional (conservative) methods of representation to challenge authority. To recall the past (or history) through its representations not only reminds us of the past but can also challenge its stake to legitimacy and authenticity. To question a narrative technique, a narrational tool, or a genre's convention is a challenge to history that is dependent on these textual devices for its ordering and existence. Subverting the representations of the past is precisely the approach taken by postmodern texts to strip these prior works of any pretense that there is a single acceptable history.

The subversive potential of parody presupposes that adopting the methods of past texts and frameworks is not the same as endorsing them. *The Hudsucker Proxy*, far from being a mere recreation of the traditions of the screwball comedy, is a parody of Capra and his typically maudlin films detailing naïve populist tales of social achievement. Capra's films are often recalled as overtly hopeful parables celebrating the ability of humanity to overcome seemingly insurmountable obstacles. The derogatory term "Capracorn" is regularly applied to his films, the expression carrying with it the implication of a rose-colored, idealistic optimism of society and human nature that ignores the harsh realities of a quotidian existence. Capra's films advocate values related to the New Deal: compassion for one's neighbor, the notion that happiness does not come from wealth but from social interaction, and the belief that no conflict is unsolvable.

Despite being Capraesque in its production, *The Hudsucker Proxy* is not reflective of the typical values espoused in Capra's films. In the tradition of postmodern representation, the Coens merely install these motifs to then subvert them. Like Capra's hick-in-the-big-city films—*Mr. Deeds Goes to Town* (1936) and *Mr. Smith Goes to Washington* (1939)—the Coens' film has "Muncie-boy" Norville arrive fresh off the bus from Indiana. Like the characters in these two Capra films—Longfellow Deeds (Gary Cooper) and Jefferson Smith (James Stewart)—Norville is then exploited by a vile capitalist system that values money above morality. And, as in Capra films, the hero of *The Hudsucker Proxy* eventually succeeds over the perils of corruption. Yet, unlike the protagonists of *Mr. Deeds Goes to Town* or *Mr. Smith Goes to Washington*, Norville is not beholden to any value system nor is he trying to expose and overturn corruption. He is a fool whose own ignorance (rather than idealism) makes him ripe for exploitation. Norville is not the repository of democratic optimism that characterizes Capra's heroes. Deeds and Smith are "little men" battling against an unscrupulous system of venality; relying on righteousness and morality, their idealism will endure as a beacon in the murky fog of duplicity. Norville, however, is an ambitious but dimwitted business major from a backwoods university. He falls into an executive position as a corporate stooge and then insipidly discards his moral code to abuse his newly acquired power. The intertextual relationship between *The Hudsucker Proxy* and Capra is characterized by subversion rather than celebration, representing a challenge to Capra's historical articulations of ideology and culture.

Todd McCarthy bemoans *The Hudsucker Proxy*'s pastiche structure and artificial aesthetic: "rehashes of old movies, no matter how inspired, are almost by definition synthetic, and the fact is that nearly all the characters are constructs rather than human beings with whom the viewer can connect." He then observes that "[Tim] Robbins calls to mind Gary Cooper and James Stewart, but there's no authentic sweetness or strength underneath all his doltishness to make him seem like a good guy the audience can get behind."[12] McCarthy's problem here is that he finds *The Hudsucker Proxy* to be a "rehash" of old movies, only to then point out the very specific distinctions between the Coens' film and those prior texts. McCarthy's inconsistency—*The Hudsucker Proxy* is just like those earlier films but also specifically different—is crucial, as it suggests not that Robbins fails to reflect authenticity but rather that authenticity has been subverted. The Coens install a pseudo-Capraesque hero to then distort him into an image that suits their critical agenda. The hope of the New Deal no longer prevails in the image of the protagonist. Rather, the Coen brothers focus on the incompetence exemplified in contemporary corporate collapse and failure. *The Hudsucker Proxy* is a period film (its setting being 1959), but it illustrates the very real concerns of a modern society disillusioned by corporate greed and incompetence.

Capra's films are highly effective in stimulating the interests of mass audiences while presenting a sense of "American-ness" and the values of democracy in a stubbornly pleasing format and structure. With *The Hudsucker Proxy* the Coen brothers transplant the format of the Capra film to a somewhat unwelcome setting, and through techniques involving repetition and difference, they scrutinize the common values of the Capra film. The protagonists in Capra's films are sympathetically drawn to maximize viewer empathy. Characters such as Longfellow Deeds and Jefferson Smith are idealistic and principled; they are symbols of integrity in a world constantly imperiled by corruption. The casting of upstanding Hollywood leading men Gary Cooper and James Stewart, respectively, confirms Capra's agenda. With *The Hudsucker Proxy*, Joel and Ethan Coen are less righteous in their representation of Norville and more sly about his motives. He does not come to New York with the noble intention of political reform but rather to find success in the vibrantly capitalistic system. Smith and Deeds are "holy fools," men whose guileless naïveté beckons exploitation, though ultimately their earthy homespun values triumph. But Norville is no holy fool, merely a self-centered simpleton. When he "graduates" to the executive floor of the Hudsucker organization, he quickly adopts attitudes of superiority, made all the more disreputable by his status as a corporate stooge. By disrupting the typical order of the Capra universe the Coens also expose what is essential to the design of his films and illuminate their elemental ideologies. Capra's films promote an idealized vision of a democratic system that flourishes with the simple application of "old-fashioned" values imported from the small towns where such tenets typically prosper. But Vito Zagarrio qualifies this assessment by noting that Capra's "populism, sticky-sweet optimism, and paternalistic demagogy [mask] a superficial democracy that fades, on close examination, into a substantially reactionary attitude."[13] The Coens engage critically with the historical setting of Capra's films—a context conceived in the shadows of New Deal politics—by employing postmodern tools that reject the conventional desire to fuse the diversity of cultural experiences into a single and universal myth. *The Hudsucker Proxy* promotes the notion that the messages of Capra's films are now irrelevant, their values no longer tenable, and a reclamation of their political ideals impossible. The transition of values in the films of Capra to those in *The Hudsucker Proxy* provides an index to the changes in values in the political and social climate of American culture. The historical investigation in *The Hudsucker Proxy* resides not in the accuracy or authenticity of its setting, design, or positioning of events but rather in its examination of the values found in the texts it parodies.

Deconstructing the Past

By adopting the modes of the past the Coens parody their assumptions, exposing their contrivances and making their frameworks transparent. Parody is a useful tool for prying open the insularity of canons and exposing the constructedness of these typical forms of representation. With *The Hudsucker Proxy* the Coen brothers are adopting a mode of self-conscious storytelling. Their use of distancing narrational modes such as voice-over explanations in *Raising Arizona* (1987) and *The Man Who Wasn't There* (2001), the direct address prologue in *Blood Simple* (1984) and *The Big Lebowski* (1998), and the rigid application of generic convention in *Miller's Crossing* (1990) serve to foreground textual construction by calling attention to the "telling" of a story. To insist on exposing the devices of construction immediately cues the viewer to the fictionality not only of that text but of all texts. Then, to in turn subvert convention demonstrates how all texts, history included, are malleable, unstable, and contingent.

The first meeting between Amy and Norville is perhaps the best example of the Coen brothers' attention to exposing the frameworks of construction in *The Hudsucker Proxy*. Amy first encounters Norville in a coffee shop, an event that is narrated by two cab drivers, Lou (Joe Grifasi) and Benny (John Seitz). The cabbies observe Amy as she undertakes a number of crafty deceptions in order to obtain Norville's attention. It will be her first involvement with her "mark" and the beginning of a series of newspaper stories in which she will ruin his reputation—a direct allusion to Capra's *Mr. Deeds Goes to Town*. The Coen brothers are acutely aware that the sequence in the coffee shop is a mass of narrative clichés. They seek to satirize the constructedness of the classic Hollywood film by drawing the viewer's attention—through the verbal narration of Lou and Benny—to its obvious conventionality. As Amy sits down at the counter next to Norville, the cabbies begin their interpretation of events:

> LOU: Enter the dame.
> BENNY: There's one in every story.

The pair of narrators go on to describe every move made by Amy to secure Norville's attention:

> LOU: She's looking for her mark,
> BENNY: She finds him,
> LOU: She sits down and orders . . .
> BENNY: . . . a light lunch.

Lou and Benny then describe the various schemes and scams employed by Amy in her attempt to obtain Norville's attention and sympathy. When he finally heeds Amy's presence, the cabbies cynically narrate the action in perfunctory tones:

> BENNY: He notices,
> LOU: She's distressed,
> BENNY: He's concerned.

The scene detailing Amy's swindle is composed of one long take and is framed from across the counter using Lou and Benny's point of view, which mirrors the audience's visual perspective. Lou and Benny are therefore stand-ins for the enlightened viewer who is aware of the methods of storytelling in the films of Capra that *The Hudsucker Proxy* mocks. The purpose of self-reflexivity in postmodern representations is to denaturalize classical modes of representation and to expose them as cultural constructions. What is significant in this scene is the way Joel and Ethan Coen expose the formulaic construction and the suspension of ethics (Amy's intentions are noble but her method is deceitful) that contribute to the pleasing idealism typical of Capra's narratives. The Coens investigate the processes of the social comedy with a satirical agenda to study its devices and examine how meaning is constructed in relation to ideology. And it is to this point that the Coens are not merely revisiting a tired old genre but rather scrutinizing its methods, exploring its limitations, and exposing its agendas.

The films of the Coen brothers are ironic in that they must be approached at two levels: one that identifies the meaning of the text and the other that recognizes the tools that are applied and employed to construct these meanings. With *The Hudsucker Proxy,* the Coen brothers are transparent in revealing the means of their own production. The film's diegetic world is paused as Moses the janitor places the handle of his broom into the cogs of the Hudsucker building clock in a literal deus ex machina. The result of this action in formal terms is beholden to both postmodern representation and to the art of parody. Parody is a form that ridicules the assumptions of texts and genres by making obvious the elements that conventionally remain implicit and hidden in their frameworks. Actors break out of character and refer directly to cinema's institutions in a move that unsettles the text's illusory status, undermining the portentousness of the parodied represen-tation. The speech Moses gives is ironic in that he addresses it directly to the viewer as if aware of the fictionality of the text that surrounds him. The dialogue is unpretentious in its affable character and seemingly homespun wisdom and also ambiguous in that it hints that even Moses is not sure how the story will play out. The character of Moses stands in for skeptical spectators who are mindful of the artifice of all texts and thus already find themselves one step removed from its conceits. Hutcheon observes that "self-reflexivity points in two directions at once, toward the events being represented in the narrative and toward the act of narration itself. This is precisely the same doubleness that characterizes all historical narrative."[14]

The Coens are aware of the processes that produce meaning, and, it seems, they demand that their audiences be aware of this too.

Foregrounding the tools of storytelling at the surface of a text exposes more than simply the methods of production; it also provides an insight into conventional modes of expression. Postmodernism invokes a study of history as a textual entity in which ideology is apparent in the means of production. The use of reflexiveness, such as that exemplified by Moses and his direct address and halting of time in *The Hudsucker Proxy*, is the type of technique that challenges the inconspicuous character of fiction and history as implied by the realist narrative. An undeniable relationship with history is established by the way such distancing techniques direct the viewer's attention to the conventions and latent ideology reflected in the seamlessness of the textual design. It is perhaps no wonder that postmodern representations are often mistakenly considered to be copies, imitations, plagiarized texts, and empty pastiches of older forms. In order to adopt a system that installs and foregrounds a narrative structure so as to scrutinize it, these representations must reflect the texts they critique. Postmodern interrogation and deconstruction, whether through artistic representation or critical inquiry, have exposed the manner by which meaning is constructed in fiction and history. By revealing the modes of production one can investigate how particular kinds of representation support values and sustain assumptions that exist within a culture. To recognize how history is constructed is to discern how meaning is made, how truth is achieved, and how the underlying ideologies that compel certain truths to the forefront may be deemed "authentic."

Where self-reflexivity and historical actuality clash, a study of representation becomes an exploration of the way in which narratives and images arrange how we view our culture and how we assemble our ideas of self, in both the present and the past. Postmodern films like those of the Coen brothers resonate with a valid and vital critical approach to modern life that typically carries a significant political agenda. Their films seek to make meaning out of past representations using parody and irony as tools in the deconstruction of ideology. As a result, the works of Joel and Ethan Coen are often censured for their refusal to engage with the "real," reproached for failing to commit to moral or ethical positions, and chastised for their perceived unreality. But it is more likely that the Coens themselves are victims of a critical establishment that considers techno-visual documentation—film and television—to be unworthy conveyers of the past. The Coen brothers do know too much about film: they know enough to recognize the conceits of its processes and to detect and challenge the values that these processes are designed to sustain. Despite its artificial visual design and hyper-affected performances, *The Hudsucker Proxy* proves to be a text that engages in historical inquiry. Through its exploration of the tenets of older forms of representation by way of parodic attitudes and ironic inversions, the Coen brothers' film examines New Deal politics, the mythology of small-town America, and the realities of contemporary corporate principles and practices. Not bad for a film that is merely about other films.

Notes

1. Linda Hutcheon, "Postmodern Film?" in *Postmodern After-Images: A Reader in Film, Television, and Video*, ed. Peter Brooker and Will Brooker (London: Arnold, 1997), 39.

2. Emanuel Levy, *Cinema of Outsiders: The Rise of American Independent Film* (New York: New York Univ. Press, 1999), 223.

3. Quoted in John Naughton, "Double Vision," in *Joel & Ethan Coen: Blood Siblings*, ed. Paul A. Woods (London: Plexus, 2000), 134.

4. Linda Hutcheon, *The Politics of Postmodernism* (London: Routledge, 1989), 94.

5. James Mottram, *The Coen Brothers: The Life of the Mind* (London: B. T. Batsford, 2000), 159.

6. Giuliana Bruno, "Ramble City: Postmodernism and *Blade Runner*," *October* 41 (summer 1987): 73–74.

7. Carolyn R. Russell, *The Films of Joel and Ethan Coen* (Jefferson, N.C.: McFarland, 2001), 114.

8. Jim Collins, "Genericity in the Nineties: Eclectic Irony and the New Sincerity," in *Film Theory Goes to the Movies*, ed. Jim Collins, Hilary Radner, and Ava Preacher Collins (London: Routledge, 1993), 246.

9. John Biguenet, "Double Takes: The Role of Allusion in Cinema," in *Play It Again, Sam: Retakes on Remakes*, ed. Andrew Horton and Stuart Y. McDougal (Berkeley and Los Angeles: Univ. of California Press, 1998), 133.

10. Thomas Schatz, *Hollywood Genres: Formulas, Filmmaking, and the Studio System* (New York: McGraw-Hill, 1981), 171 and 157, respectively.

11. Michel Foucault, "Excerpts from *The History of Sexuality: Volume 1: An Introduction*," in *A Postmodern Reader*, ed. Joseph Natoli and Linda Hutcheon (Albany: State Univ. of New York Press, 1993), 336.

12. Todd McCarthy, "*The Hudsucker Proxy*," in *Joel & Ethan Coen*, ed. Woods, 118.

13. Vito Zagarrio, "It Is (Not) a Wonderful Life: For a Counter-reading of Frank Capra," in *Frank Capra: Authorship and the Studio System*, ed. Robert Sklar and Vito Zagarrio (Philadelphia: Temple Univ. Press, 1998), 66.

14. Hutcheon, *The Politics of Postmodernism*, 76.

"A Homespun Murder Story"

Film Noir and the Problem of Modernity in *Fargo*

Jerold J. Abrams

Winner of two Academy Awards (Best Screenplay and Best Actress, Frances McDormand), the Coen brothers' film *Fargo* (1996) is a noir detective story set in Brainerd, Minnesota, and Fargo, North Dakota, about a working-class man gone bad. Jerry Lundegaard (William H. Macy) is an unethical car salesman who swindles customers into unnecessary extras like "TruCoat" sealant at the last minute of sale. Married to a Martha Stewart–like housewife whose father, Wade (Harve Presnell), is wealthy, Jerry is exploding with debt and anxiety. Frantically he looks for a way out and finds one. He hires two thugs, Carl Showalter (Steve Buscemi) and Gaear Grimsrud (Peter Stormare), to kidnap his wife, Jean (Kristin Rudrüd), and extract a ransom from his rich and miserly father-in-law. But everything goes horribly wrong when the thugs kill first a police officer (after being pulled over for improper plates and then trying to bribe him), then two witnesses to the police officer's murder, then Wade, and finally even their hostage, Jean—making Jerry not only a kidnapper but an accessory to murder. Enter Marge Gunderson (Mc-Dormand), chief of police in Brainerd. She is smart, level headed, and very pregnant, all bundled up and trudging mightily through the deep snow and freezing cold of the Upper Midwest. Hot on the criminals' trail, she tracks down her men: first Grimsrud, while he is shredding Carl's body in a wood chipper, and then Jerry as he tries to skip town.[1]

Film Noir in the Snow

What sets *Fargo* apart as a film noir is how it transforms the genre and how, in doing so, it uniquely reveals the existential isolation of the human condition within modernity. The tension at the center of modernity, which all great noir reveals, is this: civilization's advance, in the name of liberation from the dark ages of the past, brings with it alienation, social fragmentation, and individuation that dissolves first the community, then the family, and ultimately even our sense of humanity. To achieve these effects of fragmentation, individuation, and alienation, noir is typically set in the very modern context of a glass-and-steel cityscape, with its concrete jungle and towering buildings that dwarf and isolate the individual. This sense of alienation can be enhanced, however, when a director moves the noir story out of the modern city and into a more premodern setting—thus alienating (even more) the modern characters from their modern home.

One of the first major films to do this was *Touch of Evil* (Orson Welles, 1958)—widely regarded as the last of the classic noir films—which enhanced the danger of noir by relocating the action from the traditional Los Angeles cityscape to Mexico. *Fargo* uses a similar technique by placing its action in the icy reaches of North Dakota and Minnesota, in the middle of a terrible snowstorm—thereby greatly increasing the noir sense of danger and alienation. In *Fargo,* we get that creepy feeling of being in a place that is not a place, a sort of nowhere. It is true, of course, that Brainerd and Fargo are real cities—hardly nowhere—and there are, in fact, some known cultural landmarks within the film, interspersed here and there, but these are few in number, and forgettable. What dominates the screen instead is a total whiteout, blankness everywhere, with virtually no human effect whatsoever, and this serves to reveal our modern existential situation in an entirely new, but still very noirish, way.

MacIntyre's Critique of Modernity

In order to fully understand this effect, however, first we need to know something about the problem of modernity. Any of several theories might help us in this task, but one seems especially relevant here, namely that of contemporary philosopher Alasdair MacIntyre, particularly the view he develops in his major work, *After Virtue*. The reason is that both MacIntyre and *Fargo* (each in different ways) present a picture of the contemporary world in which individual subjects seem to float listlessly in a void, unable to communicate with one another, unable to connect.

The key to grasping MacIntyre's view is what he calls his "central thesis." "A central thesis then begins to emerge," he writes. "Man is in his actions and practice, as well as in his fictions, essentially a story-telling animal."[2] This view is quite different from the modern (and fairly common) view of human nature as rational agent. But MacIntyre's definition has an important advantage. All cultures tell self-reflective stories about origins and future hopes, and this cultural trait not only predates the rise of reason in ancient Greece but also, in some sense, is more fundamental because it is more formative of human experience: all children must learn stories in order to become functioning human beings. As MacIntyre puts it, "Mythology, in its original sense, is at the heart of things."[3]

In philosophy this idea goes back to Plato and Aristotle, who claimed that a culture requires a myth to give it coherence and to help ground the ethical and intellectual virtues.[4] In ancient Greek times, the myth was Homeric and centered around the gods of Olympus: Zeus, Hera, and so forth. But as time transformed the ancient world into that of the Middle Ages, Christianity replaced Homeric mythology. Much like Homeric mythology, this new story provided a kind of cultural plot, with various characters to be played by real human beings. We are these characters. "We enter human society," writes MacIntyre, "with one or more imputed characters—roles into which we have been drafted—and we have to learn what they are in order to be able to understand how others respond to us and how our responses to them are apt to be constructed."[5] These roles are the roles within a family and all the various positions within a society. People learn these roles and become integrated into the story—or they do not—and become either happy and healthy or misguided and tragic. And once again, these patterns of success and failure are all part of the dominant mythology.

But what is not part of the mythology, and what marks a fundamental distortion of the story, is the Enlightenment project of progressive modernization. Modernity is such a problem because it reacts against mythology altogether and attempts to dislocate humans as pure reason from history as narrative. The reasons for this cultural reaction are well known.[6] And no one would argue that the dominant story of the times did not have some serious problems. But rather than fixing it from within, Enlightenment thinkers somehow found a way to actually step outside the story—almost like characters leaping off the page. Once outside, these characters then proceeded to shred the text into little pieces. And with that, the story was gone—it just stopped, midsentence, halfway through. The characters then quickly declared their own autonomy from the story and their freedom to determine their own individual lives. The revolution began with René

Descartes ("I think, therefore I am") and extends up through the existentialists, such as Jean-Paul Sartre, and the current wave of postmodernity.[7] It was Descartes who declared himself an absolute "I" without any context, and it was Sartre who, three centuries later, went even further and declared the self an absolute "nothingness," entirely free of context, free of virtually all determination whatsoever.[8]

The problem with all of this is that the post-Enlightenment thinkers or "characters" seemed to lose their way. They are now lost and confused, wondering what is going on. They don't know where they are in history, and many of the most reflective thinkers, people who should know what's going on, have declared their world meaningless, nihilistic, and absurd. But, of course, it *is* absurd, MacIntyre seems to be saying. The characters have destroyed their story, the one thing that could give their lives meaning and coherence. And now they (or, rather, we) are suffering the consequences, the foremost among them being an increasing sense of isolation, because the characters are drifting ever farther and farther apart. Even the most basic modes of communication are affected. The once proficient players on the Shakespearean stage of the world no longer remember their lines and have lost all their cues and any feeling for one another upon that stage—all of them "unscripted, anxious stutterers in their actions as in their words," as MacIntyre puts it.[9]

The End of Modernity in *Fargo*

Fargo captures this descent into modernity and postmodernity perfectly, being far more than just a "homespun murder story," as the tagline goes, where "a lot can happen in the middle of nowhere." For the philosophically minded viewer, *Fargo* is a masterpiece study in darkness and nihilism at the height of modernity, set brilliantly against the premodern—almost prehistorical—background of a total whiteout, with no cityscape, no culture, barely even a road.

The first scenes of *Fargo* set the context: the middle of a blizzard that looks like it has always been blowing. Few cinematic shots achieve this sense of the abyss: no color, no life, no horizon, no bearing up or down, very sinister, very dangerous. The world is blotted out in white. Winds blow from seemingly every direction, like a primordial chaos that sucks everyone and everything down into its void. And the moment the mind attempts to impose some kind of order on the abyss, even the ground appears as a form of flux: water only temporally hardened, but which could give way at any moment to swallow the characters whole. Barely anything can live in this violent white chasm, and nothing is moving except the Heraclitean flux itself: lifeless, soulless, completely inhuman and mechanical—a blur of parts in a whirl, without Aristotelian formal causality, without any teleological end. The world is reduced to its bare, essential background, a kind of ontological tabula rasa upon which human experience can make no lasting impression.

Against this frozen, desolate scenery, the characters appear as products of a world that should never have been: wild-eyed contorted monsters, all bundled up in layers and Gortex, with gigantic gloves and "moon" boots. Like horrified astronauts on a failed mission, they float in a cold and lifeless abyss. Director Joel Coen also notes this point, how "everyone [is] bulked up, moving in a particular way, bouncing off people."[10] In this way, *Fargo* captures brilliantly the modern idea of Cartesian monadic selves. Each is ontologically splintered off from every other, drifting this way and that, hovering anywhere without geometrical context. Each one is solipsistically trapped inside a self, with access only to individual thoughts—and no real capacity to communicate.

In fact, the characters of *Fargo* speak to one another as though across the universe, hoping something gets through, desperate to connect. But virtually every conversation falls to pieces in a babble of frustration, in exactly the same way MacIntyre describes the late modern condition: everyone "unscripted, anxious stutterers in their actions as in their words." Jerry, for example, barely utters a coherent thought throughout the entire film. In his meeting with Carl and Grimsrud (at the very beginning), he shows up an hour late because of miscommunication. Then the criminals ask about the crime, but Jerry makes no sense. So Carl and Grimsrud just give up on ever understanding him.

After the meeting, Jerry arrives home to find his icy father-in-law, Wade, watching a hockey game. Jean asks Wade if he is staying for dinner, to which Wade only grunts back. Jerry (whimpering) tries to talk with Wade about the game, but again Wade only offers primate growls, as though Jerry isn't even there (in his own home). Later in the film, after Jean has been kidnapped, Marge interviews Jerry twice. In the second interview, Jerry simply cannot speak. He just starts spitting out half-sentences and subordinate clauses, nothing organized, no subjects and verbs in a row—like a robot whose wires have been crossed and who is now melting down from the inside. Realizing the malfunction, Jerry simply runs away, much to Marge's shock: "He's fleeing the interview."

A similar breakdown in communication happens with Carl. He virtually begs his co-criminal Grimsrud for conversation. But Grimsrud says nothing.

> CARL: Would it kill you to say something?
> GRIMSRUD: I did.
> CARL: "No." First thing you've said in the last four hours. That's a, that's a fountain of conversation, man. That's a geyser. I mean, whoa, daddy, stand back, man. Shit, I'm sittin' here driving, doin' all the driving, man, whole fuckin' way from Brainerd, drivin', just tryin' to chat, you know, keep our spirits up, fight the boredom of the road, and you can't say one fucking thing just in the way of conversation.

Still, Grimsrud says nothing, only smokes and stares out the window. Carl cannot take it. The pressure is building: "Oh, fuck it. I don't have to talk either, man. See how you like it. Just total fuckin' silence. Two can play at that game, smart guy. We'll just see how you like it." Again, Grimsrud says nothing. But Carl, against himself, cannot stop talking (he needs it too badly), even to the point of affirming in pain his new rule of quietude: "Total silence."

Desperate for some human connection, Carl phones an escort service and takes a prostitute out for an evening at the Carlton Celebrity Room. He wants to feel normal: to be out with a woman, enjoy a show, have a drink, and then go home with her. But Carl fails with the waiter, who just ignores him when he asks for a drink. Then he fails again with the prostitute. She asks him what he does, but he avoids the question. Then he asks her about her job.

> CARL: So, uh, how long you work for the escort service?
> PROSTITUTE: I don't know. A few months.
> CARL: Ya find the work interesting, do ya?
> PROSTITUTE: What're you talking about?

The look she gives him is cold and ostracizing. She thinks he is being condescending or ironic. But Carl is really just lonely and actually empathizes with this woman. They have things in common: both are in the middle of nowhere and stuck in jobs that are immoral and illegal; both are lonely. Unlike Carl, however, she does not want to connect; that's not why she's there. So all they can do is have sex. And even that goes wrong, as they are broken apart by the Native American car mechanic and ex-con Shep Proudfoot (Steven Reevis), who beats Carl senseless without explanation while Carl tries desperately to talk to him rationally (a total failure).

Meanwhile, Marge closes in on her suspects. But seemingly at every turn her conversations break down as well. In the middle of the night, Marge gets a call from an old school acquaintance (barely a friend), Mike Yanagita (Steve Park). On the phone he is loud, ecstatic, and generally "off." In fact, even after realizing he has woken her up, Mike does not want to let her go. Nevertheless, Marge, good soul that she is, agrees to meet him for a drink, while on her assignment. During their conversation, however, Mike can hardly put a sentence together, and just a few minutes into their reunion, he completely implodes (weeping).

> MIKE: Oh, and then I saw you on TV, and I, uh, remembered, ya know . . . I always liked you . . .
> MARGE: Well, I always liked you, Mike.
> MIKE: I always liked you *so much*. . . .
> MARGE: So, Mike, should we get together another time, ya think?
> MIKE: No. I . . . I . . . I'm sorry! I shouldn't a done this. I thought we'd have a really terrific time. . . .
> MARGE: It's okay, Mike.
> MIKE: You were such a super lady. And . . . I been so lonely. [now sobbing]

Marge is baffled. So she goes to get some fast food at a drive-thru, but again—the metaphor is plain—she simply cannot communicate. Angrily she leans out the window of her car and yells into the speaker, "Hello!" But no one answers. Like Mike Yanagita in the preceding scene, Marge is also, in her own way, a solitary voice yelling out of the abyss for help and receiving no answer.

Something similar happens with Marge in the squad car. She has caught Grimsrud, and he now sits in the back of the prowler, handcuffed. And it is here that we get the conversation that we've been waiting for: protagonist and antagonist finally meet. Marge initiates: "So that was Mrs. Lundegaard on the floor in there? . . . And I guess that was your accomplice in the wood chipper. . . . And those three people in Brainerd. . . . And for what? For a little bit of money. There's more to life than a little money, you know. . . . Don't you know that? . . . And here ya are, and it's a beautiful day. . . . Well, I just don't understand it." I think most people probably listen to this conversation and love Marge all the more for her seemingly unlimited goodness. But I see Marge very differently. I see her as morally good but intellectually vacant; instrumentally strategic, but entirely unreflective about the human condition. In fact, for all of her sweetness and light, I think Marge is actually sort of a dark character. Allow me to explain.

Marge has finally come to the end of her detective quest, and now all that remains is to nab Jerry (which is easy enough). But here her real detective quest has only begun. The questions have changed. Before they were: Who killed the police officer? Who killed the passersby? That case is over. But now notice how new questions appear in Marge's mind. Who is this man, Grimsrud? Why this? Why here? Marge is plainly bothered. So she asks him. But Grimsrud says nothing. She tries to explain to him that there are good things in the world that should have deterred him. But again, nothing. It's strange, Marge has this almost childlike innocence about her—as though it's all just so simple and easy to be good and such an awful lot of trouble being bad. Of course, Marge isn't stupid by any means. She just isn't very deep or reflective. Grimsrud may not be very deep either. But the chilling look he gives Marge in lieu of a reply says it all. She is good, and he is evil. But he can "see," and she cannot.

We recognize this absence in Marge throughout the film—McDormand lets it out bit by bit. But here it comes out clearly, especially in her remark about beauty. "And here ya are, and it's a beautiful day." The remark is strange for two reasons. First, Marge appeals to something even a criminal can understand. And we know Grimsrud appreciates beauty. Remember that he kills his hostage, Jean, for screaming during a soap opera he is watching on television. Having no coherent story of his own, Grimsrud immerses himself in romances about beautiful people in beautiful places (even if the shows are lowbrow and low budget). These are things long gone in Grimsrud's world, or perhaps they never existed at all. But now they provide him his only escape in an empty world. What's more is that Grimsrud, contrary to what Carl thinks, does indeed need to connect—and feels just as isolated and out of touch with the world as Carl. But, being a criminal, he cannot (and should not) trust Carl and knows not to talk openly with him. Only cheap and beautiful soap operas, with their tired paint-by-numbers dialogue, hold Grimsrud together. So when they are disrupted, in the form of Jean Lundegaard screaming mad with a bag over her head, Grimsrud has no choice but to kill her—and the ransom be damned.

In an earlier scene in the same cabin, Carl—having just taken their hostage—cannot get the television set to work. Grimsrud sits at a cheap TV-dinner-style table in clothing that very clearly resembles that of Alex Delarge (Malcolm McDowell) in *A Clockwork Orange* (Stanley Kubrick, 1971). The product of a hyper-modern and alienated dystopia, Alex is a murderer and a rapist who is deeply sensitive to beauty, especially the classical music of Ludwig von Beethoven. The parallel to Grimsrud is obvious. He, too, is deeply dualistic. He is a murderer on the one hand but a deeply sensitive soul on the other—and his only refuge is beauty. In this scene, there are, however, no beautiful soap operas on television, only "snow"—the chaotic scrambled mess of black and white pixilation on the screen. Snow blasting about outside, and snow blasting about inside—and on both sides, Carl simply won't stop jabbering and yelling nonsense. As he's banging his fist on the television to stop the snow, the camera slowly moves in on Grimsrud to a close-up, while soft and sad music plays in the background. We now look into Grimsrud's eyes. There's an incredible pain there, an incredible isolation, with real fear of the world. Grimsrud understands the modern condition—if only marginally (and perhaps better than Alex Delarge). And we understand him. But Marge just doesn't see it. "I just don't understand it," she says. In response Grimsrud shifts his eyes slowly back to her, breaking once again from his cold hard exterior to give her a look that says it all—and one Marge doesn't even notice. If Marge doesn't understand Grimsrud, he understands her, and he understands, too, that she will always remain on the surface of this world, without any deep understanding.

Second, and more importantly, Marge's appeal to beauty is interesting because she is just plain wrong. It is not, in fact, "a beautiful day." Actually, it is what most people, I think, would call a terrible day, and Grimsrud knows this. It's Brainerd, Minnesota, in the dead of winter, freezing cold—and dangerous by anyone's account. It's not the worst day imaginable, but it's pretty bad. So Marge's claim is simply false: the day is, in fact, horrible, and in more specific aesthetic terms, it is what philosopher Immanuel Kant refers to as "dynamically sublime," or violently overwhelming.[11] Grimsrud rightly recognizes his world as sublime. But Marge cannot see it. She just looks out of her blinkered eyes at a world that isn't there. Nor can she figure out why other people, like Grimsrud, cannot see what she sees.

But why does Marge not understand all of this? After all, she is a police officer, so she ought to know something more about the nature of crime than merely how to follow relatively easy clues to catch a low-end criminal.

Perhaps she doesn't understand the darkness because it's so far away from her—because her goodness is so complete that she might not get it if she tried. But for the philosophically minded viewer, this is not enough. And perhaps all that can be said in her defense is that her ignorance is at least, in some sense, Socratic. Marge knows that she does not know (and she knows that she should).

The absence of reflection in Marge becomes particularly evident when we contrast her character with its heritage. In terms of the genres of noir and detective fiction, Marge is quite unique because she never examines the structure of her own mind, or really anyone else's. All great detectives do this because they know that the internal mad labyrinth of the mind mirrors the external mad labyrinth of crime. And the detective, being half criminal—which makes it possible to catch the criminals—knows this isomorphism and knows, too, that mastering his (or her) own mind is essential to mastering the criminal minds of others. But Marge seems entirely oblivious to herself, in particular, and to the human condition, in general—and she seems to have little to no interest in studying either.

Her detective analysis remains entirely shallow, almost lifeless. She gathers facts and data and follows the information to the villain. But not even once do we suspect she is a philosophically deep detective like Edgar Allan Poe's Monsieur C. Auguste Dupin in "The Murders in the Rue Morgue" or Sir Arthur Conan Doyle's Sherlock Holmes, each of whom analyzes both the nature of crime and the structure of their own mad and brilliant minds. Marge has none of this philosophical madness, and none of what Poe in "The Murders in the Rue Morgue" calls "acumen" (philosophical imagination), that would allow her to picture herself as the villain and to explore the darker reaches of the criminal mind—figuring out what he will do next, figuring out where his motivations and weaknesses lie. And we never even once see her sink deep within herself, like Holmes or Dupin, to lose herself completely in what the philosopher Charles S. Peirce called "musement"—searching for the solution to the riddle in the form of a new logical abduction.

Immediately after recognizing that she does not understand Grimsrud, or the nature of crime, Marge just lets her inquiry drop. Case closed. Nothing more to do except retreat home to a kind of happy ignorance, having no interest at all in the criminal profile. A master sleuth, by contrast, would never let this go—not something as puzzling as this. The problem should plague Marge, as she sits up in bed with her husband Norm (John Carroll

Lynch). It should plague her through the night, but it doesn't. Instead, Marge sleeps well and comfortably. She is neither disturbed nor perplexed.

The main reason Marge cannot engage in this deeper level of detective analysis is that she is one of us, common folk, unlike, say, a Dupin or a Holmes, or a hard-boiled detective, or even James Bond. These detectives are always leery of the stable world of love and marriage, family and children. Such things would only cloud their judgment, and they know that. So in order to maintain their detached sense of objectivity, they stay single and cut off from the regular population. But not Marge: she immerses herself in the world. She is a loving, caring wife to Norm and a soon-to-be mother. She believes in humanity (unlike the noir detective), and she believes the world is good. She has real hope for the future, for her baby, perhaps for all of us—and, of course, we love her for it.

But we must also struggle with Marge's lack of depth as she faces the darkness of the human soul, in the form of Grimsrud. For we as viewers cannot leave things as unresolved as Marge does. Nor can we just look away from Grimsrud and Carl, Jerry and Shep Proudfoot, after a simple case is solved. And this is the real brilliance of *Fargo*—how the Coen brothers, right at the moment one mystery is solved, shift a deeper mystery back onto the viewers, as though they were detectives as well, watching privately in the theater, trying to figure out what went wrong with all of these characters. The viewer feels compelled at film's end to pick up the investigation right where Marge leaves off and follow the thread through the labyrinth of crime that leads from the world of *Fargo* straight back into the human condition.

The Deeper Crime in *Fargo*

This deeper case is, to be sure, far more abstract and difficult to solve. But there are leads in the works of philosophers of modernity, like MacIntyre. Of course, MacIntyre may not think of his books as detective manuals. Yet conceiving of them in that way loses nothing of his main point and gains us much in simplicity. So, taking some license with MacIntyre's overall philosophical view, we may consider the modern project on a par with a crime.

It all went down in the seventeenth century. In order to save the human condition, Pure Reason climbed to the top of the Ivory Tower and put two in the chest of Mythology. What Reason did not know, however, was the secret of Homer: that "mythology is at the heart of things." Reason did not know that the two were the same: mythology *was* the human condition.

Reason had, in effect, killed both: the human condition and the myths by which it lived. And for a long time, no one seemed to notice. The death was slow, and the clues were vague. So it's only been in recent years that culture has begun to examine the crime scene. One of the examinations has taken place in that same Ivory Tower, where philosophers like MacIntyre have studied the strange indexes of contemporary society: monadic subjects floating in an abyss without a story and struggling to communicate but failing miserably.

Another examination, and one I think just as valuable, has taken place in American cinema, especially the genre of film noir—where, again, monadic subjects appear to float without a story and struggle to communicate, all too often failing miserably to connect. At the height of this genre tradition, it has been the Coen brothers' film, *Fargo*, that has taken these themes of social detachment, the ontological void, and unscripted babblers to an extreme. So, while, on one level, *Fargo* certainly is a "homespun murder story," on a deeper level *Fargo* is also a philosophically spun murder mystery, shot through with ontological and historical significance, a truly masterful study of the crisis of the modern age, in all its coldness, all its isolation, and its absence of human connection.

Notes

I am very grateful to Mark Conard for reading and commenting on an earlier draft of this essay, and to Elizabeth F. Cooke and Chris Pliatska for discussions on the films of the Coen brothers. Of course, any mistakes that remain are my own.

1. Throughout the essay, I will use the names of the characters as we know them. So, for example, we know Jerry Lundegaard by his first name, Jerry. But we know Gaear Grimsrud by his last name, Grimsrud.

2. Alasdair MacIntyre, *After Virtue: A Study in Moral Theory* (Notre Dame, Ind.: Univ. of Notre Dame Press, 1981), 201.

3. Ibid.

4. Plato, for example, argues in *The Republic* (Books II and II) for a new mythology (to replace Homer): the "Myth of the Metals." This was his own "noble lie."

5. MacIntyre, *After Virtue*, 201.

6. The causes of the Enlightenment are well documented, for example, the Protestant Reformation, the rise of a reading public with the Gutenberg press (ca. 1450), the rise of science, and political problems within the Catholic Church.

7. MacIntyre writes, "For a self separated from its roles in the Sartrean mode loses that arena of social relationships in which the Aristotelian virtues function if they

function at all. The patterns of a virtuous life would fall under those condemnations of conventionality which Sartre put into the mouth of Antoine Roquentin in *La Nausée* and which he uttered in his own person in *L'Être et le néant*. Indeed the self's refusal of the inauthenticity of conventionalised social relationships becomes what integrity is diminished into in Sartre's account." *After Virtue,* 191.

8. MacIntyre also writes, "And the self so detached is of course a self very much at home in . . . Sartre's . . . perspective, a self that can have no history. The contrast with the narrative view of the self is clear. For the story of my life is always embedded in the story of those communities from which I derive my identity. I am born with a past; and to try to cut myself off from that past, in the individualist mode, is to deform my present relationships." *After Virtue,* 205.

9. MacIntyre, *After Virtue,* 201. MacIntyre offers two solutions to the problem of modernity: "Nietzsche or Aristotle?" Either we go forward with the Enlightenment project that began with Descartes and proceeded through Kant and that finds its ultimate and logical end in the nihilism and overman visions of Nietzsche, or we return to the ancient world of the virtues: we return to the story and finish it up. But either way, we cannot stay as we are. MacIntyre argues for the latter.

10. Joel Coen, "Interview with Lizzie Francke," in *Joel and Ethan Coen: Blood Siblings,* ed. Paul A. Woods (London: Plexus, 2002), 15.

11. Richard Gilmore makes a similar point in "The American Sublime in *Fargo.*" Gilmore writes, "I read the Coen brothers' movie *Fargo* as a lesson in the ways of the American sublime. I take as my starting point on the sublime Kant's discussion of it in the third *Critique.*" Gilmore, http://mcrae_tony.tripod.com/american_sublime_in_fargo .htm. In *Critique of Judgment* the philosopher Immanuel Kant distinguishes the beautiful, or that which gives harmony to the mind, from the sublime, or that which overwhelms and disturbs it. There are two kinds of sublime: mathematical (the experience of quantitative infinity) and dynamical (the experience of violent and overwhelming force). See Kant, *Critique of Judgment,* trans. Werner S. Pluhar (1790; Indianapolis: Hackett, 1987).

Part 4

EXISTENTIALISM, ALIENATION, AND DESPAIR

"WHAT KIND OF MAN ARE YOU?"

The Coen Brothers and Existentialist Role Playing

Richard Gaughran

Uncertain of All

Filmmakers Joel and Ethan Coen presuppose an absurd world. This state-ment implies more than casual viewers might imagine. True, many images in their films appear at first merely strange, incongruous, or even repulsive. An infamous scene from *Fargo* (1996) comes to mind: hired kidnapper Gaear Grimsrud (Peter Stormare) crams the corpse of his partner, Carl Showalter (Steve Buscemi), into a wood chipper, strewing his shredded re-mains across the snow. For what purpose? If Grimsrud wants to dispose of a murder victim, he could surely conceive a better plan than this one, which, rather than concealing evidence, spreads it widely. We can only conclude that Grimsrud, having a corpse on his hands, noticed a wood chipper and whimsically brought the two together. Why not?

"Why not?" is the shrug of characters who have concluded that theirs is a world without value, devoid of meaning, absurd. The very first words ever uttered in a Coen brothers film, the voice-over that opens *Blood Simple* (1984), heralds the world we enter in any of the brothers' films. It is a world divested of value, a world without hierarchies of meaning, a world of stark individual freedom:

> The world is full of complainers. But the fact is, nothing comes with a guarantee. I don't care if you're the Pope of Rome, President of the United States, or even Man of the Year—something can always go wrong. And go ahead, complain, tell your problems to your neighbor—watch him fly.
>
> Now in Russia, they got it mapped out so that everyone pulls

> for everyone else—that's the theory, anyway. But what I know about
> is Texas. . . . And down here . . . you're on your own.

We hear these words as we visually encounter the bleak, endlessly flat terrain of west Texas. The published screenplay refers to the landscape as "broad, bare, and lifeless."[1] A similar landscape provides the backdrop for the Coen brothers' second film, *Raising Arizona* (1987), though the setting is somewhat west of Texas, "'an Arizona of the mind,'" as Ethan Coen has remarked, and the film itself is more broadly comic than *Blood Simple*.[2] The flat, desolate terrain of the northern plains figures prominently in *Fargo*, and in *No Country for Old Men* (2007) the filmmakers return to west Texas, with much of that film's action playing out against, again, a desolate landscape. In each of these films the setting becomes a character at least as important as any of the human characters. In the Coen universe, we're not always specifically in Texas, but we are "down here," and we are indeed on our own.

In a groundbreaking essay on film noir—a cinematic style that, as many have remarked, the Coens have revived and revised in much of their work—Paul Schrader says of typical noir settings, "When the environment is given an equal or greater weight than the actor, it, of course, creates a fatalistic, hopeless mood. There is nothing the protagonists can do; the city will outlast and negate even their best efforts."[3] Schrader mentions the city, since, as he argues, noir settings are typically urban. Although the Coen brothers do feature cities in some films, they, like other neo-noir filmmakers, set their works in various locales. Furthermore, their merging of noir style with western settings in the films mentioned here exemplifies their genre-bending and genre-combining tendencies. In any case, the prominence given to rural settings in these Coen brothers films generates the same hopelessness of which Schrader speaks. Characters act freely, but they do so within an uncaring, hostile environment, that is, within the realm of the absurd.

If human beings "enter the new world naked," as poet William Carlos Williams says, "cold, uncertain of all / save that they enter," an individual life remains unfixed and undefined until the individual creates an identity by taking action to bring the self into being.[4] The existentialist writer Jean-Paul Sartre has famously encapsulated existentialism in the phrase "existence precedes essence," which means, he says, "that, first of all, man exists, turns up, appears on the scene, and, only afterwards, defines himself." Sartre says further, "Man is nothing else but what he makes of himself. Such is the first principle of existentialism."[5] Robert G. Porfirio, in an important essay that makes connections between existentialism and film noir, puts it this way: "Existentialism is an outlook which begins with a disoriented individual facing a confused world that he cannot accept. It places its emphasis on man's contingency in a world where there are no transcendental values or moral absolutes, a world devoid of any meaning but the one man himself creates."[6]

If, however, our efforts are doomed to failure, and if we can refer to no fixed human nature in creating ourselves, how do we choose how to act and, thereby, what to become? Numerous characters within the Coen brothers' canon dramatize precisely this dilemma. As we shall see, the individual's attempt to construct a viable identity within a hostile environment emerges as a major theme within these films, as does confusion concerning the identity of others. Even the titles themselves refer to identity, some obliquely, such as *Barton Fink* (1991), *The Hudsucker Proxy* (1994), and *The Big Lebowski* (1998), and others quite directly, such as *O Brother, Where Art Thou?* (2000) and especially *The Man Who Wasn't There* (2001), the central Coen brothers work exemplifying the dilemma of existentialist self-creation.

Albert Camus, the writer who has most pointedly articulated a theory of the absurd, explains, particularly in *The Myth of Sisyphus,* that awareness of absurdity grows from the individual's realization that the mind and the world are out of sync. We plan for the future, raise children, erect buildings, accumulate possessions, but to what end? We all die. Our best efforts are doomed. Eventually, all trace of our existence fades into oblivion. With enough time, even the greatest among us will be forgotten. Camus defines the absurd in these terms: "It is that divorce between the mind that desires and the world that disappoints, my nostalgia for unity, this fragmented universe and the contradiction that binds them together."[7]

The world offers no clues for us, and "man feels an alien, a stranger."[8] When one acknowledges this state of affairs, according to Camus, the first question is that of suicide. Since life provides no meaning, why live it? Since we know our future—death—why not embrace that future now and get it over with? Camus, of course, does not recommend suicide but an acceptance of our condition—that we are alive and desire to remain so, though we cannot. Although we are condemned to death in advance, we revolt against this inevitable future. "That revolt gives life its value."[9] Furthermore, since death is real—in fact, it is the only reality—there is no eternity for us, yet we have freedom within the earthly sphere: "Now if the absurd cancels all my chances of eternal freedom, it restores and magnifies, on the other hand, my freedom of action."[10]

Characters within the Coen brothers' films routinely engage in revolts against their doomed status. Of course, some do not. In *Fargo*, for example, Marge Gunderson (Frances McDormand), with her husband Norm (John Carroll Lynch), still clings to a belief in a priori normalcy, so in the wake of a bloodbath she shakes her head in disbelief, saying, "I just don't understand it." Marge Gunderson anticipates the bewilderment of Sheriff Ed Tom Bell (Tommy Lee Jones) in *No Country for Old Men* when he reflects on the nihilistic violence he has investigated. Concerning the lack of apparent motive or feeling within the killer of a fourteen-year-old girl, Bell says, "I don't know what to make of that. I surely don't." At the film's end, he explains his reasons for retiring from law enforcement: "I feel overmatched. I always figured when I got older God would sorta come into my life somehow. He didn't."

Within the Coen canon, the Gundersons and Sheriff Bell stand as exceptions. Most characters, whether consciously or not, stage revolts against their condition. Some of the rebels become nihilistic, such as those who adopt the "why not?" shrug mentioned earlier. Sartre refers to this attitude, expressed by Fyodor Dostoyevsky's character Ivan Karamazov (though Sartre imprecisely attributes it to Dostoyevsky himself): "'If God didn't exist, everything would be possible.' That is the very starting point of existentialism."[11] Around the same time Sartre's words appeared in English, this idea found expression in the words of the Misfit, a fictional creation of American short-story writer Flannery O'Connor. Because the serial killer of "A Good Man Is Hard to Find" finds no reason to believe in God, he concludes, "It's nothing for you to do but enjoy the few minutes you got left the best way you can—by killing somebody or burning down his house or doing some other meanness to him. No pleasure but meanness."[12]

Murdering a partner, having your wife kidnapped or murdered—all of this has as little or as much value as anything else. And a wood chipper on the premises might afford an amusing way to top off a murder. Thomas S. Hibbs says that nihilistic comedy turns inhumane atrocity "into quasi-comic expressions of exuberant amoral energy."[13] Yet nihilism does not always manifest itself in physical violence. Attorney Miles Massey (George Clooney) of *Intolerable Cruelty* (2003) is not likely to bloody his hands, but he does engage in nihilistic legal maneuvering. When offered the bromide that "life is compromise," he responds, "That's *death*. Challenge, struggle, and, of course, ultimate destruction of your opponent—that's life."

Creating a Self

As the Dude (Jeff Bridges) reminds us in *The Big Lebowski,* however, nihilism can be exhausting. Nihilistic action, furthermore, while expressing the freedom of one individual—the nihilist as murderer, kidnapper, or shyster lawyer—denies freedom to others. Many of the characters within the Coen brothers' canon step away from extreme nihilistic destruction, or temper their nihilism, by attending to the creation of a unique self. They fashion a style or a mask by means of which they can face the abyss.

Some of these self-inventions are consciously designed to deceive others, to be sure. John Goodman's Charlie Meadows in *Barton Fink,* for example, poses as a traveling salesman, when in fact he has nefarious intentions. The same actor's Big Dan Teague does something similar in *O Brother.* If Maude Lebowski (Julianne Moore) can be believed, her father, Jeffrey Lebowski (David Huddleston), is not what he seems. The thieves in *The Ladykillers* (2004) masquerade as musicians in order to deceive their landlady. Yet many Coen characters adopt a style, an aggregate of gestures, principally in order to define themselves, to create an identity.

In his essay on film noir, Schrader, speaking of the valueless universe presupposed by noir, says, "In such a world style becomes paramount; it is all that separates one from meaninglessness."[14] So it is in the Coen brothers' films. In *The Big Lebowski,* when Sam Elliott's character, the Stranger, says, "I like your style, Dude," he is acknowledging that Jeff Bridges's character has invented a self appropriate for a time and place. When the Dude answers, "I dig your style too, man. Got a whole cowboy thing goin'," he's returning a compliment and greeting a fellow role player, though these characters have adopted quite distinct roles. Walter Sobchak (John Goodman), in the same film, uses an entire palette of gestures—his obsession with the Vietnam War, his profession of Judaism, and so on—with which to define himself. Hibbs accurately summarizes the nostalgic nature of Walter's self-creation: "Walter wants to have an identity, to define himself in relation to a way of life, a tradition, larger than himself."[15] Donny (Steve Buscemi), however, has failed to take on a personal style, whether rooted in the past or not. He acts instead as a befuddled chorus for the distinct characters, and so he dies, finally reduced to ashes blown by the wind.

Although few Coen characters are as insubstantial as Donny, some attempt to squeeze themselves into roles that don't quite fit. So it is with Barton Fink (John Turturro), who imagines himself as a tortured artist advancing high principles within a crass world of commercialism. The pose is pretentious, and it reveals ignorance of the surrounding world, the world he claims to serve. So he resorts to hero worship, until he is disillusioned by the drinking and violent behavior of W. P. Mayhew (John Mahoney). In another way, *Fargo's* Jerry Lundegaard (William H. Macy) takes on an ill-fitting role. A car salesman, he assumes the pose of criminal mastermind, a mismatch that initiates a series of violent acts.

Hats, Pomade, and Hair Nets

Miller's Crossing (1990) calls particular attention to characters' styles. According to Barry Sonnenfeld, the film's director of photography, Ethan Coen said to him, "It should be a handsome movie about men in hats."[16] To be sure, in answering an interviewer's question about the significance of hats in the film, particularly the hat blown by the wind as the opening credits begin, both brothers later downplayed the significance of the image, insisting that hats are not symbols, that there is "no need to look for deep meanings."[17] Yes, sometimes a hat is just a hat, yet the hats of *Miller's Crossing* do have significance.[18] Besides evoking a period when men habitually wore certain styles of hats, the hats function as props in the process of self-creation. And, like the biblical Samson's hair, they correspond to personal power.

One of the film's early scenes shows us Tom Reagan (Gabriel Byrne) as he seeks to retrieve his hat, which he lost gambling the night before. Tom has lost more than money; he has lost a part of himself, so the film begins with his attempt to piece himself back together. Later Tom tells Verna (Marcia Gay Harden) that he had a dream about losing his hat. She romantically completes the dream, saying he chased after it and it turned into something beautiful. But he corrects her, saying he didn't go after it: "Nothing more foolish than a man chasin' his hat." Tom is arrogantly boasting here. We have already seen him chase the hat, an action that acknowledges the unfixed, fluid nature of identity and the need for vigilance in constructing a personal style. Perhaps no scene better illustrates the significance of hats than when Leo (Albert Finney) beats Tom, pummeling him down a corridor and two flights of stairs, as Tom, rather than fighting back, desperately attends to his hat, sometimes losing hold of it and then snatching it again. The scene ends with Leo's contemptuous but simultaneously sympathetic gesture of flipping Tom's hat onto Tom's chest as he lies beaten and breathless.

Miller's Crossing is indeed a handsome movie about men in hats. A man with his hat in place feels sure of who he is or, more to the point, feels sure of the man he has created for himself. So, when the boxer Clarence "Drop" Johnson (Mario Todisco) appears wearing a hat ridiculously small for him, Tom makes fun of him, relating hat size to mental capacity, in effect diminishing the threatening figure's power. Johnny Caspar (Jon Polito) also relates hats to power, complaining that he's being ill treated and disrespected by others, in his complaints continually using the expression "high hat" as a metaphor for the condescension he so resents.

To reiterate, these characters implicitly acknowledge that life lacks meaning. Johnny Caspar delivers the first extended speech of the film, comically referring to the need for a code of ethics. These are gangsters talking, so his insistence is ridiculous, but he does underscore the arbitrariness of moral standards: "Now if you can't trust a fix, what can you trust? For a good return you gotta go bettin' on chance, an' then, you're back with anarchy, right back in the jungle. That's why ethics is important, what separates us from the animals—the beasts of burden, beasts of prey. Ethics."

Referring specifically to this speech, Carolyn R. Russell says, "Friendship, character, ethics, trust, anarchy—these are concepts which are not stable in and of themselves but depend for their meaning upon the consensus of their 'user' community."[19] In other words, values are invented, not given, and the self lacks unity and definition until the individual constructs a personal style. As Sartre puts it, "To say that we invent values means nothing else but this: life has no meaning *a priori.* Before you come alive, life is nothing; it's up to you to give it a meaning, and value is nothing else but the meaning that you choose."[20] A belief system, like a personal style, is a work of art: "What art and ethics have in common is that we have creation and invention in both cases."[21]

In *The Rebel,* subtitled *An Essay on Man in Revolt,* Camus refers to the types of rebellions we've been examining under the heading "Metaphysical Rebellion." Particularly apt in the context of the Coen brothers' films is his discussion of dandyism, an attitude, a style, that grows out of romanticism. Camus writes, "Much more than the cult of the individual, romanticism inaugurates the cult of the 'character.'"[22] Camus discusses the dandy, a specific kind of "character," in these terms:

> The dandy creates his own unity by aesthetic means. But it is an aesthetic of singularity and of negation. "To live and die before a mirror": that[,] according to Baudelaire, was the dandy's slogan. It

is indeed a coherent slogan. The dandy, is, by occupation, always in opposition. He can only exist by defiance. Up to now man derived his coherence from his Creator. But from the moment that he consecrates his rupture with Him, he finds himself delivered over to the fleeting moment, to the passing days, and to wasted sensibility. Therefore he must take himself in hand. The dandy rallies his forces and creates a unity for himself by the very violence of his refusal. Profligate, like all people without a rule of life, he is coherent as an actor.[23]

Men obsessed with their hats are indeed living and dying before a mirror, as are any characters preoccupied with appearance. Within the Coen canon perhaps the most obvious dandy, at least in the conventional sense, is Ulysses Everett McGill (George Clooney), from *O Brother, Where Art Thou?* He is comically obsessed with his hair and Dapper Dan pomade, a brand name that suggests the word "dandy," as does, even more so, the competing brand, Fop, a synonym for "dandy." Everett rejects Fop, however, insisting, "I'm a Dapper Dan man!"

Significantly, though he is in the Bible Belt, surrounded by Christian culture and religious practice, even performing gospel songs, Everett pointedly rejects Christian belief. He calls his companions "fools" for submitting to baptism. Other Christians he calls "chumps," and he calls Christianity a "ridiculous superstition." When Delmar (Tim Blake Nelson) says he looks forward to "heaven everlasting" as his reward, Everett dismissively (and comically) remarks, "We have bigger fish to fry." Everett, like his model, Homer's Odysseus, stands in opposition to the heavens. He is "skilled in all the ways of contending," as the film's epigraph, from Homer, says. Everett is staging the dandy's rebellion, setting himself up as a rival to God, as Camus explains:

Romanticism demonstrates . . . that rebellion is part and parcel of dandyism: one of its objectives is appearances. In its conventional forms, dandyism admits a nostalgia for ethics. . . . But at the same time it inaugurates an aesthetic which is still valid in our world, an aesthetic of solitary creators, who are obstinate rivals of a God they condemn. From romanticism onward, the artist's task will not only be to create a world, or to exalt beauty for its own sake, but also to define an attitude. Thus the artist becomes a model and offers himself as an example: art is his ethic.[24]

For Camus, the dandy's revolt fails in that it starts with awareness of absurdity but ends by positing the self as an absolute, betraying the revolt's origins. The dandy "plays at life because he is unable to live it."[25] Furthermore, the dandy denies the values of others, even while requiring others as an audience: "He can only be sure of his own existence by finding it in the expression of others' faces. Other people are his mirror. A mirror that quickly becomes clouded, it is true, since human capacity for attention is limited."[26] As Tom Reagan says to Leo in *Miller's Crossing*, "You don't hold elected office in this town. You run it because people *think* you run it. Once they stop thinkin' it, you stop runnin' it."

Camus's discussion of the dandy's dependence on an audience for his very existence sheds light on a tendency among Coen brothers characters to loudly demand recognition on their own terms, in their own language. The Dude insists on his invented identity, pointedly instructing David Huddleston's character, "I'm not Mr. Lebowski; *you're* Mr. Lebowski. I'm the Dude. So that's what you call me. That, or Duder. His Dudeness. Or El Duderino, if, you know, you're not into the whole brevity thing." Similarly, Everett is a Dapper Dan man, and he is aghast that anyone would think otherwise. Even minor characters become adamant, as does, for example, the bank robber George Nelson (Michael Badalucco) in *O Brother*, who cannot abide the name "Babyface."

Not only is the human attention span limited, as Camus says, but also some members of the dandy's audience consciously attempt to negate his existence, refusing to applaud his performance, as it were. *O Brother*, especially, develops this theme, particularly when Everett tries to resurrect his marriage to Penny (Holly Hunter), who has other ideas. His daughters, instructed by their mother, tell him he's no longer their father, that he's been hit by a train: "Blooey! Nothin' left. Just a grease spot on the L&N." Unlike Penny's suitor, Vernon T. Waldrip (Ray McKinnon), Everett is not "bona fide," to which he insists, "I am the damn paterfamilias." The daughters, now known by their mother's maiden name of Wharvey instead of McGill, repeat, "But you ain't bona fide."

Many characters in Coen brothers films use a similar strategy to diminish or even dissolve others. In *The Big Lebowski*, when Jesus Quintana (John Turturro) threateningly swaggers before the Dude, Walter, and Donny, Walter redefines their rival, diminishing his power over them: "He's a fucking pervert, Dude. . . . Your man is a sex offender. . . . When he moved down to Venice he had to go door-to-door to tell everyone he's a pederast." Similarly, in *Fargo,* Carl Showalter denies the authority of a parking attendant by mocking his uniform, reminding him that without it he's nothing. In *O Brother,* Penny, still resisting Everett, answers a bystander's question about his identity by denying one of Everett's possible roles and assigning him a less dignified one: "He's not my husband. Some drifter. Some no-account drifter." Throughout these films, the numerous challenges to another's role imply that these characters unconsciously understand the provisional nature of identity. If character is artifice, spun from nothing, then presumably anyone can be nudged out of an adopted role into one with less power.

The Man Who Wasn't There

As mentioned earlier, *The Man Who Wasn't There,* more than any other Coen brothers film, brings these questions of identity to the fore.[27] Billy Bob Thornton has said that Joel Coen pitched him the role of Ed Crane by saying, "It's about a barber who wants to be a dry cleaner."[28] The remark's irony and self-effacement aside, it immediately announces the theme of existentialist role playing. It also provides an apt transition from previous films' obsession with hats, pomade, and hair nets. As Creighton Tolliver (Jon Polito) says, "Grooming, my friend, is probably the most important thing in business—after personality, of course." Tolliver himself is quite proud of his toupee, made from human hair, a necessary accessory for the role he has fashioned for himself.

Crane and his brother-in-law Frank (Michael Badalucco) are style assistants, so to speak, helping others create their identities. However, Crane's first words inform us that he begins the film with no substance of his own, that he's playing an assigned role in life: "Yeah, I worked in a barbershop. But I never considered myself a barber. . . . I stumbled into it—well, married into it more precisely." Not having created an identity for himself, he is a man who is not there. He is on the earth—smoking cigarettes, cutting hair—but merely existing: "Like the fella says, I only work here."

As if we need more evidence from the Coen brothers that religion provides no meaning for these lives, Crane as narrator, giving viewers a sketch of his life with Doris (Frances McDormand), announces that the couple went to church every week. But he immediately undercuts the point by saying they went on Tuesdays, for bingo games: "Doris wasn't big on divine worship . . . and I doubt she believed in life everlasting; she'd most likely tell you that our reward is on this earth and bingo is probably the extent of it."

In a world without value, humans are nothing, are "not there," until they create themselves. And, Crane, not self-created, just "the barber," is a wisp of a man, invisible to others. As Tolliver says when Crane first visits his hotel room, "'Course—the barber. I didn't recognize you without the smock."

Crane has much in common with one of his literary origins, Meursault, of Camus's novel *The Stranger* (1942). The two characters, both narrating from prison, do so in a deadpan, laconic manner, a tone that flattens events. Meursault, after killing a man for no particular reason—"because of the sun," he later says in court—tells an examining magistrate, "I don't have much to say. So I keep quiet."[29] Crane, still introducing himself in his initial voice-over, says, "Me, I don't talk much. . . . I just cut the hair."

Both characters assume, even if unconsciously, a meaningless universe. Crane tells us that his marriage was a ho-hum affair, that it took place only a couple of weeks after he and Doris met on a blind date. He doesn't mention love or emotional attachment. He merely says that when he asked Doris if she wouldn't like to know him better before marrying him, she replied, "Why? Does it get better?" He then adds, "She had a point. We knew each other as well then as now." Likewise, Meursault recounts his response to Marie when she asked him if he wanted to get married: "I said it didn't make any difference to me and that we could if she wanted to. Then she wanted to know if I loved her. I answered the same way I had the last time, that it didn't mean anything but that I probably didn't love her."[30]

Love and marriage lack meaning for these characters, but so does everything else. Meursault tells us his response to his boss's suggestion that he relocate to a Paris office: "I said yes but that it was all the same to me. Then he asked me if I wasn't interested in a change of life. I said that people never change their lives, that in any case one life was as good as another." Later he says, "Everybody knows life isn't worth living."[31] Early in *The Man Who Wasn't There* Crane stares down at a boy's crew cut and asks Frank a question that pertains to more than hair: "You ever wonder about it?" When Frank asks him to explain, he says, "I don't know. How it keeps on coming. It just keeps growing." As Crane's eyes peer down on a boy's scalp, his mind's eye gazes at the abyss.

Crane feels a faint desire to step out of this meaningless predicament, to make something of himself. Hearing Tolliver sing the praises of dry cleaning, Crane says he was "locked up in the barbershop, nose against the exit, afraid to try turning the knob." No doubt motivated by a twinge of hurt pride—he says knowledge of the affair between Doris and Big Dave Brewster (James

Gandolfini) "pinched a little"—he turns the knob, beginning with blackmail, which opens a door to a series of events that lead to the electric chair, despite the fact that Crane is innocent of the crime for which he is executed.

Meursault says that pulling the trigger on the gun that killed an Arab on a beach "is where it all started," and, like Crane, he uses the image of a door opening. The four extra shots he fires are "like knocking four quick times on the door of unhappiness."[32] Both Meursault and Crane rebel against their condition, and though they do so with destructive acts (notwithstanding Crane's misguided and futile attempt to manage a music career for Birdy [Scarlett Johansson]), they do define themselves and acquire distinct identities. After killing Big Dave, Crane notices his transformation and contrasts himself with the masses of people on the street: "It seemed like I knew a secret, a bigger one even than what had really happened to Big Dave, something none of them knew. Like I had made it to the outside, somehow, and they were all struggling way down below."[33]

When Big Dave confronts Crane concerning the blackmail, and when Frank turns on Crane at Crane's trial, they both blast him with a rhetorical question meant as an accusation: "What kind of man *are* you?" The best answer to the question is that, like Meursault before him, but unlike the ordinary citizens of Santa Rosa, Crane, though bewildered, squarely faces the absurdity of existence rather than embracing an illusion about the world. No, these absurdist antiheroes are not "normal." In fact, Meursault is convicted in part because he doesn't demonstrate conventional grief over his mother's death. They are honest about the human condition as they find it, and to some measure they take responsibility for their actions. Facing his death, Crane says, "I don't regret anything. Not a thing. I used to. I used to regret being the barber." He could have said, like Meursault, "I opened myself to the gentle indifference of the world."[34]

Of course, killing another human being is no better a way to forge an identity than is suicide. Just as Camus addresses the question of suicide in *The Myth of Sisyphus*, he takes on the question of murder in *The Rebel*. There, Camus concludes that rebellion ending in destruction is illogical because, for one thing, a killer denies another's freedom in the name of freedom. Furthermore, rebellion that takes the form of destruction violates the absurdist origins of rebellion. Rebellion, Camus says, "in order to remain authentic, must never abandon any of the terms of the contradiction that sustains it." The world's reality is death, to be sure, but the absurd man refuses "to legitimize murder because rebellion, in principle, is a protest against death."[35]

In *The Myth of Sisyphus* Camus proposes that Sisyphus, condemned forever to roll a huge stone up a slope, is the hero of the absurd. Sisyphus' punishment stemmed from "his scorn of the gods, his hatred of death, and his passion for life."[36] Rather than attempting any of the strategies employed by the characters we've examined here, strategies that attempt to unify the self and the world, Sisyphus never settles the question of the absurd. He doesn't surrender to death or choose an identity that removes him from his ongoing rebellion against death. Camus says that "Sisyphus, proletarian of the gods, powerless and rebellious, knows the whole extent of his wretched condition. . . . The lucidity that was to constitute his torture at the same time crowns his victory."[37] Or, as the Dude might say, "Fucking Sisyphus. That creep can roll, man."

Existentialism, with its roots in nihilism, struggles to present a coherent ethical system. In fiction, however, Camus presents the character Dr. Rieux, from his novel *The Plague* (1947), as his fullest, most concrete moral exemplar. Rieux knows that plague—that is, death inherent in life—always prevails in the end. But he is also one of those "who, while unable to be saints but refusing to bow down to pestilences, strive their utmost to be healers."[38]

Although the Coen brothers present numerous characters that create an identity within the context of a world without meaning, the brothers remain essentially comic filmmakers, so many of these serious issues "take shape as somewhat cartoonish."[39] To be sure, many of the absurd characters are entertaining and likeable, and even some of the Coens' nihilistic destroyers are attractive for their defiant energy. Admittedly, however, it is hard to find a Dr. Rieux among them, or even a Sisyphus, unless we can imagine him ceaselessly rolling his stone while singing the theme from *O Brother:* "I am a man of constant sorrow / I've seen trouble all my day."

Notes

1. Joel Coen and Ethan Coen, *Blood Simple* (London: Faber and Faber, 1996), 1.

2. Quoted in James Mottram, *The Coen Brothers: The Life of the Mind* (Dulles, Va.: Brassey's, 2000), 38.

3. Paul Schrader, "Notes on Film Noir," in *Perspectives on Film Noir,* ed. R. Barton Palmer (New York: G. K. Hall, 1996), 104.

4. William Carlos Williams, "Spring and All," in *The Collected Poems of William Carlos Williams: Volume I, 1909–1939,* ed. A. Walton Litz and Christopher MacGowan (New York: New Directions, 1986), 183.

5. Jean-Paul Sartre, *Existentialism and Human Emotions*, trans. Bernard Frechtman (New York: Philosophical Library, 1957), 15.

6. Robert G. Porfirio, "No Way Out: Existential Motifs in the Film Noir," *Sight and Sound* 45, no. 4 (1976): 213.

7. Albert Camus, *The Myth of Sisyphus*, trans. Justin O'Brien (New York: Vintage, 1991), 50.

8. Ibid., 6.

9. Ibid., 55.

10. Ibid., 56–57.

11. Sartre, *Existentialism and Human Emotions*, 22.

12. Flannery O'Connor, "A Good Man Is Hard to Find," in *A Good Man Is Hard to Find and Other Stories* (New York: Harcourt, Brace, 1955), 28.

13. Thomas S. Hibbs, "The Human Comedy Perpetuates Itself: Nihilism and Comedy in Coen Neo-Noir," in *The Philosophy of Neo-Noir*, ed. Mark T. Conard (Lexington: Univ. Press of Kentucky, 2007), 140. Hibbs's essay also appears in this volume.

14. Schrader, "Notes on Film Noir," 105.

15. Hibbs, "The Human Comedy Perpetuates Itself," 143.

16. Sonnenfeld makes this comment in the course of an extra feature accompanying the DVD version of *Miller's Crossing*.

17. Quoted in William Rodney Allen, ed., *The Coen Brothers Interviews* (Jackson: Univ. Press of Mississippi, 2006), 44.

18. Answering Gabriel Byrne's question about the meaning of the windblown hat, Joel Coen reportedly replied cryptically, "The hat is very significant." See Carolyn R. Russell, *The Films of Joel and Ethan Coen* (Jefferson, N.C.: McFarland, 2001), 46.

19. Russell, *Films of Joel and Ethan Coen*, 48.

20. Sartre, *Existentialism and Human Emotions*, 49.

21. Ibid., 43.

22. Albert Camus, *The Rebel: An Essay on Man in Revolt*, trans. Anthony Bower (New York: Vintage, 1991), 50–51.

23. Ibid., 51.

24. Ibid., 53.

25. Ibid., 52.

26. Ibid., 51–52.

27. Set in 1949, the film deliberately mimics the look of classic film noirs of the period, and it draws on the hard-boiled fiction of James M. Cain. See, for example, the brothers' comments in a *Playboy* interview from 2001, reprinted in Allen, *Coen Brothers Interviews*, 180. R. Barton Palmer also discusses the sources for the film's style and themes, though he overemphasizes the point that existentialist themes were peculiar to the immediate post–World War II sensibility. See Palmer, *Joel and Ethan Coen* (Urbana: Univ. of Illinois Press, 2004), 62–79. Also see Palmer, "The New Sincerity of Neo-Noir:

The Example of *The Man Who Wasn't There,"* in *The Philosophy of Neo-Noir,* ed. Mark T. Conard (Lexington: Univ. Press of Kentucky, 2007), 151–66.

28. Quoted in Allen, *Coen Brothers Interviews,* 161.

29. Albert Camus, *The Stranger,* trans. Matthew Ward (New York: Vintage, 1989), 66.

30. Ibid., 41.

31. Ibid., 41, 114.

32. Ibid., 59.

33. It may be more than coincidence that the British edition of Camus's *The Stranger* is entitled *The Outsider.*

34. Camus, *Stranger,* 122.

35. Camus, *Rebel,* 285.

36. Camus, *Myth of Sisyphus,* 120.

37. Ibid., 121.

38. Albert Camus, *The Plague,* trans. Stuart Gilbert (New York: Random House, 1991), 308.

39. Palmer, *Joel and Ethan Coen,* 79.

BEING THE BARBER

Kierkegaardian Despair in *The Man Who Wasn't There*

Karen D. Hoffman

Like so many of the films of Joel and Ethan Coen, *The Man Who Wasn't There* (2001) concerns itself with the creation of a character, Ed Crane (Billy Bob Thornton), as much as with the telling of his story. As the film's title suggests, Ed is notably absent from his own life. In the world without really being a part of it, Ed lives in despair. Taking stoic detachment to an extreme, Ed displays so little passion and engagement in life that a mere nod of his head constitutes a substantial gesture.

As the film progresses, Ed becomes more aware of the problematic ways in which he has failed to take control of his own life and to make choices that help him define himself as something other than the ordinary barber that he regrets being. Growing more reflective toward the end of his life, Ed finds himself "pulling away from the maze" and "seeing it whole." He progresses from what the nineteenth-century Danish philosopher Søren Kierkegaard characterizes as a lower type of despair to a more reflective kind. In search of new possibilities for his life and seeking some type of spiritual growth, Ed increasingly escapes despair over his minimal earthly attachments. But he does not thereby eliminate despair from his life. Instead, Ed comes to possess a type of despair characteristic of Kierkegaard's self of "inclosing reserve."[1] As a result, the Coen brothers' black-and-white, film-noir inspired *The Man Who Wasn't There* can be read as an existential meditation on despair and as a depiction of various types of despairing individuals.

Kierkegaardian Despair

To those who consider despair to be the complete absence of hope, it might appear that Ed escapes despair by the end of *The Man Who Wasn't There*. But

Kierkegaard offers a much richer understanding of despair—an understanding that helps to explain both the kind of despair Ed possesses at the end of the film and how this despair differs from the despair that characterizes his existence in the earlier scenes.

In *The Sickness unto Death*, Kierkegaard defines despair as a misrelation of the self.[2] Rather than being a feeling or an emotional state, Kierkegaardian despair is an ontological condition in which the self fails to be what it should.[3] Because humans are physical creatures, we are necessarily temporal and finite. There are limits to what we are and to what we can become. But because we are also psychical beings, Kierkegaard believes we possess an aspect of the eternal and of the infinite—an aspect that allows us to become something more than what we currently are. So we are endowed with possibility and potentiality. For Kierkegaard, the task we face is one of integrating the finite, temporal, and necessary actualities of who we are with the infinite, eternal, and possible beings we might become. It is in synthesizing these various aspects of the self and in relating the physical and psychical to this synthesis that individuals actualize and become themselves. This is what Kierkegaard means in explaining the human self to be "a relation that relates itself to itself."[4] Individuals in despair do not successfully integrate and relate these differing aspects of themselves. Thus, they are wrongly related to themselves.

Kierkegaard devotes much of *Sickness* to a discussion of the different ways in which persons can be wrongly related to themselves, even if they do not realize their error. Just as a person can be sick without realizing it, especially if there are no painful physical manifestations of the illness, Kierkegaard believes individuals can be in despair without realizing the truth of their condition. Indeed, Kierkegaard claims that ignorance that one is in despair is its most common form.[5]

Perhaps because of this, Kierkegaard begins his typology of despair by discussing the condition without regard to conscious awareness. That is, he discusses the way individuals can be in despair whether they realize it or not.

Believing as he does that despair is a misrelation of the self, Kierkegaard maintains that individuals are in despair if they live as if they lack any of the constituents of the self: finitude, infinitude, possibility, or necessity. In discussing the person who lacks infinitude, Kierkegaard explains that such a person is lost because he or she has become so completely finitized: "Surrounded by hordes of men, absorbed in all sorts of secular matters, more and more shrewd about the ways of the world—such a person forgets himself, ... finds it too hazardous to be himself and far easier and safer to be like the others, to become a copy, a number, a mass man."[6] Kierkegaard explains that such persons are "ethically narrow" and may mistakenly define themselves in terms of their occupation. Because they are so concerned with being what others would like them to be, each fails to become the self he or she should be. Instead of fashioning this self by thoughtful carving, despairing individuals who lack infinitude grind down all their intricate edges, becoming so smooth as to be indistinguishable from all the others.

The person who lacks possibility reveals similar limitations. Kierkegaard contends that such a person is either a fatalist to whom there no longer appears to be any possibility of becoming someone else or a philistine who lacks imagination and for whom everything has become trivial. Failing to raise critical questions about the future and about the multiple possibilities open to the self, this person essentially settles for the most probable future.[7] As we shall see, Kierkegaard's descriptions of individuals who lack possibility and infinitude seem to describe the Ed that viewers meet in the early scenes of *The Man Who Wasn't There*.

Introducing Ed

Set in 1949, the film opens with the iconic image of Ed Crane's profession: a barber's pole. Using the first-person voice-over narration characteristic of many noir films, Ed explains that cutting hair is not his chosen profession and that he has merely married into it. Ed's brother-in-law, Frank Raffo (Michael Badalucco), owns the shop, where Ed "just cut[s] the hair."

In contrast to Ed, who says very little throughout the film that is not communicated through narration, Frank loves to talk. A simple, corpulent man whose ambitions appear to be satisfied by working in the shop he inherited from his father, Frank "chews the fat" with anyone who will listen. Unfortunately for Ed, most of Frank's ramblings are inane. As Ed puts it, "Maybe if you're eleven or twelve years old Frank's got an interesting point of view." But, despite Ed's dislike of his brother-in-law's constant chatter and in spite of his obvious dissatisfaction with his own life, Ed tells viewers that he doesn't complain. Instead, he appears to passively accept the cards that his life has dealt him.

It's not clear in this opening scene whether Ed believes that he has the power to change the direction in which his life is going. When Frank reads from the newspaper that "the Russians exploded an A-bomb and there's not a damn thing we can do about it," he calls attention to the fact that sometimes acceptance of an undesirable outcome is the only option.

But sometimes it is not. And the shot that immediately precedes Frank's comment suggests another possibility: changing one's life and becoming a new man. While Ed's narration explains how Frank inherited the barbershop from his father, the camera focuses in on a picture of the paterfamilias. Beside the photo, taped to the frame of the mirror, is an advertisement featuring a toned man flexing his muscles beside a caption that promises, "Lend me fifteen minutes a day, and I'll prove I can make you a new man."

Thus, in an admittedly subtle way, the opening minutes of *The Man Who Wasn't There* not only establish Ed Crane's dissatisfaction with his life but also raise two possibilities for responding to this dissatisfaction: passive acceptance or becoming a new man.

As Ed introduces viewers to the more personal aspects of his life, it initially seems that he will continue to choose the path of passive acceptance. His description of his life takes us to his house, which Ed explains is "okay, I guess," largely because it possesses the proper modern appliances: "an electric icebox, a gas hearth, and a garbage grinder built into the sink."

Ed's wife, Doris (Frances McDormand), is introduced as something of an afterthought, almost as if she is just one of the important fixtures in Ed's house. Ed claims that he and his wife know each other "well enough," despite the fact that (as he admits later in the film) they "had not performed the sex act for many years." Ed offers that they attend church once a week but admits that it's usually on Tuesday night, when Doris likes to play bingo. Ed, not surprisingly, isn't "crazy about the game" but is willing to go if it makes Doris happy.

Ed is also willing to make Doris happy by having guests over to the house, even though he dislikes entertaining. But permitting guests like Doris's boss, "Big Dave" Brewster (James Gandolfini), and his wife, Ann (Katherine Borowitz), to sit at his dinner table is apparently as far as Ed is willing to go, for he doesn't actually act hospitably or engage his guests in conversation.

Perhaps because of Ed's quiet aloofness, Doris appears to have shifted her romantic interests from her husband to her boss. At Doris's dinner party, it is Big Dave who seems to step into what would otherwise be Ed's role of host, regaling the others with war stories. Even though these are much less interesting than Big Dave believes them to be, Doris appears delighted. Her excessively ebullient laughter leads Ed to correctly surmise that there is a deeper cause for his wife's mirth: Doris and Big Dave are having an affair.

Like his response to so many things in the film, Ed's reaction to his wife's infidelity is rather passive: he tells viewers that he is not "going to prance about it, mind you. It's a free country." Once again, it seems to be enough for Ed that Doris has found something that makes her happy. He seems to accept Doris's affair in much the same way that he passively acquiesces to all the other aspects of his life that he doesn't much like.

The first few scenes of *The Man Who Wasn't There* thus establish that Ed merely submissively accepts the life that others have more or less chosen for him. As viewers soon discover, Ed began dating Doris when someone else set them up on a double blind date. Ed married Doris because she thought they should wed. He began cutting hair because his in-laws owned a barbershop. Even though he does not particularly enjoy his job, he has made no attempt to leave. Indeed, despite the fact that he did not actively choose to become a barber, he identifies himself with his finite profession and finite possessions. His failure to identify himself with anything that transcends these, coupled with the implication that these are now concrete realities that must be passively accepted, suggests that Ed's initial despair consists of a joint lack of infinity and lack of possibility.

When Kierkegaard writes that one who lacks infinitude has "emasculated oneself in a spiritual sense," he seems to have a character like Ed in mind.[8] Ed doesn't exercise his agency in the world; he passively acquiesces to others' choices. It seemingly doesn't occur to him that he can choose to be someone other than who he has been. He is, as Kierkegaard puts it, someone who permits his self "to be tricked out of its self by 'the others'" and who fails to realize that the goal is to take the raw material of the self and grind it into one's unique chosen shape, not to be the everyman who is "ground down . . . as smooth as a rolling stone," pushed along well-trod paths, guided by the will of others.[9]

Ed seems to exist as a kind of everyman who is no one in particular. He doesn't initially even seem aware of the possibility that he can become someone else. Living in the world without exercising his agency in it, Ed is absent from his own life and seems to lack a strong sense of self. It is only after he realizes that Doris is having an affair—and perhaps sees that she has actualized a possibility that Ed didn't realize existed—that Ed is able to consider that perhaps he, too, can make choices that will bring his unique self into being and cast it into a different future.

The Possibility of Becoming a New Man

When Creighton Tolliver (Jon Polito) comes to the barbershop for a haircut one day, he brings one possibility of a different life for Ed. Explaining that he came to town with the hope of convincing a prospective partner to back his venture into the potentially profitable business of dry cleaning, Tolliver laments that he will have to return home without the requisite ten thousand dollars.

Perhaps because he wears a toupee and comes to the barbershop at closing, insisting that he be given a haircut, even though the little hair he has doesn't appear to need to be cut, Tolliver comes across as slightly absurd. Even so, Ed finds himself considering the possibility of becoming the man's partner. Through his narration, Ed explains that, although his first instinct was that "the whole idea was nuts," perhaps "that was the instinct that kept [him] locked up in the barbershop, nose against the exit and afraid to try turning the knob."

At this point in the film, Ed is beginning to acknowledge the possibility of changing his life and becoming aware of his own need to do so. But, because he lacks a sense of himself and his own desires, he seems capable only of perhaps taking on someone else's dreams—in this case, Tolliver's. In the words Kierkegaard uses to discuss the despairing individual who lacks possibility, Ed is still "bereft of imagination. . . . He lives within a certain trivial compendium of experiences as to how things go, what is possible, what usually happens."[10] Ed wants to make a change, but he seems to lack the ability to imagine what kind of change he should make and what type of self he should cultivate. He lacks a sense of what is possible, much less desirable, for him.

So Ed decides to take on Tolliver's dream as if it were his own. After a visit to Tolliver's hotel room confirms that the businessman needs only a silent partner who wouldn't have to do anything other than supply the start-up money, Ed initiates his plan to acquire the needed ten thousand dollars by anonymously blackmailing Big Dave with a threat to expose the man's affair with Doris. Although Ed laments the fact that obtaining the money from Big Dave will "pinch him," Ed notes that he was being "two-timed" by Doris and admits that "somewhere that pinched a little, too."

Unfortunately for Ed, Big Dave is smart enough to realize that Tolliver must have some connection to the blackmail scheme. Although Dave initially believes that Tolliver himself is the blackmailer, Dave beats the effete salesman into admitting that his newly acquired investment capital came from Ed. Big Dave then calls Ed and tells him it is important that he come down to Nirdlingers, the store owned by Big Dave's in-laws. A man of direct action, Big Dave could perhaps respect a cuckold who pummeled his wife's lover, but he cannot comprehend one who resorts to blackmail.

When Ed arrives at Nirdlingers, he finds his wife's lover seated in a dimly lit office, his face hidden by darkness. Big Dave proceeds to ask Ed a question that the film itself will attempt to answer: "What kind of man are you?"

Declining to answer Big Dave's question or to provide any explanation for his actions, Ed turns to go. But the larger man attacks him, presses him against the glass, and chokes him. When the glass cracks, it is as if something inside Ed breaks, too. With one swift, passionless, mechanical jab of his arm, Ed stabs his wife's lover in the neck.[11] He watches with stoic detachment as the violent Big Dave, whose angry attack on Ed has placed the once tidy office in disarray, falls to the ground and dies.

Leaving the murder weapon at the scene, Ed returns home to his sleeping wife. Passed out from all the alcohol she consumed at the wedding reception they attended earlier that day, she does not realize that Ed has even left the house. Continuing his narration from the point at which it was interrupted by the phone call from Big Dave, Ed details the events that led to his marriage to Doris, seemingly implying that Ed believes the sequence of events that surrounded his betrothal is more significant and worthy of reflection than his role in the death of Big Dave.[12]

Ed's life takes an unexpected turn when Doris is arrested and incarcerated for the murder of Big Dave. When Ed goes to visit her in prison, the scene begins with the camera focused not on either of the main characters but on the white line that runs the length of the table, separating inmates from visitors. Clearly marked "Do Not Reach Across," the line serves as a reminder that, despite their physical proximity to each other, the Cranes cannot overcome the distance between them. Ed is in the process of becoming a new man, though not in the way that he had hoped. Though he, like viewers, may not yet realize that Doris will never return home, he is aware of the new possibility that he may have to live his life without her.

Had the main character been anyone besides Ed, it might have been surprising that this scene is so unemotional. Perhaps to call attention to the detached character of the Cranes' encounter, the Coen brothers add to the scene another prisoner, a hysterical young woman who rocks back and forth and wails continuously in the background as she meets with her visitor. By contrast, Ed and Doris remain impassive.

In his conversation with Doris, Ed does not admit his involvement in Big Dave's death nor does he indicate that he knows why Doris changed the records at Nirdlingers.[13] He responds to his wife's offer to reveal why she altered the books by saying that she doesn't have to tell him anything. Having no intention of making any confessions himself, Ed also does not appear to have any interest in hearing his wife's. He seems to prefer that she follow his lead by remaining silent.

At this point in the film, Ed has taken a step beyond passive acceptance of his unhappy life and has attempted to take advantage of opportunities to become a new man. Even though Ed's ventures have not had the intended outcome, he has advanced his agency in the world and thereby begun to choose to become the kind of person he would like to be. Although one could argue that Ed is, at this point in the film, still despairingly bereft of imagination about his future (inasmuch as his pursuit of dry cleaning is primarily the adoption of another man's dream), it is important to note that Ed at least acknowledges that a different future for himself is possible. Even if the possibilities he attempts to actualize only involve the choice of one profession (dry cleaner) over another (barber), and even if Ed has not advanced beyond thinking of himself in terms of his profession, the mere fact that Ed comes to acknowledge the possibility that he can choose to become a different man suggests that he may be ready to move beyond the despair characterized by a lack of infinitude or a lack of possibility.[14]

Ed's Conscious Despair: A Man of Immediacy with Some Reflection

There are additional forms of despair that characterize Ed's life. Kierkegaard discusses these in the section of *The Sickness unto Death* in which he considers despair with respect to conscious awareness. That is, Kierkegaard considers how despair appears to persons who have enough of a sense of self to realize that they are in despair. Such individuals often do not want to be the selves they should become; instead, each wants to become someone else, to be the self that someone else has chosen.

At the lowest level, despairing individuals who don't will to be themselves have lives characterized by a kind of immediacy. They define themselves by things that are external to the self, such as profession, possessions, reputation, or appearance. When they are aware of being in despair, they mistakenly believe that their condition is caused by the fact that these externalities are not as they would like them to be.[15] They see themselves as subject to the vicissitudes of fortune and incorrectly conclude that their external change of circumstances, rather than their problematic identification of their particular self with contingent externalities, is the source of their newly discovered despair. So they wait for their situations to change. If a change occurs, an individual may slip back into an unconscious despair and pass up an opportunity to cultivate a more authentic self. If the situation does not change, and if an individual does not advance to another form of despair, such a person typically laments that she will never be herself again, "learns to copy others," and "wishes to be someone else." Thus, the self of immediacy does not know himself; he "quite literally identifies himself only by the clothes he wears . . . [and] identifies having a self by externalities."[16]

There is an absence of any real self here that seems consistent with the characterization of Ed early in the film. He is the man who isn't there inasmuch as he doesn't seem to have any sense of who he is apart from his profession and possessions. He has not chosen to be anyone in particular. He wants to be someone else, but only in the minimal sense of having a different lifestyle and career. He is not yet ready to choose to be a self in the more substantial sense, which Kierkegaard refers to as the self in its "eternal validity," apart from all the finite attributes and externalities the self possesses.

As the events of the film unfold, Ed arguably embodies the more intense despair that Kierkegaard characterizes as immediacy with some reflection. Like Ed, a man living with this type of despair tries to sustain himself against the ever-changing winds of fortune by using the "relative reflection that he has. . . . He does not become apoplectic when the wind blows, as the immediate person does; reflection helps him to understand that there is much he can lose without losing the self. . . . [But] he has no consciousness of a self that is won by infinite abstraction from every externality."[17] He still mistakenly believes that something finite is the source of his despair. He does not yet fully realize that the problem lies within himself and his failure to make the choices that will define him. Although he is able to retain his composure when events take an unwelcome turn, he mistakenly believes that all would be well if the wheel of fortune would simply turn again.

Ed's Deepening Despair

Ed hopes that the wheel of fortune will turn in the Cranes' favor when he and Frank hire an expensive out-of-town attorney, Freddy Riedenschneider

(Tony Shalhoub), to defend Doris. Riedenschneider reinforces Ed's decision to remain silent about the facts surrounding the case: "Keep your trap shut. I'm an attorney. You're a barber. You don't know anything." The irony, of course, is that Ed knows everything about Big Dave's death and that, since he hardly ever says anything, Ed doesn't need to be told to keep his mouth shut.

But the film suggests that Ed knows something more important than the details surrounding Dave's death. As he drives down the main street of town, watching people as they go through the routines of daily life, Ed experiences himself as being not only different from the others but above them. Able to see something that remains hidden to those focused on accomplishing their present tasks, Ed recalls feeling like he "knew a secret—a bigger one even than what had really happened to Big Dave. Something none of them knew. Like [he] had made it to the outside somehow and they were all still struggling way down below."

Although Ed is not able to fully articulate what it is that he knows that the others do not, his comment about having "made it out" suggests that he is no longer trapped in the maze, running the proverbial rat race that still occupies the others. The camera suggests as much as the film shifts from a shot of Ed languidly driving his car to people who are hurrying to reach their destinations. Interestingly, the camera takes on the perspective of Ed's gaze and tracks a woman in a black dress, keeping pace with her, never surpassing her. The Coen brothers' decision to remove the street noise and replace it with the indolent notes of a Beethoven piano sonata also serves to make the people Ed observes appear to exist in a different relationship with time. Ed seems to occupy a different world. It seems he has begun to shift from despair of immediacy—the despair that, if they are conscious of it, likely affects the people Ed watches in the street—to what Kierkegaard calls "despair of the eternal or over oneself."

Kierkegaard explains that the despair of immediacy (without reflection) and of immediacy with some reflection are different ways of despairing over "something earthly." In both types, the world and the vicissitudes of luck are mistakenly believed to be the source of despair. Something earthly has gone wrong with one's life; some external misfortune has been suffered. By contrast, an individual who lives in the qualitatively higher "despair of the eternal or over oneself" recognizes that the real problem is not external to the self.[18] The problem is that such individuals have defined themselves in terms of something earthly, that they lack a self that transcends its earthly, finite aspects. People who despair of the eternal despair over the fact that they have not developed any eternal aspects of themselves—aspects capable of transcending the loss of externalities or changes in fortune or circumstances. They lack what Kierkegaard calls the self in its "eternal validity"—the self that consists of something more than the contingent aspects of a person's life, such as an individual's profession, relationships, appearance, talents, possessions, fame, or reputation. A career, a love, beauty, talent, and the rest can be lost without losing the self. But the person who defines himself exclusively in terms of externalities fails to recognize that, because he is always more than these things, he can lose them without losing himself. So he is in despair over the possibility of losing these external goods (even if he has not yet lost them). Once a person acknowledges that he attaches too much significance to finite things and that he mistakenly defines himself in terms of something external to the self, he moves away from being a man of immediacy with some reflection; he shifts from despair over something earthly toward despair over his seeming inability to move beyond defining himself in terms of earthly, finite things and to instead define himself by the eternal aspect of himself. He begins to despair over his lack of an eternal self and over his inability to overcome his weakness.[19]

Alien Encounters

Interestingly, as Ed appears to be shifting away from despair over something earthly, the film itself introduces a literal and metaphorical other-worldliness: aliens. These beings are introduced in the next scene of the film, when Ann Nirdlinger, Big Dave's widow, pays a strange late-night call to the Crane house. Remaining outside, partially hidden by shadows, her features somewhat concealed by the veil that extends from her hat, a wide-eyed and unblinking Ann tells Ed that she and her husband had an extraterrestrial encounter while camping in Oregon. The encounter resulted in Big Dave's abduction—an event that changed him, such that he never touched Ann again. Voicing her suspicions that aliens murdered her husband and that the government wants to obscure this fact ("this thing goes deep"), Ann proclaims Doris's innocence. Confessing her hope that "perhaps now it will all come out," Ann warns Ed that "sometimes knowledge is a curse."[20]

With varying degrees of subtlety, the Coen brothers use images of the otherworldly, particularly in the form of extraterrestrials, throughout *The Man Who Wasn't There*. Considering these images in light of Ed's inclosing reserve and focus on the otherworldly helps to explain the prevalence of literal and metaphorical representations of aliens throughout the film. While images of UFOs and the paranoia that accompanies them are not unheard of in noir films, the ubiquity of their use in *The Man Who Wasn't There* might be surprising were it not tied to Ed's desire to escape the world in which he only halfheartedly dwells. When Doris is arrested for Big Dave's murder, Ann's late-night visit to the Crane house explicitly introduces extraterrestrials into the film as part of her explanation of the cause of her husband's death. After Doris's suicide, Ed sees the article "Mysteries of Roswell, New Mexico" in *Life* magazine. Among the images is a drawing of a UFO that resembles the one that Ed sees at the prison the night before his execution.

The same issue of *Life* has, on the previous page, an article about dry cleaning, proclaiming it the wave of the future. At the risk of reading too much into the connection between dry cleaning and the mysteries at Roswell, perhaps the Coen brothers are suggesting that both represent a kind of way out for Ed, with dry cleaning indicating a worldly way out and extraterrestrial encounters symbolizing an otherworldly escape.

The circumstances of Ed's subsequent execution continue the imagery of aliens. The execution chamber itself has an otherworldly appearance, with the electric chair centered in the room against a background, floor, and ceiling of solid white interrupted only by a long, curved window that resembles something one might expect to see on an alien spacecraft.[21]

Throughout the film, the Coen brothers use additional images that are reminiscent of flying saucers. The hubcap that flies through the air after Ed's car accident resembles a UFO. So does much of the lighting and many of the light fixtures that appear in the film.

In their commentary on the film, the Coen brothers admit that this imagery of flying saucers "runs throughout the entire movie."[22] They also discuss an interesting scene that was originally scripted to occur between the scene showing Ed's return home after killing Big Dave and the scene in which the officers come to the barbershop to inform Ed of Doris's arrest. The Coen brothers explain that they had planned to have Ed lie down beside Doris and close his eyes. Then an eerie, alien sound would begin. Next, the camera would show Ed on the veranda watching "tiny ant-people" come out of an alien spacecraft. After smoking a cigarette, Ed would go back inside the house. He would then get a towel, roll it up, stuff it in the crack under the door, and go back to sleep.

Having decided that the intended scene "was just taking the whole alien adventure a little too far" and would have been too much of "a Kafka break," the Coens deleted the alien dream sequence and added Ann's late-night visit.[23]

Although the Coen brothers themselves don't explain the significance of the ubiquity of aliens and UFOs in Ed's story, a case can be made for thinking that these were important to include not only because of their connection to other noir films but also because they are representations of otherworldly things. In a film in which the main character is withdrawn from the world—is the man who isn't there—it seems somewhat fitting to incorporate images of entities that are also not at home in this world.

Ed's Confession

In the next scene of the film, Ed admits to Doris and her lawyer that he knew of his wife's affair and that he killed Big Dave. Perhaps his confession is a sign that he is beginning to take responsibility for his agency and actions in the world. Interestingly, even though Ed's story is true, Riedenschneider takes it to be just an attempt to provide an alternative but ultimately untenable account of the events surrounding Big Dave's death.

Riedenschneider is not interested in knowing what really happened the night Big Dave died. Indeed, appealing to Heisenberg's uncertainty principle, he even attempts to defy the claim that there is a "reality of what happened" and suggests instead that there is no fact of the matter:

They got this guy in Germany: Fritz Something-or-other. Or is it? Maybe it's Werner. Anyway, he's got this theory, you wanna test something, you know, scientifically—how the planets go round the sun, what sunspots are made of, why the water comes out of the tap—well, you gotta look at it. But, sometimes, you look at it, your looking changes it. You can't know the reality of what happened, or what would've happened if you hadn't-a stuck in your own goddamn schnozz. So there is no "what happened." Looking at something changes it. They call it the "Uncertainty Principle." Sure, it sounds screwy, but even Einstein says the guy's on to something. Science. Perception. Reality. Doubt. Reasonable doubt. I'm saying that sometimes the more you look, the less you really know. It's a fact. A proved fact. In a way, it's the only fact there is.

In their commentary on *The Man Who Wasn't There,* the Coen brothers admit that they enjoy "writing gibberish" of the kind that Riedenschneider speaks here.[24] But, despite the incoherence—played for comic effect—of much of the attorney's speech, he does raise a few noteworthy points, one of which is that the longer (and perhaps deeper) one looks, the more open one might become to alternate interpretations and previously unforeseen possibilities. Moreover, reflection upon such possibilities might create or restrict an individual's future options in unknowable ways. In the end, we are left with a multiplicity of interpretations about what is possible and with competing interpretations of the "facts" that a postmodern view of the world suggests we cannot surmount.

Having suggested that there is no fact of the matter but merely conflicting interpretations, Riedenschneider explains that he intends to defend Doris by providing another interpretation of Big Dave, primarily by questioning the latter's service record. Riedenschneider's detectives have uncovered that Big Dave, rather than fighting on the front lines, had held merely a clerical position in the navy shipyards. He did not experience the combat that formed the subject of so many of his war stories. No celebrated military figure, Big Dave received an honorable discharge after participating in a fistfight. Riedenschneider is incredibly pleased: it is now possible for him to argue that Big Dave could have been blackmailed by someone who knew that he was not the war hero he pretended to be and that this other person—the fictitious man who wasn't there—could have killed him.

Ed's Continuing Search for a Way Out

Encouraged by the thought that Riedenschneider might be able to "fix" things for Doris and "make it all work out," Ed admits his hope that "maybe there was a way out for [him] as well." Although Ed has begun to move away from being the man of immediacy with some reflection and to move beyond the despair over something earthly, he has not yet fully given up the hope that a reversal of fortune might mitigate his despair. But his hopes now seem to be pinned largely on creating possibilities for another person: Birdy Abundas (Scarlett Johansson), the daughter of Ed's friend, Walter (Richard Jenkins). It seems to be no accident that when Ed as narrator speaks his words about finding a way out, the camera is trained on Birdy. While the exact nature of Ed's interest in the young woman remains unclear (perhaps even to Ed himself), Birdy represents youthful potential, someone who has her whole life ahead of her. Believing her to be a "good, clean kid" with a talent for playing the piano, Ed is drawn to the idea of becoming her manager. Then he could be with her "enough to keep [himself] feeling okay." He tells Birdy that "there are a lot of things that haven't worked out for me. Life has dealt me some bum cards. Or maybe I just haven't played them right. I don't know. . . . You're young. A kid, really. Your whole life ahead of you. But it's not too soon to start making opportunities for yourself, before it all washes away. . . . I can't stand by and watch any more things go down the drain. You're young, you don't understand."

Anticipating that, once the trial is over, he may be able to become a new man by directing Birdy's career, Ed still hopes for a happy ending to his story. He is not prepared for the devastating news he receives: Doris has hanged herself using the belt of the dress he brought for her to wear to her trial.[25] Already somewhat absent from his own life, Ed's despair escalates as he further withdraws from the world, fully becoming the man who isn't there. In his words, "I sat in the house, but there was nobody there. I was a ghost. I didn't see anyone. No one saw me. I was the barber." A little later he admits that he began visiting a medium (Lilyan Chauvin) because he found himself "alone with secrets [he] didn't want and no one to tell them to anyway." Eventually realizing that he was "turning into Ann Nirdlinger," Ed accepts that he "had to turn [his] back on the ghosts, on the dead, before they all sucked [him] in."

Having seen his attempt to make a new life through the dry-cleaning venture fail, having lost any possibility of resuming his life with Doris, and being unable to escape the world through the medium's interventions, Ed begins to devote himself fully to what he considers to be his one remaining chance to become a new man: becoming Birdy's manager. He arranges to take Birdy to San Francisco to play for a professional pianist in the hope that she will be able to impress the musician into taking her on as a student. But it is not to be. Although Birdy plays the correct notes, her playing is polite, formulaic, and uninspired. She has some technique but lacks the requisite soul. It is the judgment of the heavily accented professional that "perhaps, someday, she can make very good typist."

Undeterred, Ed vows to find another teacher for Birdy. But it is clear that the desire for Birdy to become a concert pianist is Ed's, not Birdy's. In the ride home, she reiterates a claim she made earlier in the film: she doesn't want a career in music. In fact, she "isn't sure that [she] wants a career at all." And, if she did, she would "probably be a veterinarian." Flattered by the intensity of Ed's desire for her to pursue a musical career, she identifies him as "an enthusiast" and, in an attempt to "make him happy," proceeds to initiate oral sex with him. Surprised by Birdy's actions, Ed veers into the lane of oncoming traffic and then off the hillside. The man who was metaphorically seeking a way out literally leaves the road.

A Modern Man? Acknowledging Absurdity

We next see Ed sitting on his porch, apparently awaiting Doris's arrival home. Approached by a man who encourages Ed to embrace "the modern way" of life by replacing the gravel in his driveway with pavement, Ed seems unsure of how to respond to the unwelcome solicitation. Soon Doris arrives home and sends the salesman packing.

Such an odd and ultimately banal domestic scene creates a jarring break for the film's audience, occurring as it does at such an important point in the film, when viewers are eager to know if Ed's car accident has been fatal. Indeed, it is not initially clear whether we are seeing Ed in an afterlife or witnessing him reflecting on an incident that might have come from his earlier life with Doris. Only as Ed regains consciousness do we learn that it is the latter.

Despite its seeming singularity, this unexpected scene from his days with Doris essentially summarizes Ed's life: he has been sitting on the porch of his life's proverbial house, marking time, failing to address the various possibilities for changing or modernizing his life, waiting for someone else to tell him what to do.

This scene also introduces questions about whether Ed is or should attempt to be a modern man. These questions recur in the speech Riedenschneider gives to the jury as part of his attempt to defend Ed against the charge of murdering Creighton Tolliver. The lawyer suggests that Ed is "too ordinary to be the criminal mastermind the D.A. made [him] out to be" and that "there was some greater scheme at work that the state had yet to unravel." Ed's narration summarizes Riedenschneider's remarks:

> He told them . . . that the closer they looked, the less sense it would all make; that I wasn't the kind of guy to kill a guy; that I was the barber, for Christsake. I was just like them—an ordinary man. Guilty of living in a world that had no place for me, yeah. Guilty of wanting to be a dry cleaner, sure. But not a murderer. He said

I *was* modern man. And, if they voted to convict me, well, they'd be practically cinching the noose around their own necks. He told them to look, not at the facts, but at the meaning of the facts. Then he said the facts had no meaning. It was a pretty good speech. It even had me going.

It is important to note that, even though it is attributed to Riedenschneider, this speech is Ed's summary of his attorney's salient points. Though the ideas might have come from Riedenschneider, the words are Ed's. Ed sees himself as someone who is not a murderer, not the kind of individual who kills people. He is just an ordinary, modern man, who, like everyone else, wants to be someone else and whose only crime consists of not wanting to be the barber.

It is likely that Ed's synopsis of Riedenschneider's defense sounds comical and slightly absurd because, in retrospect, it appears that way to Ed himself. Riedenschneider's speech may have had Ed "going" at the time of its presentation, but to the Ed who narrates the film as he awaits the electric chair, the lawyer's remarks are all style and no substance. The judge who ultimately decides Ed's fate doesn't buy "the modern man stuff or the uncertainty stuff or any of the mercy stuff either." And it seems likely that, in the end, Ed, too, doesn't really buy any of these.

Given the many postmodern elements of *The Man Who Wasn't There*, particularly the emphasis on the multiplicity of interpretations without any deeper, underlying meaning, it is tempting to wonder if the repeated references to Ed as a modern man are intended to indicate that he is not a contemporary man but is instead caught up in the antiquated modernity that serves as the setting for typical noir films.[26] Perhaps, at the end of his life, Ed, the narrator who observes the futility of attempting to live a meaningful modern life, moves beyond modernity to become a postmodern man.[27]

By the film's end, Ed's reflections on his life seem to have changed him. We learn that he has been recounting his experiences for a men's magazine that has paid him (by the word) to tell his story. Ed explains that he initially had trouble figuring out how his attempt to become a new man landed him on death row. He "knew step by step" but "couldn't see any pattern." But now he begins to see his life as a whole: "Now all the disconnected things seem to hook up. . . . It's like pulling away from the maze. While you're in the maze, you go through willy-nilly, turning where you think you have to turn, banging into the dead ends, one thing after another. But you get some distance on it, and all those twists and turns, why, they're the shape of your life. It's hard to explain, but seeing it whole gives you some peace." Apologizing for the pain he caused Doris, Ed claims that he doesn't regret anything that has happened—"not a thing." Although he "used to regret being the barber," he no longer does. Even though he is about to be executed for Tolliver's murder, which he did not commit, Ed doesn't appear to be troubled by his imminent death. He suggests that, although the "twists and turns" of his life might not be objectively meaningful, they are the patterns of his life, and they have made him who he is.

At the end of his days, the man who wasn't there for much of his own life and who was practically invisible to others for many years has become someone being featured in a magazine for all to see. It is tempting to wonder if it is partly a result of finally being recognized by others that Ed is able to jettison his regret for what might have been. He claims to be at peace as he approaches the electric chair under the watchful eye of multiple witnesses. The man who wasn't there ends his life by being the sole focus of all present at his execution.

Watched by all, Ed the narrator retains his optimism about the possibility that, wherever he is "being taken," maybe things "will be clearer there, like when a fog blows away." He expresses his hope that Doris will be there and that he will be able to "tell her all those things they don't have words for here." But, despite Ed's hope that he may awaken to a preferable afterlife, it seems doubtful that Ed has escaped despair.

Ed's Deepest Despair: Inclosing Reserve

Rather than having escaped despair, Ed seems, at the end of his life, to embody what Kierkegaard calls a despairing self of inclosing reserve—a self that is closed off from the world and may "take flight from actuality."[28] Having acquired some reflection, individuals of inclosing reserve become preoccupied with "watching" themselves, and the individual "longs for the solitude" that he or she considers essential. Drawing away from "the soothing lullaby of social life," such a person becomes increasingly isolated. Yet, despite the isolation and desire to be alone, the individual wishes for a confidant. Kierkegaard warns that the greatest danger that a self of inclosing reserve faces, particularly if no confidant appears, is suicide.[29]

In the latter part of the film, Ed seems to be seeking such an intimate. Isolated from society (initially by his own choice and finally by his prison cell), Ed repeatedly expresses his desire for someone with whom to share his secrets. After Doris's suicide, Ed visits a medium as part of his attempt to find such a confidant in his dead wife. Moreover, Ed's final narrative comment reveals that, even at the film's end, he has not relinquished this desire: he hopes that, in an afterlife, he can reunite with Doris and tell her all the things he cannot verbalize here on Earth. Finally, Ed's decision to write his story for the men's magazine gives his lengthy confession a public audience and turns readers (as well as viewers of the film) into anonymous confidants.

Importantly, what Ed confides to his audience is not only the knowledge of what really happened to Big Dave and Creighton Tolliver but the knowledge that he has gained through his constant reflection upon himself. Indeed, perhaps because of the Coen brothers' decision to use his narration throughout the film, Ed appears to be watching himself as we watch him—or to be watching us as we watch him, imagining how a third party would interpret his character. He watches himself as a kind of third party, the way a person of inclosing reserve would.

However, in addition to Ed's desire for a confidant and the fact that he spends his days watching himself and reflecting upon himself, Ed displays the withdrawal from the world and the desire for solitude that characterize the despair of inclosing reserve. He is, ultimately, the man who isn't there because he removes himself from the world. While others still occupy the world and are occupied by the business of the world, Ed has pulled "away from the maze," as he explains at the end of the film. As part of his despair, he seems to understand the futility of any attempt to find ultimate fulfillment in the finite attachments of the temporal world.

Ed does not make the movement of faith that, for Kierkegaard, constitutes the only way out of despair. He ends his life with an inclosing reserve that is only slightly mitigated by his decision to tell his story to the world. Already withdrawn from an earthly existence, Ed's attention at the end of his days focuses on his hope for an afterlife and for an end to his despair.

The Man Who Isn't There

During the course of the Coens' ninth film, the character of Ed Crane undergoes a qualitative shift in his despair that Kierkegaard's typology of despair helps to explain. Beginning as a man of immediacy, suffering from a lack of infinitude and possibility, Ed's initial despair stems from his identification of himself with the externalities and contingent circumstances of his life. Passively acquiescing to others' choices, Ed is the man who isn't there because he exercises no agency in his own life. By the film's end, Ed has begun to seize the possibilities presented to him and to make the choices necessary for creating himself as his own man. But as Ed gains a greater sense of self and as he becomes more reflective, he also becomes more aware of the meaninglessness of many finite things. He comes to see that no finite things can provide any ultimate satisfaction. So Ed begins to withdraw from the world and becomes a man of inclosing reserve. Although he now has a self, he once again becomes the man who isn't there.

Notes

I am grateful to Mark Conard for his numerous helpful suggestions and thoughtful editorial remarks.

1. Søren Kierkegaard, *The Sickness unto Death: A Christian Psychological Exposition for Upbuilding and Awakening,* trans. Howard V. Hong and Edna H. Hong (Princeton, N.J.: Princeton Univ. Press, 1980), 63–67.

2. It should be noted that the text of *The Sickness unto Death* was originally published under the pseudonym Anti-Climacus, with Kierkegaard designated as the book's editor. Although it cannot be assumed that all of Kierkegaard's pseudonymous works contain philosophical positions that represent Kierkegaard's all-things-considered view, Kierkegaard explains in his *Journals and Papers* that Anti-Climacus is a "higher" pseudonym because he is "a Christian on an extraordinarily high level." Søren Kierkegaard, "Selected Entries from Kierkegaard's *Journals and Papers* Pertaining to *The Sickness unto Death,*" in *Sickness unto Death,* 140.

Although it appears that Kierkegaard "agreed" with the positions taken by his Anti-Climacus persona, Kierkegaard seems reticent to claim to have written a text whose author seems to have found true faith in God and thereby to have escaped despair. He decided, instead, to attach his name to the monograph as its editor. As Kierkegaard elaborates in a margin in which he contemplates adding a postscript to the text, "This book seems to be written by a physician; I, the editor, am not the physician, I am one of the sick." Ibid., 162. Because Kierkegaard suggests that his reasons for not identifying himself as the author of the text are personal (in terms of its implications about his own mastery of despair) rather than theoretical (in terms of a philosophical disagreement with the content of the text), I refer to the account of despair offered in *The Sickness unto Death* as Kierkegaard's.

3. The fact that despair is not a feeling or an emotional state explains why Ed can be rightly considered to be in despair despite his emotional unresponsiveness.

4. It should be noted that being a fully functional self, for Kierkegaard, requires

more than mere synthesis of the psychical and physical poles of the self. To be a self consists of *relating* the psychical and the physical to this synthesis. This is what Kierkegaard means in defining the human self to be "a relation that relates itself to itself." He goes on to add that, as a Christian, he also believes that, in relating itself to itself, the self must also "relate itself to the power that established it, [namely] God." Kierkegaard, *The Sickness unto Death,* 13.

Also worth noting are three additional facts about Kierkegaardian despair: its universality, its connection to personal responsibility, and its contingency. Kierkegaard maintains that all human beings are in despair. Although many people are not aware of their despair, the sickness unto death is universal. Second, despite the prevalence of despair, Kierkegaard contends that all individuals are personally responsible for their condition. Despair results from a deficiency that individuals have chosen and that they continue to choose. Kierkegaard believes, then, that it is universally but contingently true that all individuals are in despair. There is nothing about human nature that necessitates despair. Indeed, one of the aims of self should be the elimination of this condition. Kierkegaard, *Sickness unto Death,* 16–28.

5. Kierkegaard, *Sickness unto Death,* 23–27.

6. Ibid., 33.

7. Ibid., 41–42.

8. Ibid., 33.

9. Ibid., 33–34.

10. Ibid., 41.

11. In their commentary on the text, the Coen brothers describe Ed's stabbing motion as "stiff and wooden and Richard-Nixon-like." Joel Coen and Ethan Coen, *The Man Who Wasn't There,* DVD commentary, 2001. Later in the story Freddy Riedenschneider (Tony Shalhoub), Doris's lawyer, suggests that one of the reasons the jury is likely to think that Doris killed Dave is that the "trimmer thing" used to stab the man was a "dame's weapon," not one that a typical man would use. Perhaps this fact is supposed to reinforce Dave's concern that Ed does not respond to his knowledge of his wife's affair in the way a typically masculine man would.

12. Like many of the other explanations of his actions that Ed proffers, his marriage to Doris also seems to have been motivated by a passive acceptance of the fact that it was what she wanted. During the blind double date in which Ed met Doris, she "put away" so much from her flask that Ed had reason to suspect alcoholism might be in her future. Claiming to enjoy Ed's frequent silences, Doris suggested—after only a few weeks of dating—that they marry. In reply to his concern that perhaps she should get to know him better, Ed recalls Doris asking, "Why? Does it get better?"

It seems fairly clear from the larger context of the film that Doris did not ask this question because she thought Ed *couldn't* be any better but because she thought that he *wouldn't* become so. Hers was a question of resignation, not exhilaration, the result of her calculation that Ed would do for a husband. But she may have calculated incorrectly and regretted her choice, leading her to have an affair with her boss and to tell the bride at a wedding reception—in a drunken voice laden with sarcasm—that married life is "just so goddamned wonderful you almost won't believe it. It's just a bowl of goddamned cherries."

It is interesting to note that the most intimate moment we see the Cranes share occurs early in the film when a bathing Doris asks Ed to shave her legs. It appears that it is in his capacity as a barber that Ed achieves greatest intimacy with his wife.

13. Although Doris does not explain why she helped "cook the books" at Nirdlingers, she does admit to Ed that she did so. She, of course, does not realize that Ed already knows that she did this to help her lover, Big Dave, come up with the ten thousand dollars he needed to pay off the person who was blackmailing him for his affair with her nor does she realize that Ed was the blackmailer.

14. A third possibility for a new profession presents itself to Ed in the form of his attempt to manage a young woman's music career. And Ed is interested in becoming Birdy's (Scarlett Johansson) manager in the hope that she will not throw away the opportunity to become a concert pianist. Despite Birdy's repeated claims to have little to no interest in pursuing a career as a professional musician, Ed seems obsessed with pursuing this possibility on her behalf. As he puts it, "It's not too soon to start making opportunities for yourself, before it all washes away. . . . I can't stand by and watch any more things go down the drain."

15. They also mistakenly believe that they are not in despair when these externalities are as they would like them to be.

16. Kierkegaard, *Sickness unto Death*, 53.

17. Ibid., 54–55.

18. Ibid., 60–67.

19. "He despairs over himself, over being so weak that he attributes such great significance to the earthly, which now becomes for him the despairing sign that he has lost the eternal and himself." Kierkegaard, *Sickness unto Death*, 61.

20. Ironically, Ed does not need to be warned about the dangers inherent in the dissemination of some knowledge—or at least in the threat of such dissemination: it was his knowledge of Big Dave's affair with Doris and his blackmailer's threat to reveal what he knew that precipitated Big Dave's death and placed the film's characters in their current circumstances.

21. R. Barton Palmer suggests that the "abstract, minimalist design" of the execution chamber "comes right from a German Expressionism as Walt Disney might reimagine it." He adds that the "cartoonish" quality of the final scene indicates that Ed's hopes for spiritual transcendence are "thoroughly ironized as unrealizable." R. Barton Palmer, *Joel and Ethan Coen* (Urbana: Univ. of Illinois Press, 2004), 79.

22. The Coen brothers also note that the lights at Nirdlingers look like flying saucers. Coen and Coen, *Man Who Wasn't There*, DVD commentary.

23. Coen and Coen, *Man Who Wasn't There*, DVD commentary.

24. Ibid.

25. Ed later learns that Doris was pregnant with Big Dave's child at the time of her suicide and that her pregnancy probably played a substantial part in her decision to take her own life. Interestingly, Ed comes to know of his wife's pregnancy when the medical examiner who performed Doris's autopsy decides that, because he "would want to be told" of his wife's pregnancy, he should tell Ed about Doris's condition. Although he wonders if he is doing the right thing by telling Ed, the doctor does not anticipate that Ed might not be the father or that Ed might prefer not to know that Doris was expecting. Because it appears that Ed would have preferred to remain ignorant about Doris's pregnancy, this scene serves to reinforce Ann Nirdlinger's contention that "sometimes knowledge is a curse."

26. Perhaps this seemingly postmodern turn is part of the Coen brothers' attempt to produce a period film that not only reflects the postwar era of classic film noir but also reflects on this era from the perspective of the twenty-first century. If so, *The Man Who Wasn't There* might be interpreted as both a tribute to film noir and a contemporary commentary on it.

27. Claiming that *The Man Who Wasn't There* is "arguably [the Coen brothers'] best film," R. Barton Palmer writes that the film "is about the hope for spiritual growth, the leap of faith made possible by the embrace of meaningless." Palmer, *Joel and Ethan Coen*, 13, 66. A Kierkegaardian account of Ed's character agrees inasmuch as it suggests that his deepening despair constitutes a kind of spiritual growth, because it both reflects a deeper degree of self-actualization and prompts a recognition of the ultimate meaninglessness of a life lived without faith in an infinite God.

28. Kierkegaard, *Sickness unto Death*, 63–67. Interestingly, the Coen brothers' decision to incorporate so much imagery of flying saucers could be interpreted as indicative of such a flight from actuality and an attempt to escape to another world.

29. Kierkegaard, *Sickness unto Death*, 63–67. Kierkegaard adds that having a confidant is one of the most successful ways for a person of inclosing reserve to fight an impulse to commit suicide.

Thinking Beyond the Failed Community

Blood Simple and *The Man Who Wasn't There*

R. Barton Palmer

Ransacking the Museum of Dead Styles

In the manner of a flamboyant postmodernism eager to ransack for re-use what Fredric Jameson has termed the "museum of dead styles," the neo-noir films of the Coen brothers offer a rich vein of allusion to both classic film noir and the hard-boiled fiction (especially that of James M. Cain) that was noir's principal narrative and thematic source.[1] Jameson asserts that post-modernist cultural production is inevitably empty, with "energetic artists" cast adrift in a kind of intellectual and social weightlessness, being forced to wear the "masks of extinct mannerisms."[2] Postmodernism may well, as Jameson suggests, foreclose the possibility of originality in the neo-romantic sense. And yet, with Peter Brooker, we may well see older styles and artistic movements as anything but extinct, as making available in fact a different form of newness that might result from "the practice of an imaginative re-making which edits, echoes, borrows from, recomposes and 'refunctions' existing narratives or images."[3]

Suitably transformed, what has been borrowed can then "work in a different medium with an invigorated social and artistic purpose."[4] Such indeed is the use the Coens make of noir texts. Their postmodernism does not accept Jean Baudrillard's pronouncement that postmodernist art, having "deconstructed its entire universe," leaves artists like them with only the bleak prospect of "playing with the pieces."[5] In three films, the Coens imaginatively remake two of James M. Cain's novels, *The Postman Always Rings Twice* (1934) and *Double Indemnity* (serialized 1936, published in book form in 1943), but the connection to hard-boiled America's most famous novelist is deepest and most interesting not in *Fargo* but in *Blood Simple* and especially *The Man Who Wasn't There*. These films can hardly be understood properly apart from the literary sources of which they are essentially re-compositions.

Such extended allusiveness may be explained, in part, by developments within the film industry, particularly the emergence of a young, cine-literate viewership eager for the self-congratulatory experience of discovering, identifying, and enjoying references to honored texts of a bygone age. Because of this niche audience, nostalgic evocations of the cultural and cinematic past are common enough in the commercial and independent films that have become such an important area of Hollywood production since the 1980s, and the Coens in particular are certainly noted practitioners of this film type. With its black-and-white cinematography, its imitation of noir chiaroscuro visuals, and its authenticating references to late 1940s American society and culture, *The Man Who Wasn't There* proudly proclaims its reconstruction of both a bygone era and that era's "mannerisms," while *Blood Simple* offers a contemporary updating of the complex, violent, and ultimately tragically self-destructive criminal scheming that is the most prominent element of Cain's narratives.[6] So much is obvious—and is meant to be. Set in a small northern California town (Cain's fiction makes use of similar locales), *The Man Who Wasn't There* is filled with references that advertise the Coens' "knowingness" and that are to be decoded only by the cognoscenti. For example, secondary characters in the Coens' film bear the unusual surnames (Nirdlinger, Diedrickson) by which *Double Indemnity*'s notorious femme fatale is known in the book and screen versions, respectively, of the story.

What has not been well recognized, however, is the way in which *Blood Simple* and *The Man Who Wasn't There* also rework and "re-function" more central elements in *The Postman Always Rings Twice* and, to a lesser degree, *Double Indemnity,* in order, somewhat paradoxically, to give vigorous voice to one of the novelist's key themes: the failure of community that engenders a desperate yearning for connection to others (the more spiritual side of Cain's scandalous foregrounding of the erotic force in human relations). These two Coen films, paradoxically enough, extend through complex gestures of restructuring and updating Cain's analysis of the socio-psychological malaise affecting Depression-era America. The result is that, in some ways, *Blood Simple* and *The Man Who Wasn't There*, especially when understood as a diptych, are more Cainian than the fiction upon which they draw so substantially. *Blood Simple* offers a penetrating reading of Cain, dramatizing how the relentless and transgressive pursuit of self-interest, because it poisons human relations, inevitably proves suicidal. The instrumentalization (or objectification) of others and the miscommunication that mars personal relations lead to fatal misunderstandings, always a dark hazard in an inscrutable world.

If this is the Cainian problem, then *The Man Who Wasn't There* stages a movement (itself inadequate, but that is perhaps beside the point) toward its utopian solution. This deepening of consciousness, though denied by Cain to his characters, is intriguingly framed by a web of references (further evidence of directorial "knowingness") to novelists who were themselves influenced by Cain. The film engages deeply, and critically, with two French works of philosophical fiction. The first, Albert Camus's *The Stranger* (1942), draws directly on *Postman,* like the Coens' own films. The second, Jean-Paul Sartre's *Nausea* (1938), treats the evolution of consciousness that comes from the hard-won perception of life's apparent randomness. Like Roquentin, *Nausea's* antiheroic protagonist, the Coens' Ed Crane (Billy Bob Thornton) is distressed by a spiritual malaise, in his case an obsession with the human abject, the hair that, neither dead nor alive, it is his job as a barber to cut and then discard. The desire to escape from the messiness of human physicality leads him to formulate a scheme for self-improvement à la Cain. And yet this plan, fed by money he blackmails from Big Dave Brewster (James Gandolfini), the man engaged in an affair with his wife Doris (Frances McDormand), is quickly defeated by unforeseen developments over which Ed has no control, thus failing to lead to what he imagines would be a less defiling way of life. His plans are to enter the emerging dry-cleaning business—all chemicals and no polluting water. Instead, much like Camus's character Meursault, Ed soon finds himself with no choice but to kill Big Dave in self-defense when the man tries to murder him after learning Ed is his blackmailer. He walks away from the scene of the crime undetected.

The killer, in spite of himself, is initially spared the consequences of his actions as his wife Doris is mistakenly prosecuted for the murder. Numbed by the absurdity of these developments (he tries to confess to the crime but is not believed), Ed now senses himself possessed of a knowledge that somehow places him beyond the realm of everydayness in which others seem mindlessly stuck. In voice-over, he comments on a scene of his fellow citizens scurrying through the town center: "All going about their business. It seemed like I knew a secret—a bigger one even than what had really happened to Big Dave, something none of them knew, like I had made it to the outside, somehow, and they were all still struggling, way down below." Though both Ed Crane and Cain's protagonist produce retrospective narratives that trace the events leading them to existential dead ends, Cain's heroes never manage such an escape from solipsism. They are never free from the powerful desires that move them, never manage to move "outside" the entanglements caused by their transgressiveness and scheming. Ed's sudden movement of consciousness owes more to Camus. As he dramatizes in *The Stranger* (and discusses at greater length in *The Myth of Sisyphus* [1942]), the realization of death's inevitability and arbitrariness strips the world of obfuscating romanticisms, revealing it to be foreign, strange, and inhuman, indifferent to human hopes and unaccommodating of any attempt to endow it with transcendent meaning. Like Ed, the absurdist finds himself living a life parallel to others, inhabiting their world but refusing to share with them the protective mythologies of everdayness, of an existence not lived in the continuous knowledge of unpredictable, unreasonable, and inevitable extinction.

Like Meursault, Ed comes to sense that others are engaged in a struggle (those motions necessary to sustain life) whose true significance—that it has no significance beyond itself—escapes them. But while Meursault is satisfied with being misunderstood by others, as he is during his trial, and actually looks forward to the uncomprehending hatred they will express at his execution, Ed is filled with a desire for human connection in some better world beyond the grave. Cain's two novels, and *The Stranger,* end with their male protagonists desperately disconnected from the world and facing imminent death, while Roquentin moves beyond human contact (dramatized in his final failed attempt to persuade the "Self-Taught Man" to accept the meaninglessness of existence) toward an artist's self-imposed isolation.

The Man Who Wasn't There, in contrast, concludes with a wish for the restoration of the community whose absence leads to the suicidal war of one against all. This is a political, perhaps moral, point implicit in Cain's analysis of the evident failure of modern society to produce bonds that satisfy and sustain. It is also a point common to the so-called hard-boiled writers in general who portray an America in which, as Sean McCann argues, "civil society can no longer contain private desire." This profanation of the liberal ideal could only be healed, McCann suggests, by a reassertion of "public values over private interests." But this is a thoroughgoing social reformation whose manner of unfolding these novelists, especially Cain, cannot begin to conceive, as they fail to provide a literary equivalent to the state social-ism envisioned by Roosevelt's New Deal.[7] On the contrary, Cain's novels call into existence fictional worlds dominated by those who can imagine bettering themselves only by betraying or destroying those to whom they are joined by bonds of loyalty, service, and *communitas*. The concept of the public sphere, at least in the sense of reformable state institutions, has no purchase in his version of America.[8]

The Marks of Cain

The place of James M. Cain in American culture, W. H. Frohock has no-toriously remarked, is defined by two perhaps contradictory propositions: "that nothing he has ever written has ever been entirely out of the trash category" and that "an inordinate number of intelligent and fully literate people have read him."[9] Similarly, Joyce Carol Oates complains that "there is always something sleazy, something eerily vulgar and disappointing in his work." And yet, doubtlessly intelligent and fully literate herself, Oates argues for the importance of Cain's fiction for the insights it offers into its eager readers in the cultural climate of the 1930s and 1940s, especially the two novels *The Postman Always Rings Twice* and *Double Indemnity*. It is, she says, the "archetypal rhythms" found in his treatments of a failing American dream that claim our attention.[10] Frohock offers a similar explanation for an extended analysis of what belongs in his view to the subliterary category of popular trash, declaring that *Postman* is "distinguished" because it has much to tell us about the "literary climate in America circa 1934."[11] It was an era fascinated by the story of "the man under sentence of death" (Oates) or, more precisely, of the hero trapped "in a predicament from which the only possible exit is the infliction of physical harm upon some other human being" (Frohock).[12]

Considered irredeemably vulgar in his own country because of his treatment of sex (which Cain finds, as Gregory Porter puts it, "primal, foun-dational, structurally and ontologically indispensable"), the novelist found more appreciative readers in France.[13] There, readers saw in his works not only the vaguely Nietzschean (or perhaps social Darwinist) perception that the pursuit of power ensures that "violence is man's lot" (a view of human nature that Cain perhaps owes to literary naturalism) but also the convincing portrayal of the irredeemable alienation of the ordinary man from social and political structures. *Postman* became, according to Camus, an important inspiration for *The Stranger*. Though Camus, like Sartre and many French intellectuals of the era, was fascinated by Cain's depiction of an energetically self-destructive transatlantic culture, he was also one of the many who profited from the revolution in form that the novel had effected.[14]

What Cain did was to displace the detective from his role as protagonist. Instead, he made the criminal the source for what, as Richard Bradbury puts it, is nothing less than "an examination of motivation." This analysis, because it is delivered by a narrator fated to die for his crimes, "eliminates the possibility of a return to normality" and provides "no informing intelligence within the text which returns the reader to the realm of external and rational explanation."[15] With *The Man Who Wasn't There*'s exclusive narrative focus on Crane, mediated by his voice-over (which often plays over sequences outside the narrative, properly speaking, that illustrate the narrator's general points or provide backstory), the Coens provide a cinematic equivalent to Cain's obtrusive narrators. In their film, too, there is no return to the external from the subjective.[16]

What this narrative method does offer is the opportunity to portray, as Camus realized, the main character's evolution in consciousness, which can be represented in content but also embodied in verbal style. Camus's Meursault verbalizes not only his own unthinking passage through a series of experiences (which is all he can come to know directly, uninterpreted by the various constructions that social mythologies impose) but also the conclusions he might draw from them. In fact, an act of unthinking and almost autonomic violence forces him to accept responsibility for the way he has lived and to contest both the character and the narrative that those in the justice system fabricate for him. Here Camus brilliantly expands and deepens the evolution in consciousness that Cain invents for two criminal narrators.

Influenced by such transatlantic admiration, a longstanding critical tradition would claim Cain and the other "tough guy writers" of the 1930s and later for modernism, disputing the claims of writers like Oates and Frohock that his books are trash or sleaze.[17] But Cain has continued to fascinate more than just the critics who see his characters as following a vaguely existentialist path toward self-understanding, however limited, and inevitable destruction in a world indifferent to their fates. Political readings of the two novels have also proven compelling. For Sean McCann, the failure of Frank Chambers and his lover Cora to make a life for themselves in *Postman* indicts the "absence of popular voice and civic freedom," for what does not appear to be restored, as it always is in the classic detective story, is that sense of "a stable order that can survive violence and abuse."[18] For McCann, *Postman* and *Double Indemnity* limn the discontents of an uncivil society as yet unreformed by New Deal liberalism; the protagonists in each case "cannot contend with a bureaucratic and commercial order—represented by courts, laws, insurance companies, and roadside restaurants—indifferent to its survival."[19]

In the manner of polemicists like John Steinbeck and the proletarian novelists of the 1930s, *Postman* and *Double Indemnity* reflect the pessimism and anomie that characterize their era.[20] Frank Chambers in *Postman* is the rootless, economically marginalized working man of the Depression, attracted by the freedom of the open road and the possibility of endless adventure but searching for something to give his life meaning. The narrative is set in motion by a sudden, physically disturbing, irresistible onslaught of primal eroticism, as Frank becomes bound, against his will, to the beautiful wife of his erstwhile employer, Nick, while she in turn rejects the husband she finds physically disagreeable for the muscular, aggressive adventurer. Needing the older man's money and property to support themselves, Cora and Frank plot to kill Nick in an attempt to make a life together that eventually fails when Cora is killed riding in Frank's car (reenacting the fate the couple make Nick suffer).

In an ironic miscarriage of justice, Frank is convicted and executed for her murder. Charged initially with the faked accident that kills Nick, Frank and Cora had been saved from prison or the electric chair because Nick (unbeknown to them) had been insured against accidental death by three insurance companies, who, facing the prospect of significant loss, connive to get Cora (who had confessed to the crime) a plea bargain on a much-reduced charge. This trick is masterminded by their public defender lawyer, Katz, who works the system in order to line his own pockets. In the second trial, however, no one stands to benefit from Frank's acquittal, though Katz is pleased enough to take as his fee, as Frank observes, "the $10,000 he had got for us, and the money we had made, and a deed for the place."[21]

Walter Huff in *Double Indemnity*, in contrast, seethes with a discontent that belongs to the more prosperous and settled wartime years (when the serialized story was issued as a novel in 1943, it became an instant success). A successful insurance salesman who lives a secure and comfortable bachelor life, Huff, like Frank Chambers, experiences his own version of *amour fou*, falling in lust with Phyllis Nirdlinger, the wife of one of his customers. This couple likewise plots to kill the inconvenient husband, mostly to collect a huge sum on his accident policy, although they do not actually need the money to make a life for themselves, something they could surely manage through an easily obtainable divorce. Walter, as he reveals, has been plotting for some time to turn the business for which he works to his own advantage: "One night I think up a trick, and get to thinking I could crook the wheel myself if I could only put a plant out there to put down my bet. That's all. When I met Phyllis I met my plant" (*Double Indemnity*, 129). Knowing that insurance companies almost always succeed in defeating those who would defraud them, Walter nonetheless wants to put down his bet, risking his life in the process. Success has given him what John T. Irwin appropriately calls an "intellectual pride, a professional's sense of superiority" that numbs him to the likely consequences of what he plans.[22] In Walter's own metaphor, he is a croupier at the roulette table from which his employers (to whom he feels superior in cunning and audacity) take all the profits. This resentment tempts him to beat his bosses at their own game, as he tries to make the system work to his advantage, much as Katz does in *Postman*. This desire for self-assertion and self-advancement, as Irwin observes, was one with which Cain's readers could readily identify: "One not uncommon resentment for American working men is the sense of being a wage slave, of being at the beck and call of that dumbbell at the office or the plant, a sense of economic dependence often experienced not just as a curtailment of personal freedom but as an impairment of masculinity."[23]

Though there are important differences between them, the two novels stage the failure of the energetic, self-reliant, and anomic protagonists to make places for themselves in a society dominated by established orders (the criminal justice system in *Postman*, the insurance business in *Double Indemnity*). If, as Jopi Nyman argues, the "ideology of individualism" depends on the possibility of self-fulfillment, then those who are excluded from the inner sanctums of civil society are bound to feel "increasingly insecure and disillusioned." These feelings are especially intense for Walter, who, unlike Frank, is in on the trick (that insurance depends on your betting on what you do not want to happen) but deprived of the opportunity for independent action and profit taking that Katz enjoys.[24] Nyman, I think, identifies a central element of Cain's novels (and of hard-boiled fiction more generally) in asserting that such characters "believe in the existence of a better or different world in which the masculine individual is properly appreciated and rewarded."[25]

Neither Frank nor Walter ever quite escapes the narcissistic self-concern that motors their desire for a society that better answers to their needs for inclusion and self-satisfaction, and this absence is strongly felt by Cora as well—if not by Phyllis, whose resort to violence is more substantially pathological and, arguably, an end in itself. A similar distressing drama of failed community, poisoned by bad faith, misunderstanding, and petty but terribly destructive venality plays out in both *Blood Simple* and *The Man Who Wasn't There*. The latter limns a similar version of early postwar America in which these same terrible failings are all too evident. But that film also imagines the possibility of their utopian transcendence. Unlike Visser (M. Emmet Walsh) in *Blood Simple*, the dysaffectual Ed Crane of *The Man Who Wasn't There* manages to break free from his initial acquiescence to a world that reduces him to numbed silence.

Emptied of his urge for self-improvement, Ed voices a desire for communion with Doris, the unfaithful wife he had barely known and who had killed herself out of disappointment with her lover, who turns out to be not a daring war hero and entrepreneur but a lying "big dope." Ed's dying wish is that he and Doris will meet again beyond the grave. In a form of expression he cannot yet conceive of, Ed hopes that together they might finally see clearly, "like when a fog blows away," what their experiences have been. Cain's characters show no interest in pursuing such mutual understanding. Awaiting his appointment with the electric chair, Frank has a different hope, asking for his readers' prayers: "send up one for me, and Cora, and make it that we're together, wherever it is" (*Postman*, 106). Walter and Phyllis, in contrast, seeing that there is no escape from an avenging law, reject any expectation that the erotic might somehow be transformed into an eternal, spiritual reconnection: "'There's nothing ahead of us, is there Walter?' 'No, nothing'" (*Double Indemnity*, 214). Their streetcar, the one named desire, ends at the cemetery. Phyllis plans to "meet my bridegroom. The only one I ever loved," whose earthly form is that of the shark following the ship on which they are escaping (215). Finishing his narrative, Walter too keeps "thinking about that shark" and the final plunge off the side of the boat he will take with his erstwhile beloved (215).

A Chilling Horatio Algerism

Cain engages with the deeper elements of the national culture, David Madden argues, by dramatizing in *Postman* the collision of "two central dreams

of the American experience—unrestrained mobility and respectable seden-
tariness—and two views of the American landscapes—the open road and
the mortgaged house."[26] If in the western what brings these visions of an
ideal life into collision is the masculine urge for self-assertion, staged in the
temporary frontier that opens up between the village and the wilderness,
in Cain's reformulation of the foundational national binary the "civilized
self" is "degraded" and "primitivized" by the violent eruption of irresistible
physical attraction.[27] This erupting desire makes irrelevant conscious wishes
such as Cora's urge "to amount to something" (*Postman*, 82) and Frank's
determination to avoid settled life and its constraining responsibilities. The
irony, of course, is that the only meaningful connection experience makes
available is one that leads inevitably to the characters' destruction.

If he discovers that he cannot take Cora on the road with him (for she
hates the uncertainties and shabbiness of the tramp's life), she in turn learns
when visiting her sick mother that Frank cannot honor the commitment
he has made to manage the restaurant, as he takes off for Mexico with another woman when opportunity presents itself. Together, they kill the man
whom Cora finds repulsive (if a solid, reliable provider), but Frank cannot
take Nick's place though he comes to occupy his bed and take charge of
his business. A more thoroughgoing antiestablishmentarianism dominates
Double Indemnity, which repeats yet decisively alters the formula developed
in *Postman*. Driven by a self-destructive desire to defy the foundations
of civilized life (the claims of family, the strictures of the law, the code of
professional behavior), Walter and Phyllis, unlike Frank and Cora, never
even consider how they might make a life together. Thrown together with
Phyllis's daughter Lola, for whom he quickly develops a deepening affection,
Walter can at least imagine a different relationship with a woman (loving
kindness) and a life not energized by a perverse and suicidal fascination
with transgression.

In effect, *Double Indemnity* splits *Postman*'s complexly dangerous woman
into two one-dimensional characters: one a pathological killer devoted to
the purposeless accumulation of property, the other an eminently sensible,
well-educated, and unworldly gamine who throws Walter over for a young
man pursuing his PhD. The Coens imitate this doubling in *The Man Who
Wasn't There*, with Ed's wife, Doris, who is eager to make a better life for
herself regardless of the pain it might cause others, contrasting with Birdy
Abundas (Scarlett Johansson), the teenage daughter of one of his customers, whom Ed thinks is a prodigy because the Beethoven sonatas she plays

bring him a kind of spiritual peace. (The salvific power of music, we might note in passing, is yet another reference both to Cain, who pursued an early career as a singer and studied music his whole life, and to his fiction; musical performers, mostly failed ones, are prominent features in his novels *Mildred Pierce* and *Serenade*.)[28]

In *Double Indemnity*, an assertiveness entirely indifferent to the suffering of others rather than *amour fou* determines the object of the criminals' desire. Frank and Cora want each other, but Walter and Phyllis are hooked on the thrill of instrumentalization, the power they can deploy to reduce others to objects, as they plot to transform her unsuspecting husband into the considerable sum denominated on his insurance policy, in one stroke defying conventional morality and, they hope at least, forcing the defrauded company to cough up a huge and legitimate payment. In *Postman*, by way of contrast, the insurance business controls the justice system (an indication that the interests of capitalism trump those of liberal democracy), disposing of the fates of Frank and Cora to its own best advantage. The doomed couple's scheme to acquire Nick's goods succeeds (if only temporarily) not because they plan and execute the perfect crime (as Walter and Phyllis do) but because they unknowingly exploit a weakness in the companies' unforeseen and unfortunate exposure to loss.

What interests the Coens in these dramas of self-improvement (which are nothing less than ironic versions of the national rags-to-riches myth of unimpeded self-fashioning) is not the central focus for which Cain is so justly famous. That focus, as Porter so aptly puts it, is the erotic: "it's desire and desire alone that makes the narrative world 'show up,' bringing its objects into a dreamlike focus and elaborating the rhythm of its unfolding."[29]

Blood Simple, it is true, does begin with the love that suddenly erupts between Ray (John Getz) and Abby (Frances McDormand), as she flees the jealous violence of her husband Marty (Dan Hedaya), at whose small-town Texas roadhouse Ray works as a bartender. But the force of the erotic is only briefly invoked and soon left behind as the film explores two related, Cainian motifs: every murder for profit, no matter how well planned, is somehow fatally flawed; and every scheme of this kind requires a partner, but success means that the erstwhile partners become, potentially at least, each other's worst enemies, possessed as they are of potentially deadly knowledge.

Informed of Abby's betrayal and Ray's perfidy by Visser, the private detective he has hired to follow them, Marty fails to force Abby to return home. Enraged and humiliated, Marty then tells Visser to murder the adulterous couple, but Visser fakes their deaths (flashing doctored photographs of the sleeping couple), collects his ten-thousand-dollar fee from a credulous Marty, and then, though they are in the man's office, shoots his surprised client with Abby's revolver. He thus collects a fee for a murder he does not commit and kills his ostensible partner, pinning the crime on the intended victims and thereby covering his tracks (an interesting variant on what Walter and Phyllis have in store for each other after disposing of her husband). Visser, however, soon discovers his plan's fatal flaw. Marty had secreted the doctored photographs in his safe, handing the detective back an envelope with a cardboard sign (the client, it seems, had his own plans for self-protection from his erstwhile employee, making sure he had evidence of Visser's involvement in the crime). Visser eventually concludes that Ray and Abby have taken the photographs and are intending to use them against him. So, ironically enough, he feels forced to kill the two of them after all. At this he fails. Though he manages to gun down Ray, Visser is himself killed by Abby with the same revolver he had used to shoot Marty, an ingenious reworking of the doubling, backtracking patterns that are such a notable feature of Cain's fiction.

"The world is full of complainers," Visser asserts in voice-over as the film begins, his world-weariness identifying what seems to be a philosophy of life Cain would endorse, "but the fact is that nothing comes with a guarantee." If the Russians, he later explains, manage to avoid the war of all against all, it is at the price of success, for no one earns more than "fifty cent a day." In Texas, however, "you're on your own," and he is thus announcing the war of all against all. Despite this freedom of action, the possibility of success is slim at best, he admits, for "something can always go wrong," even for those who, like him, have the guts to face the worst. His own plans are clever, perhaps ingenious (recalling Walter's elaborate plot to impersonate Nirdlinger on a train trip, while Phyllis drives her husband's body to dump at the spot on the tracks where Walter will jump off harmlessly, leading the police to think that the hapless victim died from the fall). In the end, however, Visser is undone by obsessive thoughts of insecurity, which are, of course, quite justified. He imagines the worst but misreads the threat he actually faces (Ray and Abby, though they have come by chance to possess the incriminating photographs, do not understand what they mean). And so Visser ironically brings on his own death, killed by a woman he tries to murder even though neither has anything to fear from the other.

The film ends with a brief dialogue between the oddly opposed pair (who have never actually met), and this darkly humorous exchange clears up a central misunderstanding when it no longer matters. To Visser, dying behind the bathroom door through which she has just shot him, Abby says, "I'm not afraid of you, Marty," showing him that the adulterous couple was not planning to blackmail or expose him. Even at this moment, Visser (the schemer who naturally knows more than his victims) is ignorant of the whole truth. Visser had not actually killed Marty. Finding the man shot by Abby's gun in his own office, Ray had concluded that she had shot her husband, and, in an attempt to save her from detection, he had removed Marty's body, only to discover the man still conscious, in which state he buries him in a cornfield. Ray assumes that Abby killed Visser, and thus he fails to explain to her clearly what he has done. Abby's puzzlement at his behavior makes her mistrust him and thus not turn off the light in the room they share when he says they are being watched; this gives Visser the chance to kill Ray. In the manner of *Postman* and *Double Indemnity*, *Blood Simple* stages a drama in which relationships are either exploitative (Marty and Visser) or poisoned by mistrust (Abby and Ray). Tellingly, no scene in the film includes all four main characters, their physical and psychological disconnection from one another belying the web of ties that bind them fatally, as it turns out.

What Kind of Man Are You?

If the erotic, Cain's principal subject, plays only a minor role in *Blood Simple*, it is even less important in *The Man Who Wasn't There*. Big Dave and Doris, it is true, are involved in an affair and they do formulate a scheme for self-promotion, but it involves only the most bourgeois of white-collar crimes and does not help separate them from that core structure of American society, the nuclear family. No impeding husband is to be removed by a violent murder meant to appear an accident; only a bit of money is to be taken from a business successful enough to stand the loss. With the aid of his ace bookkeeper Doris, Big Dave has embezzled enough money from the department store he manages for his wife's family to finance a second outlet, an "annex" that he will control directly, answering to no one, and where Doris will enjoy a promotion to comptroller. Though he does not know it at the time, Ed's crime closely mirrors that of his own victims. He too is dissatisfied with his position working at the pleasure of his wife's family (her brother owns the barbershop), and when a customer, Creighton Tolliver (Jon Polito), discusses his proposal to begin a dry-cleaning chain, Ed volunteers to be his partner. Needing ten thousand dollars to become the silent partner in the business, he immediately decides to blackmail Dave, out of anger at the man's betrayal, which furnishes him with the necessary dirty secret, for Dave stands to lose everything if his wife learns the truth. But if Dave's desire for professional advancement is thoroughly conventional, Ed's is not, motivated as it is, in large part, by an inchoate, Sartrean disgust.

A key scene in Sartre's *Nausea* records Roquentin's recall of the "nausea of the hands" he endured when handling a stone, a feeling of disgust at its strangeness and overwhelming presence, the "being" it possesses beyond his understanding of it through a conventional category. Similarly, Ed is summoned into the bathroom one night, where Doris is enjoying a long soak. She asks him to shave her legs, a task he sets about with mechanical professionalism. In his voice-over, he remembers thinking, "It was clean. No water. Chemicals." Doris is appreciative. "Love ya, honey," she coos. Perhaps Ed resents being at her beck and call (as he is, in a sense, also in his work). Perhaps he is angry at the strange intimacy of this encounter, with its complete lack of erotic charge, knowing in some sense he is preparing Doris's body for her next assignation with Dave. Perhaps he is tired of barbering, the polluting touch of harvested hair and soapy water. Ed does not say, but his narrative cuts immediately, with no explanation offered, to him knocking on Creighton Tolliver's door to draw up the partnership agreement. The defamiliarizing moment in *Nausea*, we might recall, also leads to a nagging dissatisfaction and, eventually, a drastic change as Roquentin determines to abandon his intellectual project (writing a biography of the long-dead Marquis de Rollebon) in order to live more fully in the present.

At first, Ed's scheme works well, but he soon learns that there is no pure form of life beyond the defiling, physical presence of others (interestingly enough, the plan to turn to dry cleaning would still leave him in the business of dealing with the filth and waste of his fellows). Big Dave pays up, Ed hands the money over to Creighton, but things fall apart when Dave learns the truth and attempts to kill Ed but is killed himself, an act for which Doris is arrested and arraigned. About to be acquitted, or so her hotshot lawyer predicts, Doris kills herself for reasons that are not immediately apparent (Ed will find out from the coroner some time later that she was pregnant with Dave's child). Ed's spiritual crisis deepens as he feels himself an increasingly absent presence, not noticed by the ordinary citizens he moves among. In a subjective shot, Ed moves among a crowd, none of whom meet his gaze;

indeed his image seems superimposed on a world that excludes him: "When I walked home, it seemed like everyone avoided looking at me, as if I'd caught some disease. This thing with Doris, nobody wanted to talk about it; it was like I was a ghost walking down the street. And when I got home now, the place felt empty. I sat in the house, but there was nobody there. I was a ghost; I didn't see anyone; no one saw me."

At the beginning of his narrative, Ed had affirmed that "I never considered myself a barber." But now he admits that "I was the barber," the one who is absently present, cut off from meaningful connection to others. If, in *The Stranger*, Meursault, because of his involuntary act of violence, finds himself embroiled in judicial proceedings that attempt to formulate a coherent self for him, bizarrely reading his lack of demonstrated sorrow at his mother's funeral as a sociopathic indifference to others, Ed finds himself delivered by his success (yet ultimate failure) at blackmail to freedom from his scornful, indifferent wife and her he-man paramour. And, yet, as he reminisces, "everything just seemed ruined." If Ed's movement in consciousness is archly Sartrean, the still-unfolding skein of events in which he becomes embroiled, set in motion by Big Dave's fulfillment of his demand, is vintage Cain.

Reflecting on his career, Cain found an intellectual, perhaps even an existential pattern in his fiction: "I, so far as I can make sense of the pattern of my mind, write of the wish that comes true, for some reason a terrifying concept, at least to my imagination. I think my stories have some quality of the opening of a forbidden box, and that it is this, rather than violence, sex, or any of the things usually cited by way of explanation, that gives them the drive so often noted."[30] Forbidden boxes, Pandora's especially, contain not only what we wish for but also the consequences we cannot imagine or refuse to contemplate. If he initially sought the splendid isolation of dry cleaning (a goal he attains metaphorically with the deaths of Big Dave and Doris), Ed soon attempts to reverse what he has set in motion. A visit from the coroner informs him that Doris was pregnant when she hanged herself, confirming the point that her lawyer makes that the more you look, the less you see, that the only certainty is uncertainty itself.[31] Silent most of his life, Ed now feels the desire to talk, for he is "alone, with secrets I didn't want and no one to tell them to anyway." So he consults a medium, hoping somehow to establish communication with Doris: "Well, first she told me that my wife was in a peaceful place, that our souls were still connected by some spiritual bond, that she had never stopped loving me even though she'd done some

282 R. Barton Palmer

things she wasn't proud of." Concluding that his "spiritual adviser" is merely a phony, Ed then resolves to turn his back on "the ghosts" and turn toward the living. Telling Birdy that he can't stand by and "watch more things go down the drain," he wants instead to nurture her career as a pianist and make a living as her manager; this would keep him close to the music he finds soothing. But the San Francisco concert virtuoso Ed engages to judge Birdy's work says she has no talent, and the young woman confesses to a greater desire, in any case, to train as a veterinarian. The new life comes to an even more decisive end when, on their journey by car back home, Birdy attempts to perform oral sex on him and Ed, surprised and upset, crashes the car, seemingly resolving the plot in an obvious homage to *Postman* as he awakens in the hospital to learn he's being arrested for murder. Ed thinks Birdy died in the crash, but she survived with minor injuries. So of what crime is he accused?

In *Postman*, because Cora's death in a car crash is similar to the one that killed Nick, the prosecutor and the jury at Frank's trial are convinced that he planned to eliminate her from the beginning, so that he could keep the money and the restaurant for himself. Frank is convicted, basically, for the coincidence of the two accidents in which he is involved, accidents that proved fatal to those whose deaths would profit him. The "second ringing" in *The Man Who Wasn't There* isn't the crash itself but what the police learn by chance while Ed is unconscious. Like Frank, who is convicted for Cora's "murder" but in a sense is punished for Nick's death, Ed pays for his original crime though he is convicted of a murder he did not commit, a death, in fact, of which he was ignorant until informed by the police. Big Dave, we learn, had been approached by Creighton in regard to the dry-cleaning proposition but had turned him down. When a blackmailer requests an amount identical to that of the funding needed for the dry-cleaning enterprise, the distraught businessman concludes that the blackmailer must be Creighton, whom he then beats fatally, but not before learning that Ed was the one who gave Creighton the ten thousand. When the police find Creighton and his car submerged in a nearby pond, the justice system proceeds to draw conclusions as mistaken, but perhaps as poetically just, as those arrived at by the prosecutor and jury in both *Postman* and *The Stranger:* "Inside his briefcase were the partnership papers I'd signed showing that I'd given him ten grand. For the district attorney that made it fall into place: I'd gotten Doris to steal the money, the pansy [Creighton] had gotten wise somehow, and I'd had to kill him to cover my tracks."

Because the whole truth is hardly exculpatory (Ed would have to confess to killing Big Dave), his attorney sees no reason why it should be told. He pleads instead that Ed is simply "an ordinary man, guilty of living in a world that had no place for [him], guilty of wanting to be a dry cleaner, but not of murder." Echoing the court's condemnation of Meursault in *The Stranger*, Ed's judge determines just the opposite, that he is a "menace to society, a predator on his own wife, his business associates, on an innocent girl." But Ed resists the false portrait, concluding as he contemplates execution that "I don't regret anything. . . . I used to regret being the barber." What is apparent in the film's ending, as it is in the final pages of *The Stranger*, is the contrast between the distorting constructions society puts on human behavior for its own comfort and convenience and what the first-person narration has revealed about the two protagonists. Society finds it easier to present Ed as a "menace" and a "predator" than to conceive of him, as the lawyer more correctly does, as an ordinary man for whom the world made no place, all of which lead him to a modest scheme for self-improvement that goes terribly wrong because it veers into a world where it fatally collides with other schemes (those of Creighton, on the one hand, and Doris and Big Dave on the other). The ten thousand dollars that Big Dave and Doris embezzle from his wife, that Ed then blackmails Big Dave for, and that the police find in Creighton's car—the money for which these four characters all compete unsuccessfully—stands for the zero sum of opportunity in postwar America, the cause of the war of one against all that the film traces. But that is a truth that the justice system cannot acknowledge, preferring instead to condemn the individual deemed monstrous for subverting law and social convention.

Twice in the film Ed is confronted, first by Big Dave and then by his brother-in-law and fellow barber, with a question that goes to the heart of his ordinariness: "What kind of man are you?" How could such an apparently placid conformist decide to blackmail his wife's lover, knowing that the payoff might ruin the victim? How could the man who was for years silently cutting the hair at the chair next to yours use his wife to embezzle her employer (as the brother believes, at least) and then murder an accomplice suddenly turned opportunistic predator? Ed has no answer. Why he has done what he has done falls into the category of "the things I don't understand" that, Ed hopes, will become clearer in whatever it is that waits for him "beyond the earth and sky." What he does come to know, like Meursault and Roquentin, is how the pieces of his life can be seen as constituting a meaningful pattern.

"Seeing it whole gives you some peace," he says, his words playing over the fleeting vision of a flying saucer that veers close and then shoots off, suggesting a possible path of transcendence toward that place where, reunited with Doris, the two might begin to speak about "all those things they don't have words for here," restoring something of the community that in this re-composed Cainian world seems irretrievably lost.

Notes

1. While Cain is undoubtedly the author whose fiction (and its cinematic adaptations) the Coens have shown the most interest in reworking, their film *Miller's Crossing* (1990) draws heavily on material and themes from the novels of Dashiell Hammett, particularly *Red Harvest* (1929) and *The Glass Key* (1931).

2. Fredric Jameson, "The Antinomies of Postmodernism," in *The Cultural Turn: Selected Writings on the Postmodern, 1983–1998,* ed. Fredric Jameson (London: Verso, 1998), 59.

3. Peter Brooker, "Postmodern Adaptation: Pastiche, Intertextuality, and Re-Functioning," in *The Cambridge Companion to Literature on Screen,* ed. Deborah Cartmell and Imelda Whelehan (Cambridge: Cambridge Univ. Press, 2007), 114.

4. Ibid.

5. Jean Baudrillard, "Interview: Game with Vestiges," *On the Beach* 5 (winter 1984): 19, 24.

6. For further discussion of the way hyper-authenticity plays out thematically and stylistically in the nostalgic re-creation form of neo-noir in general and the Coens' film in particular, see R. Barton Palmer, "The New Sincerity of Neo-Noir: The Example of *The Man Who Wasn't There,*" in *The Philosophy of Neo-Noir,* ed. Mark T. Conard (Lexington: Univ. Press of Kentucky, 2007), 151–66.

7. Sean McCann, *Gumshoe America: Hard-Boiled Crime Fiction and the Rise and Fall of New Deal Liberalism* (Durham, N.C.: Duke Univ. Press, 2000), 4, 5.

8. This is not true of later writers in the tradition, as McCann shows, for example, in the case of Chester Himes, who uses the hard-boiled novel to "dramatize the intimate relations between racism and American democracy." McCann, *Gumshoe America,* 252.

9. W. H. Frohock, *The Novel of Violence in America, 1920–1950* (Dallas: Southern Methodist Univ. Press, 1950), 87.

10. Joyce Carol Oates, "Man under Sentence of Death: The Novels of James M. Cain," in *Tough Guy Writers of the Thirties,* ed. David Madden (Carbondale: Southern Illinois Univ. Press, 1968), 110.

11. Frohock, *Novel of Violence in America,* 88.

12. Ibid., 8.

13. Gregory Porter, "Double Cain," *Novel* 29 (spring 1996): 285. Porter explains: "'The Cainian hero, like it or not, cannot not love; despite a casualness that makes it all seem—for the hero, at least—fortuitous, the sheer numerical insurgency of these moments indicates that for Cain there's no imaginable alternative to an originary love-bond that quite literally 'makes the world go round.'" Ibid.

14. While Camus never acknowledged his admiration for *Postman* in print, there is a wealth of circumstantial evidence, usefully examined by David Madden, that establishes the connection between the two novels beyond any reasonable doubt. See Madden, *Cain's Craft* (Metuchen, N.J.: Scarecrow Press, 1985), 79–92.

15. Richard Bradbury, "Sexuality, Guilt, and Detection: Tension between History and Suspense," in *American Crime Fiction: Studies in the Genre,* ed. Brian Docherty (Basingstoke, U.K.: Macmillan, 1988), 89.

16. *Blood Simple's* narrative pattern is quite different, as the film lacks a true main character and offers multiple focalization that creates an effective sense of dramatic irony for the spectator, who always knows more than any of the characters and is thus able to see their misunderstandings and missteps for what they are.

17. The best recent discussion is to be found in an elegant chapter on modernism and blood melodrama in James Naremore, *More Than Night: Film Noir in Its Contexts* (Berkeley and Los Angeles: Univ. of California Press, 1998), 40–95.

18. McCann, *Gumshoe America*, 19, 16, respectively.

19. Ibid., 23.

20. It hardly seems a mere coincidence that *Postman* closely resembles, in many ways, Zola's *Thérèse Raquin*, a key text of European naturalism. For a sophisticated and detailed discussion of the connection between the two novels, see Gilbert Darbouze, "L'Amour à mort dans *Thérèse Raquin* de Emile Zola et *The Postman Always Rings Twice* de James Mallahan Cain," *Excavatio* 15 (June 2001): 53–62.

21. James M. Cain, *The Postman Always Rings Twice*, in *"The Postman Always Rings Twice," "Double Indemnity," "Mildred Pierce," and Selected Stories,* ed. Robert Polito (New York: Knopf, 2003), 103. Further references to both novels will be to this edition and will be noted in the text.

22. John T. Irwin, "Beating the Boss: Cain's *Double Indemnity,*" *American Literary History* 14 (summer 2002): 260.

23. Ibid., 264.

24. Jopi Nyman, *Men Alone: Masculinity, Individualism, and Hard-Boiled Fiction* (Amsterdam: Rodopi, 1997), 243.

25. Ibid.

26. David Madden, *James M. Cain* (New York: Twayne, 1970), 109.

27. Porter, "Double Cain," 282. Porter usefully observes, "Without an initiatory object-cathexis . . . there would be no Cainian 'sociality' at all." Ibid., 285.

28. David Madden observes that "the major area of inside knowledge in Cain's novels is music." Madden, *James M. Cain,* 100.

29. Porter, "Double Cain," 285.

30. James M. Cain, *The Five Great Novels of James M. Cain* (London: Picador, 1985), 558.

31. Further discussion on this point can be found in Palmer, "The New Sincerity of Neo-Noir."

Part 5

GOD, MAN, AND NATURE

How Job Begat Larry

The Present Situation in *A Serious Man*

K. L. Evans

What gives the comedy *A Serious Man* more gravity than other similarly fatalistic Coen brother farces is this film's redefinition of the bottom line. Here we find the Coens' most resolved insistence, to date, on the essential absence of a controlling order in the universe and hence the pointlessness of man's attempts to find meaning in existence or figure out the world via divination. For this reason, it seems fair to take the film's fundamental postulates a little more seriously than usual. By distinguishing between the film's philosophical conundrums—which are posed and can only be taken in jest—and what it soberingly offers in the way of metaphysical absolutes, what it discloses about the meaningless of life, we can discover in *A Serious Man* the best cinematic example of current critical discourse's adopted style. This style reflects the logical end of an intellectual movement that appeared in academia in the 1960s, and (though in 1990 John Searle called the spread of post-structuralist theory a "silly but noncatastrophic phenomenon") its principal theme and overall effect is neatly expressed by the Jefferson Airplane lyrics that play throughout *A Serious Man* and constitute its thesis:

> When the truth is found to be lies
> And all the hope within you dies
> Don't you want somebody to love?[1]

Thus the film shares with much contemporary theory the sense that man's confidence in some kind of true order is fittingly spent, and with it belief in a positive outcome to life's troubling events. And it advances the view that rather than let ourselves be tormented anew each time we confront the absence of divine providence, we should quit all theological speculation, including the fruitless attempt to categorically know right from wrong, and instead turn our attention to everyday pleasures and responsibilities.

Like its biblical source Job, in other words, *A Serious Man* is a "distilled, hyperbolic account of the human condition."[2] We identify it as a Job story because it opens with a framework narrative told in a classic style, its central character is tormented by his failure to account for the miseries that befall him, and what happens to him and his family brings to mind the painful awareness that inexplicable misfortune is the lot of man. In most other respects, however, the Coens' Job is unrecognizable to readers of Kethubim, the third section of the Hebrew scriptures in which Job, Psalms, and Proverbs together form "the great writings." That is because the obvious lesson of Job and *A Serious Man*—awareness of the prevalence of disorder in the government of the world, of the purposive and nonpurposive, playful and uncanny—is the same, but the function of the lesson is not. In Job, the outcome of the drama is that the collapse of a complacent view of divine economy can be overcome.[3] Job exposes, so as to offset, the meaninglessness of life. But in the film this second step is never taken. The upshot of *A Serious Man* is also that the attempt to find meaning in human existence is futile, but not as in Job, because this would be to misunderstand the reality of God's relation to man. For the Coens, looking for meaning is futile because it's futile: because truth is a fabrication, a cultural construct—hence the need for somebody to love.

In this way *A Serious Man* adopts the conclusions of one of the most popular approaches in academic fields concerned with the analysis of language, culture, and society. In the second half of the twentieth century, critical discourse in these disciplines adopted a certain style, one in which "it became *de rigueur* to place the word 'reality'—always—in inverted commas, to signal awareness that this so called reality was a cultural fiction," or in which absolute truths, and with them the basis for the distinction between right and wrong thinking, were summarily dispensed with.[4]

Consequently it wasn't just the "new freedoms" of the 1960s (sex, drugs, and rock 'n' roll) that "kicked holes in the conformist patterns of middle class life."[5] The era also ushered in what Foucault describes as "the immense and proliferating criticizability of things, institutions, practices, and discourses; a sort of general feeling that the ground was crumbling beneath our feet, especially in places where it seemed most familiar, most solid, and closest to us, to our bodies, to our everyday gestures."[6] The practice of analyzing human culture semiotically (i.e., as a system of signs) eventually led to what

Derrida calls "a rupture in intellectual life," as those who studied the underlying structures of cultural products such as texts came to hold that there was no transcendent meaning to those texts other than what was created by the readers of them.[7]

This is the world in which we find Larry Gopnik (Michael Stuhlbarg), who is the protagonist of *A Serious Man* but not, we suspect, its eponymous hero. Larry is a physics professor at a local midwestern university. Rather than espouse Theory, however, Larry lives it. Dutifully he searches for clues, answers, or signs that might explain his progressively more cringe-inducing misfortunes: the charge of his unemployed, unlovable brother Arthur (Richard Kind), sebaceous cyst all a-drip in the family bathroom; a mysteriously threatened tenure application; a wife, Judith (Sari Lennick), who is both faithless and accusing; and worst of all, forced closeness with his wife's new lover, the oleaginous, excessively earnest, and insincerely virtuous Sy Ableman (Fred Melamed).

As these clues fail to materialize and the people to whom Larry turns for help prove increasingly ineffectual (the junior rabbi advises Larry to "look at the parking lot," with the eyes of someone "with the capacity for wonder"), Larry's hope of making sense of his experiences gives way to the feeling that the brute irrationality of life is all he can really count on. Though it is tempting to read the fast-approaching tornado of the film's final scene as retribution for Larry's decision to accept a bribe, Larry's back-to-back conversations with Arlen (Ari Hoptman) from the tenure committee and his family doctor suggest otherwise: Arlen tells Larry that he has indeed been awarded tenure (though by now we know him to be an ineffective teacher with no publications), but the doctor's news, we understand, is about to make that decision incidental. From this, Larry learns that you don't get what you deserve—you get what you get. There is no reliable relationship between good actions and good fortune or wickedness and punishment.[8] More precisely, if evildoers do sometimes suffer and goodness brings blessings, then, as Moshe Greenberg writes, "the manifestation of this causality can be so erratic or so delayed as to cast doubt on its validity as the single key to the destiny of men and nations."[9]

This at least must be the film viewer's conclusion. Larry himself seems too empty-headed to undergo any kind of realization, too much like a fish behind glass. Unlike Job, Larry is not a complainer and a denouncer, not a man tortured by concepts his experience doesn't support; when things get really unbearable, Larry gets stoned. Or if he experiences confusion, this confused state is where his thinking will likely terminate. Larry is not working toward a finer comprehension, that is to say, nor does he ever benefit, as Job does, from sudden revelation. Job's flood of insight comes about in a storm, or transpires through a sudden overwhelming awareness of the complexity of God's manifestation in reasonless phenomena.[10] However, the oncoming storm of the film's final scene hardly suggests Larry's immanent intellectual and spiritual transformation, nor do we ever know him to be a man whose sensibility can absorb or even affirm the contradictions of a world that clearly does not operate on a straightforward model of retributive justice. That storm will simply flatten Larry and his lousy offspring—and the inexorableness of that fact is where the differences between *A Serious Man* and the Book of Job start to matter. Since the film and Job share the same lesson (encapsulated in the film's epigraph, to which we will now turn), there must be a glaring difference in the *use* the authors of these works wish us to make of it. Which use, then, ought we to avail ourselves of? And if Job promotes a religious sensibility and *A Serious Man* shares or reflects the foundational assumptions of largely secular critical discourse, is Larry the Job this film's disproportionately secular and academic audience prefers? Is Larry the Job we choose?

A Circular Logic

The lesson that ends *A Serious Man* is the same that begins it: "Receive with simplicity everything that happens to you." The epigraph is from Rashi's commentary on Deuteronomy 18:13, and the context there is of not doing magic or sorcery—but of rather awaiting or expecting God, as opposed to trying to figure out the world using divination.[11] This warning sets in motion the film's extended critique of any attempt to understand how providence works, mockingly illustrated in the failed lessons and roundabout logic of a story Rabbi Nachtner (George Wyner) tells Larry about a dentist who found a Hebrew message inscribed in a gentile's teeth. Larry demands an explanation of the story's meaning, which the rabbi is unable to provide. Viewers are obviously meant to identify with Larry's frustration with not receiving a clear answer from the rabbi about either his situation or the bizarre parable of the goy's teeth. Larry's lawyer (Adam Arkin) voices this identification when he inquires about Larry's visit to the rabbi: "What—did he tell you about the goy's teeth?" he asks, in a tone suggesting that the rabbi often tells this story and it is never appropriately helpful.

But if the insight about the wrongness of theological maundering on is an important one, and in keeping with the story's biblical sources, what happens when this initial assertion becomes the film's ultimate assertion? Though profoundly skeptical about the merits of instruction, *A Serious Man* does offer a kind of final lesson, a line of reasoning Larry the physics professor describes as "the uncertainty principle." It proves that "we can't ever really know what's going on," as Larry tells his students, "but you'll still be responsible for it on the midterm." This is *A Serious Man*'s punch line, the source of its comic/anguished mood. True wisdom is hidden from humans. Man cannot discern any justice in his rewards and punishments, nor does he attain any wisdom on the topic from his friends and neighbors. For the Coens this fact is both acceptable, the cause for a lot of fun, and intolerable—which explains why "a deep anxiety lurks beneath the jokes," as A. O. Scott writes, "and though *A Serious Man* is written and structured like a farce, it is shot (by Roger Deakins), scored (by Carter Burwell), and edited (by the Coens' pseudonymous golem Roderick Jaynes) like a horror movie."[12]

This underlying anxiety is warranted, and not simply because the universe turns out to be inexplicable in human terms. There is in fact something worse than the collapse of a complacent view of divine economy, or the disintegration of the idea that God rewards people for their virtue and punishes them for their sins. In *A Serious Man*, this more terrifying prospect takes the form of Sy Ableman: Sy Ableman making love to your wife; Sy Ableman living in your house, parenting your children, offering moral instruction. Because when the wisest rabbi can only mouth Jefferson Airplane lyrics, or when speculation about the limits of human knowledge becomes an occasion not for examining the whole theological enterprise but for abandoning the attempt to live ethically, then an unctuous moralizer like Sy Ableman has just as much right as anyone else to call himself "a serious man" and insinuate himself into his neighbors' lives. When truth is reconstrued as "truth," in other words, "then—Sy Ableman," as Judith nicely puts it.[13]

That is to say, it's worth noting the splendidly archetypal quality of Judith's abridged explanation for the dissolution of her marriage to Larry, a story all the more decipherable for its ellipses, and to take this story to be offering a kind of instruction. "You know the problems you and I have been having," Judith tells Larry one evening, in the family kitchen. "Well, Sy and I have become very close." The more contracted this story becomes, the more effective it is. "In short," Judith remarks in even tones, "I think it's time to start talking about a divorce." To Larry's pathetic appeal that he hasn't "*done* anything" and also that he's "probably about to get tenure," Judith replies:

"Nevertheless . . . things have changed. And then—Sy Ableman." Although the Coens clearly do not mean for Judith to display any special wisdom (she is introduced in the script as "a woman of early middle age" and in this form embodies marital shortfall, as these filmmakers see it), Judith's simultaneous declarations about Sy and her criticism of Larry's response to the news bring us closer to a good theological reading of Job than anything else in the movie. That is because Judith is right to point out that all of Larry's appeals—not just what he says on this occasion but his outburst to Arlen of the tenure committee ("I'm not an evil man!"); even his decision to consult a lawyer about an encroaching neighbor—belong to the context of the neat, orderly system to which he has somewhat blindly subscribed and that Judith is right to belittle. "You always act so surprised," she tells Larry, when he registers shock at the news she's just delivered. "I have begged you to see the rabbi."

Judith is an active member of her congregation, while Larry's zeal for religious instruction seems to be on the wane, and the film's viewers are meant to scoff at the hypocrisy of Judith's conjugal faithlessness.[14] Yet what Judith reminds Larry in this scene is that exercising retributive justice is not what God does. It is rather what people imagine God does, what they want God to do. Thus "seeing the rabbi" will not provide Larry with an explanation of the events in his life, as he indeed finds, nor is it meant to. Seeing the rabbi should confirm that there is no account (certainly there is not one in Job) of the actual nature of divine providence, only a reaffirmation of human ignorance about God. This lesson is of consequence because any man who is fixated on the notion of cosmic justice will undoubtedly find himself in a universe that has lost all meaning. The reason for that is obvious: loyal spouses are often betrayed; more deserving academics than Larry don't get tenure, et cetera. What "seeing the rabbi" should accomplish, then, is not what Larry thinks it should, but what Judith thinks it should: reconfirmation that appalling, penalizing things happen to blameless people all the time.

The view that the purported design of the universe is a *human* invention is not, however, one the rabbis in the film are allowed to teach. For the filmmakers, this lesson is given expression by current critical discourse or is a lesson embodied in the new freedoms of the 1960s or the flight from the suburbs and what they offer in the way of a benighted religiosity.[15] It is moreover *A Serious Man*'s only lesson, its raison d'être, which leaves the film nowhere to go once it shows how the orderly fabric of Larry's life has been irreparably rent.[16] At the film's end, Larry's death sentences stack up senselessly: he's likely to be a casualty of the oncoming storm; the sufferer of a fatal disease; the permanent caregiver of his despondent brother; the reinstated other half of a lifeless marriage; and the teacher of innumerable Clives—students demanding "C"s for "F"-level work. He'll suffer all these fates for the reason that everything that happens to a man is literally beyond his understanding. Painful, perplexing events occur, but there's no good reason for thinking or saying they shouldn't, since, if no claim has any truth value, then there can be no criteria for distinguishing proper from improper behavior, and hence for knowing the difference between a good life and a wretched one.

Thus runs the film's circular logic: if divine governance is beyond human understanding, then there's no justification for saying that there is any kind of true order and no way to determine right from wrong. Only now it is the case that by following its implications logically to an absurd consequence, *A Serious Man* disproves the very proposition it tries to establish. The film becomes a reductio ad absurdum of the proposition that if God's ways are inscrutable, truth is a hollow concept. For if there really is nothing that allows the concept of objectivity any traction, if all truths are "truths," then there's no reason why Sy Ableman, spokesman for all that is false and inaccurate, author of baseless accusations, shouldn't be called "a serious man"—why Sy shouldn't be seen as a legitimate substitute for the man whose life he usurps. *A Serious Man* replaces Job with Larry, and then, as Larry himself points out when he and Sy have synchronized car crashes and Sy alone dies, it invites the possibility of replacing Larry with Sy. It grants Sy's replacement of Larry a modicum of sense, or renders sensible-sounding Sy's suggestion that he move into the house while Larry moves into the Jolly Roger. ("It's not expensive," Sy croons, "and the rooms are eminently livable.") We might also put it this way: if silly things are afforded a degree of seriousness because speculation about God's ways fails as an explanation for anything, then—Sy Ableman.

The Lesson of Job

How differently the Book of Job must strike us. What readers learn from Job isn't what they began it knowing, what conventional wisdom teaches: that there is disorder in the government of the world. What we learn—and in addition to the detail that it is possible to absorb the contradictions experience offers in the way of senseless calamity while maintaining a relation to God—is that there is something fundamentally wrong, something inaccurate in *reality,* about saying unreasonable things.[17]

The chief way the text of Job accomplishes that difficult lesson is by introducing an ironic distance between the story's readers and its protagonist. If Larry is our everyman, an ordinary schlub with whom we can all identify, Job is as far removed from us as the clouds. Job is impossibly righteous, rich, fatherless, and unfamiliar (he's not even Jewish!); and for this reason he is easy to turn into the abstract parabolic figure he must become. We know him to be this way because that is how he is presented in Job's framework story—the prologue (chapters 1 and 2) and epilogue (42.7–17)—that encases the main body of work, which is the poetic disputation. The framework narrative has a very different style, one that reflects epic elements that go back to an earlier prose tale. In the prologue, readers learn about Satan's wager with God, which has the consequence of destroying Job for no good reason, and thus know why dire misfortune falls on blameless Job and also why his friends' arguments regarding why he is being punished are inaccurate. Moshe Greenberg tells us: "Without the prologue we should lack the essential knowledge that Job's misfortune really made no sense; without the prologue the friends' arguments that misfortune indicates sin would be plausible, and Job's resistance to them liable to be construed as moral arrogance. The prologue convinces us from the outset of Job's integrity, hence we can never side with the friends. For Job is a paradigm ('He never was or existed,' says a Talmudic rabbi, 'except as an example')."[18] "From the very outset, then," as Allan Cooper argues, "the sole cause of Job's suffering is revealed to the reader, who thereby assumes an ironic distance from the book's uninformed characters."[19]

This corrective is lost, however, if readers cannot by means of the prologue bring about or acquire an ironic distance. In contrast to Job's framework narrative, the prologue to the Coens' film settles nothing about the story that is to follow. *A Serious Man* begins with a Yiddish-language ersatz folktale in which a husband and wife get help from, and then murder, Traile Groshkover (Fyvush Finkle), who may or may not be a dybbuk (ghost). Yet in an interview, the Coens say that the prologue "doesn't really have any direct relationship to the rest of the movie."[20] The prologue's disconnection from the body of the film is further emphasized by the fact that it is not truly a Yiddish folktale but a fabrication of the directors. As Ethan Coen remarks, "We didn't know any suitable Yiddish folktales, so we just kind of made one up."[21] The Coens' parable—this is presumably their point—does not help the viewer understand the meaning of the film any more than Rabbi Nachtner's parable of the goy's teeth helps Larry understand his situation. Like the other stories told within the film, the folktale is inexplicable, or points once more to the brothers' view of parables as an essentially unsuitable means of addressing any of the world's mysteries.

On the other hand, perhaps the brothers' remarks about the prologue are disingenuous, and viewers are meant to argue about its meaning without the benefit of any key the Coens' might provide. Some viewers, suffering through Larry's suffering, cannot help but wonder if the reason for his misery has to do with his ancestors' guilt. (Especially since it was the wife who stabbed Finkle. Wives are not a source of joy in this film.) Others may imagine the parable to be a reading of Schrödinger's cat dressed up in Yiddish garb: is Finkle alive or dead? Conceivably, the Coens could be suggesting that religion fails as an explanation of anything and its commonly understood corrective, natural science, fails just as completely.[22] But is the generation of a potentially endless or unresolvable debate what Rabbi Sklar, a consultant for the film, means when he calls *A Serious Man* "the most Jewish film I've ever seen"?[23] As he explains it, "You leave the theater with a host of questions, no easy answers and . . . arguing about what it all means." Has Jewishness come to stand for the business of "arguing about what it all means" on the grounds, or on the basis, that the texts which inform our lives (the films we watch, the books we read, the tenure applications we file) have no actual meaning?

What we have already said about the Book of Job, of course, shows why, as Bernard Harrison writes, "personal judgment, hunch, intuition—subjectivity, in short" may enter into the critic's initial sense of what to do with a text, "but at some point subjectivity must begin to ground itself in argument, rebuttal and the presentation of evidence drawn from the text."[24] This view of reading "allows a substantial foothold to the concept of objectivity," not because it is ever possible "to provide a finally correct reading of any given text" but because reading in a way that does not neglect the plain meaning of a text can show the "objective *inadequacy*" of an unacceptable interpretation—in this case, for example, that the arguments of Job's friends may have some merit. The plain or literal meaning of Job's framework narrative proves to be of particular importance when readers discover that, like Larry and his misguided friends, Job *also* has a complacent view of divine economy, or generally believes that God rewards people for their virtue and punishes them for their sins. Job knows himself to be both innocent and punished and is thus from the beginning in the position to cast off his complacent view, and yet many of the book's verses involve a seemingly endless argumentative dialog between Job and his friends, both sides essentially holding that God is just by human standards but disagreeing over Job's appropriate righteousness. In this part of the text, all speculation on this matter eventually runs down into ceaseless squabbling and name-calling—a far cry from answering the question of theodicy.

The prologue makes it impossible to get embroiled in the debate between Job and his friends, who as Allan Cooper writes, "claim to know what they know on the basis of revelation, tradition, or experience," even while "it is obvious to the reader that they know nothing."[25] That is why

> the reader, armed with information that is withheld from the characters, should be troubled by their presumption: On what basis do they make all sorts of wild assertions about what God does—assertions that are plainly false? What do they perceive to be the basis of their knowledge? If we begin by asking these questions, we may get around to asking another one: How do we ourselves justify the claims that we make concerning God? And if, in our zeal to explain the nature of things, or because of our desire to account for problems of human existence, we continue to make such claims, can they possibly have any value?[26]

Readers of Job are thus in the position to see how silly and presumptuous the things people say about God can sound. That is the function of God's speeches near the end of the book, as Cooper argues:

> Their main purpose, in my view, is to undermine the truth value of *all* theological statements, which naturally encompasses (if only by inference) those that have been made throughout the book concerning providence, the suffering of the innocent, and retributive justice. Human ignorance is brought to the fore from the outset: "Who is this [not directed at anyone in particular—the "this" is for emphasis]—who darkens counsel, speaking without knowledge?" "Darkening counsel" means "saying unreasonable things," either denying the evidence of reason and observation, or claiming to know what one cannot possibly know.[27]

Thus the lesson about divine providence is not the Book of Job's conclusion, according to this reading, but its premise. This lesson provides the basis for much harder instruction on the subject of human misconception, for in Job we learn that wrong thinking about God is to be expected, and also that wrong thinking is reprehensible, or has ethical repercussions. That is why we must say that in the Book of Job, awareness of the prevalence of disorder in the government of the world does *not* lead to the conclusion that objective truth is a delusion. Job does teach that all theologies are ultimately false—but then the text goes one crucial step further when it shows how it is nevertheless "necessary to correct wrong thinking about God, and to put a stop to the verbal expression of that wrong thinking."

How does the Book of Job do this? Why isn't the text offering, as if it were a lesson, a simple contradiction? To make sense of the fact that "although all theologies are ultimately false," as Allan Cooper argues, "theology may still be of value when placed in the service of the ethical," we must look at the meticulously drawn portrait of Job's character, provided in the prologue.[28] Here we learn that Job is "virtuous but ignorant" or that "despite the excellent qualities that the narrator observes (1:1), which God calls to the attention of Satan (1:8, 2:3), and even Eliphaz acknowledges (4:6), no one says that Job is wise." Job doesn't understand what is happening to him, and he shares with his friends a mistaken theology of retributive justice, but *at no point* does he use what he thinks he knows to bludgeon his friends. Job's friends' error in judgment induces them to castigate him mercilessly. As Job then says to them,

> Ten times you have humiliated me,
> And are not ashamed to abuse me.
>
> Pity me, pity me! You are my friends;
> For the hand of God has struck me!

That the friends do not pity him or hold their tongues, as Job asks, is the reason why, in the epilogue, God is angry with them and declares them in need of forgiveness. There God tells Job's friends that they have not "spoken rightly" of Him. To "speak rightly" of God is not, then, to speak knowingly of Him, since Job, who is not rebuked in the epilogue but rewarded, is also incapable of this knowledge. Speaking rightly means not using your non-knowledge to bludgeon others; it means not speaking to one's friends in punitive or humiliating ways. For if Job "represents virtue without wisdom," as Cooper argues, "then surely the friends represent 'wisdom'—in quotation marks—without virtue. That is, 'wisdom' in the sense of authoritative traditional teaching, mindlessly taken up and used as a cudgel with which to beat an innocent man. The friends are not to be differentiated in terms of the content of their arguments, but by the manner in which they justify them." Thus, although "nothing that people say about God is true," some of what they say can be of benefit and some will make a bad situation worse. "That is the lesson of Job, and it makes good sense."[29]

Suffering Cats

In *A Serious Man,* Sy Ableman is of course a friend who "darkens counsel," or does not "speak rightly," while Larry, more modestly, reveals his ignorance but never uses it against anyone. The difference between Larry and Sy is such that Sy is the one who brings to life the ethical implications of "wrong thinking" or shows, as he deals with his distraught friend in totally inappropriate ways, that there are objectively wrong things to say. (That is, you don't need to think God's got his eye on you to agree that Sy treats Larry terribly or that you shouldn't act like Sy in similar circumstances.) The fact that we *know* Sy's arguments should not count as arguments gives the lie to *A Serious Man*'s final premise, that there are no real injustices in reality if there is no divine model of justice.

This explains the flatness or falseness of the film's conclusion—Larry's capitulation to his disgruntled student's view of things. When the collapse of retributive justice has the rather uncomplicated effect of rendering the universe meaningless, or when, as Larry's student Clive Park says, true understanding is "mere surmise," any "F" grade can become a "C," just as any man can be called serious. If all the judgments we make turn out to be arbitrary or subject to elastic criteria, then specious arguments count as arguments, and nothing presses us to look uncongenial facts in the face.

In the assumption that there *are* facts that may be looked at in this way, careful readers will recognize a reference to reality—and not the "reality" that expresses itself through social consensus or the conventions of language but the reality that transcends these practices and determines their correctness. There is proof in *A Serious Man* that this reality is something even secular intellectuals might want to consider seriously—though it arrives in the strange form of a lesson that Larry gives his students but obviously does not himself understand. Perhaps the Coens do not understand it either, as they seem to believe that "Schrödinger's paradox" or "Schrödinger's cat," like "the uncertainty principle," puts into effect a kind of skepticism, or legislates *against* a conception of the world that takes objective reality into account.

This is unfortunate for the reason that Schrödinger's thought experiment was intended to highlight the *absurdity* of interpretations of quantum states that failed to account for reality. By applying quantum mechanics to a living entity (and thus reminding physicists who had lost track of the fact that a dead cat was not the same thing as a live cat), he showed what happened when the traditional interpretations of quantum entanglements were followed to their logical ends—smeared, exploded cat as an indistinguishable substitute for "cat."

Thus the question Schrödinger's reductio ad absurdum raises is not "Is the cat alive or dead?" as Larry asks, or even, less stupidly but just as literally, "When does the cat change from live to dead?"—but "Why isn't anyone considering the cat, an object that can, after all, in the way of cats, be seen with one's actual eyes?"[30] (Here "considering the cat" doesn't mean thinking of the cat's *feelings* or overall well-being but thinking of the cat as a demonstrable aspect of reality; that is to say, as a reminder that conceiving of reality as microscopic particles is perhaps useful for certain purposes in physics, but it can lead to a real misunderstanding of what reality is, which is in actuality made up of the everyday objects of our experience—things like cats.) Thankfully Einstein's famous response to the thought experiment goes some way toward clarifying Schrödinger's intentions:

> You are the only contemporary physicist, besides Laue, who sees that one cannot get around the assumption of reality, if only one is honest. Most of them simply do not see what sort of risky game they are playing with reality—reality as something independent of what is experimentally established. They somehow believe that the quantum theory provides a description of reality, and even a *complete* description; this interpretation is, however, refuted most elegantly by your system of radioactive atom + Geiger counter + amplifier + charge of gunpowder + cat in a box, in which the Ψ-function of the system contains both the cat alive and blown to bits. Is the state of the cat to be created only when a physicist investigates the situation at some definite time? Nobody really doubts that the presence or absence of the cat is something independent of the act of observation.[31]

But Schrödinger's own comments, by way of an illuminating metaphor, offer the best corrective to the Coens' faulty theorizing: "It is typical of these cases that an indeterminacy originally restricted to the atomic domain becomes transformed into macroscopic indeterminacy, which can then be resolved by direct observation. That prevents us from so naively accepting as valid a 'blurred model' for representing reality. In itself, it would not embody anything unclear or contradictory. There is a difference between a shaky or out-of-focus photograph and a snapshot of clouds and fog banks."[32]

Job offers a snapshot of clouds and fog banks in order to emphasize how it is still possible, given the absence of a retributive model of divine justice, to conclude that specious arguments don't count as arguments or that the things some people say are objectively wrong. But the Coens gather together some of the world's best filmmaking talents to take an out-of-focus photograph. This blurry quality stems partly from the fact that the religious and scientific texts they use to deny the reality and essential meaning of the world actually promote quite a different view, or validate an idea of reality (not "reality") that can and does provide an ethical framework for our lives. In this way the Coens' movie may be darkly entertaining, but it is not particularly practical. It never encourages an animated "where next?" but fixes on the ultimately exhausting "what now?"

Notes

I could not have written this essay without the help of Daniela Aaron, an undergraduate at Stern College for Women, Yeshiva University. In addition to excellent translations of Hebrew texts and retrieval of crucial source material, she contributed substantively to this essay's composition and its line of reasoning. Were it not for the exigencies of her end-of-term pressure, this project would have been the first of what will hopefully become several formal collaborative projects. Also, I thank Mark Conard for his invitation to write on *A Serious Man* and for his many helpful comments on an earlier version of this essay.

1. The song's third line, "Don't you want somebody to love?" is rhetorical, since we know what the answer to this question must be, given the wholly disabling premise that has generated it.

2. In a shrewd review of *A Serious Man*, A. O. Scott offers this discerning comment on the Coens: "Their insistence on the fundamental absence of a controlling order in the universe is matched among American filmmakers only by Woody Allen. The crucial difference is that the Coens are compulsive, rigorous formalists, as if they were trying in the same gesture to expose, and to compensate for, the meaninglessness of life." A. O. Scott, "Calls to God: Always a Busy Signal," *New York Times*, October 2, 2009 (nytimes.com).

3. In this essay I rely on the elegant overview of Job's theology that Moshe Green-berg offers in "Reflections on Job's Theology," from *The Book of Job: A New Translation According to the Traditional Hebrew Text* (Philadelphia: Jewish Publication Society of America, 1980).

4. A. D. Nuttall, *The New Mimesis: Shakespeare and the Representation of Reality* (New Haven: Yale Univ. Press, 1983), vii.

5. David Denby, "Gods and Victims," *New Yorker*, October 5, 2009 (newyorker .com). The "new freedoms" is the term Larry's tempting neighbor Mrs. Samsky (Amy Landecker) uses for, among other things, pot-smoking and nude sunbathing.

6. From a January 7, 1976, lecture in which Foucault briefly summarized the general impetus of the post-structuralist movement. Michel Foucault, *Society Must Be Defended: Lectures at the Collège de France, 1975–1976*, trans. David Macey (New York: Picador, 2003), 6.

7. This depicts with absurd brevity structuralism's evolution toward post-structuralism, as well as the close resemblance of this intellectual movement to formalism. The Derrida reference is from a 1966 lecture, "Structure, Sign and Play in the Discourse of the Human Sciences," published in *Writing and Difference*, trans. Alan Bass (Chicago: University of Chicago Press, 1978), 278–94.

8. This deduction is supported by the happy fate of Larry's cursing, thieving son Danny (Aaron Wolff), who seems to get away with a lot and is worthy of very little. At least, even if Larry's son is lost to the storm, Danny the paradigm—Danny who got one over on his Hebrew teacher, and the kid who supplies him with pot, and his parents, and his community—lives on as the undeserving hero of any number of Hollywood films, as well as the successful director of many of them. (That is, Danny is the character who most closely resembles the Coens themselves, the character with whom they can be said to identify. Thus, Danny's escape from this world and his adult success is in a way encoded in the Coens' success.)

9. Greenberg, "Reflections on Job's Theology," xxiii.

10. Ibid., xix.

11. The verse states "you should be 'tamim' with the Lord your God," and Rashi comments: סימת היהת סע 'ה—ריהלא— דלהתה ומע בתממות נצפה ול ולא תקחור רחא תעדיתו, אלא לכ המ ישבא עילד ךבל בתממות ואז תהיה ומע ולחלקו. Daniela Aaron translates the line thusly: "Walk with him with 'temimut' and wait expectantly for him [maybe 'anticipate' him], and don't try to determine the future. Rather, accept everything that comes to you with 'temimut' and then you will be with Him, and [be part] of his portion." However she notes that the word "temimut" in Rashi's commentary gets translated in the Coens' epigraph as "simplicity," and it is difficult to translate this way. In English, "simplicity" suggests the quality of being uncompounded, whereas the connotation in the original is closer to "wholeness" or "perfection." Grammatically, "temimut" as Rashi has it here is an adverb: "with perfection, completion, innocence."

12. Scott, "Calls to God."

13. *A Serious Man,* shooting script written by Joel Coen and Ethan Coen, June 2007 (IMSDb.com), 28–30.

14. For what it's worth, in this respect Judith and Larry echo the sentiments, or imagined sentiments, of the Coens' own parents: "She towed the line in terms of Party dogma," Joel reports, referring to his mother. "My father, Ed, just went along for the ride. We were shocked to learn he ate Welsh rarebit at the campus club. I thought, 'welsh rarebit—that's made with bacon, isn't it?' It was an early disillusionment." For the record, Welsh rarebit does not contain bacon. We might then take this scene of remembered infraction as a reminder that Joel's knowledge of kashrut is as thorough as his knowledge of British comfort food.

15. "The context of the movie, the setting and community in which it's set," the Coens report, "are drawn from personal experience. Because it's where we grew up and how we grew up. The story's all made up but the setting—we were definitely thinking about our own experience and probing that in a way." These remarks come from a short film linked with A. O. Scott's review "Calls to God."

16. This phrase is Greenberg's ("Reflections on Job's Theology," xix), and I like it even more for the way it resonates with the kind of language a post-structuralist like Derrida admired and used.

17. This argument about Job's real purpose is Allan Cooper's, and those interested in it should read in entirety his excellent essay, "The Sense of the Book of Job," *Prooftexts* 17.3 (1997): 227–44.

18. Greenberg, "Reflections on Job's Theology," xvii–xviii.

19. Cooper, "The Sense of the Book of Job," 235.

20. Ethan Coen, "Becoming Serious," included in Special Features of *A Serious Man* DVD (Universal Studios, 2011).

21. Ibid.

22. I appreciate Mark Conard's articulation of this reading of the relationship between the Jewish parable and Schrödinger's cat.

23. Rabbi Sklar explains his comment in Franz Lidz, "Biblical Adversity in a 60's Suburb," *New York Times,* September 23, 2009 (nytimes.com).

24. This line and the next come from Bernard Harrison's chapter, "Reactive versus Interpretive Criticism," from his forthcoming but as yet unpublished work, "What Is Fiction For?"

25. Cooper, "The Sense of the Book of Job," 235.

26. Ibid.

27. Ibid.

28. Ibid., 234.

29. Ibid., 237.

30. This is not unrelated, of course, to questions Larry asks himself and their difference from the ones he might have asked. As Daniela Aaron writes in private correspondence, "the Jewish view of divine justice focuses very little on answering the

question 'Why does this happen?' and far more on the question 'How must I act when this happens?' Whatever injustices we may perceive as happening in reality, let's say, the things we see as under divine jurisdiction, there is an assumption that we must create justice in the mortal realm. God may punish one person for the actions of his ancestors—but the Torah forbids people from doing the same in their own courts. This view seems to be the subject of a good deal of criticism in the Coens' movie *A Serious Man,* or is at least the subject of much confused frustration."

31. Nicholas Maxwell, "Induction and Scientific Realism: Einstein versus van Fraassen Part Three: Einstein, Aim-oriented Empiricism and the Discovery of Special and General Relativity," *British Journal of the Philosophy of Science* 44 (June 1993): 290.

32. Erwin Schrödinger, "The Present Situation in Quantum Mechanics: A Translation of Schrödinger's 'Cat Paradox' Paper," trans. John D. Trimmer. Originally published in *Proceedings of the American Philosophical Society* 124 (1980): 323–38.

"A LEAD BALL OF JUSTICE"

The Logic of Retribution and the Ethics of Instruction in *True Grit*

David LaRocca

A father tells his child a story of the nineteenth-century American West in which a child wants to avenge her father's murder. What lessons is the child supposed to learn from the story? To leave justice to God's judgment? To depend on the law and courts for the right application of punishment? To become the agent of vengeance? In their film adaptation of Charles Portis's *True Grit,* Joel and Ethan Coen—one of whom, in fact, read the novel to his child—answer with the last option: the child takes on the mantle of a vendetta and succeeds in fulfilling it through murder. The man who killed the father is killed by the child. But this isn't how the story goes in Portis's novel. Why do the Coen brothers, otherwise so faithful to the book, deviate from it on this crucial point, and what can their heterodox reading reveal to us about the logic of retribution and the ethics of instruction?

Many of the Coen brothers' films engage questions at the heart of ethical theory, though usually with an ironic sense of how we act instead of how we ought to act. Sometimes, as in *Miller's Crossing* (1990), the characters make manifest this pervasive but often latent feature: "I'm talking about—hell Leo, I ain't embarrassed to use the word—I'm talkin' about ethics," says Johnny Caspar (Jon Polito). Of course, this is ethics from the mouth of a criminal, and the Coens' ethical meditations often take place in a criminal context—hence the irony. While the nature and consequences of criminal activity predominate in their work—from the earliest *Blood Simple* (1984) onward to the Academy Award–winning *No Country for Old Men* (2007)—most of the criminal activity is committed by adults. In *True Grit,* there is a posse of them, including Tom Chaney (Josh Brolin)—a hired hand who in a drunken frenzy kills his unarmed boss, Frank Ross; steals from his corpse; and flees.

Ross's fourteen-year-old daughter, Mattie Ross (Hailee Steinfeld), is forced to decide how to respond to her father's unexpected death and his unprovoked murderer. Where we might expect to find a girl shattered by her loss, numbed to inaction by the extreme trauma of the egregious act, we instead find the resolute Mattie Ross, whom Charles McGrath describes as "humorless, righteous, and utterly without either self-doubt or self-consciousness."[1] This is the first time in the Coens' lengthy and celebrated corpus that a teenager occupies a starring role. And perhaps in order to step into that position, the child must decide, even while set on edge by the death of her beloved father, whether or not to become a criminal herself: to do whatever it takes to bring Chaney to justice. "I am trying to get action," she says.[2] But what would that mean exactly? To see him imprisoned, hanged, or shot? And if killed—by what force, by whose hand? Will she be the proximate cause of Chaney's death (a role she may not be in a legal position to inhabit) or its broker? Are we meant to think that in the West, in the wake of the Civil War, it doesn't matter much if a child takes on the mantle of retribution?

Film critics usually take Charles Portis's critically acclaimed 1968 novel to be about a daughter's vengeance—that somehow in avenging her father's murder by committing a murder of her own she achieves retribution.[3] This kind of retribution might be called "blood vengeance" since it involves punishing the body or taking the life of the guilty. Mattie makes evident that this kind of vengeance is a possibility for her and presumes that she is capable, if need be, of sustaining its moral demands as well as its legal and psychological effects. But she's fourteen years old and thus not fit to take on the responsibility of blood vengeance in any of these senses. And yet Mattie may be a sufficiently clever rhetorician to have convinced her readers, including the Coen brothers, that hers is a tale of blood vengeance—vengeance satisfied—and that we should not just give credence to her story but marvel at it. But that's not what Portis meant to show us in *True Grit*.

While Mattie speaks of blood vengeance as part of her mission to avenge her father's murder, she in fact pursues what we can call economic retribution—a quantitative or literalized form and thus a simplistic and reductive approach to punishment. Economic retribution as a kind of *restitution* seems to be what is within her control and, importantly, also within the law and sanctioned by business practices—although even then she is recurrently faced with adults who either question her capacity to do business or doubt the legality of her authority as a minor. Stonehill (Dakin Matthews) nervously objects to her demands by saying: "I cannot make an agreement with a child. You are not accountable. You cannot be bound to a contract."[4]

As we seek to understand the imprimatur of "retribution" and "punishment" used to promote the film and the frequent reference to the story as a "revenge" plot, we should look through the Coens' film to its source material, Portis's *True Grit*.[5] In dialogue that is described as "poetically arch," "oddly formal faux-Mark Twain," imbued with "formal diction," a combination of "eager fulsomeness" and "tetchy reserve," and a "mixture of quasi-biblical dialect," Portis creates a narrative voice of such tremendous distinction and definition that it attracts our interest, even as its pronouncements may confound us.[6] In addition to the literary innovations in the prose style of *True Grit,* Portis dramatizes several models of retributive justice, with many of the figures in the story—lawmen and outlaws—expressing some opinion or variation on the topic (and even marginal characters register their views). But it is Mattie Ross's version—informed as much by her age (and therefore inexperience) and her understanding of scripture—that comes under critique by the "the meanest" marshal, "a pitiless man, double-tough," Rooster Cogburn (Jeff Bridges).[7]

While the Coens—known in their other work for crafting inventive and entertaining plot and dialogue—keep their screen adaptation very close to Portis's text, they depart from it on two decisive occasions. If, as David Denby suggests, *True Grit* "isn't exactly brimming with plot and character complications," we might be surprised to discover how the Coens' departure from Portis's novel creates them.[8] As a result, while J. Hoberman claims that the film's "most serious lapse is more aesthetic than ethical," I suggest—on the basis of the Coens' changes—just the opposite.[9] Of course there are many necessary elisions from the Portis text; film adaptations customarily must leave out scenes and passages for the sake of keeping to a predetermined running time and preestablished budget and eliminate passages of text that are inelegant or distracting if translated to film. My concern is not so much with what the Coens left out but instead with instances of *reversal* from Portis's novel. In a few changes, the Coens have created consequential adjustments to the ethical notions in the novel. As a result they undermine Portis's meditation on the *illogic* of retribution and render a conventional, we might say immature and naïve, understanding of retributive justice. If Mattie Ross pays attention to Rooster, as Portis phrases it, she should learn that there is no such thing as the kind of vengeance she seeks—it is, in Rooster's experience, an empty concept, a promise that can't be fulfilled. The Coens deny the chance to explore, and even celebrate, Portis's rare insight—especially within the genre of westerns—into the false aspects of retribution, and instead change his account to something Rooster might call a "stiff-necked" and "wrongheaded" idea of vengeance.

A Prehistory of the Coens' "Sanguinary Ambuscade"

Unlike so much of their work, *True Grit* is not an original screenplay by the Coens but rather "written for the screen" from Portis's novel.[10] *True Grit* is only the second remake undertaken by the Coens, the first being the underwhelming adaptation of Alexander MacKendrick's Ealing Studios production of *The Ladykillers* (1955). Feted with ten Oscar nominations (though no wins), the Coen's *True Grit* is already the most commercially successful film of their twenty-seven-year careers. The Coens' version has a venerable antecedent in Henry Hathaway's 1969 film of the same name starring John Wayne, the only role for which the Duke won an Academy Award for Best Actor.[11] Even before *True Grit* was released, the Coens publicly claimed "they only dimly recalled having seen the earlier movie when they were young, and they did not watch it in preparing their own." Ethan Coen added, "We didn't do our homework."[12] Nevertheless, as with *O Brother, Where Art Thou?* (2000) and *No Country for Old Men*, the Coens do show interest in written texts—Homer's *Odyssey* and Cormac McCarthy's novel—and now Charles Portis's book. Joel Coen said he and his brother were intrigued by the book after he (Joel) "re-read it out loud to my kid." The brothers concluded that no film starring John Wayne "would possibly reflect the very acid sensibility" they discovered in Portis's novel. And they encouraged their actors, including Jeff Bridges, to eschew the Hathaway version: "When the brothers invited me on board," Bridges relates, "I was curious as to why they would want to make the movie again. And they said, 'We're not making it again. We're making the book, as if the movie never existed!' So I took them up on that, and I didn't refer to the original movie at all."[13] Taking a cue from the Coens and Bridges, then, I will focus on the relationship between the 2010 film and the Portis novel.

Describing the nature of their adaptation from the Portis novel, Joel Coen said that the film is "formal in the sense that it is a straightforward presentation. We weren't trying to tune it up stylistically. When we were thinking about how to shoot the scene, the default position was more pretty, more classical."[14] The Coens, then, did not seek to transform Portis's novel so much as translate it to film: to visualize the prose.[15] The Coens said that they were "shooting the story that was on a page written by someone else, not a quirky one that was conjured in the space between them."[16] And we should praise their effort to be good and close readers of Portis's novel, which they clearly admire; in most respects their adaptation is faithful to his book. Thus, while there is much in the Coens' adaptation that confirms their judgment of "shooting straight," there are two deviations that upset the moral order of their work, divide it from Portis's understanding, and catastrophically undermine the ethical value of the film.

This change in the moral order of the film is interesting for several reasons, including the interpretive and pedagogical role the Coens create for themselves. It is rare that a father who reads a bedtime story to his child can proceed to make a feature film adaptation of the story starring Oscar-winning actors. The adaptation is itself a form of parenting or parental instruction insofar as the film confirms the Coens' reading of the novel. Most would agree that *True Grit* is a bedtime story of an exceptional sort; like Solomon's book of proverbs, which so significantly informs the novel, it is full of wise lessons and reminders about the challenge of being wise in the midst of potentially compromising circumstances. Could it be that one of those lessons sanctions, or even glorifies, murder by a child?

Given the sophistication of Portis's reading of the Judeo-Christian scripture, his novel deserves more than a paraphrase gloss as a story of revenge. Like Cormac McCarthy's novels of men on the American frontier, and Marilynn Robinson's novels of the spiritual lives of midwestern men and women, Charles Portis's novel is full of characters whose outlook is informed by religious ethics (even the bandits know the scripture they contravene) and constrained by brutal economic realities. The characters inhabit a world defined by unforgiving scarcity in the midst of a bountiful but often overwhelming and ungenerous Nature, and further compromised by the greedy and lawless. It is, in other words, not a great place for business—moral and otherwise; as Stonehill says in the novel, they seem to go together: "The civilizing arts of commerce do not flourish there."[17] And it is certainly a difficult place to raise children in so far as notions of justice and the rule of law are still under negotiation. When LaBoeuf (Matt Damon), a proud Texas Ranger—who has, in Mattie's parlance, been "ineffectually pursuing" Chaney for months—proposes to "throw in" with her and Rooster, his most effective argument rests on the promise of "mutual advantage." LaBoeuf, deploying his charm and displaying his competence, appeals to her desire for success in the face of tremendously daunting obstacles.

A child who takes up the mantle of avenging a parent's death in a contemporary story—such as Luc Besson's *The Professional* (1994)—will know unequivocally that the law is being transgressed. But in the 1870s, on the frontier side of the Mississippi River, it's not always clear whose laws one is appealing to: the laws of the state or territory, the laws of the court, the laws of man (his mores and culture norms), or the laws of God. It is clear, however, that such ethical considerations inform the Coens' thinking as they add to the screenplay the distinction between *malum prohibitum* and *malum in se*—respectively, that which is wrong by statute and that which is wrong in itself. But these ambiguities and conflicts persist in the present, so we can resist condescension to "simpler" times, much less claim any moral superiority. In fact, through their adaptation, the Coens usefully illustrate how we remain confounded by the criteria that might determine the right thing to do and are thus often unsure how to be loyal, brave, and morally justified.

Historically there are two dominant and opposing theories of punishment—a utilitarian one and a retributive one. A third option, restorative justice, may not seem overtly present in *True Grit* primarily because key factors such as bilateral consensus and identity sharing are not part of the cultural, moral, legal, or religious context of the time depicted in the novel. Yet Portis does indicate the possibility that Mattie unwittingly or vaguely desires a restorative solution to her crisis.[18]

The utilitarian view employs a straightforward criterion: if good consequences come from punishment, then it is justified—even if the innocent are punished! Retributive theory ignores consequences (good or ill) and focuses squarely on the "deserved suffering of the guilty." As moral theorist C. L. Ten notes, however, "retributivists have difficulty explaining why the guilty should be punished at all if punishment fails to produce any good consequences."[19] Even if we are certain about a person's guilt, there may be mitigating circumstances that affect the rendering of justice. Was the criminal acting of his own free will? Was he coerced? Did he have reason to harm? Was he inebriated or otherwise mentally impaired? What unknown circumstances and persons might have contributed to the crime? To what extent could the conditions beyond the guilty party's control lead to misunderstanding and accident? The courtroom proceeding where we meet Rooster Cogburn for the first time is a fairly robust disquisition on these questions. The defense attorney, Mr. Goudy (Joe Stevens), wants Rooster to articulate how he goes about making decisions regarding who to punish—and more especially, how he punishes or how much punishment it takes. Rooster's answers are entertaining but crude and suggest that he shoots first and asks questions later. The sheriff (Leon Russom) contrasts Rooster's style with that of L. T. Quinn, who "brings his prisoners in alive. He may let one get by now and then but he believes even the worst of men is entitled to a fair shake." Mattie would appear to choose Rooster over Quinn not because of differing moral sensibilities but because she would not willingly choose the lawman who "lets one get by now and then."

Mattie's choice of Rooster over other marshals gives an indication of the meaning of grit—especially as *true* grit implies there might be something like false, affected, or insincere grit. Mattie tells Rooster: "They told me you had grit and that is why I came to you." Grit is Mattie's criterion for selecting her tracker, because a man without grit will cower at a moment when he needs to charge ahead. Rooster narrates as much when describing how a few bold men can overcome "a full troop of regular cavalry": "You go for a man hard enough and fast enough and he don't have time to think about how many is with him, he thinks about himself and how he may get clear out of the wrath that is about to set down on him."[20] Rooster demonstrates just this kind of grit when he puts the reins in his mouth and charges after Lucky Ned Pepper (Barry Pepper) to "throw down on him."

"The joke—the Coens' touch of sardonic black humor," writes David Denby, "is that . . . the proper talk merely decorates the savage moral incoherence of the West. Here, if you want someone punished, you shoot him."[21] If the ethical nature of Portis's story is also incoherent (being as it is a rendition of the larger story—and myth—of the West), why is it so quickly and assuredly deemed to be about revenge? Why not the business of settling an estate? Or the pursuit by the young of knowledge from elders? Part of the "moral incoherence," savage or not, lies in the simple fact that lawmen are getting paid as mercenaries or bounty hunters instead of as impartial officers of the law. There may not be a conflict of interest if the marshal's interests and those of the law are perfectly coincident, but it seems rare that the two points of order should regularly match. Commenting on the Wharton case, in which Rooster would be paid more for delivering a live fugitive, he tells Mattie: "I should have put a ball in that boy's head instead of his collarbone. I was thinking about my fee. You will sometimes let money interfere with your notion of what is right."[22] In this case, Rooster kept to the law (and got his fee) but deems it a failure of justice.

As a retributivist, Rooster might be called a moral sense theorist—someone who intuits, as Jeffrie G. Murphy describes it, "the fittingness of guilt and punishment."[23] Early in Portis's novel there is a moral parable in Rooster's violent destruction of rats, a scene the Coens do not feature in their film. Rooster tells Mattie: "You can't serve papers on a rat, baby sister. . . . These shitepoke lawyers think you can but you can't. All you can do with a rat is kill him or let him be."[24] If Rooster is correct, then is retributivism (at least his intuitionist sort) "a bit of primitive, unenlightened and barbaric emotionalism"? If there is no care or concern for the utility (that is, the promotion of good consequences), it seems that retribution is nothing but "pointless vengeance."[25] But then part of Portis's exploration of the "savage moral incoherence of the West" poses precisely this question or doubt about the logic of retribution.

The Logic of Retribution

The novel *True Grit* is a revenge story in the way *Moby-Dick* is a revenge story: superficially—for those who seek a quick plot arc, sorting and settling the psychological motivation of disparate characters, and achieving a satisfying and simplistic end. Portis's novel, like Melville's, is narrated by one of the survivors of the tale. As it was for so many wives and daughters on the nineteenth-century American frontier, the death of a patriarch was as much a devastation to the heart as the pocketbook. A more penetrating look at Mattie's immediate, sure-footed decision to seek out Chaney bypasses the notion of vendetta and reveals her motivation for pursuing him and a better way to think about her understanding of retribution in Portis's terms: to settle accounts. From her first encounter with Stonehill, Mattie is fixed on the condition of what is due her and her religious education that defines what is due.

As in *Moby-Dick*, the touchstone of the novel *True Grit* is not the law of man but the law of God, so it is another mark of the Coens' faithful reading that Stanley Fish declares their work "a truly religious movie."[26] In *No Country for Old Men, A Serious Man, True Grit,* and the decision to adapt Michael Chabon's *The Yiddish Policemen's Union,* we see an emerging attention to the presence of religion in the Coens' work and its influence on one's frames of mind and frames of reference. In Portis's protagonist we meet a child of the Church, a reader of the Bible—an interested reader of that book, though importantly a young reader and not necessarily a good interpreter of its lessons. In the novel *True Grit,* that "old-time religion" animates everything from the idea (or prospect) of retribution to the way one educates children or parents them. Mattie does not presume to do God's work—to achieve some kind of ultimate justice. She keeps squarely to what she believes is within her control.

The Coens' first act of reading, or adapting, Portis's *True Grit* comes in their choice of epigraph, an incomplete extract from Proverbs that concludes the first chapter of the novel: "The wicked flee when none pursueth."[27] And within the first minutes of the film, we learn that no man of the law has set off to apprehend the wicked Tom Chaney. The rest of the extracted verse— "but the righteous are bold as a lion"—applies then to the undaunted and pursuant Mattie Ross. Portis's novel can be read as a narrative that illustrates and forms a commentary on many verses from Proverbs; indeed, verses throughout Proverbs, but especially in chapter 28, parallel the story of Mattie Ross and her search for the murderer, Tom Chaney.[28] Portis's novel is, in important ways, a dramatization of Hebraic wisdom and warning, but it is also a reconsideration of the inherited lessons. Consider how the novel begins with Mattie's self-understanding that she is out to "avenge her father's blood" and ends with her sense that she has offered a "true account of how I avenged Frank Ross's blood."[29] The Coens, along with many critics of the book and film, emphasize the pursuit of blood for blood (taking Chaney's blood as the only fitting exchange for Frank Ross's), but the real interest of Portis's tale lies in the account *he* gives of her very different sort of vengeance—its nature and its limitations.[30]

"Shooting Foolishness"

Watching Rooster and LaBeouf shooting corn dodgers, aiming to impress each other with their marksmanship, Mattie notes: "It was entertaining for a while but there was nothing educational about it."[31] In the last minutes of the film, at the core of its denouement, the Coens make the first of two changes to Portis's novel that greatly undermine the moral nature of their adaptation. In the film, Mattie kills Chaney; in the novel, she doesn't. While Mattie declares in the novel that she fires—with her second bullet—the "lead ball of justice, too long delayed, into the criminal head of Tom Chaney" it is, in fact, "Rooster Cogburn's rifle stock smashing the wounded head of Tom Chaney" that does the dreadful deed of killing him.[32] Rooster sends Chaney, as so much dead weight, plummeting down the shaft toward Mattie and the den of rattlesnakes and scurrying bats. As Rooster pulls Mattie from that same pit (an image featured in the same chapter from Proverbs that begins the film), he also "delivers" her from the hell of having blood on her hands; as the final cause of Chaney's death, he exculpates Mattie from the charge of murder above the law.[33] Freed from that horrible fate, Mattie is liberated from the pit—"blameless" in the language of Proverbs—while Chaney, his guilt translated into his death, descends into oblivion for eternity. As Portis writes it, Mattie does not achieve the kind of retribution the Coens have chosen for her; she does not avenge her father's death. Rather, "the law" (in the form of a U.S. marshal) takes care of her unlawful desire and spares her from transgression.

Unlike the Coens' reading, in Portis's imagination the "lead ball" is not for killing but for weighing the scales of justice. The bullet Mattie delivers to Chaney's brain adds to his weight, even as the arm she loses to snake venom subtracts from hers. Despite an apparent equilibrium, on Portis's account, nothing is gained by Chaney's death, but something is lost; this is part of the logic of retribution that Portis dramatizes and criticizes. Chaney should be punished, but to do so herself means that Mattie will lose something—at the very least innocence, at the most her own life, and much in between, including her arm. Killing Chaney may seem to her like the right thing to do, but it will not leave her as it found her. Her father remains dead whether she goes home to Dardanelle and lets the "wicked flee" or whether, "bold as a lion," she hunts Chaney down and delivers him out of this world.

The second plot element that the Coens change precedes Tom Chaney's death and transforms our understanding of his character. In the Coen film, Chaney lurches toward Mattie and lands on her with a knife in hand, open blade pressed to her throat. Seemingly seconds away from taking her life, Chaney speaks angrily through gritted teeth to Mattie: "I do not regret killing your father." In Portis's novel, Chaney does not attack her and is instead repentant: "'I regret that shooting,' said he. 'Mr. Ross was decent to me but he ought not to have meddled in my business. I was drinking and I was mad through and through. Nothing has gone right for me.'"[34] Of course, Chaney's last line complicates things further, since his self-pity gets in the way not just of the expression of his regret but also our assurance that he understands fully the nature of his apology. Killing someone by accident, as it were, should not be followed immediately by a commentary on how one—as the killer—is a victim.

These two changes to Portis's story have a profound effect on the understanding of retributive justice the Coens put forward—a notion that, despite their assurance of staying close to their source material ("shooting the story that was on the page written by someone else"), leaves their film at a great moral distance from the sentiment and insight of Portis's novel.[35] Usually creators of moral ambiguity, challenging viewers to consider the ironies, paradoxes, and confusions at the heart of ethical experience, the Coens in *True Grit* seem to give over to a celebration of stock genre conventions of the western. That is not necessarily a bad thing, just unexpected from the Coens, and a feature of their latest film that we should take note of. Clearly general audiences have responded favorably to the Coens' reading by making it their highest grossing work to date; yet the popular success of the film has become a strange commentary on the Coens' previous work and a confession of audience desire for this kind of storytelling. We have in their *True Grit* an accomplished film that is nevertheless detached from their customary sensibility: they have chosen to make an old-fashioned western instead of a work that would more naturally align with their other innovative engagements with the genre, which have also transformed it: *Blood Simple, Raising Arizona* (1987), *The Big Lebowski* (1998), and *No Country for Old Men.* At the end of the Coens' *True Grit*, Mattie Ross is a gunslinging murderer who deposits that "lead ball of justice" into her father's killer. At the conclusion of Portis's novel, Mattie is a "blameless" daughter spared the burden of Chaney's death, free—as the narrator who tried but failed to kill a man—to put the account of her experience in her own words, on her own terms.

The Vengeance Business

Retribution means the delivery of punishment that is morally right and justly deserved. As a moral idea, then, it entails not a literal replacement of the lost thing but the imposition of punishment as a form of payment for the loss. Punishment is a surrogate that enables the transfer of suffering; and that transfer is a mode of exchange. In the moral language surrounding ideas of retribution we should become conscious of the way the terms suggest an economic scenario. But this is, of course, a kind of symbolic manifestation of the human desire to restore; in legal proceedings, the effort is to translate the symbolic into the literal: how much is this life worth? Who should pay? And how—in time? in money? with one's life?

The economy of revenge in *True Grit* takes place, as Stanley Fish notes, on "two registers of existence"—the earthly, where events, actions, and property can be weighed and measured, and the godly, where everything is beyond assessment.[36] Mattie often quotes biblical passages that emphasize the nature of God's grace—that it is not something that can be earned, but only given by God. While telling her story, she implores her reader to dwell on how the Lord "hath saved us, and called us with an holy calling, not according to our works, but according to his own purpose and grace."[37] Mattie concentrates on what might be deemed empirical or economic restitution: the counting of ponies, gold slugs, mercenary fees, and the like. As Deirdre McCloskey has described them in "Bourgeois Virtue," we could say Mattie is an exemplary combination of *homo petens* and *homo loquans*—that is, someone not focused on rendering ultimate, providential justice but "seeking . . . the maximization of known utility under known constraints" by means of persuasive speech.[38] What is unknown Mattie leaves to God's grace.

The revenge plot, as Portis writes it, is a foil for illustrating the incoherence of retribution as a form of rendering justice. He achieves this by drawing a portrait of a girl who uses her preternatural business skills and her biblical wisdom to orchestrate the conditions in which her father's killer will be apprehended—alive or dead. When Mattie herself declares, in the final line of Portis's book, "This ends my true account of how I avenged Frank Ross's blood," we ought to dwell on her notion of "how," since it is not the "how" we may think it is.[39] Throughout the novel, Mattie is an instigator and negotiator of business deals, and all the while she keeps her old-time Presbyterian theological training close at hand to define her terms and conditions. Mattie is moved not so much to kill the man who killed her father as to square accounts: consider her preoccupation with trying to retrieve the other "rectangular slug of gold" that Chaney stole and that remains at large; or the early scene of negotiation to sell back to Stonehill her father's recently purchased ponies—where prevailing over Stonehill requires an elegant braid of appropriated marketplace rhetoric and confident litigious threat.

Mattie's drive to lay Tom Chaney low is motivated by her economic and theological judgment—manifested in her legalistic, contractarian approach—not derived from her moral sense. When Mrs. Floyd brings Mattie her father's things she says, "I went through them and made an inventory." Her cataloguing does not lead her to Proustian reflections or recollections; neither does she cry nor register sentimental thoughts of her kind and now dead father. Instead, she makes a list, she takes stock. Upon seeing her father's corpse she laments only that such an able man—a man in the midst of business, of being useful—was cut down: "I stood there looking at him. What a waste!" Thus, despite all her attention to the economy and theology of her actions, at no point in the novel or the film does Mattie ever pause to consider the long-term moral—much less the emotional and psychological—implications of killing Chaney by her own hand; her attention, instead, is squarely and unequivocally on balancing the books and relying on the direction of scripture. As Mattie concludes, now nearly forty years old and looking back on the events of a quarter-century ago, "I love my church and my bank."

In the novel, Mattie senses the judgment of her readers: "Some people will take it wrong and criticize me for not going to my father's funeral. My answer is this: I had my father's business to attend to." The Coens, along with the critics, take this to be the business of blood vengeance. But that is a kind of metaphysical reading of Mattie's declaration. Rather, we do better to take her words at their plain meaning: in the wake of her father's death, she immediately assumes the mantle of his business concerns.[40] She dons his jacket and hat, wears his watch and pistol, and as his self-appointed heir and representative heads for Stonehill's office to continue—or conclude in a right fashion—the business her father had been occupied with.

Mattie is described as "headstrong" (Lawyer Daggett), "contrary" (LaBoeuf), "an unnatural child" and "impudent" (Stonehill), unwilling to "varnish" her opinion (Lucky Ned Pepper), and she characterizes herself as having "spunk" and a "mean streak"—what could be read as synonyms for "true grit" in a fourteen-year-old.[41] These qualities might be as advantageous in business as in the business of vengeance, but they are uniformly meant to suggest Mattie's exceptional nature: that she is responsible and perceptive in ways that others, even adults, are not. Mattie, it would seem, is the opposite of the character she reads about in *Bess Calloway's Disappointment*: "She made trouble for herself because she would never say what she meant."[42] Mattie, contrariwise, finds trouble because she only says what she means.[43] Because she is led by a feeling of righteousness (instead of fear) she doesn't worry that her straight-talking, no-nonsense demands might cause offense. She will not be "used" by others, as her father had been. Still, and quite importantly, a child's precociousness—exhibited either as savvy business sense or confident knowledge of her rights—should not be mistaken for moral wisdom.

Though Mattie continually reminds the reader that her mind is set to her father's business, in the economic sense, the Coens translate her mission into a grander, more violent, and more mythical undertaking. But for Mattie, even cosmic destiny is understood as a kind of economy—seeing prisoners in chains alighting in Fort Smith she says: "And now justice had caught up with them to demand payment. You must pay for everything in this world one way and another. There is nothing free except the Grace of God. You cannot earn that or deserve it." Heavenly accounting is mirrored by worldly accounting. The only free thing—the only gift—is given by God; all mortal dealings come at a price. And Mattie says: "I want Chaney to pay for killing my father." When she makes her proposition to Rooster, she tells him "I mean business," and he likewise prioritizes the economics of the situation before weighing its ethical implications: "'Don't crowd me,' said he. 'I am thinking about expenses. . . . There will be expenses.'" Rooster is not thinking of what's right—in an important sense he already *knows* Chaney should hang—but what it will cost him to find the man. Rooster's hesitation is based squarely and solely on whether Mattie's paid mercenary expedition is a good business decision.

In a scene not included in the film, Mattie shows herself to be a competent bookkeeper. She quickly dispatches one of Rooster's objections to accepting her job by noting the convoluted "fee sheets" that need sorting and tabulating. "There was nothing hard about it," she tells us, "only I had to rub out most of what he had already done." Her accounting skills win her Rooster's praise and ultimately his accession to the job—straight upon which, not surprisingly, Mattie draws up a formal contract: "I wrote out a short agreement regarding the business between us and had him sign it." (Later she will advise Rooster to draw up a contract to protect himself from the risk of being cheated: "Smallwood was a gentleman but gentlemen are only human and their memories can sometimes fail them. Business is business.") Not to be missed, when Tom Chaney first recognizes her in the river, moments before she first shoots him, he calls out: "You are little Mattie the bookkeeper."

As she was with Stonehill, Mattie is attentive to the description of business relationships and responsibilities and also to the importance of a man's promise—his name, his signature, his reputation inscribed in ink. When Stonehill tells a girl whose father has just been murdered, "We must each of us bear our own misfortunes," Mattie implicitly accepts the truth of this in existential affairs—the contours of life and death, the judgment of God—but is wholly deaf to it in business affairs. For her, a contract, with its exposition of terms and conditions, should be sufficient for carrying out one's business; there is no need to appeal to God's judgment when the contract is in hand. As any fastidious and driven boss might say, Mattie notes with frustration: "If you want anything done right you will have to see to it yourself every time."

The Ethics of Instruction

The film, as the novel, begins with a man about to be hanged given a chance to have last words. Admitting his guilt, his short speech could be taken as a second epigraph to the story, an admonition as much as a description: "If I had received good instruction as a child I would be with my family today and at peace with my neighbors. I hope and pray that all you parents in the sound of my voice will train up your children in the way they should go." Not one to give over to weeping, Mattie confesses: "He was in tears and I am not ashamed to own that I was too" (tears that do not come in the Coens' visualization).[44] Moved by the man's words and tears, but also at realizing that she is in a state without a father to give her good instruction, to train her up in the way she should go, she experiences a shock worthy of tears. In the novel, her emotive weeping is self-reflexive: she cries not just for the loss of her father but for the loss of her own education from him. In the Coens' version, the shock of witnessing the hanging agitates her blood lust; it is in the immediate wake of *seeing* the hanging that Mattie begins to speak of hanging Tom Chaney, as if the experience gave her a picture of what retribution might look like.

Mattie, in some sense, does not know what she has lost in losing her father. Aristotle says of his teacher in the *Nicomachean Ethics:* "As Plato observes, men should have been trained straight from their childhood to receive pleasure and pain from proper objects, for this is right education."[45] The man about to be hanged laments his own lack of "right education" even as he warns the audience to embrace the responsibility of this kind of instruction. When talking with Lucky Ned Pepper, while being in his custody, Mattie thinks to herself: "I had not thought before of this disfigured robber having had a childhood. . . . When he needed a firm restraining hand, it was not there. An old story!"[46] A story Mattie is now in danger of living—if not for Rooster, LaBoeuf, Lawyer Daggett, and other sources of advice, "firm" or otherwise effective.

Jeff Bridges, who took the Coens' Jeffrey Lebowski role and transformed it into a character worthy of mythic status, sufficiently profound to spawn several books of philosophical criticism, does much the same with the literary antecedent Rooster Cogburn.[47] Rooster can at times seem nonchalant, a man dangerously comfortable with his power as marshal, lazy in his faithfulness to his own judgment (instead of due process)—characteristics shared, we might note, with William Hickok, whom Bridges portrayed in the 1995 film

Wild Bill. Despite his slovenly ways and his penchant for "pulling a cork,"[48] he is not "takin' 'er easy for all us sinners." If anything, as a man who rode among Quantrill's Raiders in Lawrence, Kansas, he is likely as afflicted by guilt for things he did as by the trauma of involvement in events beyond his control and comprehension. Unlike the Dude, Rooster is a man of action whose pain stalks him—a pain that sometimes impairs his deportment while it often motivates his better instincts.

We learn that Rooster has no wife and no child, or rather that he once did but lost them. He tells Mattie of his ex-wife's disappointment in him. She bought him a book—*Daniels on Negotiable Instruments*—but he wasn't interested in it.[49] And when she left with their son, she said: "Goodbye, Reuben, a love for decency does not abide in you."[50] Rooster reports indifferently, without blame, that his son did not like him: "I guess I did speak awful rough to him but I didn't mean nothing by it." As a husband and as a parent, Rooster appears unfit. And yet in telling Mattie his story—in the thoughtful, self-knowing descriptions he generously offers (perhaps "generously" is a euphemism here, since Mattie notes, "Rooster talked all night. I would doze off and wake up and he would still be talking")—Rooster gives instruction to Mattie and demonstrates his decency. He tells her of a father's failed ways and in that gesture exhibits an unexpected facility as a guide and mentor—fathering the wayward, orienting one in need of direction.

But is Mattie in need of adult or parental advice? Does her clarity of mission—"I intend to kill Tom Chaney if the law fails to do so"—mitigate the murkiness of her logic in pursuing it? Rooster thinks so and says as much to Mattie when she objects to LaBoeuf's desire to return Chaney to Texas—"That is not what I want. That was not our agreement."

> "We will be getting him all the same. What you want is to have him caught and punished. We still mean to do that."
>
> "I want him to know he is being punished for killing my father. It is nothing to me how many dogs and fat men he killed in Texas."
>
> "You can let him know that," said Rooster. "You can tell him to his face. You can spit on him and make him eat sand out of the road. You can put a ball in his foot and I will hold him while you do it. But we must catch him first. We will need some help. You are being stiff-necked about this. You are young. It is time you learned that you cannot have your way in every little particular. Other people have got their interests too."

> "When I have bought and paid for something I will have my way. Why do you think I am paying you if not to have my way?"[51]

In this exchange, we see how Mattie loses touch with the scope of the economic framework she adopted at the onset of her crisis. And Rooster corrects her. She doesn't own Chaney and she doesn't own Rooster or LaBoeuf. Though she understands very well the boss/employee relationship, she can't discern how this case is different—for example, how many things are beyond her control, and not just divine judgment but the comings and goings of men. Her desire for Chaney to be arraigned and punished in Arkansas, for wanting him to know that *she knows* of his guilt, is a metaphysical slippage in her thinking about vengeance—and the Coens take that misjudgment as an occasion to intensify the error instead of countermanding it.

Rooster speaks and exemplifies the core wisdom of vengeance's varieties, illogic, and inconsequentiality: there is no way to "get back" the person you lost or "get back at" the person who took him. He understands Mattie's illicit desire, for he has shared it—of the Wharton case he reflects: "It is too bad they cannot hang him three or four times." This is, we might say, an *emotional* economy—when passion for punishment outstrips its realities and limitations—and it deeply informs the model of blood vengeance.

It is some measure of Mattie's naïveté—perfectly understandable given her age—that she sees tracking and killing Tom Chaney as not much different than hunting an animal. As if to give credibility to her fitness for joining him on the trail, she tells Rooster about "coon hunting" with her dad. Rooster replies sharply: "Blast coon hunting! This ain't no coon hunt, it don't come in forty miles of being a coon hunt." And Mattie replies briskly: "It's the same idea as a coon hunt. You are just trying to make your work sound harder than it is." But Rooster is right (in a moral sense), and he aims to correct Mattie's understanding of their undertaking. It is a man they seek, not a raccoon. Retribution of the wider, metaphysical, godly sort is not something one can buy; and retribution of the economic sort is not ultimately very satisfying, since it diminishes the lost, loved object to brute facts and figures. Retribution is, it would seem, a way of relating to facts beyond one's control, and invites a necessary myth of resolution. Mattie imagined that she could settle her accounts with Chaney's life the way she did with Stonehill's ponies. But they are on different registers, not conducive to reduction or conflation.

Rooster might as well have taught this lesson to the Coen brothers, given their modification of the narrative—especially in Chaney's lack of repentance and Mattie as the final cause of his death. By putting a conventional notion of blood vengeance in the mouth of a child, Portis created a story in which he could school the reader indirectly by making Mattie's correction a matter of being educated, growing up, becoming wiser (in the sense we find in Proverbs). As readers, we are reminded or perhaps learn for the first time that inherited notions of legal, religious, moral, economic—but especially violent—punishment are as difficult to discern and make coherent as they are easy to uncritically accept and promulgate. By taking up Mattie's errant view—featuring it, stylizing it, celebrating it—the Coens missed an opportunity to give credence to Portis's mature, considered, and much-needed analysis of retribution—perhaps even to make it attractive and intelligible to a wide audience. The Coens have mistaken Portis's novel for a typical western, not the critique of frontier life and logic that it is, and thereby have created yet another clichéd and misleading portrait of retribution in a long tradition of them, especially in the film genre of westerns.[52]

Given the penitent criminal's opening speech about the need for parents, and of support for orphans, it is worth considering how *True Grit* offers a substantive account of how orphans require protection, parental proxies, and other forms of guidance. By this reading of Portis's novel, pursuing retribution is not the subject of the story but the means of its principal action: the proximate reason for seeking or testing out a new parent or parental-proxy, a new teacher or guide. The Coens are true to this aspect of the novel and repeatedly emphasize not only a child's need for parents (a search that may exist even when they are alive; Mattie's mother, for instance, is not a source of guidance but a charge Mattie must assume responsibility for until the end—"Mama was never any good at sums and she could hardly spell cat" and is now "indecisive and hobbled by grief") but also the way adults try to understand their own capacities as parents or moral guides.[53] The reluctant but effective parent is almost a character type. One does not train to be a parent but discovers the vocation through the activity.

Rooster's presence in the story suggests that being parented in some way is a better hope for the harmed than the actualization of retribution (in any form), and in this way hints at the promise of a form of restorative justice not yet sensible to the characters. Mattie may not realize how much her attraction to Rooster—early on expressed as an attraction to his reputation for violence—is caught up with an instinctive desire to find an *alternative* to violence, an option that takes her away from having to kill a man herself (since Rooster is proven more than competent in that respect) and into a realm of campfires and storytelling, adventures like she used to share with her dad. Tracking Chaney with Rooster becomes a nightmarish parallel to Mattie's fond memories of coon hunting, but a meaningful surrogate nonetheless.

The logic of retribution in the novel *True Grit* has less, almost very little, to do with the nature of punishable wrongdoing than with the pursuit of a kind of equilibrium based on a judgment of value; thus not the replacement of what was lost but the discovery of something or someone who can give it sense.[54] In addition to standard forms of retribution (viz., blood vengeance, economic restitution, and divine punishment), Portis suggests a nascent model of restorative justice—wherein the primary victim is prompted to a different kind of pursuit, the search for a new protector or parental proxy. Seemingly unaware of this herself, Mattie undertakes a process of inviting, then testing, adults who might want the responsibility of lending her protection and counsel. Figures present themselves for the role—sometimes accidentally and unwittingly, other times consciously, often with some degree of reluctance, perhaps aware of conflicts of intention and interest, or fears of incapability. And looking at it from the potential proxy parent's perspective, there is rightly a sort of panic about the nature of parenting and obligation to the young who are not "one's own" (and who are as self-possessed as Mattie Ross). Why, for example, would a man such as Rooster Cogburn want to care for a child? Because, as a man of the law, he might be in a position to keep Mattie from going above it? Because he can find in her a proxy for his own lost son, a second chance to guide and love the young? What would he teach her? Or perhaps it is she who can teach him to parent her, for example, to take a child seriously—to talk to her instead of talk "awful rough" to her; to find in her a person worthy of trust and respect instead of a distracting and debilitating responsibility.

Rooster's parental protectiveness of Mattie reaches its crescendo when he must rush to save her life from the venom that poisons her blood. More than anywhere else in the story, it is here that Rooster acts as an unmatched protector, infused with the adrenaline it would seem only a parent of a threatened child is capable of summoning. How else to explain heavyset, heavy-drinking Rooster's Olympic sprint for medical help to save the waning Mattie Ross? For good reason, then, Mattie remains faithful to Rooster's character for the quarter century that passes before she retrieves *him* from oblivion and plants him honorably in her family plot, beside her own father.

Mattie dubs Rooster a "resolute officer," which is tombstone-speak for true grit: the man had it, and Mattie wants to testify to it in stone.[55]

The End of Retribution, the Beginning of Sense

We know Mattie Ross survives the ordeal with Tom Chaney because she narrates it (in the book and the film). Otherwise *True Grit* would be a ghost story. But then, in a way, it is: Mattie wears her dad's hat and jacket for practical reasons (because he had equipment that would aid her pursuit of Chaney) and perhaps for instinctive though unarticulated sentimental reasons (because she can feel closer to him as she acts as his agent and seeks to restore balance in herself). Frank's clothes, though ill-fitting, offer her borrowed authority—and as the costume of Frank's ghost, they remind us of his absence on every page and in every frame. At the end, Mattie's outfit makes it seem as if Frank Ross himself has come to settle up with Chaney. But, as Mattie says of herself, her approach is not her father's—where he would have been meek and forgiving ("If Papa had a failing it was his kindly disposition"), she is bold and righteous. Still, Mattie's approach is not for blood vengeance; rather she wants to see accounts settled. Mattie's naïve notion of retribution in economic terms—which is as much on display as under critique throughout the novel—suggests that her father's death is quantifiable in earthly terms. For her, then, achieving justice is a matter of making sense of cents, whereas it should suggest the impassable gulf between the two—and "that we're all haunted by things we can't understand."[56] We would be better off considering how Mattie's economic relationship to death (and life) is her way of coping with the trauma of losing her father. If, as Stanley Fish says, "she has faith in the righteousness of her path," it is not a path that leads to avenging her father in blood but in laying Chaney low—putting him out of business.[57] Mattie explains: "Some people might say, well, what business was it of Frank Ross to meddle? My answer is this: he was trying to do that short devil a good turn. Chaney was a tenant and Papa felt responsibility. He was his brother's keeper."[58] Well, Mattie feels a responsibility too; she also is her brother's keeper—the keeper of her father's accounts as much as his memory. And so just as Chaney made a withdrawal from her accounts, she will make one from his.

Mattie Ross, especially the young Mattie Ross, isn't waylaid by skepticism about the range of difficult consequences that come from executing a man—guilty or not. Her lack of doubt reinforces the estimation that she also, even as the elder Mattie Ross, doesn't possess a sophisticated moral sense. She was in need of that kind of instruction, and she got some in the form of Rooster's provocation to moral intuitionism, and their unexpected encounter with a mode of restorative justice. But it was a short-lived association, and while Mattie dearly remembered it, she doesn't seem to have sought new forms of counsel—but instead remained quarantined in her church and her bank. It is not clear that Mattie ever fathoms the complications Rooster's lessons make for moral life; she relates them to us as if passing on a campfire story instead of confessing a teaching that transformed her perspective on the events in the Winding Stair Mountains. In the end, as this bedtime story comes to a close, as a father reads the last lines of Portis's novel to his child, the mature Mattie's loss is literal and evident, while her moral growth remains elusive and unexpressed; we are, however, as readers, as listeners, privy to the implications of her unanticipated and concise tutelage as a child. The elder Mattie is physically marked by the event: her lost limb a sign of her success in achieving a survivable equilibrium—an ever-present reminder of the economies that rule her life. She paid bodily for her participation in the killing of Tom Chaney, but one would hope that with the help of men such as Rooster she might have also developed a mature sense about the nature of retribution. But such lessons don't come easily, and Mattie certainly would not expect them to come cheaply. If only she had found someone after Rooster, someone who amplified her moral education by reading a story where the response to the death of a loved one was not recourse to blood vengeance. With this kind of instruction, the mature Mattie Ross might acknowledge her now more developed disdain for the weighty effects of delivering that punitive lead ball of justice. While Charles Portis wanted his account of Mattie Ross to convey such an insight to his readers, the Coen brothers' rendering of Mattie Ross obscures the lesson. We are perhaps all served to recall Lucky Ned Pepper's droll assessment of life lived by the gun: "It will embarrass you every time."[59]

Notes

Please note that I wrote this essay while the Coen brothers' *True Grit* was still in theatrical release, beginning December 22, 2010, and as a result I cannot provide time-code references for the film. I'm very grateful to Mark T. Conard for the invitation to write on the Coen brothers' latest film. I thank him, K. L. Evans, and Lorna K. Hershinow for helpful comments on an earlier version of this essay.

1. Charles McGrath, "True Grit, Odd Wit: And Fame? No, Thanks," *New York Times,* December 19, 2010 (nytimes.com).

2. Charles Portis, *True Grit* (1968; repr., New York: Overlook Press, 2004), 33.

3. See, for example, Michael Cieply, "Coen Brothers Saddle Up a Revenge Story (or Two)," *New York Times,* December 3, 2010 (nytimes.com); Manohla Dargis, "Wearing Braids, Seeking Revenge," *New York Times,* December 22, 2010 (nytimes.com); David Edelstein, "Punch, Drunk, Love," *New York Magazine,* December 20–27, 2010 (nymag .com); J. Hoberman, "Old Men, Young Girls, and Tall Tales Once Thought for Dead in *True Grit* and *The Illusionist*," *Village Voice,* December 22–28, 2010 (villagevoice.com).

4. Portis, *True Grit,* 36.

5. During late 2010, promotion for the film declared "Retribution this Christmas" and "Punishment comes one way or another." The song used to promote the film in previews, but which does not appear in the film, was "God's Gonna Cut 'Em Down," with verses such as "Go tell that long tongue liar, go tell that midnight rider. / Tell the rambler, the gambler, the back biter. / Tell 'em that God's gonna cut 'em down."

6. David Fear, "True Grit," *TimeOut New York,* December 16–29, 2010 (timeout-newyork.com); Hoberman, "Old Men, Young Girls"; David Denby, "Roundup," *New Yorker,* December 20 and 27, 2010 (newyorker.com); Carlo Rotella, "True to *True Grit*," *New York Times,* December 10, 2010 (nytimes.com); and Edelstein, "Punch, Drunk, Love."

7. Portis, *True Grit,* 25.

8. Denby, "Roundup," 144.

9. Hoberman, "Old Men, Young Girls."

10. The phrase in the subject heading is from Portis, *True Grit,* 33.

11. Only a few weeks after its release, *True Grit* had outperformed all of the Coens' previous box office results; see Michael Cieply and Brooks Barnes, "As a Hot Ticket, Will *True Grit* Sway the Oscars?" *New York Times,* January 4, 2011. Pertaining to antecedents, I mention that Richard T. Heffron directed a television pilot in 1978 for a series entitled *True Grit: A Further Adventure,* which never materialized.

12. Cieply "Coen Brothers Saddle Up." This is also the source for the next two quotations from the Coen brothers.

13. Joshua Rothkopf, "The Hot Seat: Jeff Bridges," *TimeOut New York,* December 16–19, 2010, 172.

14. David Carr, "The Coen Brothers, Shooting Straight," *New York Times,* December 10, 2010 (nytimes.com).

15. As a result, the celebrated cinematographer and frequent Coen brothers collaborator Roger Deakins should be credited when considering the artistry with which the film was photographed.

16. Carr, "The Coen Brothers."

17. Portis, *True Grit,* 33, 74.

18. For more on restorative justice, including an extensive bibliography of secondary

resources, see Tyler G. Okimoto, Michael Wenzel, and N. T. Feather, "Beyond Retribution: Conceptualizing Restorative Justice and Exploring Its Determinants," *Social Justice Research* 22.1 (2009): 156–80.

19. C. L. Ten, "Crime and Punishment," in *A Companion to Ethics*, ed. Peter Singer (Oxford: Blackwell, 1993), 366, 367. The retributivist is interested neither in the ways that punishment may serve as a "treatment" or therapy for the guilty nor as a deterrent to further criminal behavior. See Ted Honderich, *Punishment: The Supposed Justifications Revisited*, rev. ed. (London: Pluto, 2006), 112.

20. Portis, *True Grit*, 25–26, 87, 145.

21. Denby, "Roundup," 144.

22. Portis, *True Grit*, 84.

23. Jeffrie G. Murphy, *Retribution, Justice, and Therapy: Essays in the Philosophy of Law* (Boston: D. Reidel, 1979), 77.

24. Portis, *True Grit*, 66–67.

25. Murphy, *Retribution, Justice, and Therapy*, 78.

26. Stanley Fish, "Narrative and the Grace of God: The New *True Grit*," *New York Times*, December 27, 2010 (nytimes.com).

27. Portis, *True Grit*, 17. Proverbs also features prominently in the James Mangold remake of *3:10 to Yuma* (2007). In that film Ben Wade (Russell Crowe) quotes from Proverbs 13:3 and chapter 21.

28. See especially Proverbs 28:4, 5, 7, 9, 10, 17, 18, and 24.

29. Portis, *True Grit*, 11, 224.

30. It is worth remembering and emphasizing that Portis authored Mattie's tale, and thus it refracts his more mature ethical sensibility, including his ability to critique Mattie's adolescent moral understanding even as he articulates it in her speech. Donna Tartt, novelist and lifelong fan of *True Grit*, misdescribes and undermines Portis's achievement when, trying to praise the work, she claims his novel "reads less like a novel than a firsthand account." *True Grit* is a novel, not an autobiography, and it should not be conflated—even as a gesture—with what Lawrence Weschler calls "rhapsodic nonfiction," where (for example, in Tartt's reading) we find the elder Mattie telling a story of her youth "in a different register" than it would have been told by her fourteen-year-old self. Both registers are Portis's. Despite the novel's compelling realist attributes, among them its distinctive prose style and its compelling characters, it is crucial to an appreciation of Portis's contribution to ethical thinking that readers keep him in mind as the creator of the work. (Donna Tartt, afterword to *True Grit*, 230; Bob Garfield interview with Lawrence Weschler, "Lawrence Weschler on the Fiction of Non-Fiction," *On the Media*, December 24, 2010 [onthemedia.org].)

31. Portis, *True Grit*, 170. The phrase in the subject heading is from this page as well. Subsequent quotations from Portis, *True Grit*, 204, 211.

32. In the film Mattie does not act in self-defense when she shoots Chaney for the second time. She takes the occasion of having him, apparently unarmed, in her gun-sight to say "Stand up Tom Chaney" and then proceeds to execute him.

33. Proverbs 28:10, 17.

34. Portis, *True Grit,* 180.

35. Carr, "The Coen Brothers."

36. Fish, "Narrative and the Grace of God."

37. II Timothy 1:9 (KJV). See Portis, *True Grit,* 115.

38. Deirdre N. McCloskey, "Bourgeois Virtue," *American Scholar* 63 (Spring 1994): 177–91.

39. Portis, *True Grit,* 224. Subsequent quotations from Portis, *True Grit,* 136, 11, 29, 24, 224, 27.

40. For all her concern with money, Mattie is not cheap, and she apprehends when others attempt to defraud her. When Yarnell tells Mattie that the undertaker is "trying to stick you," she replies: "Well, we will not haggle with him. . . . We will let it go." When Rooster doubles Mattie's proposed payment for the job, she accepts, in the Coens' wording: "I shall not niggle." Mattie has a sense for when it is indecorous or unproductive to argue about money, and when it is fitting, as with Stonehill, when she scolds him: "I will not be pushed about when I am in the right"; and when she puts Rooster on the level: "You are trying to take advantage of me." Ibid., 24, 35, 63.

41. Ibid., 78, 99, 36, 35, 41, 12. Lucky Ned Pepper's line is a Coen addition.

42. Portis, *True Grit,* 70.

43. "It was a cashier's check for $2,750 drawn on the Grangers Trust Co. of Topeka, Kansas, to a man named Marshall Purvis. I said: 'This is a cashier's check for $2,750 drawn on the Grangers Trust Co. of Topeka, Kansas, to a man named Marshall Purvis." Ibid., 194. Subsequent quotations from Portis, *True Grit,* 12, 40, 75, 60, 62, 88–89, 166, 178, 79.

44. Portis, *True Grit,* 22.

45. I use a translation from Aristotle's *Nicomachean Ethics,* book 2, chap. 2, 1104b10 that shares some of the cadence of the Portis text, 10th ed. (Project Gutenberg edition by Ted Garvin and David Widger, July 2005). Consider also translations by W. D. Ross (N.p.: World Library Classics, 2009), 24; Martin Ostwald (Englewood Cliffs, N.J.: Library of Liberal Arts, 1962), 37; and Richard McKeon (New York: Random House, 1941), 944.

46. Portis, *True Grit,* 193.

47. See for example *I'm a Lebowski, You're a Lebowski: Life,* The Big Lebowski, *and What Have You,* ed. Bill Green et al. (New York: Bloomsbury, 2007); *The Year's Work in Lebowski Studies,* ed. Edward P. Comentale and Aaron Jaffe (Bloomington: Indiana Univ. Press, 2009); and Adam Bertocci, *Two Gentlemen of Lebowski: A Most Excellent Comedie and Tragical Romance* (New York: Simon and Schuster, 2010).

48. Portis, *True Grit,* 25. Subsequent quotations from Portis, *True Grit,* 143, 147, 60, 97–98, 84, 86, 11.

49. The Honorable John Warwick Daniel is the author of a work titled *A Treatise on the Law of Negotiable Instruments,* 2 vols., 3rd ed. (New York: Baker, Voorhis & Co., 1886).

50. In the film, it sounds as if the Coens give Rooster two wives—a first wife with whom he had a child, and a second who gave him the *Daniels* book.

51. In the Coens' version, the "ball in his foot" line is replaced with the more graphic flaying of feet and adding of "Indian pepper."

52. As for genre conventions, *True Grit* would be a buddy film if not for the presence of Mattie Ross. With her, the film, like the book, makes what would be squabbling between men into scenes of instruction, scenes in which a child can witness how men behave, learn what they believe, and develop a sense of judgment about positions offered and refuted. Without Mattie, *True Grit* would be much closer in tone and temper to the bickering couple scenarios we find among the principal male pair in *Butch Cassidy and the Sundance Kid* (George Roy Hill, 1969), *Open Range* (Kevin Costner, 2003), and *Appaloosa* (Ed Harris, 2008).

53. Portis, *True Grit*, 15.

54. LaBoeuf himself is confounded by his situation and confides as much to his trail mates: "I don't understand this conversation. It is not sensible. I am not used to consulting children in my business." Ibid., 98.

55. The Coens emphasize the parallel between Frank Ross and Rooster in the way they visualize the handling of their corpses and coffins: these men are claimed by Mattie, and then sent home to share a final resting place (the coffins chalk-marked in both cases to the appropriate destination). The parallel between Ross and Rooster (here even sensing in the sequencing and saying of their names a homophonic similarity) lends weight to the parental, not the romantic, nature of Rooster, and his effect on Mattie's life and consciousness.

56. Hoberman, "Old Men, Young Girls."

57. Fish, "Narrative and the Grace of God."

58. Portis, *True Grit*, 16.

59. Ibid., 186.

CONTRIBUTORS

JEROLD J. ABRAMS is associate professor of philosophy at Creighton University in Omaha. His research focuses on aesthetics, philosophy of film, pragmatism, and ethics. His publications include essays appearing in *Philosophy Today, Human Studies, The Modern Schoolman,* and *Transactions of the Charles S. Peirce Society.* His essay "From Sherlock Holmes to the Hard-Boiled Detective in Film Noir" appears in *The Philosophy of Film Noir* (Univ. Press of Kentucky, 2005).

SHAI BIDERMAN is a doctoral candidate in philosophy at Boston University and a lecturer in Colman's Law School, Israel. He graduated magna cum laude from Tel Aviv University with a master's in philosophy, having written a thesis focusing on knowledge and subjectivity. His primary research interests include philosophy of culture, philosophy of film and literature, aesthetics, ethics, existentialism, and Nietzsche. His recent publications include several essays on philosophy in contemporary film and television.

MARK T. CONARD is associate professor of philosophy at Marymount Manhattan College in New York City. He is coeditor of *The Simpsons and Philosophy* (Open Court, 2001) and *Woody Allen and Philosophy* (Open Court, 2004), and the editor of *The Philosophy of Film Noir* (2005), *The Philosophy of Neo-Noir* (2006), and *The Philosophy of Martin Scorsese* (2007), all published by the University Press of Kentucky. He is also the author of the novel *Dark as Night* (Uglytown, 2004).

PAUL COUGHLIN is a writer and researcher who earned his PhD in visual culture from Monash University (Melbourne, Australia). He has written extensively on the work of Joel and Ethan Coen and on postmodernism. His articles have appeared in *Literature/Film Quarterly, Scope: An Online Journal, Journal of Popular Culture, Film Journal,* and *Senses of Cinema.*

WILLIAM J. DEVLIN is assistant professor of philosophy at Bridgewater State College in Massachusetts and visiting summer lecturer at the University of

Wyoming. His fields of interest are the philosophy of science, theories of truth, Nietzsche, and existentialism. His essays appear in *"South Park" and Philosophy* (Blackwell, 2007), *"Family Guy" and Philosophy* (Blackwell, 2007), *"Lost" and Philosophy* (Blackwell, 2007), *The Philosophy of TV Noir* (Univ. Press of Kentucky, 2007), *The Philosophy of Science Fiction Film* (Univ. Press of Kentucky, 2007), and the forthcoming *"Star Trek" and Philosophy* (Open Court).

MATTHEW K. DOUGLASS received a master's degree in theological studies from Asbury Theological Seminary in Wilmore, Kentucky, in 2006 and is currently working toward a PhD in philosophy at Baylor University in Waco, Texas. His philosophical interests include logic, the philosophy of religion, and the philosophy of physics. In his spare time, he especially enjoys lounging at home with his lovely wife, Angela. In fact, like the Dude, most of his preferred pastimes involve laziness and loved ones.

K. L. EVANS is associate professor of English at Yeshiva University, where she teaches literature and philosophy, American literature, and film criticism. She is the author of *Whale!* (University of Minnesota Press, 2003) and the forthcoming *The Missing Limb*, a Wittgensteinian reading of *Moby-Dick* in which she takes seriously, or takes as a piece of logic, Ahab's disemboweling of the proposition that anything a man knows can be tested. Recent publications include "Charlie Kaufman, Screenwriter," in *The Philosophy of Charlie Kaufman*, ed. David LaRocca (University Press of Kentucky, 2011); "A Rest from Reason: Wittgenstein, Drury, and the Difference between Madness and Religion" (*Philosophy* 85 [2010]); "A Machine for Becoming Decent" (*Denver Quarterly* 42 [2008]); and "While Reading Wittgenstein," in *Stanley Cavell: Philosophy, Literature, and Criticism*, ed. James Loxley and Andrew Taylor (Manchester University Press, 2011).

RICHARD GAUGHRAN is assistant professor of English at James Madison University in Harrisonburg, Virginia, where he teaches courses in American and world literature. Among other things, he has published articles on baseball literature, popular film, and the literature of the American South. He received his PhD from Lehigh University in Bethlehem, Pennsylvania. He lived and worked in Eastern Europe between 1997 and 2002, first as senior Fulbright lecturer in American studies at the Ss. Cyril and Methodius University in Skopje, Macedonia, then in Bratislava, Slovakia, working as an editor and literary translator.

RICHARD GILMORE is associate professor of philosophy at Concordia College in Moorhead, Minnesota. He is the author of *Philosophical Health: Wittgenstein's Method in "Philosophical Investigations"* (Lexington Books, 1999) and *Doing Philosophy at the Movies* (State Univ. of New York Press, 2005).

REBECCA HANRAHAN is assistant professor of philosophy at Whitman College in Walla Walla, Washington. Her current areas of research include modal epistemology, feminism, and applied ethics. She has an article forthcoming in *Philosophical Forum,* entitled "Imagination and Possibility," and another article forthcoming in the *International Journal of Applied Philosophy,* entitled "The Decision to Abort."

BRADLEY L. HERLING is assistant professor of religious studies at Marymount Manhattan College in New York City. He has recently published *The German "Gita": Hermeneutics and Discipline in the Reception of Indian Thought, 1778–1831* (Routledge, 2006) and *A Beginner's Guide to the Study of Religion* (Continuum, 2007). Herling has also written a number of reviews, articles, and items available online. His work has focused on the interchange between East and West, comparative religious and philosophical ethics, the challenge of evil and unwarranted suffering, and theory and method in the study of religion.

THOMAS S. HIBBS is distinguished professor of ethics and culture and dean of the Honors College at Baylor University in Waco, Texas. In addition to teaching a variety of interdisciplinary courses, he teaches in the fields of medieval philosophy, contemporary virtue ethics, and philosophy and popular culture. He is the author of, among other works, *Dialectic and Narrative in Aquinas: An Interpretation of the Summa Contra Gentiles* (Univ. of Notre Dame Press, 1997) and *Shows about Nothing* (Spence Publications, 2000). He is currently finishing two books: *Aquinas, Ethics, and the Philosophy of Religion: Metaphysics and Practice* (Indiana Univ. Press) and *Arts of Darkness: American Noir and the Lost Code of Redemption* (Spence Publications). He has published articles on film, culture, and higher education in the *New Atlantis, Weekly Standard, Dallas Morning News, National Review,* and *Chronicle of Higher Education.*

KAREN D. HOFFMAN is associate professor of philosophy at Hood College in Frederick, Maryland. Specializing in ethics, she has a particular interest in the work of Søren Kierkegaard and is the author of "Evil and Despairing

Individuals: A Kierkegaardian Account," which appears in *Minding Evil* (Rodolpi, 2005). She is also interested in film and the philosophy of film and has essays in *The Philosophy of Stanley Kubrick* and *The Philosophy of Martin Scorsese* (both Univ. Press of Kentucky, 2007).

DAVID LAROCCA is a Fellow at the Moving Picture Institute in New York and writer-in-residence at the New York Public Library. He is the author of *On Emerson* (Wadsworth, 2003) and the editor of Stanley Cavell's book *Emerson's Transcendental Etudes* (Stanford University Press, 2003) and of *The Philosophy of Charlie Kaufman* (University Press of Kentucky, 2011). His articles on film, autobiography, and aesthetic theory have appeared in *Epoché, Film and Philosophy, Afterimage*, the *Midwest Quarterly*, and the *Journal of Aesthetics and Art Criticism*. LaRocca, who lives in New York, has made documentary films in the Intellectual Portrait Series with Academy Award–nominated director William Jersey and master cinematographer Robert Elfstrom and attended Werner Herzog's Rogue Film School. More details at www.DavidLaRocca.org.

DOUGLAS MCFARLAND is chair of the English and Comparative Literature Department at Oglethorpe University in Atlanta. He has published on Rabelais, Montaigne, and Spenser. He is currently working on a book-length study of the early films of Peter Bogdanovich.

R. BARTON PALMER is Calhoun Lemon Professor of Literature at Clemson University, South Carolina, where he also directs the PhD program in film and international culture. He is the author, editor, or general editor of more than thirty books devoted to film and literary subjects. In addition to numerous articles and book chapters on the American cinema, he has published *Hollywood's Dark Cinema: The American Film Noir* (2nd rev. and expanded ed., Univ. of Illinois Press, forthcoming) and *Joel and Ethan Coen* (Univ. of Illinois Press, 2004). He has also edited *Perspectives on Film Noir* (G. K. Hall, 1996). He has just published (with David Boyd) the edited collection *After Hitchcock: Imitation, Influence, Intertextuality* (Univ. of Texas Press, 2007), as well as the edited collections *Nineteenth Century American Fiction on Screen* and *Twentieth-Century American Fiction on Screen* (both Cambridge Univ. Press, 2007).

DAVID STEARNS is a senior philosophy major at Whitman College in Walla Walla, Washington. After graduating, he plans to move to China to teach

English at Shantou University. Aside from thinking about philosophy and movies, he enjoys playing lacrosse.

JERRY L. WALLS taught philosophy at Asbury Theological Seminary in Wilmore, Kentucky, for twenty-one years. In addition to his PhD in philosophy from Notre Dame, where his mentor was Tom Morris, he has degrees from Houghton College, Princeton Seminary, and Yale Divinity School. He is Senior Speaking Fellow in the Morris Institute for Human Values, under whose aegis he has spoken to many business and professional meetings in America and abroad. He is also a member of the Dulles Colloquium of the Institute for Religion and Public Life. He is the author or editor of many articles and books, including *Heaven: The Logic of Eternal Joy* (Oxford Univ. Press, 2002); *The Chronicles of Narnia and Philosophy* (coedited with Gregory Bassham, Open Court, 2005); *Basketball and Philosophy: Thinking outside the Paint* (coedited with Gregory Bassham, Univ. Press of Kentucky, 2007); and *The Oxford Handbook of Eschatology* (Oxford Univ. Press, forthcoming). He has also published several poems and in college won first place in a national poetry contest. He has two children, Angela Rose and Jonathan Levi. He is a big fan of college football and basketball and the proud owner of a 1973 TR6.

ALAN WOOLFOLK is dean of academic affairs at Flagler College in St. Augustine, Florida. He has recently edited and written an introduction to Philip Rieff's posthumous work, *The Crisis of the Officer Class: The Decline of the Tragic Sensibility* (Univ. of Virginia Press, 2008). He has also recently written several articles on film.

INDEX

CPSIA information can be obtained at www.ICGtesting.com
Printed in the USA
BVOW02s2309181213

339184BV00002B/21/P